Henry Christopher McCook

American spiders and their spinningwork

A natural history of the orbweaving spiders of the United States

Henry Christopher McCook

American spiders and their spinningwork
A natural history of the orbweaving spiders of the United States

ISBN/EAN: 9783337132118

Printed in Europe, USA, Canada, Australia, Japan

Cover: Foto ©Andreas Hilbeck / pixelio.de

More available books at **www.hansebooks.com**

AMERICAN SPIDERS

AND

THEIR SPINNINGWORK.

⁂

A NATURAL HISTORY

OF THE

ORBWEAVING SPIDERS OF THE UNITED STATES

WITH SPECIAL REGARD TO THEIR INDUSTRY AND HABITS.

BY

HENRY C. McCOOK, D. D.,

VICE-PRESIDENT OF THE ACADEMY OF NATURAL SCIENCES OF PHILADELPHIA;
VICE-PRESIDENT OF THE AMERICAN ENTOMOLOGICAL SOCIETY;
AUTHOR OF "THE AGRICULTURAL ANTS OF TEXAS,"
"THE HONEY AND OCCIDENT ANTS,"
ETC., ETC.

VOL. I.

PUBLISHED BY THE AUTHOR,
ACADEMY OF NATURAL SCIENCES OF PHILADELPHIA.
A. D. 1889.

THESE STUDIES IN NATURAL HISTORY

ARE DEDICATED TO

THE VENERATED MEMORY

OF MY FATHER,

JOHN McCOOK, M. D.,

A LOVER OF NATURE, A FRIEND OF SCIENCE,

A GOOD PHYSICIAN, A SERVANT OF

HIS FELLOW MEN

WHOSE FAITH IN THE UNSEEN

NEVER FALTERED.

PREFACE.

THE studies whose results are here given have been prosecuted throughout the last sixteen years. I have largely limited my investigations to the habits and industry of spiders, as the matters which seemed most important at this stage of scientific knowledge.

None but the field naturalist can fully know and appreciate the difficulties of my task. To these ordinary obstacles have been added special

A Field Naturalist's Difficulties. hindrances of my own. The cabinet or laboratory student, with his pinned and alcoholic specimens, is largely independent of outward conditions; but he who studies nature as a living thing is the servant of seasons, hours, moods. He must live amidst the life which he would see, and seize the opportunities as they come, or lose his venture for that season or year, or perhaps wholly. The duties of my calling in a large city have held me rigorously away from the open country except during two months of the year. Summer vacations, and such leisure hours as a most busy life would allow, have been given to the pleasant task of following my little friends of the aranead world into their retreats, and watching at the doors of their fragile domiciles for such secrets of their career as they might happen to uncover. Occasional excursions at other times were unavoidably brief, and often broken off at the point of promised discoveries. I have, in part, indeed, overcome this obstacle by transporting and colonizing specimens, and by directing the observations of others. But, at the best, artificial conditions fall short of Nature's fullness, and no faithfulness of assistants can quite equal personal investigations.

Then, again, the natural disposition of the spider is a great hindrance to the prosecution of field studies. It is a solitary and secretive animal,

The Spider's Solitary Nature. and the most ingenious device for winning its confidence is as apt to drive it into hiding as to persuade it to revelations. In this respect there is a great difference between these solitary creatures and those sociable and demonstrative insects, the ants, whose life history I have heretofore been permitted to give to the scientific world. The success which was readily obtained by spending a few weeks or months encamped among formicaries of emmets, continually eluded me when trying like methods with araneads.

To be sure, in some respects the Orbweavers and Lineweavers are more approachable than other tribes of spiders; for, as they are sedentary creatures, and are found continuously upon their webs, one often has the opportunity to observe them with comparative freedom and comfort. But this is only true of the commoner species, and of that part of their life which concerns the structure of snares and trapping of food. In other, and even more interesting fields, these sedentary spiders, like all the wandering groups, persistently conceal their manners.

When it is considered that most of the facts presented in my books consecutively, as a connected history, have been collected under such difficulties, and at widely separated periods and places, it is not strange that some gaps in the life record may be found. But, if in some parts the connecting links are lacking, and the story is incomplete, it is no more than ordinarily befalls other naturalists when investigating the habits of other animals. While, therefore, no one can regret more than I the blanks which here and there occur in the pages of that wonderful history of industrial life and art which I have attempted to unfold, I venture to urge the above reasons for indulgence towards any failures which may appear.

The general plan of my work, as it will be given to the public, may briefly be stated as follows: The first volume is chiefly taken up with descriptions of those parts of aranead spinningwork which are generally known as the web or snare, and the nest or den. The former concerns the nurture of the spider, as the snare is its manufactured tool for capturing insects. The latter concerns the protection of the animal from changes of weather and assaults of enemies. In my studies of the snares of Orbweavers, I have tried to obtain the fullest possible details of the spinning methods of every species; to mark the striking differences which exist among the various groups; and to associate these, as far as my knowledge would permit, with the general habits of the various families. Furthermore, I have brought to bear upon these, in a comparative way, the spinningwork and habits of other tribes, so that the reader may be able to trace resemblances and differences, and to perceive what relations, if any, exist between the general life habits of all spiders.

General Plan of the Work

Plan of Volume I.

The consideration of these topics has necessarily suggested the degree of intelligence and the variety and adaptation of methods shown by spiders in their ordinary and special behavior. Thus have come into view the profound and interesting problems relating to animal mentalism.

Finally, I have endeavored, in the closing chapters, to present a bird's eye view of the entire field of industrial life treated of in the volume, with special bearing upon a common origin, whether from the one standpoint of a single originating Mind, or from the other standpoint of a genetic evolution from common ancestral actions and tendencies.

In the second volume I shall take up and treat in the same way the habits and industry associated with mating and maternal instincts, the

Plan of Volumes II. and III. life of the young, the distribution of species, and other general habits indicated in the appended table of contents. The third volume of the series will be a systematic presentation of the Orbweavers of the United States, and this I hope to make tolerably complete. The descriptions will be accompanied by a number of plates drawn in the best style of lithographic art, and painted by hand in the colors of nature.

The above plan is the result of an entire change in my original purpose, which was to write a natural history of all American spiders, following consecutively and separately the several tribes, beginning with the Orb-

Original Plan. weavers. A vast amount of material has been gathered with this purpose in view, but I have found that the work thus marked out is so great that I doubt my ability to accomplish it all. For, even should my life be sufficiently lengthened to overtake the entire field mapped out, the expense of the undertaking appears to be an impassable barrier. I have, therefore, concluded to introduce, in the comparative way referred to, such notes of tribes, other than Orbweavers, as seemed most desirable and important for solution of the various problems which have arisen as my studies progressed. Thus, while the Orbweavers are treated fully, the natural history of all other tribes of our spider fauna comes well into view. Although I confess some regret at the abandonment of the original plan, I am confident that most naturalists will agree with me that the present treatment adds to the value of the volumes now published, and is, perhaps, after all the best that could have been adopted.

There is another point at which this work departs from my original plan. As my observations have especially traversed the spinning habits of

Study of Spinning Organs. spiders, it seemed important to make a careful study of the spinning organs, not only of Orbweavers, but of all other spider tribes. It was thought that such a comparative study would not only give valuable hints in the systematic determination of the animals, but would have an especial bearing upon the variations in spinning habit. It was inferred that there must be some connection between special function and the organs thereof. In this line work was begun and prosecuted far enough to see how promising and interesting is the field. But a severe attack of sickness, whose consequences were felt for several years, compelled an entire cessation of work with the dissecting knife and microscope. I was, therefore, reluctantly compelled to omit from the opening chapters much material which I had hoped to present, and to limit my illustrations to the few which are really necessary to give the reader a correct idea of the structure of the spinning organs and the manner in which the spinning material of spiders is formed. Even these illustrations I have borrowed in part from others. I venture to express the hope that some one who can thoroughly prosecute this line of studies will be led to take it up and give the results to the scientific world.

I have made a point of illustrating all descriptions with drawings whenever the proper material was in hand. During my studies of aranead spinningwork, I have made thousands of original sketches **Full Illustrations.** in my note books, from which I have selected those that seemed best suited to make clear the points treated of. Judging by my own experience, even an outline drawing is better to communicate certain facts than pages of verbal explanation. Acting upon this belief, I have preferred to risk excessive illustration rather than fall upon obscure description. Indeed, I cherish the hope that the contents of some of the following chapters might be fairly understood by a simple examination of the cuts with their explanatory legends.

I have not been unmindful of the artistic sense of my readers, which, I trust, has been measurably satisfied; but I take it for granted that those who honor me by looking at my work will understand that the chief object of the engravings is to make plain what I have to say. In other words, the figures are for illustration and not for embellishment. Many of the cuts have been redrawn by competent artists, but a large number remain as figured by myself on block or paper. Among those who have assisted in making the drawings are the well known artists and arachnologists, Mr. J. H. Emerton, of Boston, and Dr. George Marx, of Washington; also, Messrs. Edwin Sheppard and Frank Stout, of the Academy of Natural Sciences of Philadelphia; and the Misses Bonsall, of this city.

It may not be out of place to allude to the fact that, in order to give my investigations to the public in any form that would satisfy me, I have **Why the Author is Publisher** been compelled to undertake the entire burden and expense of publication. Few things could be more inconvenient and distasteful than the business details thus imposed; but I have accepted them as a part of the sacrifice required of one who, as a prophet of the mysteries of Nature, feels called to declare, at whatever cost, the truths known to him.

Those who have undergone a like experience need not be told that the amount of loss to fall upon an author will be largely determined by the interest which friends and associates take in procuring for his book a place on the shelves of scientific societies and leading libraries.

I have received many favors and much generous help in procuring information and specimens from various naturalists and friends, for which **Thanks.** I express my thanks. I have tried to give full credit to all in the appropriate place in text or foot note, but will make deserved personal acknowledgments in a succeeding volume.

H. C. McC.

The Masse,
Philadelphia, November 1st, 1889.

TABLE OF CONTENTS OF VOLUME I.

PART I.—STRUCTURE AND SPINNING ORGANS.

CHAPTER I.

GENERAL CLASSIFICATION AND STRUCTURE.

CHAPTER II.

THE SPINNING ORGANS.

PART II.—GENERAL CHARACTERISTICS, CONSTRUCTION, AND ARMATURE OF WEBS.

CHAPTER III.

GENERAL CHARACTERISTICS OF ORBWEAVERS' SNARES.

CHAPTER IV.

CONSTRUCTION OF AN ORBWEB.

CHAPTER V.

ARMATURE OF ORBWEBS: VISCID SPIRALS.

PART III.—CHARACTERISTIC FORMS AND VARIATIONS OF SNARES.

CHAPTER VI.

ARGIOPE AND HER RIBBONED ORB.

CHAPTER VII.

EPEIRA AND THE ROUND VERTICAL WEB MAKERS.

CHAPTER VIII.

COMPOSITE SNARES AND SECTORAL ORBS.

CHAPTER IX.

HORIZONTAL SNARES AND DOMED ORBS.

PART IV.—UNBEADED ORBS AND SPRING SNARES.

CHAPTER X.

THE FEATHERFOOT SPIDER, ULOBORUS PLUMIPES.

CHAPTER XI.

THE TRIANGLE SPIDER AND ORB SECTOR.

CHAPTER XII.

THE RAY SPIDER AND HER SNARE; ACTINIC ORB.

PART V.—MECHANICAL SKILL, INTELLIGENCE, AND EQUIPMENT.

CHAPTER XIII.

ENGINEERING SKILL OF SPIDERS.

CHAPTER XIV.

MECHANICAL STRENGTH OF WEBS AND PHYSICAL POWERS OF SPIDERS.

PART VI.—PROVISION FOR NURTURE AND DEFENSE.

CHAPTER XV.

PROCURING FOOD AND FEEDING.

CHAPTER XVI.

EFFECTS AND USES OF POISON.

PART VII.—NESTING HABITS, PROTECTIVE ARCHITECTURE, AND DEVELOPMENT.

CHAPTER XVII.

NESTING HABITS AND PROTECTIVE ARCHITECTURE OF ORBWEAVERS.

CHAPTER XVIII.

NEST MAKING: ITS ORIGIN AND USE: DEVELOPMENT IN VARIOUS TRIBES.

CHAPTER XIX.

GENESIS OF SNARES.

CONTENTS OF VOLUME II.

CHAPTER I.

GENERAL CLASSIFICATION AND STRUCTURE.

I.

The order Araneæ has given the name of the true spiders, which it embraces, to the class of invertebrates to which it belongs, Arachnida. This

Origin of the Name

name, again, is due to that special function by which the spider is and has ever been popularly known. According to the Greek myth, Arachne was transformed into a spider by Pallas Minerva because she had boasted her superiority over that goddess in the use of the distaff. Hence the Greek name for spider (ἀράχνη), arachne. The English name is doubtless derived from the same function which led the unhappy Arachne upon her doom.[1] Spider is a corruption of "spinder," the spinning one. The word survives in a different form in the term "spinster," by which the virgin mistress of the distaff was commonly known in the days of our grandsires. There is therefore a popular and philological as well as natural fitness in the general classification of the order Araneæ which we adopt after Thorell,[2] who in turn has substantially followed the arrangement of Latreille.[3]

This classification is based upon the web making characteristics of the various groups

General Classification.

and is as follows: The order may be divided into two principal groups, the Sedentary spiders and the Wandering spiders.[3] The former group includes those whose habit it is to remain, for the most part, upon or within their webs and take their prey by means of snares. The second group includes those which stalk or pursue their prey

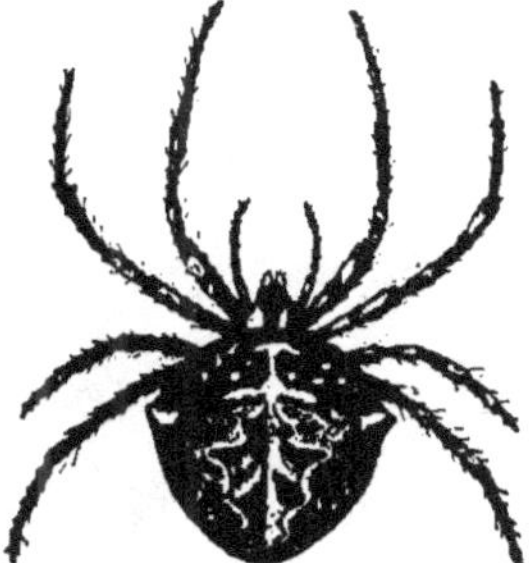

Fig. 1. An Orbweaver, Epeira gemma.

---

[1] See Ovid's Metamorphoses, Chap. vi. The story is told in the first 150 lines.

[2] On European Spiders, by T. Thorell. Nova Acta Reg. Soc. Scientarium Upsaliensis. Upsala, 1869.

[3] Latreille: In Cuvier's "Le Regne Animal," edition 1817, Paris. Sedentaires (Sedentary), page 79; Vagabondes (Wandering), page 95; Territèles, page 79; Tubitèles, page 81; Inequitèles (Retitelariæ), page 84; Orbitèles, page 86; Laterigrades, page 91; Citigrades, page 95; Saltigrades, page 98.

afield, upon the ground, water, or trees, and as a rule have no fixed domicile, except at the brooding time and during winter. These principal groups are subdivided into seven secondary groups, sections or suborders.[1]

Sedentary Group. The four tribes comprising the Sedentary spiders are named strictly from the chief characteristics of their spinningwork, viz.: the Orbitelariæ, from their orb shaped web; the Retitelariæ, from their net like web or snare of crossed lines; the Tubitelariæ, from the tubular web which they spin, and from the opening of which, in some species, a close textured snare spreads out in all directions; the Territelariæ, from the silken cylinder with which the typical species line their burrows in the ground.

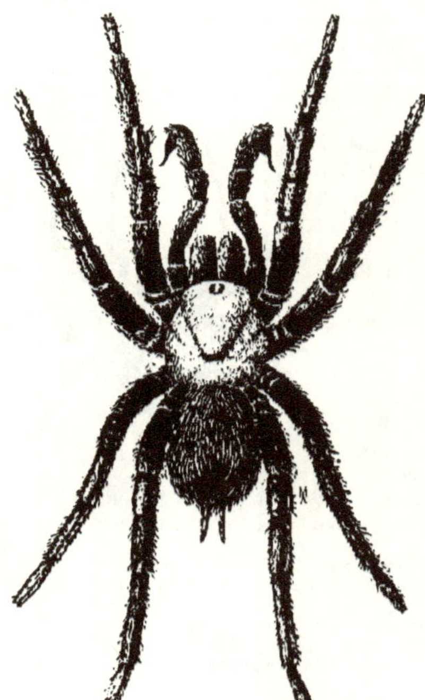

Fig. 2.   Territelariæ: Eurypelma Steindachnerii Ausserer.
(Dr. Marx, del.   Natural size.)

The Wandering spiders include three tribes, which are conspicuous by their ordinary independence of snares for the capture of prey, and have been named from certain peculiarities of motion. The **Wandering Group** Laterigradæ have legs so inserted as to permit a motion sidewise, as well as forward or backward. For this reason Latreille called them also Crab spiders. The Citigradæ include those species that keep chiefly to the land and water, upon which they run with great rapidity. The Saltigradæ, or vaulting spiders, are named from their hopping movement in ordinary progress. The individuals of these three tribes are almost equally entitled to be called citigrades, for they all move swiftly, but the Citigrades technically so termed are habitually running spiders, keeping closely upon the ground, while the Laterigrades and Saltigrades are arboreal, habitually dwelling upon plants and vertical surfaces. The three are also quite distinct in their structure, and the systematic position of any one, as far as above indicated, can commonly be told by a glance at the form.

[1] Thorell uses the term "suborders" in his European Spiders for these principal groups, but adopts the term "sections" in his "Descriptions of the Araneæ of Colorado" (Bulletin U. S. Geological Survey, Vol III., No. 2, page 477, note), and still later the name tribe (tribus).

The following tabular exhibit is given of this classification, or grouping, if that word seems to any one more suitable:—

CLASS ARACHNIDA.

ORDER ARANEÆ.

I. First Division.—Sedentary Spiders.

Tribe 1. Orbitelariæ,[1] Orbweavers.   Tribe 3. Tubitelariæ, Tubeweavers.
" 2. Retitelariæ,[2] Lineweavers.   " 4. Territelariæ, Tunnelweavers.

II. Second Division.—Wandering Spiders.

Tribe 5. Citigradæ,[3] Citigrades.   Tribe 6. Laterigradæ, Laterigrades.
Tribe 7. Saltigradæ, Saltigrades.

This arrangement is the best, perhaps, that can be adopted, and seems more natural and satisfactory than that which commanded the approval of

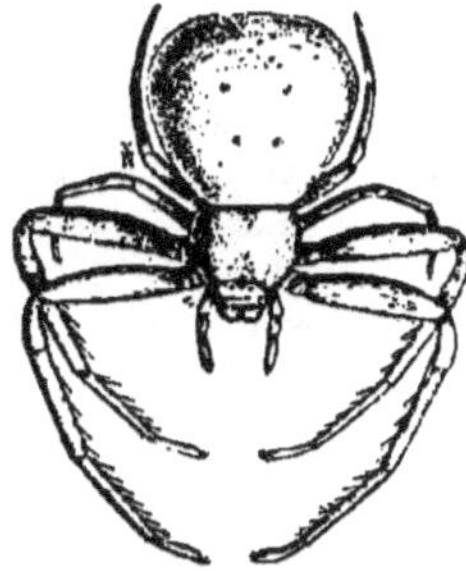

Blackwall's Classification.

such a distinguished arachnologist as Blackwall, and which is based upon the number of the eyes. Blackwall founded three tribes, within which all the species known to him are included. They are: (1) Octonoculina, eyes, eight; (2) Senoculina, eyes, six; (3) Binoculina, eyes, two. In the first tribe, Octonoculina, which is the most extensive of the three, he included all the genera having eight eyes, without regard to other characteristics or to the considerable differences in organization and economy. The second tribe, Senoculina, as known to Blackwall included but ten or eleven genera, and

FIG. 3. Laterigrade Spider, Misumena rosea Keyserling.

embraced all tribes having six eyes, with the same disregard to other characteristics. The third tribe, Binoculina, contained the single genus Nops, instituted by Mr. W. S. McLeay for the reception of two remarkable species of extra European spiders.[4] The Latreillian classification, which Thorell

---

[1] Araneæ Orbitelariæ: Perty, Delect. Anim. Art. Bras., page 193.

[2] From retus, a net. The word "net" very well expresses the knotted and meshed character of most spinningwork of this group. But since it is used popularly as a general term for the webs of all spiders, I have preferred "Lineweavers" to "Netweavers" as a distinctive popular name of this tribe.

[3] Prof. Thorell assigns the Laterigrades to the fifth tribe, the Citigrades to the sixth. I have ventured to so far change this arrangement as to reverse the positions of the Laterigrades and Citigrades. The Citigrades appear to me to approach the Tunnelweavers and Tubeweavers, both in structure and economy, more nearly than the Laterigrades. So also the step from the Citigrades to the Laterigrades through the genus Dolomedes appears more natural than the reverse, as Thorell has it; and the step to the Saltigrades from the Laterigrades is quite as, if not more, natural than from the Citigrades. From the standpoint of economy alone the passage is certainly easier.

[4] Blackwall. "Spiders of Great Britain and Ireland." Preface, page 6.

has so admirably expressed as above, will at least be preferred by those who set as much store upon the habits and functions of the creatures as upon their forms. The latter indeed will not be undervalued by a wise and careful student; but the systematists and anatomists will doubtless bear with those who would fain keep natural history from swinging too far away from the paths which earlier naturalists trod, and which so thoroughly traversed the life history of created things.

A general classification based upon the spider's behavior, especially in relation to its chief function, has the advantage that it compels attention to the creature's habit without at all neglecting its structure. It is not claimed that this classification is without objections. There are, indeed, some incongruities, more or less serious, which will appear hereafter. **The Classification Justified.** But until these interesting animals shall have received from naturalists that attention which their character and importance in nature justify, and which will enable some future arachnologist to show us a better way, we shall, perhaps, be best repaid by accepting this general grouping of the great families of the spider fauna. At least it is that which best serves my own purposes in the special lines marked out for this treatise.

Students who are interested in a more thorough consideration of this point will find the objections to the above system well stated, and a classification proposed based more upon anatomical structure, by Dr. Philip Bertkau, of Bonn.[1] A very satisfactory answer to these objections has been published by Prof. Tamarlan Thorell, M. D.,[2] who adheres substantially to his former system but, confessing his indebtedness to Prof. Bertkau for certain modifications, proposes a rearrangement which, he thinks, answers to our present knowledge of this order, as follows:—

ORDO ARANEÆ.

SUBORDO I. TETRAPNEUMONES.

Tribus I. Territelariæ.

SUBORDO II. DIPNEUMONES.

Tribus II. Tubitelariæ.

Ecribellatæ.   Cribellatæ.

Tribus III. Retitelariæ.

Tribus IV. Orbitelariæ.

Cribellatæ.   Ecribellatæ.

Tribus V. Laterigradæ.   Tribus VI. Citigradæ.   Tribus VII. Saltigradæ.

The scheme embraces European families for the most part, but includes a few exotic ones.

[1] See especially his "Versuch einer natürlichen Anordnung der Spinnen," in Archiv für Naturgeschichte, xliv., i., page 351, sq., 1878; and his treatise "Ueber das Cribellum und Calamistrum. Ein Beitrag zur Histiologie, Biologie, und Systematik der Spinnen," ibid., xlviii., i. page 316, et seq., 1882.

[2] Annals and Magazine Nat. Hist., Apl., 1886. "On Dr. Bertkau's Classification of the Order Araneæ or Spiders," by Prof. T. Thorell.

II.

The propriety of beginning the series of spiders with the Orbweavers has been generally recognized by authors. Perhaps some have had no better reason than that which popularly associates this group with the name spider; but others have thought that the highest forms in the order Araneæ are really included within the Orbitelariæ.

Highest Forms.

The suggestion of Thorell can hardly be allowed that the more artistic construction of web shows higher development of instincts in Epeïroids than in other families of the order. Surely the nests of some Lineweavers, as Theridium riparium and Linyphia marginata; of such Citigrades as our Turret spider, Lycosa arenicola Scudder; and such Tunnelweavers as our California trap door spider, Cteniza californica Cambridge, show a grade of instinct quite as high as that of the Orbweavers, and which, moreover, as it seems to me, exhibits a wider range of voluntary action and variation than the more mechanical spinning of a geometric web. With greater justice Thorell, when speaking to the point of structure alone, disallows the claims of the Orbweavers to the highest position in their order.

Fig. 4. Saltigrade Spider, Epiblemum scenicum Clerck.

Thorell's Views.

If we consider (he says) as we reasonably ought to do, more the harmonious development of the body's various parts, the superior development of the organs of sense, and such like, we see that the Epeïroidæ, with their weak cephalothorax and heavy abdomen, their slow and clumsy motions, and their comparatively small eyes, are surpassed by more than one of the other families usually looked upon as lower. The Lycosoidæ are distinguished by their well proportioned forms, their powerfully developed cephalothorax, by the quickness and force of their movements, and highly developed organs of sight.

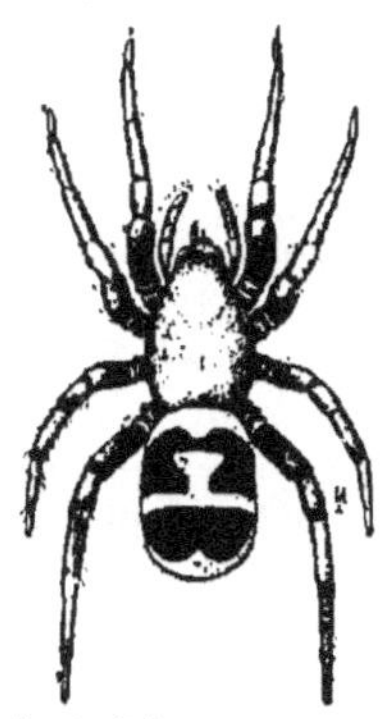

Fig. 5. Tubeweaving Spider, Gnaphosa variegata Hentz. (Marx, del.) Much magnified.

The Attoidæ also, as may be easily remarked by a casual observer in the little striped, jumping spider (Epiblemum scenicum) familiar around all our rural and suburban homes, have a striking expression of intelligence. This may be an optical effect solely due to the peculiar eyes and nervous jerking action of the animal, but certainly one is strongly reminded thereby of the "expression" of the Hymenoptera, as ants and wasps, the most highly developed of the order of insects.

The Attoidæ.

As regards the other reasons adduced to support the preëminence of the Epeïroids above all other spiders, such as the number and beauty of the species, the small number of transition forms, etc., they hold equally true of the Attoïds. These form a unit quite as close, compact, and rich in species as the Epeïroids; in brilliancy and variety of colors they surpass both these and other families of spiders, and may even be compared with the showy families of Coleoptera.[1]

Great as is the weight which this justly distinguished arachnologist carries toward the Attoïds, I am inclined, in consideration of both instincts and structure, to place the Lycosids at the head of the order. **Superiority of Lycosids.** The organization of this family is, to say the least, but little inferior, if at all, to that of the Attoïds; and in their spinning habits I have no hesitation in pronouncing them to be superior. Indeed, the Saltigrades are by no means remarkable for their spinning-work, in this respect scarcely equaling the Tubeweavers, perhaps the lowest of the spiders. The Citigrades, however, exhibit most interesting industries; and especially in the personal care of their young, from the egg cocoon to the period when the spiderlings can shift for themselves, the Lycosids seem to me to show a higher order of instinct than the Attoïds, certainly one as high. The whole subject, however, is one which includes difficulties too numerous and serious to allow a full discussion in these pages.

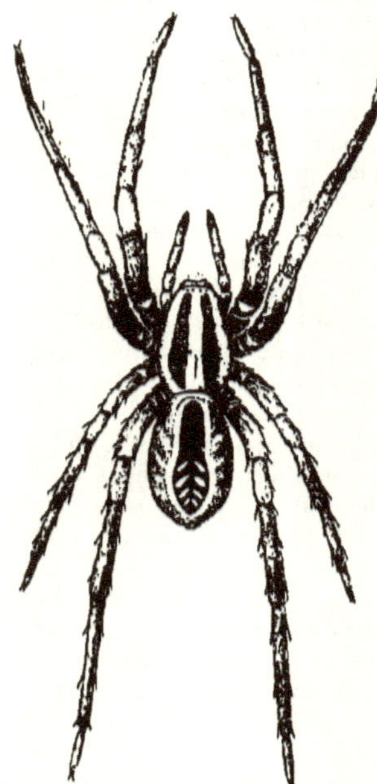

Fig. 6. Citigrade Spider, Lycosa scutulata Hentz. (Marx, del.) × 2.

Fig. 7. Lineweaving Spider, Theridium tepidariorum. (Marx, del.)

The Orbweavers have their nearest relations in the Lineweavers, whose snares of netted lines are familiar in the angles of our houses, forming largely the domestic "cobwebs." **Orbweavers and Lineweavers.** In most cases the two tribes can be distinguished by a practiced eye by the general form. But they can most easily be separated thus: The Epeïroids have a low forehead, not transversely impressed; from the margin of the clypeus to the middle front pair of eyes the distance is less, or at any rate not greater than the distance between the middle front and middle rear eyes. In the Retitelariæ, on the contrary, the distance from the margin of the clypeus to the middle front eyes is greater than that from the middle front to the middle rear eyes.[2]

[1] European Spiders, page 10.

[2] There are exceptions in the case of some Epeïroid males with strongly projecting forehead, and in the genus Tapinopa, among the Retitelariæ.

Thus Fig. 8 represents the eyes of an Epeïra, and Fig. 9 the eyes of the Retitelarian genus Theridium. Dr. Bertkau distinguishes these two tribes by the presence in the Epeïroids of what he calls a basal spot (Basalfleck) upon the mandibles.

III.

For the convenience of readers not acquainted with the anatomy of spiders, a general description of the animal is here given. It is not in accord with the purpose of this work to enter into the details of structure; for these the studies of anatomists and histologists must be consulted. But some knowledge of the principal organs, especially in their relations to the spinning industry, is necessary to the understanding of much of what follows.

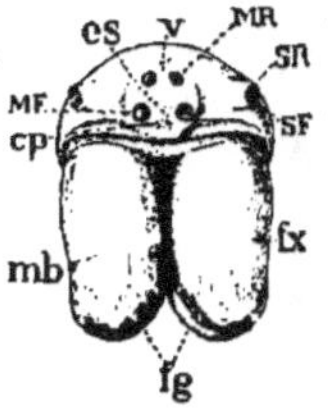

The principal parts are the cephalothorax and abdomen. The cephalothorax consists of the cephalic part (cp, Fig. 11) and the thoracic part, tp; the two parts

Fig. 8. Face of Epeïra.

are united directly, and not by a neck, the caput being set immediately upon the thorax, whence the name cephalothorax. The point of juncture is marked by a suture, more or less distinct, extending along the lower margin of the caput backward, on each side, and converging in a depression more or less profound at the summit of the thoracic part. The cephalothorax is externally a hard, chitinous case composed of two principal plates, resembling more nearly than any other part of the body the tough shell of true insects.

The front and upper portion of the cephalic part is the caput, which in Orbweavers is sometimes depressed, more frequently elevated. On the

The Caput. fore part of the caput are situated eyes, which in this group are eight, but in other groups sometimes number six and even two. The arrangement of the eyes upon the caput forms good generic and specific characters. The eyes in the Orbweavers are disposed across the caput in two rows of four each, known as front and rear rows (Fig. 8);

The Eyes. they are again divided into three groups, of which the middle group contains four eyes, known as the middle eyes, those in front being mid front or middle

Fig. 9. Face of Lineweaver, Theridium tepidariorum.

front (M.F.) and those behind, the mid rear or middle rear eyes (M.R.). The remaining four eyes, known as the side eyes (or lateral eyes), are placed in two's on either side of and equidistant from the middle group. They are known as the side front (S.F.) and side rear (S.R.); they are generally quite near to each other, frequently touch, but occasionally are well separated; for the most part they are smaller than the middle eyes. They, as well as the middle group, are often placed upon tubercles more or less prominent.

The part of the caput included between the two rows of eyes is called the eye space. The space between the front row of eyes and the lower margin of the face where it joins upon the mandibles is the clypeus (Cp). That between the upper row of eyes and the vertex (v) of the caput is the forehead. The entire space thus occupied, from the vertex to the margin of the clypeus, is the face or facial space.

Mandibles. The mandibles (mb) are two jaw like organs attached to the head beneath the margin of the clypeus, within which they articulate laterally. They are placed perpendicularly, or inclined more or less backward or toward the sternum. In shape they are conical or subovate. Each mandible is composed of two parts, the base or falx (fx) and the fang (fg). The fang is a curved movable tooth, smooth, hard, and pointed. It is hollow, pierced on the inner side near the point with a small hole, which opens into a slight furrow. The hollow of the fang is occupied by a membranous duct which leads upward to a gland lodged within the falx. This gland is supposed to secrete a poisonous liquid.

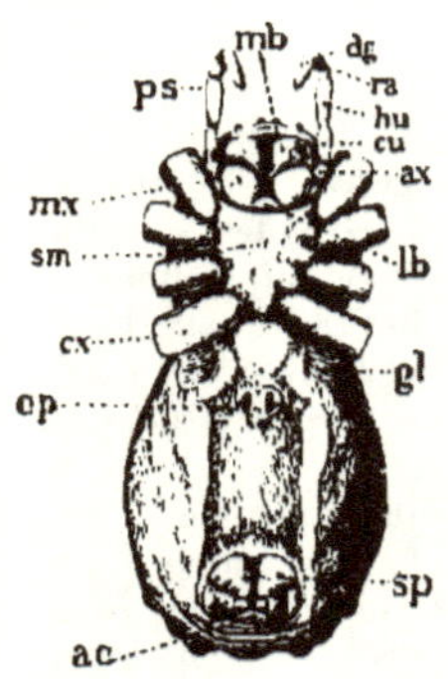

Fig. 10. Ventral view of Argiope argyraspis. ps, palps; mb, mandible; dg, digital joint of palps; ra, radial joint; hu, humeral; cu, cubital; ax, axillary; mx, maxillæ; lb, labium; sm, sternum; cx, coxa of the leg; gl, breathing gills; ep, epyginum; sp, spinnerets represented closed; ac, anal closure.

Falx. The falx is covered with hair, especially near the base, and at the apex is formed into a toothed groove or sheath into which the fang is folded down when at rest.

Sternum. **Labium.** The sternum (sm) is a cordate plate which forms the under part of the shell of the cephalothorax. It has four indentations on each side, which mark the insertion of legs. On the forward part at the middle is placed the labium or lower lip (lb), a subtriangular or semi-ovate organ of the mouth. (See Fig. 10.)

Maxillæ. Opposed to the labium and above it is the upper lip, a slight hair tipped projection, which is the termination of the palate. On either side of the labium is placed one of the maxillæ or lower jaws. They vary in form, the variation giving good generic characters. They have a

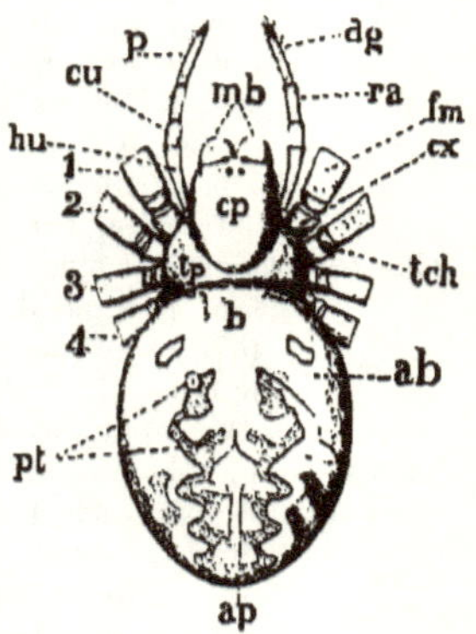

Fig. 11. Dorsal view of Epeira insularis. ab, abdomen; b, base; ap, apex of abdomen; pt, pits which mark the attachment of abdominal muscles; cp, cephalic part of cephalothorax; tp, thoracic part; mb, mandibles. 1, 2, 3, and 4, the legs represented in their order, first, second, third, and fourth. Tch, trochanter of the leg; cx, coxa; fm, femur; dg, digital, ra, radial, cu, cubital, hu, humeral joint of palps.

rotary motion upon the fore part of the sternum, moving toward and against each other, thus crushing the interposed prey.

The palps (ps) or palpi are two organs inserted into the free end of the maxillæ, of which they are an organic part.[1] Each palp has five joints of various lengths named in order from the maxilla, (1) axillary, ax, (2) humeral, hu, (3) cubital, cu, (4) radial, ra, and (5) digital, dg. The axillary joint is the shortest of the five and corresponds to the second joint of the leg or trochanter, the maxilla being the equivalent of the coxa.[2] The humeral joint is much longer than the axillary; the cubital again is short, being a sort of knee joint. The radial is one and a half or twice as long as the above, and the digital is usually the longest joint of all.[3]

Palps.

The palps vary greatly in the two sexes. In the female each digital, dg, terminates like the foot and is usually armed with a well developed curved claw (palpal claw) pectinated or serrated. These organs are prehensile, are used variously as hands or feet to hold and turn the prey, to dig, to sustain the body when suspended upon webs, to grasp the cocoon, etc., and even to aid in locomotion. In the male the digital joint contains the genital organ; it is

Sexual Forms of Palps.

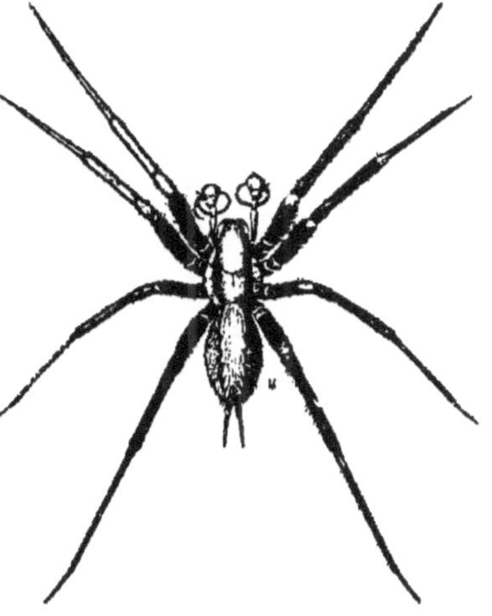

Fig. 12. Male of Agalena nœvia: the speckled Tubeweaver. (Marx, del.)

enlarged, often very greatly, into a bulb whose structure is complicated and subject to great specific variations. (Fig. 12.) It is always more or less covered on top by a plate, which may be distinguished from other parts by a more or less dense pubescence scattered upon the superior surface and

[1] On account of the curved process upon the top of each maxilla whose convexity is toward its fellow, the palp may be said to issue from the side instead of the end of the maxilla.

[2] Westring, "Araneæ Svecicæ," Termini Technici, page 11.

[3] I have adopted the terminology of Walckenaer, which is followed also by Blackwall and Cambridge. That of Westring is (in the same order as above): (1) basal, (2) femoral, (3) patellar, (4) tibial, (5) tarsal. The analogy between this terminology and that of the legs, perhaps has some advantage to the memory, but the Walckenaer names appear to me to be preferable, as being quite distinctive, and thus preventing confusion with names given to the joints of the legs.

sometimes under the apex. This genital plate or lamina corresponds to the apical part of the female digital, but the digital claw is entirely wanting, or rudimentary and hidden by pubescence. The genital organ is placed under the base of the lamina. It is furnished with processes varying in form, size, and number, and with a hook or tube (or tubes) which fit into corresponding cavities in the female organ, and transfer the seminal fluid thereto. This peculiar formation does not appear until the last moult, when the spider is mature. Previous to that the male digital is simply a hairy bulb. The term genital bulb is also applied to the genital

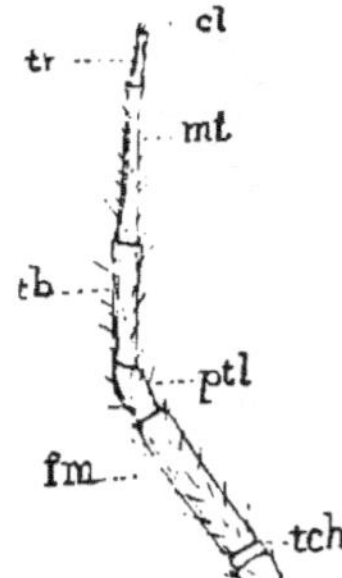

Fig. 13. Leg of Epeira magnified. Cx, coxa, the joint which unites the leg with the sternum; tch, trochanter, small joint by which the femur articulates upon the coxa; fm, femur; ptl, patella; tb, tibia; mt, metatarsus; t, tarsus; cl, claws.

organ. Sometimes the bulb is quite one with the lamina in which it is muffled, in which case the bulb is called the clava.[1]

During the interval between the third and fourth moulting a considerable change takes place. In the male the extremities of the palpi swell like clubs and develop into different indentations, teeth, threads, or leaves, which later on serve as transmitters of the semen. At first the clubs are filled with semitransparent fluid, while the forming inner organs are yellowish or brownish; at first the skin is quite soft, but soon hardens and forms a shell, which turns darker by the action of the air. Inasmuch as these organs are almost devoid of soft parts it follows naturally that as the shell cannot come off, no further moulting can take place.

Moulting Changes.

At the time the palpi become fully developed a great change takes place also in the female genitals; the immediate surroundings become roughened and somewhat hardened, presenting little humps which serve partly as rests for the male palpi and partly as receptacles for the semen, and is what is designated as "vulva."[2] When fully matured the sexes, hitherto separated, come together, and the copulation takes place in a different manner by different varieties.[3]

The legs of the spider are eight, symmetrically disposed, four on each side of the sternum to which they are articulated. Their relative lengths give one of the best characters for systematic arrangement. They are numbered from the face backward as first (1), second (2), third (3), and fourth (4) pairs. (Fig. 14.) The relative lengths are indicated by a formula composed of the above numerals arranged in the order of greatest lengths from highest to lowest, thus: 1 2 4 3 is the formula which expresses the prevailing order among Orbweavers and de-

The Legs.

[1] Westring, Araneæ Suecicæ, page 12.

[2] Menge, "Die Preussische Spinnen."

[3] See Chapter on "Wooing and Mating Habits," Vol. II.

clares that the first leg is the longest, then the second leg, then the fourth leg, and lastly the third leg. When two pairs of legs are of equal length the numerals expressing them are united by the sign of equality: thus, 1 2 = 4 3 indicates that the second and fourth legs are of equal length.[1] For the most part the third leg is much the shortest of the four, and the first pair decidedly the longest. This rule, however, varies in certain genera, as Acrosoma, in which the fourth pair is as long as, or longer than the first, a variation which seems to be adapted to the peculiar form of the spider. The males have legs longer and slighter than the females, and in some species have a special armature in the shape of a comb of stout spines upon the tibia of the second pair, which probably serves as a clasping organ in the act of pairing.

The legs have seven joints, which are arranged in the following order, counting from the point of union with the sternum: First, the coxa (cx, Fig. 13), the short joint which unites the leg to the body. It is partly concealed beneath the cephalothorax, and sometimes carries short, pointed processes. Second, the trochanter (tch), a minute joint which really serves for the articulation of the leg upon the body, the coxa being fixed. Third, the femur (fm), usually the longest and stoutest joint of all. Fourth, the patella (ptl), which nearly corresponds in length with the coxa, and serves as a sort of knee joint. Fifth, the tibia (tb), whose length is usually a little less than that of the femur. Sixth, the metatarsus (mtr), the penultimate joint, which approaches the length of the femur, is commonly longer than the tibia, but much slighter. Seventh, the tarsus (tr), the ultimate joint, which is usually shorter than the metatarsus. The last five of these joints are armed with a great number of spines, bristles, and hairs, which are placed more freely along the inner surfaces of the legs, and thus are disposed for the greatest advantage of the animal in manipulating its prey, embracing its mate, or fighting its enemies. They are also used in spinning the snare.

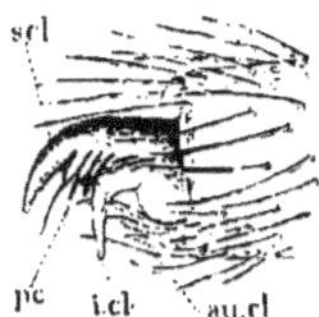

Fig. 14. Foot of Epeira insularis. s.cl, superior claw; pc, pectinations upon the superior claws; i.cl, inferior claws; au.cl auxiliary claws upon the tarsus.

Orbweavers have three strong, genuine claws upon their tarsi, of which the two superior are pectinated, and (with rare exceptions) the inferior is armed with two close and blunt comb teeth (cb.th). The superior claws are of equal size, placed side by side. The inferior claw is smaller than the others and is below them, bent down near the base. The extremity of the tarsus is always provided with two or more auxiliary claws (au.cl).[2] One of these, a strong spine, has the

Tarsal Claws.

---

[1] I have taken this formula as more convenient for expression in type. In most authors the equal members are joined by a bracket above, thus: 1 2 4 3.

[2] Thorell, European Spiders, page 47.

power of motion toward the claws beneath which it is situated, thus acting as a sort of thumb, which is used especially in grasping the spinningwork.[1]

In the armature of the legs must be reckoned also the calamistrum which characterizes the family Uloborinae among the Orbitelariae, in common with certain Ciniflonidae. This is a double row of curved spines, placed upon the inside of the metatarsus of the hind pair of legs, in form not unlike the old fashioned "flyers" of a spinning wheel. (Fig. 15.) They are used for the flocculation of the threads as they pass from the spinning tubes, thus forming the peculiar cross lines which characterize the spinningwork of the above families, and serve the purpose of viscid beads.

Fig. 15. Calamistrum of Ciniflo. (After Blackwall.) a, upper row of spines; b, lower row; c, the spur.

The Abdomen. The second principal part of the spider is the abdomen. Among Orbweavers it assumes widely varying forms, being globular, ovate, subtriangular, cylindrical; sometimes flat, sometimes convex above; on the ventral surface nearly flat or slightly convex. Thus, the face of a section cut transversely through the middle would, for the most part, be properly or approximately described as semicircular, except in the case of gravid females. The integument is soft, sometimes leathery; usually hairy, but not densely so, sometimes naked and glossy. The organ is generally smooth, but in some species is marked with conical tubercles upon the base, and in some genera is bordered with sharp, hard, spinous processes, and in some is ridged or striated along the rear. The base generally overhangs the cephalothorax as much as one-third or even one-half the length of that organ with which it is united by the pedicle, a short cartilaginous tube through which pass the organs of nutrition and circulation.

Pigment-Colored Hairs. In the female the size of the abdomen is large, as compared with the cephalothorax, a proportion which is greatly increased during the period of gestation. In the male spider the relative size of the abdomen is even less than, or is equal to the cephalothorax. The markings upon the tergum are various, and are more or less uniform with every species, though subject to some decided specific variations. They are caused, when present, by a pigment under

[1] This arrangement gives a strong color of justification to the use of the word "hands" in the familiar quotation from Holy Scripture, Proverbs, xxx., 28: "The spider taketh hold with her hands, and is in king's palaces." In various palaces in Europe, and in many public buildings of America, I have never failed to observe spider's webs, usually some species of Lineweaver, whose occupants hung by their "hands" within their silken domiciles. I hesitate to think, notwithstanding the philological objection that the Hebrew שְׂמָמִית (Semamith) means "lizard," that Solomon had any other animal in view than the spider. The natural history of the text so exactly harmonizes with the habits of spiders, especially Lineweavers and Orbweavers, that I have difficulty in believing that so careful an observer of nature as the Royal Proverbialist could have used the above language concerning any other animal.

the translucent epiderm, rather than by pubescence. These colors are often very bright, shades of yellow and red prevailing, and bright metallic white or silver being frequent.

The tough integument which covers the abdomen consists of three layers; the external one is a thin, transparent, horny membrane, nearly colorless, but more or less densely covered with colored hairs. Beneath this lies the soft layer of pigmentary matter upon which the peculiar color of the body largely depends. The third or inner layer consists of an expanded network of muscular fibres, which are irregularly interlaced, and which must enable the spider forcibly to compress the abdomen. The muscles forming this layer are very faintly, if at all, marked with transverse striæ. (Meade.)

On the ventral side or venter near the base (anterior part) are situated two gills, breathing holes, or pulmonary sacs (bg). They are scales or plates symmetrically apposed on either side, form-

Pulmona-ry Sacs. ing the covering of cavities communicating with the tracheæ or air tubes. Externally they present the appearance of simple transverse slits in the venter. Each cavity contains about fifty extremely thin, triangular, white leaflets, fastened together at the edge of the breathing hole. Each is double, being in fact a flat pouch with an opening on the lower side communicating with the outer air. The spiracular plates are usually conspicuous objects upon the venter, differing in color therefrom, sometimes slightly pubescent, but more commonly smooth, and of harder substance than

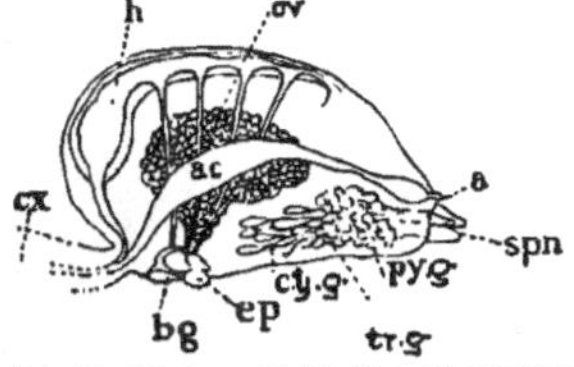

Fig. 16. Diagram of location of spinning organs and their relations to other organs of the abdomen. spn, spinnerets; py.g, pyriform glands; tr.g, treeform glands; cy.g, cylindrical glands; ep, epigynum; bgl, breathing gills; ac, alimentary canal; a, anus; ov, ovaries, showing the eggs; h, heart; cx, cephalothorax. (After Underhill.)

the surrounding surface. (Cambridge.) In the male spider a minute orifice which leads to the seminal organs is located between the spiracular plates.

Epigynum. In the same situation in the female is an aperture usually rather conspicuous, which is surmounted or surrounded with a corneous process of greater or less development. This aperture is the vulva. The process is known as the epigynum, and probably has the function of an ovipositor. The form and structure of the epigynum are characteristics highly valued by systematic arachnologists in the determination of species. But the organ is not present in immature spiders, and until the female reaches maturity no aperture is visible. The organs of reproduction in the female consist of two long ovoid plates, longitudinally placed within the ventral surface of the abdomen. These unite and form a short broad oviduct, whose external opening between the spiracular orifice is the epigynum (ep), Fig. 16.

The ovaries, which shortly before the deposition of eggs occupy a large portion of the abdominal cavity, are seated in the central and posterior part. The intestinal tube runs through it in nearly a straight direction from the base to the apex, and the sacs and tubes which elaborate the material for forming the webs are placed in the lower, lateral, and anterior parts. In the male, the organs for the secretion of seminal fluid consist of two long, narrow, convoluted tubes, occupying the same relative position as the ovaries in the female. They also open outwardly into the minute orifice noted above.

The manner in which the act of pairing between the sexes occurs is a matter of doubt, and probably differs among different species. Mr. Cambridge[1] reports a case in which a perfect apparent coition was effected between sexual apertures of the male and female spider, the palpi not being used at all; and I have observed what seemed to be a similar act in the pairing of the sexes of Agalena nævia. On the other hand, it is evident that the spermatic fluid is conveyed to the female parts of generation by the male palpi. I have seen and recorded this action in the case of Linyphia marginata. Menge and Ausserer have observed that the male spider before the act of union emits from the sexual aperture a drop of sperma on a web made for the purpose, which drop he then takes up in the genital bulb of the palpi and then communicates it to the female.

Male Organs.

Fig. 17. Collecting a spider in a box.

With regard to the function exercised by the remarkable organs connected with the digital joint of the palpi of male spiders, there exists some difference of opinion. Taking anatomy as his guide, Treviranus arrived at the conclusion that the parts in question are used for the purpose of excitation merely, preparatory to the actual union of the sexes by means of appropriate organs situated near the anterior part of the inferior regions of the abdomen. This view of the subject, which is very generally adopted, is opposed to that derived from physiological facts by Dr. Lister and the earlier systematic writers on arachnology, who regarded the palpal organs as strictly sexual; and recent researches, conducted with the utmost caution, have clearly established the accuracy of the opinion advanced by that distinguished Englishman.[2]

Digital of Male Palpi.

[1] For valuable anatomical notes see his "Arachnida," Encyclopædia Britannica.
[2] Blackwall: "Reports 14th Meeting British Association Adv. of Sci.," pages 67-69. Also "Spiders of Great Brit. and Ireland." Introduction, page 5.

IV.

Perhaps a few of my readers may become sufficiently interested in the subjects considered in this volume to wish to make personal observations on the habits of spiders, and collections of species. A few hints for the benefit of such persons may be given. For collectors a small satchel or hand-bag with a strap by which it can be slung across the shoulder is a most convenient arrangement. This should be furnished with a number of small paper or wooden boxes, such as are used for putting up pills and like drugs. Wide mouthed vials and bottles may also be used.

In capturing a spider, the lid should be removed from the box and the two parts placed one upon one side and another upon the other side of the orb, or above and below, as circumstances may require. **Capturing Specimens.** When they are gradually approached they may be suddenly closed, and the spider will be captured inside the box. Care should be taken to get the spider well inside before the cover is closed, as there is danger of crushing the specimens. Any note or record may briefly be made upon the top or bottom of the box, or it may be numbered and the memorandum kept in the note book. The imprisoned spider will keep without injury until the collector has reached his home, when he can make a further personal examination by opening the box carefully and dropping the spider into

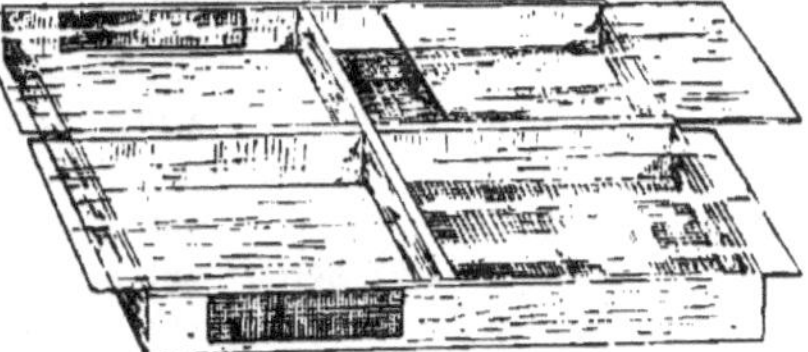

Fig. 18.   Example of a trying-box.

a glass vessel with steep sides. Long test tubes of several sizes are very convenient for decanting collections from the boxes and, after examination, into alcohol.

If one wishes to observe the habits under artificial conditions, a series of wooden boxes may be made with sliding glass covers, as represented in the accompanying cut. **Trying Boxes.** These may be ventilated by fine wire cloth or gauze. Such boxes may be made of sizes to suit the habit of the species. For cocooning purposes, eight by ten inches will be large enough ordinarily, and also quite large enough to observe the spinning habits of the smaller species. Large glass jars of any sort make good homes for trying the manners of many species. When the creature's habit requires, earth and sticks should be inserted. (See Fig. 18.)

What is still better, if circumstances will permit, the collecting boxes may be opened upon vines and shrubbery in the garden or grounds. It is not a difficult thing to establish a spidery in this way. The observer may open the boxes promiscuously and allow the spiders to settle their own habits in their own way; or if he wish, he may deposit all those of one species upon certain parts of the ground, in which case they will be very sure to permanently colonize. In this manner the most interesting species of an entire neighborhood or district may, in the course of a couple of years, be so thoroughly domesticated upon a small space that observation of habits will be greatly facilitated.

Natural Spidery.

There are many other points of practical value which might be mentioned, but, as a matter of fact, the collector's experience will soon show him what is the best thing to do. A few failures in capturing prizes will teach caution, and successes will in like manner show the best way of procedure. Caution is always necessary. While looking for spiders one needs to move with his eyes thrown well in advance, and to be careful to disturb as little as possible the bushes and surrounding shrubbery, upon which the greatest prizes may be domiciled and may be lost by careless or too rapid approach.

In searching for spiders, one should take such a position toward the sun as to enable the light to fall upon the webs in the direction towards which he is moving. Frequently the head should be turned to one side and lowered towards the ground in order to catch the sheen of the spinningwork hanging in secluded places, or even in quite open places. A soft black hat or something that will be a good substitute therefor, is a necessary part of the spider collector's outfit. Placed behind a web, it brings out all its white lines clearly, and one can thus study the structure with greater ease.

How to See Webs.

As a rule the evening is the best time to observe the netmaking habits, and, indeed, many other habits of the spider fauna. Some species begin to spin early in the evening, as early as four or five o'clock. Others are rarely found abroad until a later hour. These actions, however, are always more or less conditioned by the weather. During the night spiders are nearly always out upon their webs, and by means of a lantern one can make good collections and observations after nightfall. A dewy morning is perhaps the best time of all for finding webs. Provided with a stout pair of shoes or rubber boots, one may tramp through the dew laden fields of a summer morning, and find myriads of webs, great and small, of all species, hanging from every part of bushes, trees, grasses, weeds, and even spread in great multitudes upon the fresh soil of an upturned field. At such times the Orbweavers will not always be found upon their webs, at least certain species of them cannot conveniently be out, but the character of the webs can thus be readily perceived, and the habitat of the spider known. Little bits of paper should be carried in the satchel, and they may be fastened upon twigs in the neighborhood of the webs which thus are well located. A little slit in the centre of the patch of paper, thrust over a forked twig, will stay for many days, and will at once mark the

Best Times.

Marking Localities.

desired position. A note to identify the species may be scratched upon this paper guidon. A cotton string will answer the same purpose in a small field of observation. Another method is to puncture a leaf with a pencil point, making a letter, figure, or symbol. The holes leave a dry border which easily identifies a particular spot for many days.

Larger boxes should be placed in the satchel to be used for collecting cocoons and nests. The nests are often difficult to preserve, but some of them are so beautiful that they are well worth the effort. I **Taking Nests.** usually take special boxes for this purpose, or when not so provided, carry the nests free in my hand, or wrapped in little paper bags. Cotton should always be kept in the satchel, and when the nests are taken they should be carefully filled in with the cotton wool until the natural proportions are fully marked out. Of course, the leaves will rapidly dry up and wither and the nests will lose their form unless this precaution be taken.

In collecting spider nests, it will nearly always be necessary to cut away carefully a part of the adjoining foliage, in order to prevent the collapse of the whole when the supporting lines are cut. It is better to fill a nest with cotton before it is cut away from its site, or immediately thereafter. Tissue paper or even crushed leaves will answer where cotton is wanting.

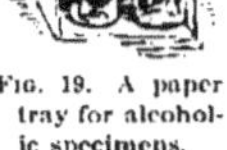

Fig. 19. A paper tray for alcoholic specimens.

An ordinary pocket rule, a strong knife with a good, big blade for taking out ground spiders, should also go into the hand bag. Pencils, several of them, for one is apt to lose a pencil in the excitement of collecting unless it be tied to the neck or button; a hand lens for the satchel, and two or three others to carry in the pockets, are almost necessary. A good objective may be carried in a vest pocket, and will give one an opportunity for rough microscopic observations while he is afield. Provide also a pair of shears for clipping off twigs and branches; and a few elastic bands for fastening the boxes whose covers are a little loose.

For one who wishes to collect spiders without particularly observing the habits, a glass bottle or good sized glass tube filled with alcohol, is the chief requisite. If one is collecting Orbweavers or Line- **Cabinet Speci- mens.** weavers, by placing the open bottle beneath the spider and gently touching the creature, it will frequently drop into the alcohol, or the bottle can be placed rapidly beneath the spider, and with the sudden impulse to drop which is characteristic of it, it will fall directly into the alcohol. A cyanide bottle, such as is used by collectors of Lepidoptera may be used instead of alcohol.

After the spiders have been collected in the bottle, they may be assorted and placed in separate tubes. No special method of mounting spiders can be satisfactorily recommended. I have found nothing better for my own purposes than glass bottles, well corked, with a bit of paper inside to indicate the species, and these placed in small paper trays (see Fig. 19), bound in by two India rubber bands slipped over the box. These trays are placed upon end inside of my cabinet boxes, and the name **Preserving Specimens.** of the species marked distinctly on the top. Any other notes as to date, locality, etc., can be jotted upon the back or on the inside of the tray. The trays may be readily stored in boxes with stiff pasteboard or wooden partitions, according to the width of the tray, and the whole kept in a small cabinet. (Fig. 20.) A quite small cabinet will suffice to contain all the species of any neighborhood.

A stout umbrella is a very important implement in collecting. The open umbrella should be placed (handle upwards) underneath the bushes, and these beaten in the ordinary way. When the umbrella is lifted aside, there will be found numbers of insects of various kinds, along with bits of leaves, twigs, etc., and more or fewer spiders of various sorts. These can readily be taken in boxes or in the collecting bottle. I have often found advantage in holding the umbrella off a little distance and inverting it slowly. The rubbish will drop on the ground and the spiders will also fall, but hold on to the little dropline which they instinctively throw out when falling. The bottle can then be rapidly placed beneath these swinging individuals, who are thus secured. The ordinary ento-

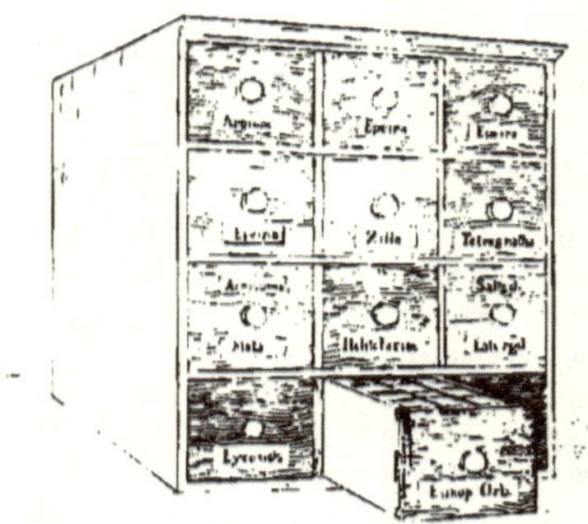

Fig. 20. A collector's cabinet.

mologist's bag may also be used for sweeping the grasses and hedge rows. Many species will be found by sifting the fallen leaves and other rubbish of the woods and fields, within which they hide. Others will be found underneath the bark of old trees and fallen logs.

A cupping glass and a card usually answer for collecting large ground spiders. I have taken the great tarantula of Texas in this way, watching my opportunity to slip the glass over the animal. The card is **Ground Spiders.** then gradually introduced between the glass and the ground, and the spider can thus be lifted up in the hand. A small vial of chloroform or ether for such purposes may be carried in the satchel. A pellet of cotton, moistened in either of these drugs, if slipped underneath the card within the cupping glass, will soon overcome the animal, which may then be dropped without inconvenience into the alcohol.

I have never had any hesitation in handling our indigenous spiders in order to collect them, though, of course, I should not care to lay hands on a tarantula, and am careful with our largest species of Lycosids. But there are few spiders, perhaps there are none, in our Northern and Middle States, that may not be seized with comparative impunity and disposed of according to the wishes of the collector. I have (I suppose I may say thousands of times) picked out of their snares or from the ground all sorts and sizes of spiders; even the largest orbweavers, as Argiope cophinaria and Epeira trifolium, I have collected and carried in my hands. Yet only on one occasion do I remember to have been bitten. In point of fact my respect for the good nature of my aranead pets has been greatly increased by my experience of their forbearance and general harmlessness under extreme provocation. I state the facts in my own case, but do not take the responsibility of advising any one to follow my example.

Of course the above hints are bare outlines of what my own experience has suggested as satisfactory. Others, doubtless, have better ways, and all may find modes better for themselves. No man's methods will quite fit another; and, after all, experience is the best teacher for all. I have only tried to give the tyro arachnologist a helpful start.

CHAPTER II.

THE SPINNING ORGANS.

I.

THE external spinning organs or spinning fingers, are located under the posterior or apical extremity of the abdomen in most species. In some, however, they are placed a little more underneath, and in such **External Spinning Organs.** genera as Acrosoma and Gasteracantha they are located at or near the middle point of the ventral part of the abdomen, forming the apex of the inverted pyramid or cone, which it then assumes. In the orbweaving species the external spinning organs consist ordinarily

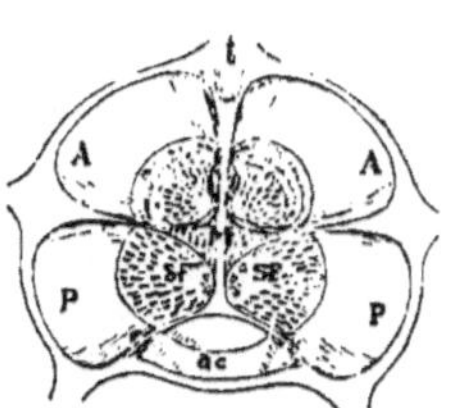

Fig. 21. View of the spinnerets of Argiope cophinaria, represented closed, but the parts not quite in contact. A, anterior, P, posterior, M, middle spinnerets. SF spinning field; ac, anal closure.

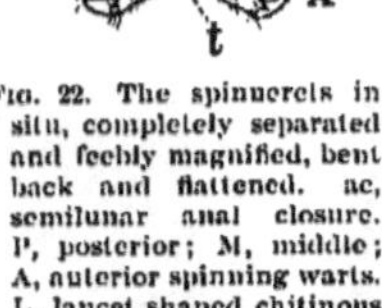

Fig. 22. The spinnerets in situ, completely separated and feebly magnified, bent back and flattened. ac, semilunar anal closure. P, posterior; M, middle; A, anterior spinning warts. L, lancet shaped chitinous leaf, between the two anterior spinnerets.

of six spinnerets, which are divided into pairs arranged symmetrically on either side of the median line of the venter, occupying a small circular space immediately forward of the anal opening. The hindermost pair (nearest the apex), will be known in this work as the posterior or outer spinnerets; the foremost pair, as the anterior or inner spinnerets; and the pair located between these two, as the middle spinnerets.[1] (See Figs. 21 and 22.) With Orbweavers the spinnerets are short, and the anterior and posterior pairs

[1] The nomenclature of these organs has become very much confused, and I have hesitated as to what terms I should adopt, but finally have concluded to call the six "spinning mammulæ" of Blackwall by the term which has now passed into common English use, namely, spinnerets; and the minute tubes upon the tips of the spinnerets, out of which the silk directly proceeds, by the name which they commonly receive among German writers, namely, spinning spools. These latter organs, Blackwall has called spinnerets, but his name has been transferred by naturalists and by the lexicographers to the larger organs which he called spinning mammulæ, and which the Germans generally name "spinning warts." The names of the several groups of spinnerets, as determined by their relative position, are also much confused. I have concluded to drop the titles prevalent among German histologists and others, namely, inferior, intermediate, and superior, and speak of them as the anterior or inner, the middle, and the posterior or outer spinnerets. I also occasionally speak of these organs as the spinning fingers, a name whose propriety has often been impressed upon me by their use.

(34)

about equal in length. In form these organs are somewhat conical and cylindrical, widened at the base and gently sloped or flattened at the tips.

The Spinnerets. The three pairs differ somewhat in appearance and size, the middle pair being shorter and less in size and more closely approximated. The posterior and anterior spinnerets have two joints (Bucholz and Landois); the middle ones are unjointed cones.[1] They are movable, particularly the posterior and anterior pairs, articulating with the integument of the body, and can be closed in upon each other until the tips touch at the spinning fields, as when one closes the thumb upon the four fingers of his hand. The spinning fields, Fig. 21, SF, are those portions of the tips and sides of the spinnerets on which are placed the sessile tubes out of which the silk passes.

In repose the spinnerets are generally closed (Fig. 21), forming a sort of rosette of five divisions; but when the spider is engaged in active operations, the posterior and anterior spinnerets are thrown well back, and the two middle ones open up, and thus,

1. Posterior Spinnerets. to quote the language of Dugès, "this singular flower unfolds." The posterior spinnerets (Figs. 21 and 23, P)[2] are well separated from each other, and lie directly forward of the semilunar anal covering (Fig. 21, ac). They are movable horizontally toward each other, so that their long oval

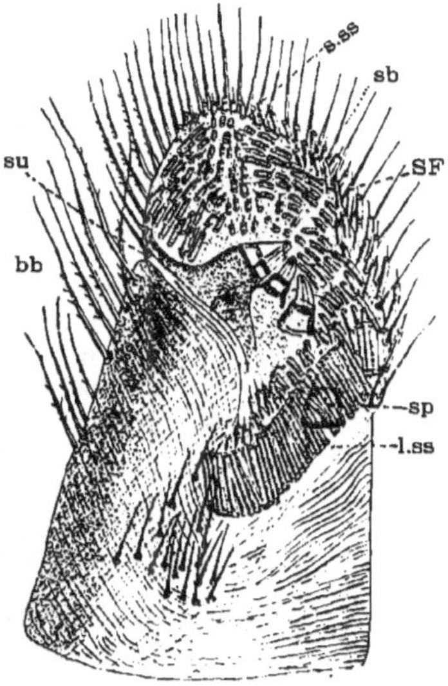

Fig. 23. Posterior spinneret of Ep. diademata, greatly magnified. su, sutine between joints; SF, spinning field; bb, branched bristles; sb, simple bristles; sp, spigot spool; l.ss, long spinning spools; s.ss, short spools. (After Bucholz and Landois.)

spinning fields approximate and, indeed, may be said to lie upon the corresponding middle spinnerets. They may be described as thumb shaped organs; are of a long, cylindrical form, and towards the free end are conically rounded. The terminal joint is divided from the base by a suture, Fig. 23, su, which extends along the inner and hinder edge, much farther than on the opposite edge, so that the spinning field extends on that face much farther towards the base.

---

[1] Meckel and Oellinger both attribute three joints to the posterior and anterior, and two to the middle spinnerets.

[2] To prevent confusion and the multiplication of references to figures the same lettering is preserved for like organs and parts thereof in all the anatomical figures.

The spinning field, SF, is an elliptical slope, which is situated on the inner side of the spinneret, and extends across the summit to the opposite **Spinning Field.** face of the lip. The basal part of the spinneret is cylindrical and gradually grows smaller toward the spinning field. At the lower or inferior edge is a row of long, strong branched bristles, bb. On the inner surface, and at the border of the prolonged spinning field, is a group of much shorter, stiff, simple bristles, sb.

On each posterior spinning field is placed a number of spools, which may be estimated roundly at one hundred and twenty. Besides these, there are five larger spools, sp, which after Bucholz and Landois we may distinguish as spigots. Through these spigots issue a corresponding number of cylindrical and treeform glands presently to be described. That part of the spinning field which runs downward toward the base is composed of numerous rows of long, closely placed spools, l.ss.; while that part of the field on the summit is covered with short spools, s.ss. (See Fig. 23.) Of the spinning spigots (Fig. 23), four stand close together in one group towards the middle of the spinning field, and one of them is situated in the lower part of the field (near l.ss.), and appears to be covered by the long spinning spools. Of the four grouped spigots, three give exit to treeform glands; and the one farthest towards the base is connected with a cylindrical gland. The isolated spool sp, (near l.ss.) also discharges a treeform gland.

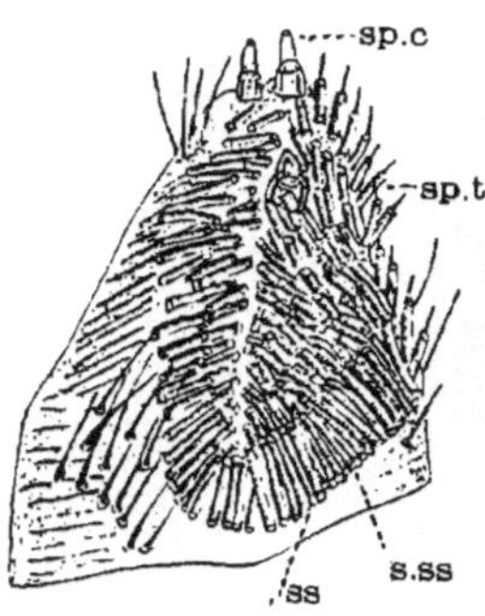

FIG. 21. Middle spinneret, largely magnified. sp.c, spigot discharging cylindrical gland; ss, and s.ss, spinning spools of pyriform glands; sp.t, spigot of treeform gland.

The middle spinnerets are of a three faced pyramidal form. (Fig. 22, M, and Fig. 24.) The bases are directed towards the front, while their points, lying closely together, are turned immediately backward. They are unjointed.[1] The spinning field is triangular, and occupies almost the entire slope **2. Middle Spinnerets.** of the spinneret from base to point. It contains quite a number of long spinning spools, which may be approximately estimated at one hundred and fifty. On each middle spinneret there are also three spinning spigots, of which two are close together at the tip, sp.c, and give issue to cylindrical glands. A little further back, another spigot gives exit to a treeform gland, sp.t. Along the inner base **3. Anterior Spinnerets.** are rows of bristles. The anterior spinnerets are of stouter proportions and more conical shape than the posterior, from which and the middle spinnerets they are divided by quite an intervening space. (See Fig. 22, A, A.) Their inner bases are almost in contact and are divided only by a tongue like chitinous leaf, Fig. 21, t.

[1] See Bucholz and Landois. Merkel describes them as with two joints.

The spinnerets articulate obliquely from the outer side and the front, inward and backward, so that their tips approximate the corresponding spinning fields of the middle spinnerets. The base is covered on both of its side faces with many rows of bristles (Fig. 25, b); it is divided from the terminal field by a suture, su, and a brown chitinous zone, z. The terminal joint is cap-shape, and is only partially occupied as a spinning field.

On the top of the spinning field are from sixty to seventy very short spinning spools, s.ss, and a spinning spigot, connected with a cylindrical gland, Fig. 25, sp.c. The base of these spigots is surrounded by a pair of chitinized stripes, which originate in the chitinous zone, z. Close to this place is inserted a very strong

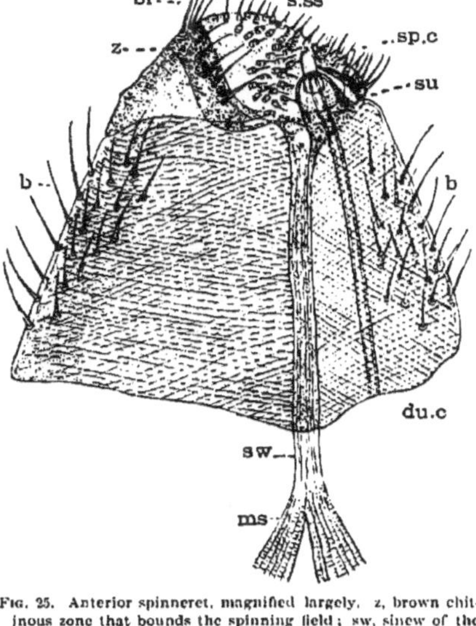

FIG. 25. Anterior spinneret, magnified largely. z, brown chitinous zone that bounds the spinning field; sw, sinew of the bending muscles of the anterior spinning wart; du.c, duct from cylindrical spinning glands; sp.c, spigot discharging cylindrical gland; sp.t, spigot of treeform gland; s.ss, spinning spools of pyriform glands. (Bucholz and Landois.)

and long sinew, sw, which unites with the chitinous border of the spinning field at the furrow (su) between the base and the terminal joint. This sinew passes beyond the root of the spinneret into the strong, motor muscle, ms, which controls the movement of the spinneret towards its fellows. Within the bases of the spinnerets are bundles of muscles which contribute both to the general movement of the spinneret and to the movement of the individual spools on the tip. On the chitinous edge of the spinning field is a single row of strong bristles, br.

On examining the spinnerets with a lens of ordinary power, the tips or spinning fields are found to be covered with a great number of fine movable spinning tubes, already mentioned, known as spinning spools (Fig. 26), which are regularly disposed over the surface.

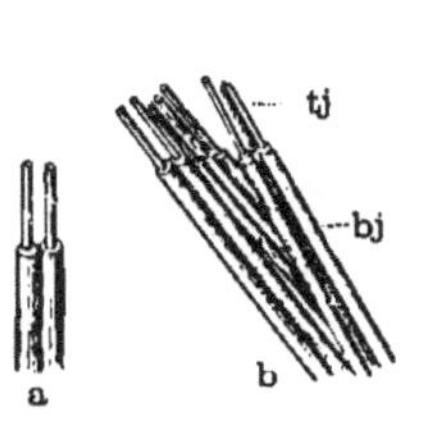

FIG. 26. View of the spinning spools of Argiope cophinaria, as they appear in clusters. a, short spools; c, long spools; b, a small cluster; tj, terminal joint; bj, basal joint.

As many as one hundred and fifty or two hundred may be counted upon
the tip of a single spinneret of an Epeïroid spider, as for example, Argiope cophinaria. These spinning spools are two jointed, at least they are
divided into two parts, of which the base is the thicker,

Spinning Spools. and sometimes the longer. They are hollow
tubes, through which the delicate ducts connected
with the silk glands convey the liquid silk to the
surface. These spinning spools are of several sizes and
shapes (Fig. 26), and differ somewhat according to their
position upon the several spinnerets. Thus those upon the
anterior spinnerets have the basal part (bj) of a conical
shape and rather shorter than the point or terminal joint,
tj. (Fig. 26 b, c, compare with Fig. 27.)

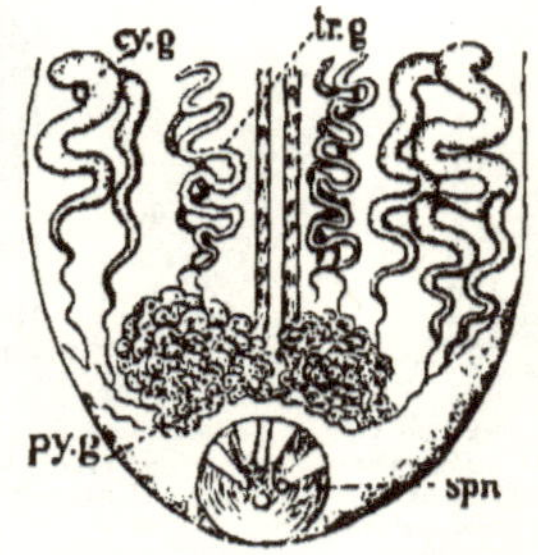

Figs. 27, 28. View of a spinning spool and spinning spigot of Epeira diademata. (After Meckel.)

Distributed here and there among these spools of ordi-
nary size are a few which are larger and stouter. (Fig. 28.) In Argiope
cophinaria there are three of these on each of the middle spinnerets, four
upon each of the posterior, and one upon each of the anterior ones. A
detailed description of these instruments will be given further on.

These groups of spinning spools are surrounded by ranks of hairs and
bristles (h, bh, br), both simple and branched, which are movable and

Hairs and Bristles. appear to have some important part in spinning. Possibly they
serve to direct the course of the threads as they issue from the
spools, or it may be that they form a protection to the more
delicately organized spinning spools themselves.

II.

The spinning spools are connected with a system of glands and ducts
constituting the internal spinning organs, the reservoir within which is
formed, and from which is secreted the material for all spinningwork.
When the integument of the lower and front
part of the abdomen is removed, to-

Internal Spinning Organs. gether with the thin layer of fat and
the muscles that move the spinner-
ets, a large bunch of minute vesicles
visible to the naked eye in a large spider such
as Argiope cophinaria is brought into view.
Examined by the microscope they are found
to be small, transparent, oval sacs. These are
the silk glands. They are about one two-hun-
dredth of an inch in diameter, in Epeira diademata (Meade); or 0.22 millimetre (Bucholz
and Landois). In Argiope cophinaria they are
of various lengths, averaging about (0.3 mm.)
three-tenths of a millimetre.

Fig. 29. View from beneath of the location of spinning glands in Epeira diademata. (After Meade.) spn, spinnerets; py.g, pyriform, cy. g, cylindrical, tr.g, treeform, glands.

They are placed in a mass just above the spinnerets, and within their bases and the abdomen, and along the venter forward and laterally. See Fig. 30. The pyriform glands, which are smaller and very much the most numerous, are arranged in five roundish clusters, about two millimetres in diameter in A. cophinaria, each corresponding to one of the exterior spinnerets, one cluster being devoted to the two middle spinnerets, al-

Silk Glands: Number. though even in this case the clusters can be separated into two. The number of glands precisely corresponds with the number of spinning spools and spigots. Bucholz and Landois give about seven hundred for Epeira diademata and they are as numerous in Argiope cophinaria. Mr. Blackwall expresses the opinion that the total number of spinning spools does not greatly exceed a thousand, even in adult females of Epeira quadrata, whose weight is about twenty grains, and in many other species it is smaller. As the spools correspond in number with the glands, this gives an indication of the number of silk glands within our best known

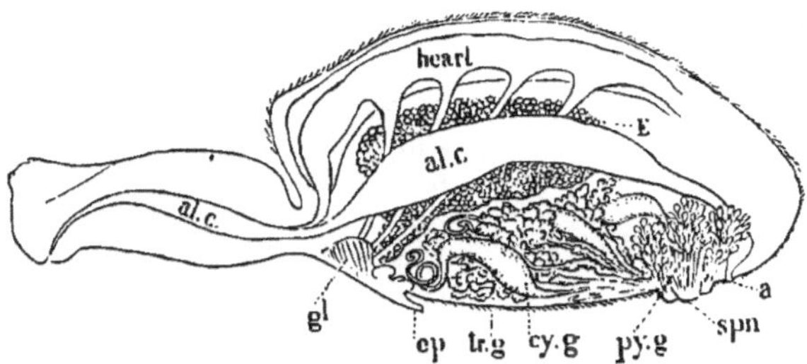

Fig. 30. Partly diagramatic view of the location of the spinning organs in Argiope cophinaria. spn, spinnerets; py.g, pyriform glands; cy.g, cylindrical glands; tr.g, treeform glands; ep, epigynum; gl, gills; E, eggs; al.c, alimentary canal; a, anus. Th figure is a composite one.

Orbweavers. Each gland terminates in a long, delicate duct, and one duct enters one of the spools; a distinct duct belongs to every spool, without any connection, as a rule, with other ducts or glands.

Under the microscope the liquid silk can be seen very distinctly within the glands, and presents the appearance of minute, yellowish, translucent globules of thickish oily or viscous substance. Some of the glands of Argiope cophinaria appear to contain material which is rather smoother and of a

Liquid Silk. lighter color than that above described. The contents of some glands in this species have a reddish brown color, which indicates that they supply the brown silken padding that envelops the eggs of this species and lie just within the outer cocoon case. Where the glands have been broken, or the contents spilled on the mounting cover, the liquid silk generally shows stringy or fibrous, but sometimes maintains the globular appearance retained within the gland. It is very probable that these differently formed glands prepare different secretions. However, the only difference which Meckel obtained by applying a few reagents was that the cylindrical glands became more coagulated through alcohol and acids than others. We may now enter upon a detailed description of these silk glands, for which I am particularly indebted to the admirable studies of Drs. Bucholz and Landois,[1] and of Meckel.[2] In some measure, also, I have drawn upon the English microscopists, Messrs. Underhill and Meade. I have tried, however, to confirm all statements accepted by me by independent studies of our own fauna.

Detailed Description.

The secretions of Epeira diademata on which spider most of the valuable studies here referred to have been made, are in not more than a thousand glands, which are connected with an equal number of independent ducts. There are three different sorts of these glands, which are distributed to their own especial spinnerets. Each spinneret possesses a large and somewhat variable number of small pyriform glands, and besides this one or more larger glands. Concerning these I have adopted substantially the conclusions of Bucholz and Landois, which are confirmatory, for the most part, of the principal statements of Meckel, and which are almost wholly in accord with my own studies as far as they have been prosecuted. The pyriform glands py.g, vastly exceed the other forms in number, as there are present in every spinneret one hundred or more. However, they may not exceed the less numerous but considerably larger gland forms in quantity of secretions. They are arranged, as has already been said, in round clusters of about two millimetres

Pyriform Glands.

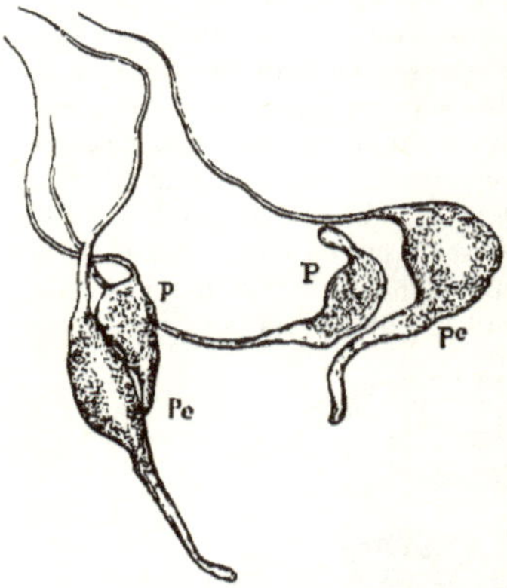

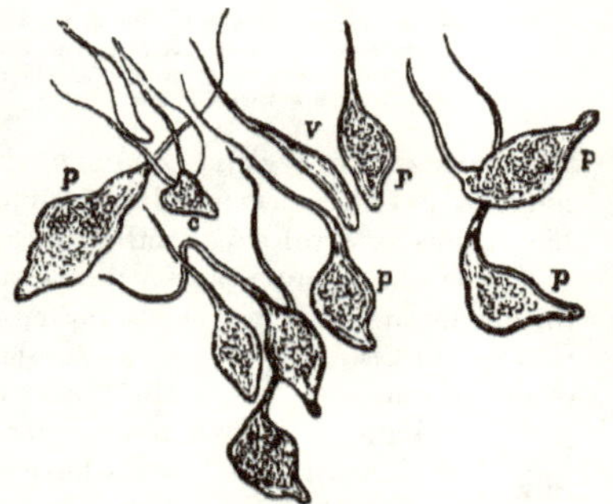

Fig. 31. Pyriform glands, caudate; A. cophinaria.

Fig. 32. Pyriform glands of Argiope.

[1] Anatomische Untersuchungen über den Bau der Araneiden: von Dr. Reinhold Bucholz und Dr. Leonard Landois. Archiv Anatomie, Phisiologie und Missch. Med. Jahrgang, 1868, page 240 sq. (Leipzig.)

[2] Heinrich Meckel: Mikrographie einiger Drüsen Apparate der niederen Thiere. Archiv f. Anat. Phys. (Berlin.) 1846, page 1 sq., Pl. III.

in diameter (about one-twelfth of an inch), lying close to the bases of the spinnerets. (Fig 30, py.g.) In form the individual glands are long, oval, pear shaped vessels, 0.22 mm. long, or, expressed approximately in linear measure, say one hundred and fifteen of average length would make an inch. In Argiope I find the average length about one eighty-fifth of an inch. At the inferior end they diminish gradually, passing into a duct which narrows towards the point of discharge, and which, together with a compact bundle of similar ducts, enters the interior of the spinneret, each one to discharge through its appropriate separate spinning tube. The wall of the gland contains a single cell stratum of a diameter of from 0.020 mm. to 0.024 mm. These cells contain a quantity of small drops, which consist of a strong refractory substance that agrees in appearance with the spinning material within the ducts. This glandular

Fig. 33. Pyriform silk glands.

wall incloses a large middle cavity, which is entirely filled with a viscous liquid spinning substance. The duct which projects from this gland possesses at the beginning a diameter of 0.024 mm.; narrows very soon after exit from the gland to the diameter of 0.01 to 0.012 mm. That is to say, the termination of the duct is about one twenty-five-hundredth of an inch in diameter. At this width it runs unaltered to its place of exit from the spinning tube.

Pyriform Ducts.

These pyriform glands, as preserved in Argiope cophinaria, while agreeing in general form vary a good deal in details, as shown by comparing the figures, 31, 32, and 33. Some of them are vermiform in shape, Fig. 33, v; some are strictly pyriform, p; some are cordate, Fig. 32, c; and some have long caudal parts, Fig.

Argiope's Glands.

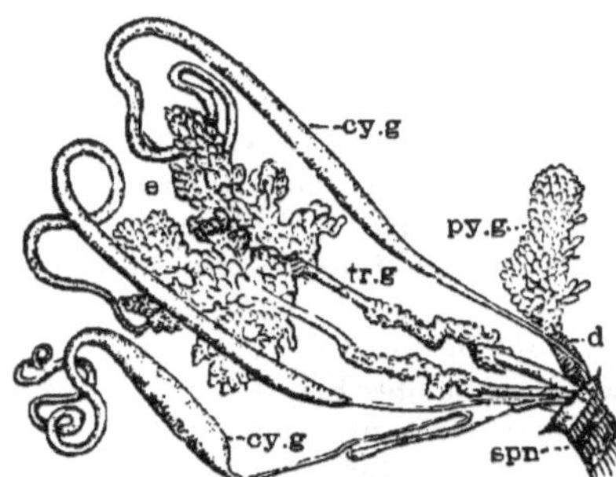

Fig. 31. View of the cylindrical glands, cy.g, and treeform glands, tr.g, of Epeira diademata. py.g, cluster of pyriform glands. d, bundle of ducts leading therefrom. spn, a spinneret into which the glands lead. (After Meckel.)

31, pc, which in general appearance resemble the cylindrical glands, but are on a much smaller scale. The vermiform glands contain a yellowish white substance. The other glands contain a somewhat similar material, but of a deeper yellowish color, and broken into distinct globules; while others contain a brownish liquid which has already been alluded to. This difference in size and form is perhaps largely due to the presence in greater or less quantities of the liquid silk contained within the glands. The caudate extensions of the pyriform part manifestly permit the secretion and storage of larger quantities of spinning material.

The Cylindrical glands, cy.g, have been considered by Meckel under two distinct forms, according as they have in one case an ampullate extension towards the duct, or in the other case are simply cylindrical tubes. These forms he denominates Cylindrical and Ampullate. They appear, however, to be the same glands, exhibited under different conditions; and even according to Meckel they have the same structure and discharge from the same character of spinning spigots. They appear to be, as Bucholz and Landois regard them, but one gland. The difference in their form is probably due to the same cause by which the somewhat similar difference in the form of pyriform glands has been explained, namely, the presence of more or less of the secreted spinning substance. The number of cylindrical glands is eight, four of which are located on each side of the body.[1]

Cylindrical Glands.

These glands represent very long cylindrical tubes, which extend from the root of the spinnerets to the fore part of the body, near the breathing organs. Thence, bending with waving convolutions, they return to their origin. If they were stretched out entire, their length would almost equal the length of the animal itself, of which, perhaps, they occupy only a third part. This extraordinarily long gland terminates with a double fold beneath the lower end of the gland and the spinneret, which if stretched out straight would exceed the length of the whole gland section. On the walls of the gland is a simple stratum of gland cells, whose diameter is 0.020 to 0.024 mm. They are precisely like the cells of the pyriform glands, and like them are filled with a great number of minute shining globules of spinning substance.

In the direction of the duct, the tubular part of the gland enlarges greatly into an elliptical, ampullate extension, am, Fig. 35, from which the duct proceeds. The construction of this ampullate swelling is the same as that of the cylindrical section, and in fact the swelling may be caused simply by the accumulation of spinning material in the lower part of the gland, which thus rounds out that part into an ampulla, am.

The Ampullæ and Duct.

The duct of the cylindrical gland, c.du, has at its origin a width of 0.065 to 0.070 mm. (one three-hundred-and-fiftieth of an inch) and runs, quickly narrowing at first, to the root of the spinneret; thence it returns again, folded like a bent knee, k, and once more doubling (do.) and proceeding downward discharges through its appropriate spinning spigot, a brown obtuse cone on which stands a clear trans-

Cylindrical Duct.

---

[1] Meckel and Oeflinger both report six glands of this kind on either side.

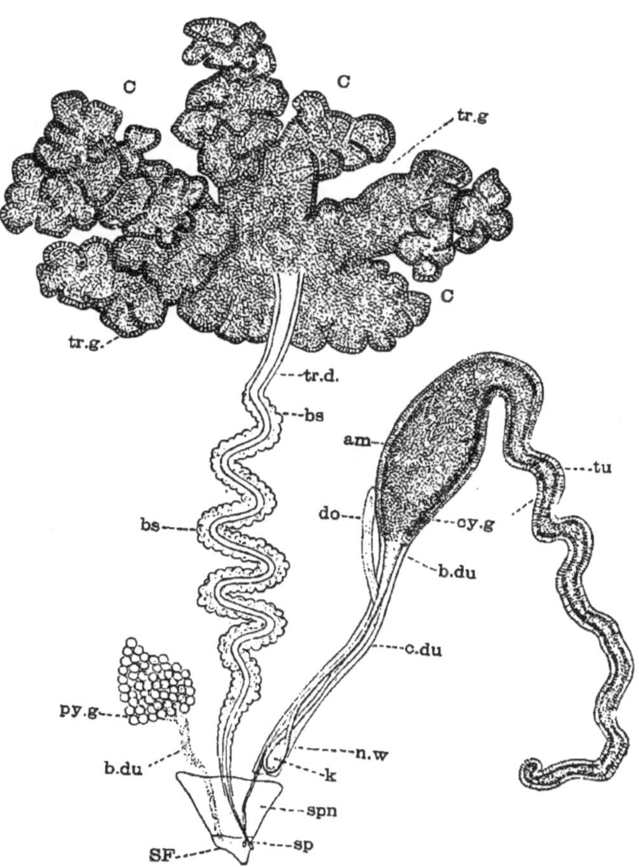

FIG. 35. Three forms of spinning glands opening into the posterior spinneret, spn. The middle one enlarged in different proportion from the others. py.g, a group of pyriform glands. b.du, a bundle of ducts opening into the spinneret through the spinning field, SF. tr.g, treeform gland; tr.d, excretory duct with brownish glandular walls or boundaries, bs; cy.g, cylindrical gland; tu, its tubular part; am, ampullate expansion of the same; b.du, beginning of duct from the ampulla; c.du, cylindrical duct; do and k, the noose shaped twist of the duct continued in an external envelope, n.w, derived from the ampulla.

parent tube from which proceeds a thick thread. In its course it runs between the delicate external net like walls (n.w), which originated as a continuation of the ampulla, and terminate close at the base of the spinneret. The walls are without ordinary cell formations. There is no difference in construction between the cylindrical and ampullate part of this gland. Of the Treeform, or as Meckel denominates them Aggregate glands, tr.g, there are five on either side, of which four discharge at the anterior spinneret, and one at the middle. The secreting part of these **Treeform Glands.** glands consists of a large, white canal, widening into many sacs, which form together a roundish cluster, c, c, c. The duct, tr.d, runs quite close to the middle of the cluster, like the umbilical cord from the placenta in mammals. In the beginning it is straight and smooth, but farther on is accompanied on its superficial part by a number of small blind saes (bs), with thin necks. Towards the end, the duct becomes smooth again, and enters the spool destined for it, which is somewhat larger than that of the cylindrical glands. Soon after its exit from the gland the duct has a diameter of 0.160 mm., but greatly narrows toward the spinneret to 0.04 mm. The duct appears, throughout its entire length, spirally twisted, without forming such folds as are seen in the cylindrical glands.

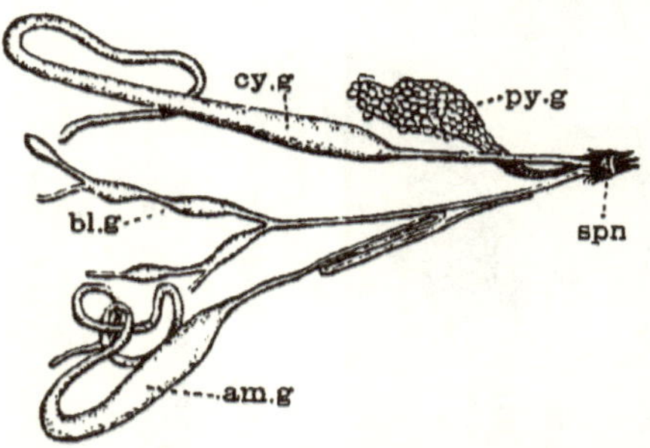

Fig. 36. Glands of Epeira diademata. (After Meckel.) cy.g, Meckel's cylindrical glands; am.g, ampullate glands; bl.g, bulbous glands; py.g, cluster of pyriform glands leading into the spinneret, spn.

Meckel further describes what he calls the Tuberose or Bulbous glands (glandulæ tuberosæ), of which he says there is one on either side. (Fig. 36, bl.g.) According to this author they are small, and consist of a few branching tubes with knotted enlargements at short intervals, which pass finally into a duct that unites with the duct of the large cylindrical gland (Ventricose gland of Meckel), which leads into the middle spinneret. Bucholz and Landois, however, declare that they have never been able to detect this gland, and doubt its existence. I have seen somewhat similar glands in Argiope cophinaria, but have simply regarded them as one of the various forms of the pyriform glands.

A valuable study of the internal spinning organs of spiders was made by Mr. R. H. Meade, and reported to the British Association as early as 1844.[1]

---

[1] On some Points in the Anatomy of the Araneida or True Spiders, especially on the Internal Structure of their Spinning Organs, by R. H. Meade, F. R. C. S.; British Association Reports, 1858, page 157, sq.

The immediate purpose of these anatomical studies was to throw light upon the question, then much discussed, whether spiders actually possess the power of shooting out threads to a greater or less distance into the air.

Can the Spinnerets Dart Threads? The question is considered elsewhere, although it is now hardly worthy of a very serious discussion. As is often the case, both parties were right though they appeared to be at opposite poles of the subject. In other words, spiders do not possess the power of darting threads into the air to any considerable distance, and are dependent upon the atmosphere to elevate those lines upon which they ascend, and those which they extrude for web foundations. But in the act of swathing insects, and on other occasions also, it is possible for the aranead to expel liquid silk with great rapidity and violence, and at least for a short distance. This I have often observed. Mr. Meade abundantly demonstrated that the muscular apparatus furnished to the internal spinning organs was sufficiently formidable to produce such a result. Independent of this question, Mr. Meade's somewhat extended studies, during which he compared the external spinning organs of Orbweavers with those of other tribes, have a real histological value, and I have made use of some of his results, particularly for comparison with the more perfect work of others.

According to Mr. Meade, the nature and construction of the silk glands are essentially the same in all species of British and foreign spiders dissected by him, though they differ greatly in form and number. As might be expected, they are most highly developed in the web spinning species, while in those that hunt for their prey, as the Lycosids, they are few and small in comparison, with the exception of those species which are aeronautic in their young state.[1] They appear to be similar in the males and females. In Agalena labyrinthica the silk glands are of a large tubular or clavate shape (see Fig. 37), as is also the case in Tegenaria domestica. (See Fig. 38.)

Fig. 37. Three glands, g. and the long triarticulate spinneret, sp, of Agalena labyrinthea. (After Underhill.)

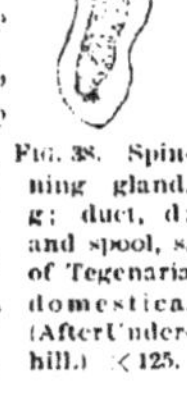

Fig. 38. Spinning gland, g; duct, d; and spool, s, of Tegenaria domestica. (After Underhill.) ×125.

III.

This detailed description of the spinning glands may be appropriately followed by a somewhat more detailed description of the organs through which they discharge for the purpose of forming the silken lines of

[1] I have supposed that all Lycosids practice ballooning; but the subject is open for inquiry, and it would be interesting if histology should point the way to a wider knowledge of natural habit.

which the spider's spinningwork is composed. The ordinary spinning spool is a hollow, cylindrical, chitinous formation, and consists of two joints: first, a shorter or longer basal cylinder, bj, whose walls are strongly brown colored; and second, a much smaller and transparent terminal joint, tj, which terminates in a very fine point, provided with a minute opening. The spools in which the pyriform glands terminate, s.ss and l.ss, Fig. 24, stand in large number on all the spinning fields. They are not alike in form of the several spinnerets, and those of the anterior spinneret especially, are quite differently constructed from those of the posterior pairs. On those spools of the posterior spinnerets which receive pyriform glands, the basal joint (Fig. 39, bj) forms everywhere a regular cylindrical tube of even thickness, which seems to be obliquely cut at the exterior end where the terminal joint is united to it. This interrupted space is, as Fig. 39 (i.s) shows, a very little flat in the middle, and towards the edge slightly curved. The base of the tube is joined to the surface of the spinneret by a ring formed enlargement, and, as elsewhere, bristles and hairs with chitinous rings are seated upon the skin.

Into the base of each spool enters a single duct of a pyriform gland, and this duct can be followed as a straight tube to the end space of the base of the spool, where it ceases to exist as a canal, and is merged into the cavity of the terminal joint.

The terminal joint (tj) is in the larger tubes, about half the length of the basal joint, bj, and sits precisely in the centre of the summit of the basal joint. The terminal joint is hollow, gradually diminishes, and terminates in a very fine, round opening at the tip. The thickness of a single thread, coming from this spinning spool, would be about 0.001 mm., or one twenty-five-thousandth part of an inch. This form of spinning spool undergoes changes at different places of the spinning field, caused by the basal cylinder varying in length. The central parts of the spinning field especially are covered with very short spools. The terminal joint, however, remains unchanged in length, notwithstanding the varying lengths of the basal joint. (Fig. 39.)

Spinning Spools.

Pyriform Spools.

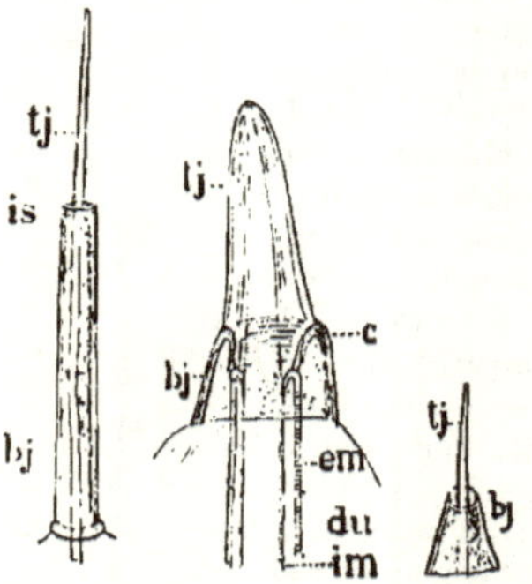

Fig. 39. Fig. 41. Fig. 40.

Fig. 39. Spinning spool of the usual form from the posterior spinneret, and connected with pyriform glands. Multiplied greatly, 2000 times. Fig. 40. Spinning spool from the anterior spinneret. × 2000. Fig. 41. Spinning cone or spigot into which a cylindrical gland empties. The whole taken from the apex of the middle spinneret. × 2000 times. bj, basal piece; c, circumference or ring of the chitinous wall of the basal piece, constituting a ring formed chitinous thickening on its apex; em, the exterior membrane of the chitinous wall of the duct, du, with vertical striation; im, inner membrane of the duct passing into the canal of the basal piece.

Somewhat different from the above are the spinning spools which are found on the anterior spinnerets. On these (Fig. 40) the bases consist of a short, more conical segment, which diminishes considerably from the broader base toward the free end. This conical basal joint, bj, is provided with a strongly concave end space. The terminal joint is almost double the length of the base, and is not straight as in the spools of the posterior spinnerets, but is a little curved. It stands in the centre of the concave end space of the basal cylinder.

Dispersed among these smaller spools of the pyriform glands are shorter and thicker spools, sp, through which discharge the cylindrical **Spigot Spools.** and treeform glands, Fig. 35. Those belonging to the cylindrical glands differ from those of the treeform glands in the character of the end space, which is in the former longer and considerably thicker. In general, however, the construction of all these formations is similar. Figure 41 shows the discharging spigot of a cylindrical gland, situated at the tip of the middle spinneret. This spigot like spinning tube consists of a basal piece, bj, formed by brown chitinous walls and a cylindrical end piece, tj, which tapers more sharply towards the point.

We are now better prepared to consider these beautiful instruments in their relation to their several silk glands.

Close by the lower end of the spinning field of the posterior spinneret stands a large spool (Fig. 33, sp) into which leads a cylindrical gland. Farther above are the spools of two treeform glands, and close by are the two spools of two cylindrical glands. Besides these, innumerable spools of the pyriform glands cover the spinning field, and they are here all very long, especially those placed at the inferior position of the spinning field.

Fig. 12. Epeira diademata.

On the spinning field of the middle spinneret stand many long spools which are connected with the pyriform glands. The number, however, is **Middle Spools.** here less than on the other spinnerets. Just below these smaller spools, stands toward the upper side of the field (Fig. 24) a very large spool which is the mouth of a cylindrical gland. The point of the entire spinneret is formed by a rounded projection at the extreme end of the oval space, constituting the spinning field. On this none of the smaller spools stand, but only two larger ones, of which the one is the mouth of a cylindrical gland (ventricose of Meckel); the other gives exit to a tuberose gland. Besides these, there is also a short, solid horn of unknown use. The spinning field of the anterior or inner spinneret is **Anterior Spools.** covered with short small spools, whose number exceeds that of the other spinnerets. The chitinous epiderm which bounds the spinning field forms a zone not entirely closed, and in the open space is a horny cone (Fig. 25, sp.c) on whose point stands a spool of a

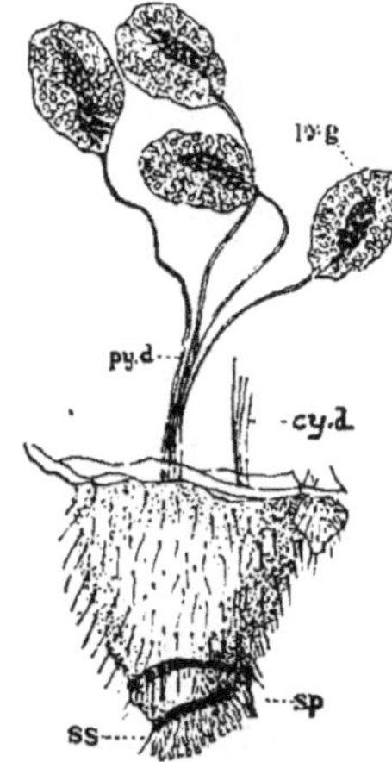

Fig. 43. Anterior spinneret of Epeira diademata. (After Underhill.) ss. spinning spools; sp, spigot; py.g, pyriform glands with their ducts, py.d. The glandular epithelium is represented. cy.d, ducts belonging to the spigots; sp, probably of cylindrical glands, cy.g.

cylindrical gland, the only larger gland which discharges here. On the inside of this horny cone is attached a long yellowish cord or point, upon which strong muscles are inserted in order to move the cone against the spinneret.

Mr. Underhill figures the spigots or large spinning tubes which issue upon the posterior and anterior spinnerets.[1] The former are situated upon the interior margins and are connected with two very large glands which are doubtless the cylindrical glands as heretofore described. These spigots are shown at Fig. 43 together with a portion of the ducts leading to their appropriate glands (not represented) which lie below the pyriform glands. Fig. 44 shows one of these anterior spigots, a.sp, compared with two spools ss. of the same spinneret. Mr. Blackwall announced the fact for the first time, so far as I know, that the spools vary greatly in number in different species, and also differ considerably in size not only in individuals of the same species, but often even on the same spinnerets. The larger species of the Epeiroids have the spinnerets most amply provided with spools, and Blackwall ex-

Spools Vary.

presses the opinion that the total number does not greatly exceed a thousand, even in adult females of Epeira quadrata, whose weight is about twenty grains, and in many other species it is smaller.

As illustrating the difference in various genera it may be stated that Tegenaria domestica and Tegenaria civilis, for example, have less than four hundred spinning spools each. In Textrix agilis and Lycosa saccata the number is below three hundred. In Segestria senoculata it scarcely exceeds one hundred, and in many of the smaller spiders it is still further reduced.

Numbers Vary.

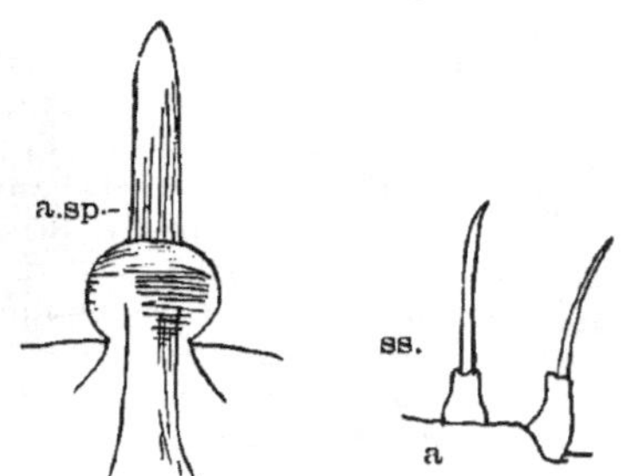

Fig. 44. a.sp, spigot on anterior spinneret of Epeira diademata leading to cylindrical gland; ss, spools of pyriform glands, same spinneret. (After Underhill.) × 165.

The difference in the number and size of the spools connected with the several parts of the spinnerets in the same species, and with similar pairs in different species, is also very apparent. In spiders constituting the

[1] Science Gossip, 1874, page 181.

genera Epeira, Tetragnatha, Linyphia, Theridium, Agalena, and many others, they are generally large, more numerous and minute on the anterior spinnerets than on the posterior and middle ones. The last are the most sparingly supplied with them, and in the case of Segestria senoculata each has only three large spools at its extremity.

On each of the posterior spinnerets Mr. Underhill found three spigots differing in character from those of the anterior spinnerets. Fig. 46, sp. Their form and size as compared with the spools of the anterior pyriform glands (ss.p) is shown in the figure. These spigots are evidently the ones connected with treeform glands; which glands Underhill estimates at five millimetres (three-twentieths to four-twentieths of an inch) in length, while the common pyriform glands are about one millimetre (one one-hundredth of an inch). The ducts which connect those glands and spigots are shown at tr.g, Fig. 45, where their covering of curious globular cells is indicated. These cells according to Underhill are so slightly attached as to be easily rubbed off during manipulation. He had not seen anything analogous to this gland on any other genus than Epeira except the exotic Orbweaver Nephila; and for this reason conjectured that through these spigots and from this gland the viscid beading of the Orbweaver's spirals may be drawn.

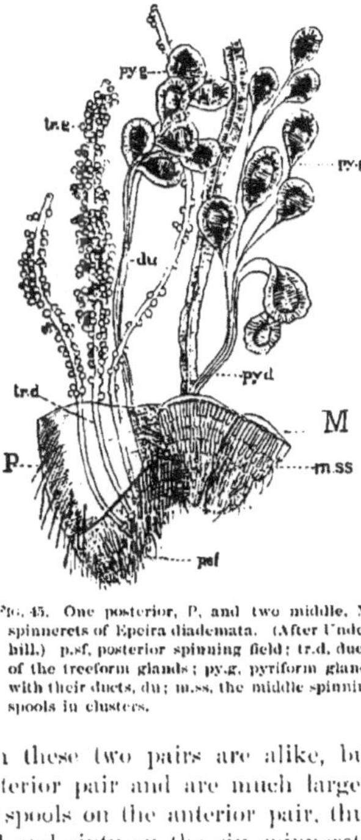

Mr. Underhill has stated that in a large Tegenaria domestica, one one-hundredth of an inch is the average length of the silk duct. On the posterior pair of spinnerets are about sixty tubes: on the middle pair, although the spinnerets are smaller, about eighty. The spools on these two pairs are alike, but they differ in shape from those of the anterior pair and are much larger. There are nearly two hundred and twenty spools on the anterior pair, thus making altogether three hundred and sixty on the six spinnerets.

Spools Vary with Age. Blackwall also made the discovery that the number of spools varies with the age of the female. In specimens of Drassus ater, which had attained nearly a third of their growth, they amounted to five or six. In others, which were two-thirds grown, to six or seven. In adults which had acquired their full complement, they

FIG. 45. One posterior, P, and two middle, M, spinnerets of Epeira diademata. (After Underhill.) p.sf, posterior spinning field; tr.d, ducts of the treeform glands; py.g, pyriform glands with their ducts, du; m.ss, the middle spinning spools in clusters.

were uniformly eight, two of which were situated on the inferior surface of the spinneret at a greater distance from the extremity than the rest, and were minute and almost contiguous.

It is a fact deserving notice that the spinning spools are not always developed simultaneously on these spinnerets, six, seven, and eight being sometimes observed on one, while five, six, or seven are to be seen on the other. This remark is applicable not to the anterior spinnerets alone, but to the intermediate ones also, which, in mature individuals, are further modified by having the extremities of the terminal joints directed forwards at right angles to their bases. The same condition was observed in a species of Drassus and in Segestria senoculata. It is not improbable, therefore, that other species, and perhaps all spiders, follow the same law of development.

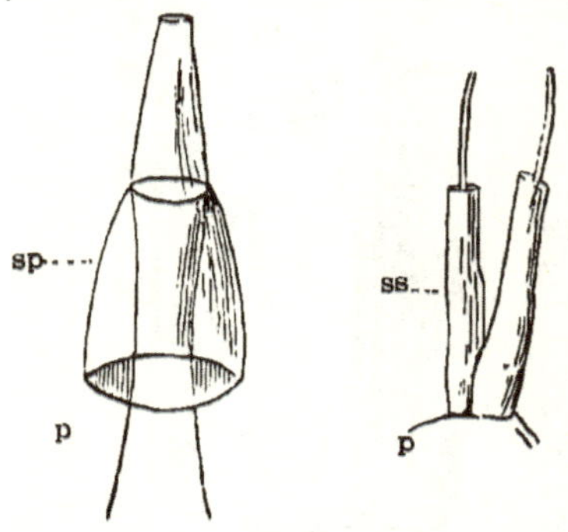

Fig. 46.   Epeira diademata.   sp (p), spigot of treeform gland on posterior spinneret; ss (p), spools of pyriform glands on same. (After Underhill.)   × 165.

This whole system of liquid silk supply is regulated by the compression of surrounding muscles, which act upon the several glands in the manner of the hand when squeezing upon the rubber bulb of a spraying tube. The contents are forced out of the glands in this liquid condition, through the long, delicate ducts, into the hollow spinning tubes, whence they issue in minute jets through the exterior openings or mouths of the spools.

Muscular System.

As the points of the spools or tips of the spinnerets are approximated, a number of these jets flow together, and hardening instantly upon contact with the air, form the thread or line familiarly known as the spider's web.

The excretory ducts, as well as the silk glands themselves, are encircled by a fibrous or muscular coat, which loosely surrounds them, and seems to be a continuation of the outer coat or sac itself. The spinnerets are connected with, or surmount the integument of the abdomen, by means of diverging bands of muscular fibres, which enable them to move in different directions. These muscles are placed immediately beneath the skin, and their expanded extremities are inserted into it so that they are separated with it, unless dissected very carefully.[1]

All the spinnerets are thus provided with many muscles which cause the approachment of all the spools of one spinneret against one another, as also the convergence of all the six spinnerets towards a central point, in order to produce in this way a single thread. For this purpose the

[1] Meade.

exterior spools of the spinning field are always bent a little towards the centre.[1] The spider, of course, possesses the power of regulating the flow of silk as to quantity, and can graduate it from the most delicate gossamer thread to the thickest blanket which is used for the rapid enswathment of insects. She can also play upon the special glands as occasion requires, and extrude the viscid substance which forms along the spiral lines of an orbweb, or the variously colored silk used in cocooning.

The field of comparative anatomy, and especially of histology, affords innumerable examples of the wonderful beauty of structure and adaptation of organs to the various uses of living creatures. But there are few objects better calculated to awaken admiration, even to the point of enthusiasm, than the machinery by which the Orbweaver is enabled to prosecute her spinningwork.

[1] Meckel.

CHAPTER III.

GENERAL CHARACTERISTICS OF ORBWEAVERS' SNARES.

The so-called "geometric web" which one sees in art work and book illustrations has no place in nature. Were that taken as the standard one would decide that there is little need of comparison, and no room for classification, since in the books no more differences exist among Orbweavers' snares than might be found in the four wheels of a wagon.

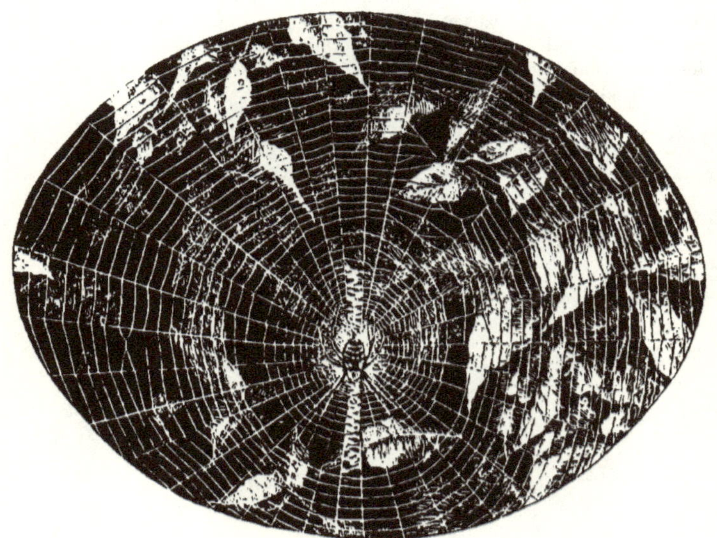

Fig. 17. A vertical snare, full orbed. Snare of Argiope cophinaria.

Unfortunately our artists, and indeed the same is largely true of naturalists as concerns cobwebs, are too much intent upon general effects to attend to such small details as variations in the web architecture of a spider. As common a figure as is the wheel shaped snare of the Orbweaver, I remember but one which gave proof of having been drawn from a natural web by one who knew its characteristics.[1] In point of fact, we shall see that there are very striking differences in form and structure among the snares spun by the Orbitelariae. In the following chapters these differences will be pointed out and illustrated, and an attempt made to group and arrange the various snares in some natural order. I define an **Orbweb Defined.** orbweb as a snare constructed of right lines radiating from a common centre, and crossed spirally, for the most part, by numerous circular lines, or lines forming arcs of circles.

The round web of the Orbweaver probably deserves the distinction of having given the popular name cobweb to the whole spinningwork of spiders. One easily sees how the Anglo Saxon word cop, a head, could have been appropriately applied to objects which, by their rotundity and size, suggest the contour of the human face.[2] The orb is the figure which quite unconsciously rises when one speaks of the spider's web, an indication that it is perhaps the most striking, although it is by no means the most common form of araneal

FIG. 48. A horizontal snare, full orbed.

spinningwork. Nevertheless, all orbwebs are not round, as will be seen hereafter, hence the qualified terms of the definition given above.

Orbwebs fall naturally into two great groups, Vertical Snares and Horizontal Snares. In Vertical Snares the orb is habitually perpendicular to the plane of the horizon, or nearly so. In Horizontal Snares **Great Groups.** the orb is habitually parallel with the plane of the horizon, or nearly or approximately so. The normal positions of these snares are as described, and they often appear thus in nature; but location compels more or less variation. The exigencies of construction frequently force such an arrangement of foundation lines as inclines the orb to the plane of the horizon more or less sharply. Thus it may occur that a true vertical and a true horizontal web may be stretched upon nearly the same plane. The careful observer, however, will rarely fail to note and allow for the peculiarities of the site which cause these deflections, and easily give each web its proper classification.

Vertical orbwebs may be arranged under four subdivisions: first, Full Orb; second, Sectoral Orb; third, Ray or Actinic Orb; fourth, Orb Sector.

[1] For example, I have collected, without much effort, quite a number of samples of wall paper, into whose patterns the orbweb is introduced, showing how favorite a figure this is in decorative art. Orbwebs also abound in embroidery and hammered ware.

[2] The German has kopf, the Welsh cob, and the Greek κεφ, knbe. The word cob, however, has been applied to the spider herself, as a round or head-shaped object, just as we give the name "cobble stone" to boulders.

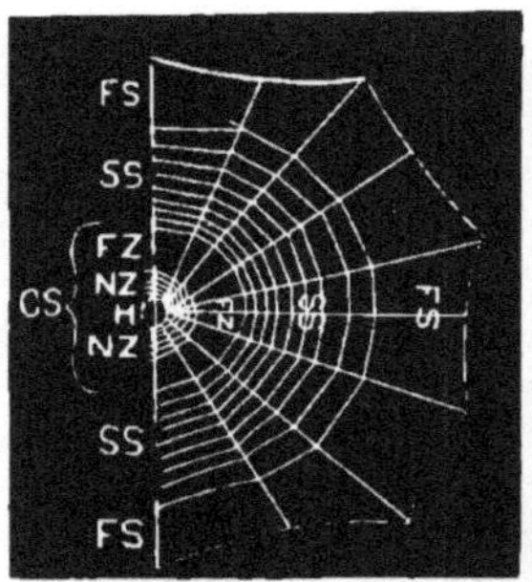

FIG. 49.   Subdivisions of an orbweb.

1. In Full Orb snares the spiral concentrics cross all the radii, appearing to form complete circles. (See Fig. 47.) They are divided into Simple and Compound snares.

a. A Simple orbweb is simply an orb of radiating straight lines crossed by spiral or looped lines. The snare of the Furrow spider (Epeira strix) is a typical example.

b. A Compound orbweb adds to the simple orb a system of netted or retitelarian lines crossed and joined at different angles, and placed above and on either side of the upper part of the orb, or placed below the orb. The snare of the Labyrinth Spider (Epeira labyrinthea) is an example. Simple orbicular snares may be approximately arranged into three groups according as they have the Hub Meshed, Sheeted, or Open.

I am not aware that any arrangement, description, or nomenclature of the various parts of the orbweb has ever been attempted apart from the following, which will therefore be found convenient and perhaps sufficiently comprehensive.[1] The orb may be naturally divided into the Central Space, CS, the Spiral Space, SS, and the Foundation Space, FS. (See Fig. 49.)

Parts of the Orb.

The Central Space is included between the centre of the orb and the origin of the Spiral Space. It has three distinct parts, the Hub, the Notched zone, and the Free zone. The Hub is a small circular part immediately surrounding the centre, which is either wholly open, or covered in whole or in part by spinningwork.

1. The Meshed Hub is wholly or partly covered by a series of irregularly shaped meshes, through which one can often trace the continuation of the radii as zigzag lines. In fact, it may be considered as a small rudimentary and irregular orbweb (Fig. 50). Usually it nearly corresponds in size to the length (including the legs) of the spider that has woven it.

The spider when waiting for her prey upon her snare is frequently and at night generally stretched upon or near this hub.

FIG. 50.   Meshed hub and central space.

[1] First published in "Our Continent," Philadelphia, No. 33, page 362, 1882, and "Proceedings of the Academy of Natural Sciences," Philadelphia, 1882, page 257.

and a close observation of her feet will show that the claws grasp, and even draw out somewhat the lines which represent the radii continued.

Meshed Hub. Every motion of the net is thus communicated more readily through the taut lines to the sensitive feet. The brushes or tufts of delicate hairs with which these organs are provided, and which are in contact with the lines, must greatly increase the sensitiveness of the creature to every movement.

This natural telegraphy is, perhaps, also aided by a short line extending from the spinnerets to the upper part of the hub. This line is apt to divide into two, or radiate into several branches near the hub. In this position, of course, the apex of the spider's abdomen is slightly elevated (Fig. 51). However, the chief design of this habit is probably to hold the aranead to her snare when she rushes after her prey, or to give her a point of attachment for dropping out of the web, or running from it in case of assault, with similar advantage when she may wish to return.

2. The Sheeted Hub is wholly covered by a closely woven sheet of white silk, against which

Sheeted Hub. the under part of the spider is placed as she hangs thereon. The type of this form of hub is that made by the Basket Argiope, A. cophinaria, (Walck.), the largest and one of the most beautiful of our indigenous Orbweavers. It is shown at Fig. 52, where a thick, irregular shield like piece two inches long and one and a half wide, covers the entire hub. Above, it extends in a broad ribbon of the same consistency to the spiral space, a distance of

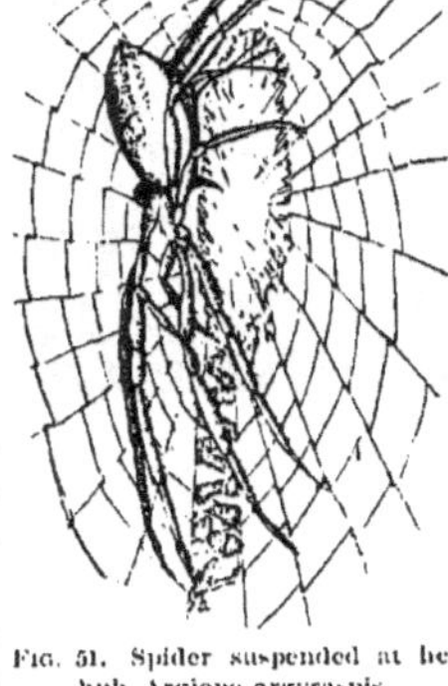

Fig. 51. Spider suspended at her hub, Argiope argyraspis.

one and seven-eighths inches; and below, it terminates in a narrow, zigzag ribbon two inches in length. (Fig. 52.)

3. The Open Hub is entirely free from any spinningwork, being a small opening in the centre of the orb, that is, the point toward which

Open Hub. the radii tend. It is characteristic of snares spun by the genus Acrosoma, and prevails largely in horizontal orbs. But it is frequently found in the webs of spiders whose general habit is to spin a meshed hub. Such variation in habit of course prevents us from taking these peculiarities of the hub as characteristics of absolute determinative value. Nevertheless, they are valuable, and will

Notched Zone. be found generally distinctive. The Notched Zone (NZ, Fig. 49) is a short series of spiral lines, ordinarily from four to ten in number, immediately surrounding the hub. These spirals do not cross the radii directly, but diagonally, thus causing a notch or angle on each side when they are drawn taut. In other words, the spiral line overlays the radius longitudinally for a minute space at the point of crossing. The precise effect of this arrangement may be produced thus: Stretch a cord tightly; then take a second cord, loop it by one twist around the first, and draw its two loose ends in opposite directions. The appearance of these notches is shown at Fig. 53.

The Free Zone (FZ, Fig. 49, see also Fig. 50), the third division of the Central space, is **Free Zone.** that portion of the orb which, for the most part, lies between the notched zone and the spirals, and consists simply of the radii without any crossing lines. Its outer boundary appears always to be marked by the last or innermost of the foundation spirals. Blackwall[1] objects to the statement of Kirby and Spence concerning a free zone as characteristic of geometric webs, that this is true of but one species. But the greater part of our vertical orbs have the free zone. It seems strange that Blackwall[2] should speak of the nets which are destitute of the free zone as having the centre entirely closed up (meshed

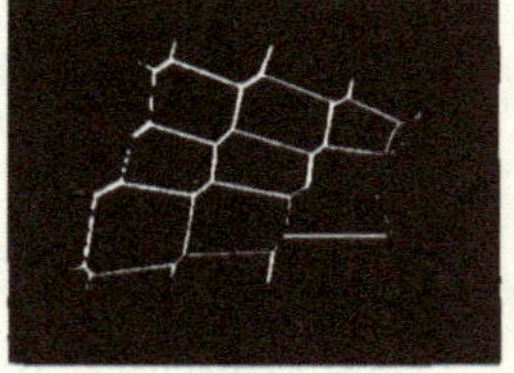

hub, for certainly in America the orbs spun by the genus Epeira, which are by far the most frequent, have both the closed centre and the free zone, almost invariably. (See Fig. 50.) I must doubt the accuracy at this point of the distinguished observer, and the doubt is confirmed by my limited observation of the spinningwork of British spiders.[3] **Use of the Central Space.** The economy of the Central Space in its several parts must be a matter of conjecture, but there are some good grounds for the following opinions:

1. It must be noted, first, that no part of the Central space has viscid beads. This permits the freer motion of the spider around the centre without liability of entanglement upon her own snare. She is, indeed, able to run over the beaded spiral space with apparent impunity, yet her

<hr>

[1] "On the Construction of the Nets of Geometric Spiders." Zoological Journal, Vol. V., 1832-4, page 184.

[2] As above, page 185.

[3] Mr. Cecil Warburton writes me from Southport, England, that the snares of Meta segmentata are distinguishable at a glance from those of most common English Epeiroids, as Zilla atrica, Epeira diademata, Ep. quadrata, etc., by the presence of a notched zone and the absence of a meshed centre. Evidently, his observation of the common species showed a closed centre.

movements there, always when capturing an insect, and often in bringing the captive to the Hub, do at times result in the marring and breakage of the snare. The fact that the prey are taken to the centre to be fed upon and sometimes to complete the swathing is a reason why that portion of the web should not be covered with viscid beads, which are obviously a hinderance to feeding upon and swathing the victim. In fact the viscid parts have to be cut out in order to permit the revolving of the captured prey when it is being swathed.

2. Moreover, the struggles of insects ensnared upon the beaded spirals, and subsequent actions of the spider to capture its prey, invariably break up more or less of the web. In the case of large insects the damage done is quite serious. Were the Central space also beaded it is evident that the very seat and throne of the aranead at the hub of the snare would

Fig. 54. The ribbon brace of Acrosoma.

be greatly liable to invasion, to her sore discomfort and disadvantage, especially in cutting off her avenues of approach to the main portions of the snare. This would be no less true in cases where her retreat is a leafy or silken castle outside the limits of the orb but connected with the hub by a trapline. The breaking of the radii at the point of their attachment to the hub of course must cause all the connected parts towards the circumference to relax, entangle, and drop away. Repair in such cases is difficult or impossible. The farther from the centre is the point at which the insect is entangled, the less injury ensues, the longer does the web remain serviceable, and the more easily is it mended. Thus, the absence of beads from the entire Central space gives added security to the snare.

Fig. 55. Semicircular zigzag cords in the hub of Argiope.

3. In like manner the economy of the Free zone may be considered as protective. The absence of spiral lines enables many insects to pass quite through the net, with little or no impediment. When there is a momentary arrest or entanglement, the subsequent escape or capture is accompanied by very slight, if any, destruction.

4. Here, too, it may be observed that the necessity for viscid beads near the centre is not as manifest as upon the outlying parts. The momentary pause caused by an insect striking upon the naked radii of the Free zone

near the hub where the spider waits, is commonly quite long enough to allow the active creature to reach and secure her victim, when capture is desirable. When for any reason capture is not desirable or prudence suggests caution, the nearness of the spider to an insect thus arrested on the naked radii brings it within her vision, which at the best seems to be limited. On the contrary, insects who strike upon the outer margin are not only detained by the viscid beads, but made comparatively harmless.

5. The Free Zone gives the further advantage of allowing the spider

Fig. 56. Flossy ribbon braces of Uloborus.

easy access to the under part of the snare, a convenience which is sometimes important. It is perhaps worth noting here that vertical snares which have an open hub appear quite commonly to have no free zone, that part of the web being occupied by the notched zone prolonged to the inner boundary of the spirals.[1] Thus in either case, although by an interesting variation in spinning habit, the way is left open for the spider to pass from one side of her orb to the other. I have watched with great interest the agility of a large Argiope in swinging herself from one side of her shield to the other when threatened by danger. I could always by demonstrations with finger or pencil cause her to change sides. This was done invariably by crawling through the free zone. The space seemed over small to give passage to such a large creature, but the elasticity of the threads readily permitted the transfer, which was made with remarkable deftness and dexterity.

The chief purpose of the Notched Zone seems to be to strengthen the web, and particularly to brace

Notched Zone.

and hold in position the radii before the spirals are wrought in. My observations indicate that the notched spirals are invariably woven in before the beaded spirals. The outer

Fig. 57. Flossy circular braces of Uloborus.

or diverging ends of the radii being supported by the Foundation lines, the inner or converging ends by the notched space, the spider begins to lay in her foundation spirals from the inner margin of the spiral space, working toward the circumference. Thus her operations are conducted somewhat after the architectural modes of a human builder erecting a large scaffolding.

[1] I make this statement with some qualifications and cannot positively say that it is true of all snares with open hubs. That it is with many I know. The point is one for further investigation.

Certain species (indeed, the habit has its representatives among several genera) further strengthen the notched space by a close, plain band of white silk, which ordinarily extends between two radii, along the perpendicular diameter upward from the hub to the spiral space. (Fig. 54.) Sometimes also the ribbon reaches both upward and downward from the hub, and takes the form of a scalloped band or thick winding cord. This peculiarity prevails in all our indigenous examples of the genus Acrosoma, and is also quite characteristic of the exotic species of the same genus. Our beautiful and familiar representatives of the genus Argiope (A. cophinaria and A. argyraspis Walck.)[1] have the same habit. (See Figs. 55.)

Some species, as frequently Argiope argyraspis, add to this perpendicular ribbon, on either side thereof, one or more semicircular zigzag cords, which further tend to strengthen the central part of the orb. Some species of Uloborus have a similar habit, but also at times throw the cord entirely around the notched space, making a series of circles. (Figs. 56 and 57.) The perpendicular cords are sometimes extended above and below the notched space, and terminate in serpentine folds, bulb shaped tufts, or tapering points. They give a striking and beautiful appearance to the web, the graceful lines, and thick, white, flossy texture showing in pretty contrast against the radii and spirals. Examples of these peculiarities will be found among the descriptions of characteristic webs. (See Chap. VI.)

These bands and cords, besides probably serving as braces, are used by the spider as supports when she hangs at the open hub. Acrosoma rugosa will generally be found hanging by her hind pair of legs to the lower end of the ribbon.

[1] Epeira fasciata Hentz. and Argiope transversa Emerton.

CHAPTER IV.

CONSTRUCTION OF AN ORBWEB.

I.

A DESCRIPTION of the remaining part of the orb will be better reached by a detailed account of the manner in which an orbweb is constructed.

Laying Out Frame of Snare. There are some variations in methods among different species, as might be expected from the varieties of webs, but the process is substantially the same in all species observed. The first step is to secure a suitable framework upon which to hang the orb,

which is known as the Foundation or Frame, and the several parts composing it, as Foundation Lines. The spider has two methods of accomplishing this.

First, the frame lines are laid down "by hand." The spider crawls along the objects over and upon which she purposes to spin her snare,

FIG. 58. Epeira moving with dragline and anchorage.

A Frame Laid Down. drawing after her a line which at various points she fastens to the surface in this wise: the spinnerets, which are grouped in a little rosette at the end of the abdomen, have a large number of minute hollow tubes or spinning spools upon their tips, out of which issues a liquid silk of which all spinningwork is formed. The spinnerets and their hundreds of spools are movable at the will of the spider. When they are held closely together, the numerous threads emitted by them blend into one. When they are held apart, on the contrary, various separate threads are formed. As the spider runs along she stops here and there, expands her spinning organs, and at the same time thrusts them downward and touches the surface. The clustered threads thus issued stick to the surface and at once harden.

Then the spider closes together the spinnerets, as one would close the points of his fingers against his thumb, lifts them, moves on, and the con-

Drag-lines. tinuous threads dragged behind her again converge into one thread as shown in Fig. 58. An ordinary pocket lens, if applied to one of the little white dots which mark the point of adhesion, will easily resolve it into various parts and show the above construction. At Fig. 59 are magnified drawings of two of these spots.

Dr. Hulse, as early as A. D. 1670, noticed the habits of spiders to make various anchorages of their drag line as they moved along. He thus wrote to Mr. Ray: "They will often fasten their threads in several places to the things they creep up: the manner is by beating their bums or tails against them as they creep along. This line will express the way :—

By this frequent beating in of their thread among the asperities of the place where they creep, they either secure it against the wind, that it is not so easily blown away; or else whilst they hang by it, if one stitch break, another holds fast, so that they do not fall to the ground." [1]

In this way the Orbweaver proceeds, with more or less variation, until she has described the irregular polygon which forms the foundation of her snare.[2] Each of these boundary lines, according to Blackwall's observation, is composed of five, six, or even more united threads.[3] It is always sharply distinguished by its thickness and strength, and often by its color, from the other lines of the snare. The upper foundation line is quite commonly much the strongest. The framework thus formed is braced by various cords passing diagonally from line to line across the corners, and sometimes also by numerous threads attached to surrounding objects. The entire foundation thus hangs taut, and presents a framework having the requisite degree of strength and elasticity upon and within which to suspend the true snare.

Prime Foundation.

Fig. 59. Dragline and anchorage magnified.

This work is not always done rapidly and as though by an engineering instinct that readily perceives the quickest and most advantageous sites and courses. Often there is much preparatory pioneering: the laying out or dragging out of tentative lines which appear to be to no purpose; a groping or "feeling" the way, so to speak, toward the best location, and at last the seeming accidental determination of the frame lines.

Of course, even under such behavior there must be a general instinctive movement in the direction of the polygonal or triangular outlines which are the prevailing forms one sees. It has been said that the spider seems careless about the shape of the area which the foundation lines inclose.[4] But the fact that these two forms do prevail well nigh universally, places the architect's action outside the pale of mere chance. Moreover, examples are frequently found of

Intelligent Selection.

[1] Correspondence of Ray, page 58.

[2] See an article by the author in "Our Continent," Philadelphia, September 27th, 1882.

[3] Blackwall, Zoological Journal, Vol. V., 1832-4, page 182. "On the Construction of the Nets of Geometric Spiders."

[4] Introduction to Entomology, Kirby & Spence, Vol. I., Set XIII., page 411.

Orbweavers who move at once from the beginning of a foundation to its completion as though directed by a sure knowledge; one cannot say by a sure experience, for in point of fact this behavior is not the result of experience, inasmuch as it is observed in the youngest animals, and on the other hand adults are quite apt to show the confused and indeterminate action above referred to.

The second mode of securing an orb foundation is by means of air currents. It has been questioned by naturalists whether the Orbweaver ever pursues any other method than that of carrying around the **Foundations by Air Currents.** foundation lines. As recently as A. D. 1881, so good an arachnologist as Mr. Cambridge expressed the belief that this is the usual mode of proceeding, and that air currents are never utilized for the construction of orb foundations.[1] This opinion, however, he shortly afterward abandoned, yielding to the facts presented by other arachnologists.[2] I have elsewhere treated the question at some length,[3] and now present the evidence that the prime foundation lines of orbwebs are often laid by means of air currents.

In a great number of cases I have observed the Orbweavers **Bridge Lines.** passing from point to point by means of lines emitted from their spinnerets and entangled upon adjacent foliage or other objects.

Fic. 60. Orbwebs on water plants in a pond.

Any one who will note with ordinary carefulness the movements of orbmakers among shrubbery towards the close of a fair evening, may see such examples. These mimic "suspension bridges" are of various lengths, owing to the direction of the wind and the position of the spider relative to the standing objects around it. Lines of two, three, and four feet are frequent; lines from seven to eight feet occur often; I have measured one twenty-six feet long, and in several cases have seen lines strung entirely across country roads thirty or forty feet wide.[4] Many of these lines I have seen carried by

[1] Spiders of Dorset, Rev. O. Pickard-Cambridge, Vol. I., Introduction, page 21.
[2] Op. cit., Vol. II.
[3] Proceedings Academy Natural Sciences of Philadelphia, 1881, page 430, seq.—"How Orbweaving Spiders make the Framework or Foundation of Webs."
[4] Lister, the father of English araneology, observed such lines stretched between trees and over streams. Tractatus Araneis, page 8.

the wind directly from spiders' spinnerets, have observed the entanglement, have seen the animal draw the threads taut and then cross upon them. That all the lines are similarly formed and used I have no doubt.

Mr. Terby, in a paper contributed in 1867 to the Royal Academy of Belgium, makes a number of intelligent and accurate observations upon the **M. Terby.** habit of spiders to throw out their floating threads in order to secure passage from point to point. He demonstrated by numerous experiments that these threads could not be projected by the power of the spider without the aid of the wind. I regret that I only happened to fall upon this paper after the completion of my manuscript, so that I can insert here but a brief allusion to it.[1] Blackwall also had ob- **Black-wall.** served as much and gives a brief and accurate description. The manner, he says, in which the lines of spiders are carried out from the spinners by a current of air appears to be this: as a preparatory measure, the spinnerets are brought into close contact and viscid matter is emitted from the spinning spools. They are then separated by a lateral motion, which extends the viscid matter into fine filaments, connecting the spools. On these filaments the current of air impinges,

Fig. 61. A colony of spiders domiciled over water.

drawing them out from the spinnerets to a length which is regulated by the will of the animal, and on the spinnerets being again brought together the filaments coalesce and form one compound line.[2]

It is a more difficult matter to determine whether the lines used for the foundations of orbwebs are formed in the same way. I have seen an orbweaver, after traversing a considerable space by a series of successive bridge

[1] M. F. Terby, sur les procédés qu'emploient les araignées pour relier des points éloignés par un fil. Bull. l'Académie Royale de Belgique, 1867, page 274, sq.

[2] Researches in Zoology, page 269.

lines, settle upon a site between the forked twigs of a bush and carry her foundation lines around in the manner described. But, on the other hand, I am prepared to say that the air laid bridge lines are also used for the foundations or frames of orbs. The following are my reasons for this opinion:—

1. First, the hours in the evening at which the greatest activity of web-weaving begins are those in which also begin the formation of the bridge lines. The latter action quite invariably precedes the former.

2. Again, a study of the foundation lines of very many webs has given me almost conclusive evidence that they must have been laid by the aid of air currents. For example, the webs of some species, as Acrosoma mitrata, A. spinea, and A. rugosa, are frequently found strung between young trees separated by two or three yards of space. That these builders might have dropped to the ground, crept over the wood, grass, or dry leaves carrying the thread in the free, out-stretched claw is, perhaps, not impossible, but does not seem to me at all probable, although short spaces over smooth surfaces might be passed in this way. I once found an orb hung upon lines which stretched from the balustrade of a bridge that spans a deep glen in Fairmount Park, to the foliage of a tree that springs out of the glen at least twenty-five feet below the bridge. Unless the foundations of this orb were formed by line bridging the interspace of a yard or more, it must be inferred that the spider had dropped from the balustrade to the glen, crossed the interval to the trunk of the tree, ascended it, and, having made a detour of nearly sixty feet to the point directly opposite that from which she started, all the while carrying her line with her and keeping it free from entanglement, have drawn the line taut and so completed her foundation. Such a supposition could not well be entertained, and it is clear that a breeze carried the line across from the spider's spinnerets.

I have noticed stronger examples of circumstantial evidence. Very many webs of Tetragnatha extensa and T. grallator have been seen spread upon bushes overhanging pools and streams of water; others were stretched between separated water plants or from such plants to the shore. (See Fig. 60.) Either the foundation lines were borne by air currents, or the spiders must have crossed upon the water, carrying their lines. The latter supposition is not wholly untenable, but will hardly be raised by any one who has studied the spinning economy of the creature.

One other example may be cited. At Atlantic City, by the boat-landing where pleasure boats used for sailing upon the Inlet are stored, there is (or was) an immense colony of Epeïroids, chiefly Epeira strix, E. sclopetaria, and E. benjamina (domiciliorum Hentz). During the summer months of 1880–81 great numbers of these spiders had their lines strung between the opposite exterior walls of the boat houses, which were built upon piles driven into the water. These lines were about nine feet long, and were stretched over the water at heights varying from one to ten feet. Most of them passed from wall to wall; many were fastened at one end upon piles and sticks driven here and there between the houses. (See Fig. 61.) It was a curious association, not to say analogy, which started in the observer's mind, as he saw the picturesque methods of the ancient "Lake dwellers" thus used by modern men, and appropriated, with befitting modification, by the orbweaving araneads. Certainly their silken domiciles were well secured above the inlet on their silken frames, and were happily placed for obtaining ample food supplies

Fig. 62. Spider suspension bridge over a stream.

of green-head flies and other insects hovering over the water. But when we ask ourselves, how were these snares built? we are constrained to call in the aeronautic habit and the air. It passes belief that these Epeiras carried their lines back and forth upon the rough waters of an inlet of the Atlantic Ocean. One must conclude that the foundations were formed by air currents.

One must draw the same conclusion concerning those orbs found suspended over streams. I have seen these cobweb bridges at various times; and they are not unfamiliar objects to wanderers in summer fields, woods, and mountains. (See Fig. 62.) This habit is not limited to American spiders. Vinson[1] says that in Madagascar Epeira (Nephila) tuberculosa throws from one bank to the other of streams of considerable size her lines of prodigous length, in which are arrested numbers of Libellulæ and large Agrions. He had observed this phenomenon upon running streams of forest interiors. One might call them, in truth, aerial bridges. In the island of Réunion it is to the wrinkled trunks of the huge Pandanus that the gigantic Orbweavers attach their long silken lines, and stretch them from one tree to another at a distance of many metres.

Cobweb Bridges.

3. I have greatly desired, but heretofore without complete success, that to the above cases of circumstantial evidence might be added actual observations of the use for foundations of lines stretched by air currents. Three summer evenings were once entirely devoted to endeavors to obtain this result. On one evening I was interrupted and called off at a very critical period of my observation; on the two other evenings the wind was unfavorable; but some valuable results were obtained. The webs of three adult individuals of Epeira strix, one male and two females, were selected, the den or nest of each spider located, and the web entirely destroyed.

The latter precaution was made necessary by the fact that Orbweavers use the same foundation lines during many successive days for the erection of their new webs. The great value which may attach to these old foundations appeared strikingly in subsequent studies, and also the difficulty if not impossibility of procuring suitable foundations for the webs of large spiders without the aid of the wind. In fact, a good foundation frame is a "good property," and it is accordingly treasured and used as long as it remains. I have noted many cases of snares continuing on the same site as long as the foundation lines endure. Their destruction is generally followed by a shifting of position.

Old Foundations Preserved

Two of the above webs (one of the females) were so situated that the prevailing air currents carried the lines in such wise that they could not possibly find entanglement. In consequence neither of these spiders succeeded, during two entire evenings up to half-past ten o'clock, in making a web. They frequently attempted it in vain. One spider that was more closely watched, was in motion during the whole period, passing up and down, from limb to limb, apparently desirous of fixing her web in its former site, but completely confused and foiled. The site was one, moreover, which would have allowed her to carry around a thread with comparative ease, being a dead sapling that forked near the ground.

Failures.

This spider domiciled during the day on the ground, but had her orb at the top of the forks, a height of six feet. Thus the space to be

<hr>

[1] Araneides des les Isles La Réunion, &c., page XIX.

traversed in passing from the top of one of the forks to a similar point on the opposite one, presented comparatively few difficulties. But no attempt was made to carry the line around, and as the wind had evidently not changed during the night, no web appeared on the tree in the morning. During the next evening the same restless movement along the bare limbs of the sapling was repeated, and was terminated at a late hour by a rare accident. A large moth, attracted by the lantern, became entangled upon a single short thread strung between two small twigs, whereupon Strix pounced upon it, swathed and fell to feeding on it. Next morning a tiny orbweb had been built around the shell of the moth at the point of capture.

During both evenings this spider at frequent intervals poised herself at the extremity of twigs, and emitted threads from her spinnerets which

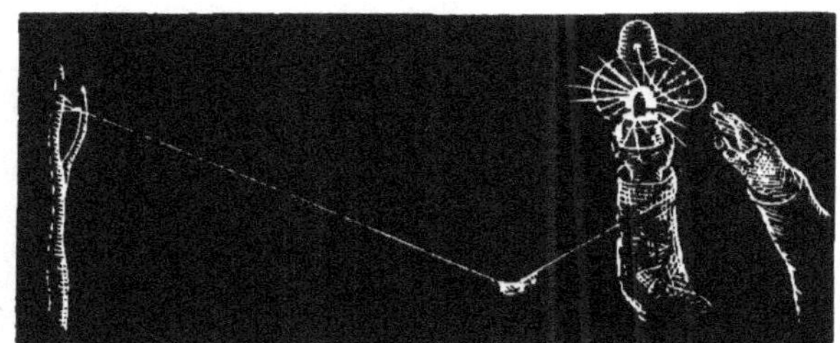

Fig. 63. Seeking attachment for foundation lines.

entangled upon some of the short twigs, but never upon the opposite fork, **Trial Air Lines.** as the wind was steadily contrary. No other entanglement was secured, as there was no elevated object in the direction of the wind for a great distance. However, I could at any time obtain an entanglement upon my hand by arresting the thread. By imitating the motion of a swaying leaf or limb, the spider was caused to perceive the attachment, and immediately ventured upon the line. (See Fig. 63.) Once the thread fastened upon my face, and the animal was allowed to cross the line, a distance of four or five feet, until within a few inches of the face, when she took in the situation, instantly cut the line and swung downward and backward over the long arc, and, after a few oscillations, climbed up the line to the point of departure. Her willingness to use air currents for making transit lines was thus quite as manifest as her then inability to get a foundation thereby. The second spider exhibited a like behavior.

4. The third individual, a male, did not attempt to spin an orb in the former site; the wind was unfavorable, but there would not have been much difficulty in carrying the cord around. He came out of his rolled leaf den at 7.20 P. M., and for more than an hour labored to secure a web foundation. He was located upon a dead end of a bough with many

branching twigs. As with the former individual, so with this; many efforts were made to obtain foundations by sending out threads from the spinnerets, and to this end he tried most of the numerous points of the twigs covering the territory which he seemed to have chosen as his general range.

One of these, a little pendant, which hung in the centre of the group, was taken as the basis of a most interesting operation. The spider dropped from the pendant by a line three or four inches long, grasped the line by one of the second pair of feet, and rapidly formed a triangular basket of threads by connecting the point of seizure with lines reaching to the feet of the remaining second leg and the third and fourth pairs. (See Fig. 64.) In this basket he hung head upward, the body held at an angle of about 45°, the two fore feet meanwhile stretched out, and groping in the air, as though feeling for the presence of obstructions, of enemies, or of floating threads. At the same time he elevated his

Swinging Baskets.

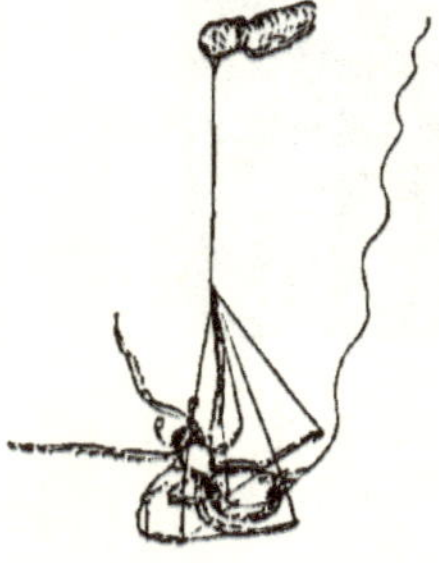

Fig. 64. The swinging basket used in issuing trial cables.

spinners and emitted a line which was drawn out at great length by the air, but secured no entanglement. The body of the spider had a gentle lateral oscillation that appeared to the observer to result from a voluntary twisting of the central rope by the animal, but may have been caused by the air; the effect was to give the output line a wider swing, and much increase the chance of entanglement.

However, there was no entanglement, and the spider dropped several inches further down and repeated the process as described above. This was repeated again and again, and when I allowed the line to attach to my person the spider at once proceeded to satisfy himself of the fact, and then to venture a crossing. In all these actions there were evidences of an habitual mode of securing transit by bridge lines. Since the first observation of this most interesting habit I have frequently seen the construction of these "baskets" or "hammocks" by adults of various species, and for a similar purpose by baby spiderlings reared indoors and colonized.

I had supposed, for several years, that the observation and record of this use of a swinging basket was original with myself, until one day reading Master Jonathan Edwards' description of flying spiders. I was surprised there to note that this remarkable character, when but a child, had probably anticipated me by one hundred and sixty years. I quote his language, and reproduce his rude figures, which while perhaps leaving the matter in doubt to the ordinary reader, will doubtless satisfy an arachnologist that the nimble-witted lad really saw this interesting habit: "I have been so happy as very frequently to see their manner of working; that when a spider would go

The Observation Anticipated.

from one tree to another, or would fly in the air, he first lets himself down from the twig he stands on by a web as in Fig. 1, and then, laying hold of it with his fore feet, and bearing himself by that, puts out a web as in Fig. 2, which is drawn out of his tail with infinite ease in the gentle moving air, to what length the spider pleases, and if the farther end happens to catch by a shrub or the branch of a tree, the spider immediately feels it, and fixes the hither end of it to the web by which he lets himself down, and goes over by that web which he put out of his tail as in Fig. 3, and this my eyes have innumerable times made me sure of."[1] (See Fig. 65.) The habit indeed prevails and is utilized for many func-

Use of Swinging Basket. tions; sometimes to secure a convenient attitude for cleansing the limbs and abdomen; sometimes as a position of guard or rest when the spider through fright has cast itself from its snare or nest, and has paused midway of the ground; sometimes as a favorable point of departure on a ballooning excursion. But most frequently the swinging basket serves, as here, when exploiting surroundings for an available orb site, and to work in the prime foundation line. While suspended thus she keeps one, or yet more frequently both fore legs extended slightly curved in the attitude of "on guard," and either held rigidly or occasionally waved to and fro feeling for the indications of the presence of the friendly trial line, or of unfriendly objects.

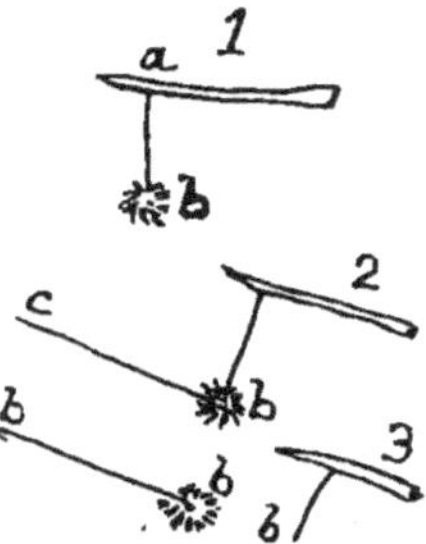
Fig. 65. Jonathan Edwards' illustration.

This use of the fore legs is habitual in all movements of spiders from point to point. While engaged **Fore Legs as Antennæ.** in dragging a foundation line around vines and twigs, over leaves or other surfaces, she will often pause and wave the extended fore legs as though prospecting her way not only, but testing the safety of

Fig. 66. Antennal use of the fore legs.

her surroundings. The action frequently reminded me of the characteristic use of the antennæ by ants and other insects; and, indeed, I have little doubt the fore legs of spiders do have in part the function of antennæ. (See Fig. 66.)

[1] Am. Jour. Sci. and Arts, Vol. XXI., 1832, pages 112, 113.

During the intervals of the attempts above described, and, indeed, preceding them, our Furrow spider passed back and forth along the branching twigs, leaving behind him trailed threads or lines connecting the ends, many of which seemed to be purely tentative. At last a central point was taken, a short thread dropped therefrom and attached to one of these tentative lines. The confused network of circumjacent lines was gathered together in a little flossy ball at the point of union, which was now made the centre of the orb, the first dropline and two divisions of the cross line constituting the three original radii. From these the spider proceeded to lay in the radii and complete an orb. The time occupied in constructing the web proper was half an hour, while the work of prospecting for and obtaining a foundation consumed more than an hour. Even then the orb was very irregular, and showed decided traces of the want of the usual well and orderly laid foundations. An examination of a number of web sites which I had marked upon the same grounds, showed that in every case where the surroundings had allowed an easy and good entanglement by the wind, the spiders had made webs at an early hour, and with straight and regular foundations.

I feel justified in saying that the above observations which might be indefinitely multiplied, are sufficient warrant for the belief that air currents have a large part in placing the original framework or foundation lines of orbwebs, and that spiders habitually make use of them for that purpose. I doubt, however, whether there is anything like a deliberate purpose in any case to connect the point of occupancy with any special opposite point. The spider seems to act in the matter very much at hap hazard, but with a general knowledge that such behavior would somewhere secure available attachments. Many of her bridge lines are evidently tentative and chiefly at the mercy of the breeze, although some observations indicated a limited control of the thread by manipulation.

This use of air currents is depended very much upon the site chosen, the condition of the wind, the abundance of prey, etc. Webs built in large open spaces are perhaps always laid out by bridge lines, at least as to the first and principal line or lines. In more contracted sites the frame lines are generally carried around, and often a foundation is the result of both methods.[1] The above observations have been fully confirmed by the behavior of spiders colonized upon the vines and shrubbery in my manse yard. The securing of one principal line is the important desideratum. This obtained, the remainder is generally easy. In carrying around a frame line the largest spider will move with great deftness over the leaves and

---

[1] Blackwall, Constr. Nets Geom. Spiders, page 186, and Kirby and Spence, Introduction, i., page 413, knew that spiders could form foundation lines by means of air currents.

tendrils, frequently securing an anchorage by attaching her dragline, and all the while holding aloof from contact with the foliage the new foundation line which is spun after her as she moves.

Kirby and Spence describe this curious variation of the habit. A spider isolated upon a stick set within a vessel of water dropped from the top of the stick to which the usual dragline attachment had been made, and emitted two threads as it descended. Having reached a point near the surface of the water, it stopped, and by some unobserved means, severed one of the threads close to the spinnerets. The free end of the released filament floated up and outward from the top of the stick, and was caused to entangle upon a pencil held in the observer's hand. The spider, which had meanwhile mounted the summit of the stick, perceived the line to be taut, and having tested it by pulling, crept over it to the pencil, dragging another line behind her as she moved.[1] This is an isolated example, and may, of course, have been a simple coincidence, as it is not certain that the spider designed to secure a bridge line by the above behavior. Yet it is worthy of notice as suggesting a line of observation that may yield good results.

A Variation of the Habit.

II.

We may now construct the diagramatic figure, Fig. 67, to show the process by which an orb frame is laid when the prime foundation is obtained by an air current. We suppose that an Orbweaver in the act of web-making has stopped upon the leaf at the left of the cut. Turning her abdomen toward the course of the wind, she issues a line (a, a) that floats outward until it entangles at x. This fact is at once perceived, and the spider (ss) ventures over it as at bb, dragging behind her a thread which unites with and strengthens the original line, which had been drawn taut, as c, c, c, x. This may be repeated several times, until, at last, the prime foundation line is formed.

This strengthening by means of overspinning is not necessarily, perhaps not generally, done in immediate succession of threads, but from time to time. At various stages of working in the radii of other parts, the creature seems to perceive the need of strengthening the supporting lines, and proceeds to stretch a new strand or two. Then she resumes work upon the orb, to return as occasion requires, and adds strands to her cable. When the upper line is completed, especially if it be one which has been used for several days, it presents the appearance of a white or yellowish white thread as thick as a bit of sewing silk. It may readily be reeled upon a stick or spool, and its numerous filaments can be seen and even separated. It has a glossy appearance, and may often be found several feet in length.

First Line.

[1] Introduction to Entomology, Volume I, set XIII., page 415.

From some point in this first line, as d, the spider makes an attachment and drops down, paying out her thread as she goes, until she reaches the ground or touches the first object directly underneath her. If the air is quite still and the spider large, the line will be nearly perpendicular, as d dd. It will vary more or less from the perpendicular according to the spider's weight and the wind's force.

This vertical line, d dd, is lashed to the grass, foliage, or other object, and then is reascended to a point, o, where an attachment is made and a new line begun. This is held out in one of the hind feet quite free from the

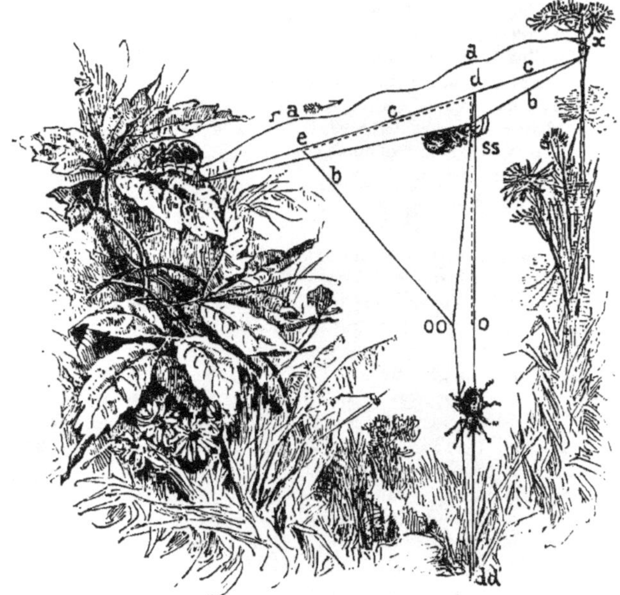

Fig. 67. Laying foundation lines by air currents. (First lines.)

dropline, d dd, as the ascent is continued. The new free line (the dotted line odcc) is thus carried up dd and along cx to the point c, where it is fastened, after having been drawn taut. This last act pulls out the line dd until o reaches the point oo, and the deported (dotted) line, o d c thus becomes the line, c oo. There is then completed the triangle, cd oo, within which the spider at once proceeds to spin her orb. When a four sided frame is spun instead of the three sided one here illustrated, precisely the same method is pursued, the line cb oo being simply carried farther around and down the bush until it forms the lower boundary of a trapezoid, and is parallel to ccx.

It must be understood that I have only taken a case that may be considered fairly typical of the general plan of construction. It will explain the ordinary principles and a common mode of proceeding; but in point
The Plan Variable. of fact the details continually vary, according to the local peculiarities of the orb site, the conditions of the wind, and I suppose to some extent the individuality of the spider. Some incident will cause a variation; the advent of an insect, the presence of an enemy, the neighborhood of another web, a falling leaf, a fright or excitement of any sort may divert the spider's attention, and cause a variation in her plan. In short, her "plan" is to some extent elastic, and variable by the stress of accidents and circumstances; but as a general fact the exterior frame of the orb will be found to be a more or less regular quadrilateral or a triangle.

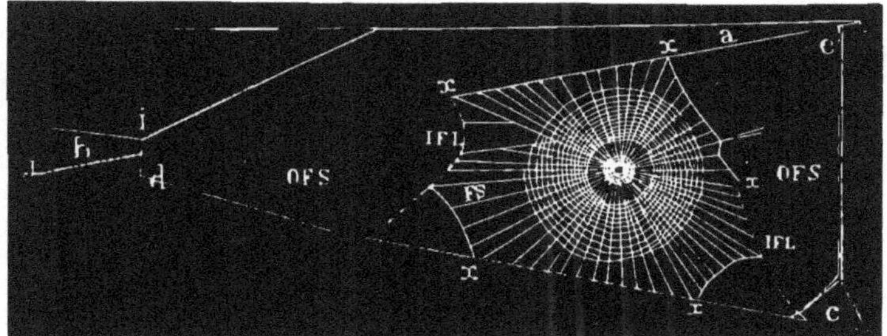

Fig. 68. Double foundation lines.

The foundation lines most commonly observed take the form of a trapezoid, whose sides are directly anchored to surrounding objects. Webs
Double Foundations. frequently occur, however, in which the orb with its trapezoidal frame is hung within an outer foundation of strong cords usually, but not always, triangular in arrangement, as illustrated in Fig. 67. This form prevails in cases where the snare is hung within large open spaces, or stretched between two trees or bushes in woods. Some species appear to hang their snares quite habitually in this way, as with all the indigenous species of the genus Acrosoma whose industry is known to me.

An example of this style of foundation is shown at Fig. 68, which is a snare of Acrosoma rugosa. Here we have two strong cords, ab, cd, united at d in a point, and joined at the base by cc, which was probably the line used in securing the union of the two long cords at d. The lower line, cd, is caught up by a short perpendicular line, id, and stayed upon a cross line ti, which again is supported by an upper straight cord attached to the leaves of the grapevine in which the orb hangs.

The trapezoidal foundation lines, x—x, are woven within the basilar part of the triangle thus formed. We have here the usual Foundation Space, FS, and indeed might aptly apply that term to the entire Foundation system. But it will be convenient, in webs of this form, to name the inner side of the trapezoid, IFL, the Inner Foundation Lines, and the large exterior cords, ab, cd, the Outer Foundation Lines, and the intermediate space, OFS, the Outer Foundation Space.

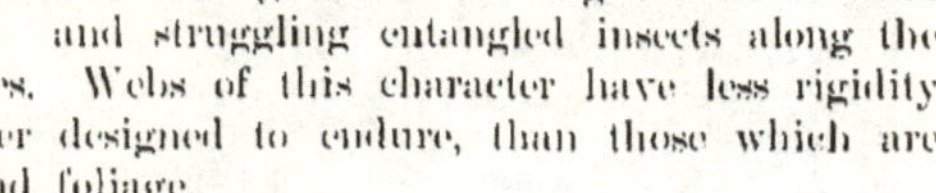

Fig. 69. Spinning the initial radii.

Use of Inner Lines. The inner foundation lines are of course necessary to the construction of the orb under such circumstances, but they are plainly so adjusted as not only to allow the nicest balance of the beautiful snare, but also to afford the greatest power of resistance by distributing the disturbing forces of wind and struggling entangled insects along the elastic inner foundation lines. Webs of this character have less rigidity and would seem to be better designed to endure, than those which are directly attached to limbs and foliage.

A foundation having been secured, the spider proceeds to place in the radii. To this end a position is taken at or near the centre of the orb, usually by dropping down from a top line, dragging **Placing in the Radii.** after her a thread which becomes the initial radius, Fig. 69, a. At the central terminus of this radius a little ball of floss (H) is formed by emitting a thick ray of silk or by gathering together into a wad the many tentative lines with which the space within the frame is frequently matted. This ball evidently serves as an anchorage for the radii and perhaps also as a guidon for the animal herself. Sometimes as the work proceeds and the strain of the new laid radii is felt upon the centre, the bit of floss is pulled out into an irregular frayed mass with interlacing filaments, as at Fig. 70, which shows a hub of a snare of Epeira vertebrata arrested when nine radii had been spun. The spider hung at the centre, and the positions of the feet in their order (first, second, etc.) are indicated by the numerals.

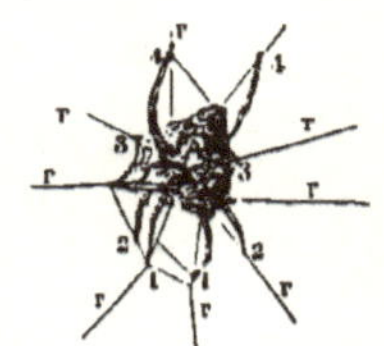

Fig. 70. Pulled out guidon.

The spider may now proceed in two ways: first to drop downward from H along c, to the foundation line, and attach thereto the thread, which is done by touching the spinnerets to the point of attachment, the natural viscidity of the exuded silk causing it to adhere. This gives the second radius. Thence the spider returns along c to the centre H, and ascends a, to form the third radius Hk or Hi. If, however, the tentative lines which net the enclosed space have such an entanglement with the guidon ball as to brace it sufficiently from beneath, the spider instead of dropping down may first climb up the radius a, carrying a free thread in one of her hind feet which is held out quite well from the radius for this purpose as shown at Fig. 71. When a desired point of attachment, as K, has been reached, the deported line x is drawn taut, fastened, and the radius

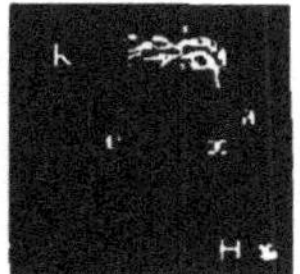

Fig. 71. Putting in a radius.

c is now formed, which in this case will be the second radius. Next the spider returns to the guidon H by c, or more likely by a, and thence drops to the line, mn (Fig. 69), forming a third radius, e. The radii are all inserted in the above manner, and not consecutively, but alternately on the opposite sides of the included space, by single lines or successive couplets. The behavior of different individuals of the same species or of the individuals of different species may show variations more or less decided, but the above action is fairly typical.

Blackwall says[1] that the radii are formed by the spider "without observing any regularity in the order of her progression." On the contrary there seems to be at least so much order in this act that a sort of alternation as to the orientation of the lines is observed, which I have called the alternate apposition of the radii. A purpose to maintain a balance in the radial framework during its construction is thus suggested, although, certainly, an absolute regularity of alternate progression cannot be asserted.

Alternate Apposition of Radii.

The order in which the radii are spun into the frame of the orb was quite fully shown in the work of an Epeira sclopetaria observed at Alexandria Bay, New York. When the observation began the foundation lines

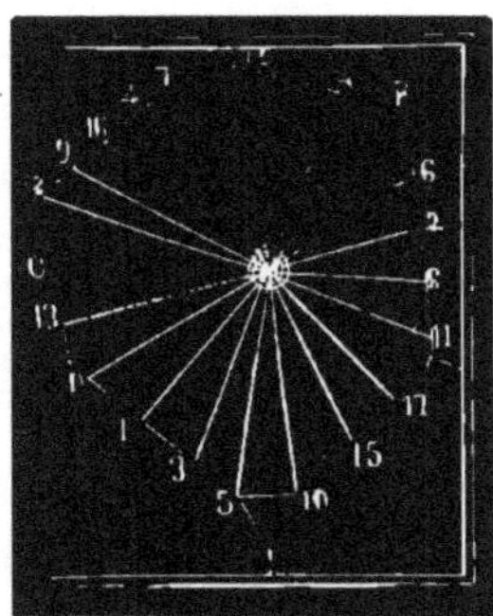

Fig. 72. Alternate apposition of radii.

were already laid, and also the original radii marked A, B, C, D, Fig. 72. These cords were united at the centre by a tuft of silk, and braced by a few concentric lines, which formed the basis of the hub. I counted seventeen radii before the spider ceased. Their alternate apposition can easily be seen by tracing them in the order of the numerals in Fig. 72, which are arranged in the order of construction. That is, radius 1 was formed by carrying the line along D to 1 and tightening it. Thence the spider went to the centre, ran along B, which had previously been inserted, thence down to 2, where the radius 2 was formed. From 2 again she went to the centre, passed down 1 and along D to 3, where attachment was made, and radius 3 was formed. Once more the centre was sought, and passing along the line A the point 4 was reached and another radius there fastened. Thus on from 4 to 5, from 5 to 6, and so around the entire circle. The mechanical advantage of this order is apparent. Several times the central termini of the radii were strengthened by lapping threads across them.

This tendency to alternate apposition I have frequently observed in various species, and its character will be better shown by giving several other schemes of the order of progression in spinning radii. The **Order of Radii.** schemes do not present a complete sequence of the radii from the very beginning, but number from the point at which I happened to catch the spider at work. They are to be read as in Fig. 72, the order of numerals showing the relative position of the radial lines in the order of their spinning. The series will show, I think, that while no absolute mathematical regularity marks the succession, some method of alternation evidently dominates the spider's movements. She knows the necessity

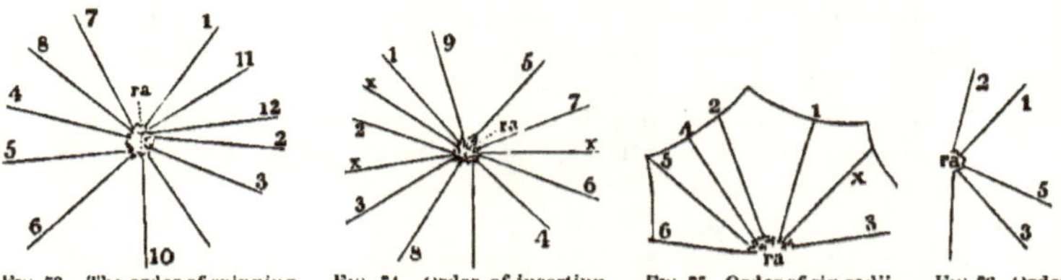

Fig. 73. The order of spinning in twelve radii. Epeira vertebrata.

Fig. 74. Order of inserting nine radii.

Fig. 75. Order of six radii.

Fig. 76. Order of five radii.

which exists for balancing such a peculiar and delicate structure, and adopts her mode of spinning to the exigencies of her spinningwork.

Blackwall states that after the completion of the radii the spider proceeds to the centre, turns around and pulls each radius with her feet to ascertain its strength, breaking such as are defective, and replacing them by others. I have never seen anything of the kind; the spider in settling herself and gathering the radial lines into her eight claws naturally jerks them somewhat. But no such purpose was ever suggested to my mind as that declared by Blackwall. He also says that the radii are composed of double lines, a statement which my observations contradict.[1] I have seen very many radii spun, but have never observed any one overlaid or doubled (if that be the meaning) as is often the case with foundation lines. On the contrary they were always composed of one thread drawn out in the usual way from the spinning spools.

Rennie in his remarks upon the construction of an orbweb expresses the opinion that the most remarkable circumstance in the process is that

---

[1] Nets of the Geometric Spiders, page 182.

the spider uses her limbs as a measure to regulate the distances of her radii or "wheel spokes," and the circular meshes interweaved into them.[1]

Legs no Unit of Measure. The above method of alternate apposition shows that the distances between radii, at least, are not determined by any such mensuration, which of course would only apply on the supposition that the lines were spun consecutively. Moreover, having frequently measured the distances between the radii at their circumference or attachment to the foundation lines, I have found that there is often great irregularity therein; the interspaces sometimes vary in the proportion of three to one on the same orb. The fact that the number of radii is not constant in the successive webs of any individual spider, but varies from day to day (although within a narrow limit), is also against this hypothesis.

It has already been intimated that the notched zone serves an important end in bracing the radii while they are yet in outline. This appears distinctly while observing the above described behavior. The first **Forming Notched Zone.** radii that are inserted bend and sway under the weight of the spider, which, as she clambers over them, suggests the idea of a carpenter engaged upon a scaffolding in its first crude state. In some cases the aranead stops at the guidon, after having placed the first few radii, and swings her spinnerets around their bases as though to strengthen them. This act may be repeated several times; and in fact the spider whenever she comes to the centre is apt to make two or three of these gyrations. However, when all the radii are inserted she proceeds to complete the notched zone, laying in the spirals thereof from the centre outwardly. These vary in number from four or five to ten or even more. This variation holds in webs of the same species; for example, in seven webs of Argyroepeira hortorum, the spirals in the notched zone numbered, successively, 8, 10, 10, 10, 6, 8, 5. I have counted as many as twenty in the web of Epeira gibberosa. In the group of Orbweavers, of which Epeira insularis[2] is the type, the number of notched spirals is quite persistently less, commonly five or six. The width of the notched zone is about equal to, or a little greater than that of the free zone, and about twice that of the hub. In at least one example noted (an orb of Tetragnatha extensa) three wide notched spirals were first spun before the others were laid in. These appeared to be the analogue of the spiral scaffold, referred to in the next section; but this is not the ordinary rule of construction.

Mr. Romanes[3] quotes Dr. Leach as giving, on the authority of Sir J. Banks, a case of a web-spinning spider which had lost five of its legs,

---

[1] Insect Architecture, page 313.

[2] This familiar and beautiful spider Dr. Thorell declares quite identical with the Epeira marmorea of Europe. I have no specimens of E. marmorea with which to compare, but have no doubt of Dr. Thorell's identification. However, I retain Hentz's name in the two volumes on Habits, and will endeavor to adjust the nomenclature of this and other species in the final volume.

[3] Mental Evolution in Animals, page 209.

and as a consequence could only spin very imperfectly. It was observed to follow the habits of the hunting spider, which does not build a web, but catches its prey by stalking. This change of habit was only temporary, as the spider recovered its legs after moulting.[1] Mr. Darwin also alludes to this incident.

My observations are wholly contradictory of this. I have placed upon my vines an Epeira domiciliorum that had lost all the legs on one side, and found it to weave a serviceable web, although necessarily some-what imperfect. It hung upon its snare and trapped flies with fair success. I have often noted similar defects in various species always with the same result. Mr. Romanes' inference as to the plasticity of instinct needs a little more confirmation. Indeed, the inference was long ago fully exploded by the observations of Dr. Heineken, a surgeon in the Island of Madeira during the early part of this century. This gentleman, in order to test the ability of orbweaving spiders to spin after mutilation, removed at intervals, successively, the legs of various individuals, with the following results: Epeira (Argiope) fasciata, with all the legs removed except the second and last on the left side and the last but one on the right side, thoroughly mended its web when two-thirds of it had been torn away. It maintained the same position and attitude as before mutilation, and in every respect had the manner of an Orbweaver.

Spinning after Mutilation.

Another Epeïroid spider had all the legs removed except the first on the right side and the second and last on the left side, leaving the spider with but three legs. On the following day, filaments appeared in several directions. These were constantly added to, and in the course of two weeks a geometric web was formed equally perfect, but more sparing in quantity than one made by a spider in the same species and under the same mode of confinement, but healthy and unmutilated. The entanglement and taking of flies, and the conduct of the two spiders was in every respect similar. They were confined in large glass jars. A number of individuals were experimented upon with the same result. In the case of one tubemaking spider, the number of limbs was reduced to two, and the web entirely destroyed. Even then enough web was spun to cover the spider imperfectly and occasionally to entangle an exhausted fly. It lived for five weeks after mutilation.[2]

[1] Transactions Linnæan Society, Vol. XI., page 393.

[2] Dr. Heineken, On the Reproduction of Members in Spiders and Insects. Zoological Journal, Vol. IV., page 428. 1828–29.

CHAPTER V.

THE ARMATURE OF ORBWEBS: VISCID SPIRALS.

I.

THE next step in orbmaking is to prepare for the spinning of the concentric lines or spirals. This is done by starting a line at or near the **The Spiral Scaffolding.** notched zone and carrying it around spirally toward the circumference, attaching it by the spinnerets to the intersected radii. This forms the spiral scaffolding. The distance between these lines is about equal to the width of the notched zone, the space between which and the first scaffold spiral is in fact the free zone. The absolute width differs of course according to the size of the web. In large orbs of Epeira domiciliorum from which the explanatory figure (Fig. 77) was drawn, the distance was about an inch between any two of the eight spirals

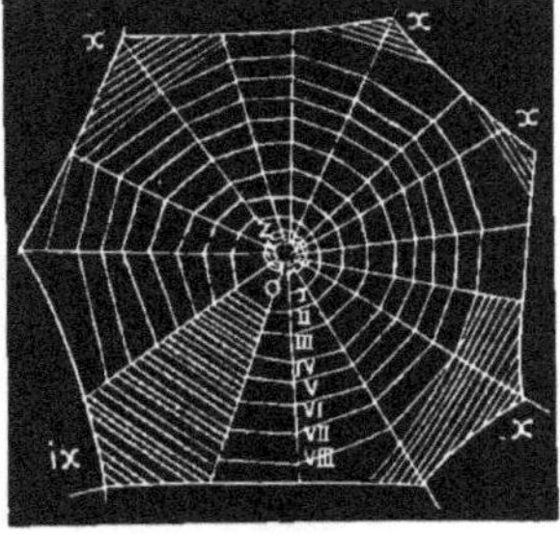

Fig. 77. Spiral scaffolding. Lines I-VIII are the scaffold; ix, a section filled in; x, corner loops.

(I-VIII) except between I-II, where it was about three-fourths of an inch. These wide spirals, as will presently be seen, are the scaffolding upon and by which the true spirals are laid in, and from which they differ by being destitute of viscid beads.

Before the beaded spirals are spun, however, which is the completion of the snare, a preliminary act sometimes occurs. Very many orbwebs are not perfect orbs; in some the entire space circumscribed by the foundation lines and the foliage or other objects to which they are attached, is filled with true viscid spirals, thus nearly eliminating the Foundation Space proper. In other orbs only the lower part of the snare is netted with spirals to the very foundation lines. In others again the angles formed by the interior margin of the Foundation Space (the inner foundation lines) represented by letters ix and x, in the figure, are filled with spirals. In such cases these corners or angles have usually been covered first. For example, in the orb at Fig. 77 the animal first spun the spirals which fill up the angle ix. She then passed to the right hand corner x which was in like manner covered; and so moved around the web until all the corners (at x) were filled in, leaving the open circular space occupied by eight scaffold spirals.

The lines thus covering the angles are not strictly "spirals" although they belong to the spiral space, and have precisely the characteristics of the true spirals from which often they cannot be separated by the eye, without close attention. They are put in by "loops;" that is, the spider passes back and forth over the ends of the radii, as at x, ix, carrying her thread, and looping it at the extremities of corner spaces. These lines have therefore been designated corner loops. In point of fact the concentric lines are complete circles only when the framework of the snare allows an unobstructed movement entirely around the centre. This example is not the invariable rule of procedure, for spiders vary their modes. Some start at once upon the spiral concentrics and make loops (particularly at the lower part of the orb) before the final finish. The case is simply illustrative of the ordinary method of dealing with the corners and angles.

In the act of spinning the spirals the spider moves from the circumference toward the centre, precisely the reverse of the direction taken when placing in the spiral scaffolding. The rapidity with which the spiral line is spun and the peculiar manner in which the spider's eight legs appear to be intermixed, make it extremely difficult to observe and describe the actual method.

Spinning Viscid Spirals.

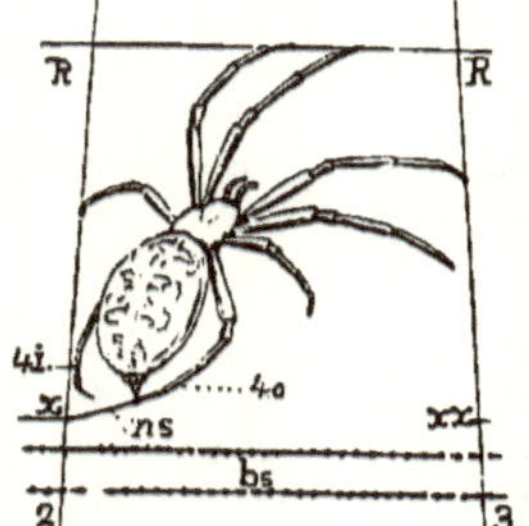

Fig. 78. Starting a spiral string.

But the process, as it is ordinarily pursued, is substantially as follows: The two hind legs are used exclusively to aid the spinning fingers in the work of spinning. The other legs are used for locomotion alone. The moment one string is fastened at the upper point upon a radius, which is done by the application of the spinnerets thereto (see Fig. 79), the spider lifts its abdomen, thus of course drawing out after her a thread, one end of which is the last point of attachment (x, Fig. 78) to the radius (R 2), and the other the closed spinning fingers. The hind foot (4 o) nearest the spinnerets is now bent under and grasps this thread, which, as the spider moves, it holds and appears to pull out with great rapidity. Next, the inner hind foot (4 i) is bent under and seizes the thread, which it holds aloft, stretching it out until it is almost double its proper length, as represented in Figs. 79 and 80. If the distance between the radii be great, and the spiral string therefore much lengthened, the two hind legs will be used alternately several times to draw out the line.

In the meantime, the outer hind leg, which had first aided the spinnerets in paying out the thread, is reached downward towards the radius, which the spider all the while has been rapidly approaching, and grasps it with the claws just beneath the point where the new string will cross. This then is the attitude of the spider at this point of her operations, Fig. 79. One hind foot (l.o) grasps the radius near and below the point (xx) just opposite the last point of attachment.

Paying out the Thread. The other hind leg (l.i) is reached out beyond and above the spider's abdomen, holding the new string (ns) so that the two parts form an angle. Now the abdomen drops towards the radius. The raised foot lets go the stretched string at the very moment that the spinning fingers grasp the radius (at xx) and clamp the string thereto. The string being released at the same moment, contracts with a sudden snap, and thus forms the little interradial or portion of the spiral line between the two radii.

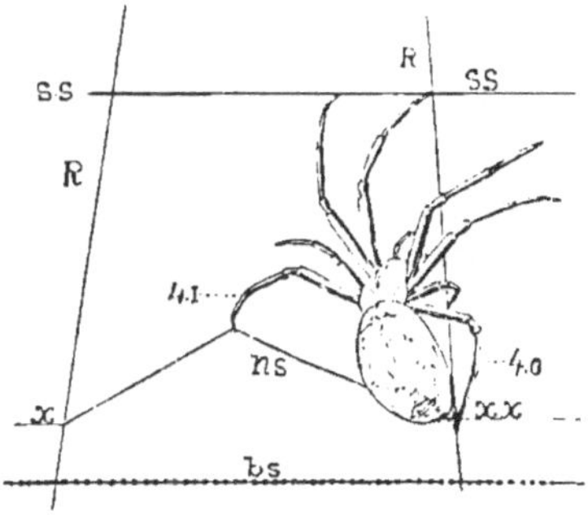

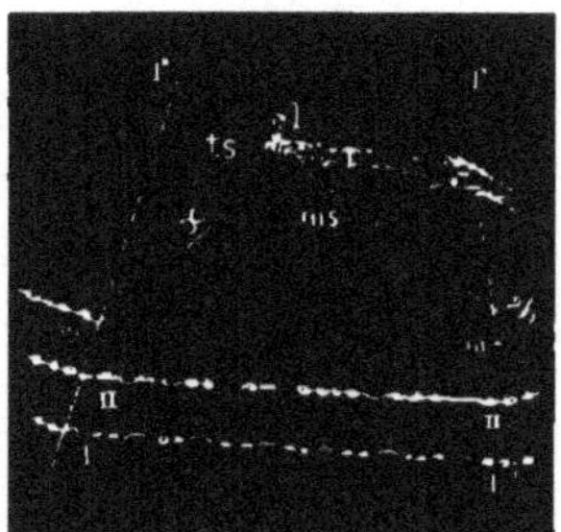

Fig. 79. Clamping a spiral string.

Fig. 80 shows the first action in this process. The strings I I, II II, are sections of a finished spiral line, and III x III is a string in the act of being spun. The line x is caught up by the claw, cl, upon a tarsal spine, ts, (apparently) or a metatarsal spine, ms, and pulled out from the abdomen to which it is attached by ab. The foot (there greatly exaggerated) moves rapidly towards ab, and the line is fastened at the point III, indicated on the right hand radius, r. The large tarsal spines which arm the terminus of the tarsus of Argiope cophinaria are continually used by that species to hold the beaded string as it is thus drawn out. In the meantime, of course, the remaining limbs of the spider have been carrying her forward. The **The Forward Progress.** legs on the side towards the centre of the hub reach upward and grasp the spiral scaffold (ss) if the scaffold happens to be within reach. This is frequently the case during the whole process of spinning; but frequently also during the placing in of the first spiral strings included between two scaffold lines the spider is unable to reach so far, and therefore must go around the radius, as will be described presently. The legs on the side of the body towards the

Fig. 80. Drawing out a beaded spiral. The leg much exaggerated.

circumference of the orb grasp the radius as it is approached. This describes in a general way the method of locomotion. In other words, the legs towards the circumference reach forward toward the approached

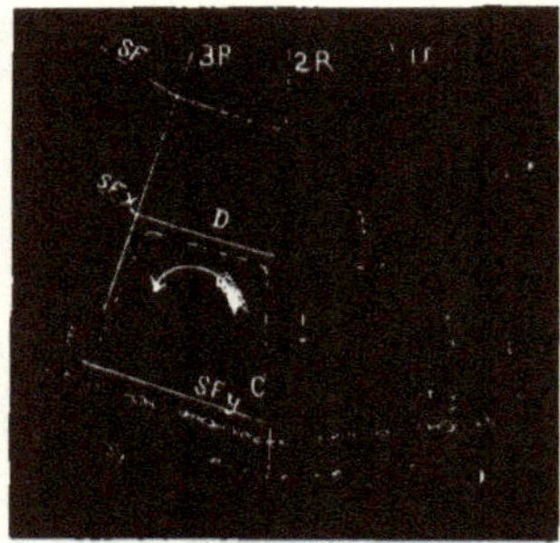

Fig. 81.   Movements of the body while spinning spirals.

radius. At the immediate instant when the spinnerets clamp the new made string upon the radius the whole body is at rest and is balanced by the legs in the position just described (Fig. 79), that is, on the upper side supported by the two fore legs; on the forward side (towards the head of the spider) by the other **The String Clamped.** two fore and third legs, holding to the radius; and on the lower side by the hind foot, which also grasps the radius just below the point of intersection. Of course, this period of poise, as a rule, is so brief that it is scarcely noticeable. At times, however, when the spider appears to be moving more sluggishly, for one reason or another, the moment is sufficiently prolonged to permit the observation. I have often seen that the spider would make a quite noticeable pause before the hind foot let go the new spiral string, permitting it to snap into its position between the two radii. Sometimes the position of the spider will differ from the above in detail; for example, when the beaded strings have been brought up close to the scaffold line, they can be fastened while the spider hangs with her sides nearly parallel with the scaffold. In such case the legs on one side will hold on to the scaffold, while at least two legs on the under side remain free, and grope about with the restless motion of feeling after something, heretofore described. In these operations the scaffold line is generally well bent downward instead of being taut as shown in the cuts.

The general line of progress of the Orb-weaver's body while spinning the spirals is illustrated at Fig. 81, where R represents the radii, SF, SFx, SFy are spiral scaffold lines, and SP true beaded spirals. The spider engaged upon the spiral A fastens it to the radius 1R at the point of contact; then the

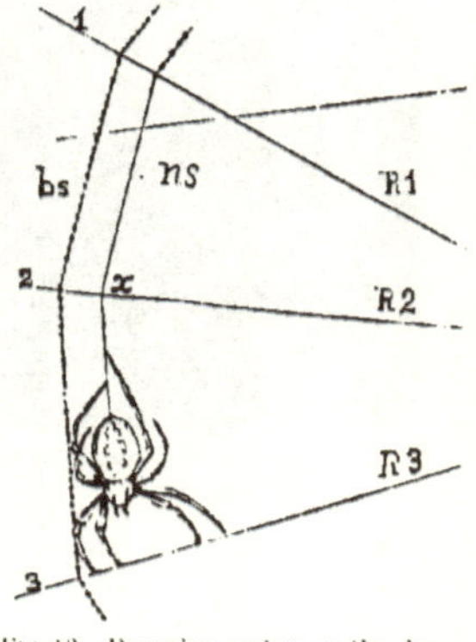

Fig. 82.   Dropping action on the downward course.

course of the body is upward along 1R to the spiral foundation SFx; thence across the section B thereof; thence downward along radius 2R, until at the point C opposite A she can tighten and fasten the line which she has carried around with her. This makes one section or string of her beaded spiral. The next string, C-D-E, is completed in the same way, the general course being in the direction of the arrows.

Course of Spider. As the space between the newly made viscid spirals (as A) and the next occurring foundation spiral (SFx) is diminished, the spider does not need to walk along the intervening radii, 1R, 2R, etc. The distance between the spiral foundation and the new points of operation is then short enough to allow her to grasp the former with her fore feet; and thus she strides along, oscillating between the viscid spirals and the foundation spiral, and between the two radii separating the beaded string which she is weaving in. Very often, indeed, there is no need to walk along the radius at all, but from the beginning to the end the spider is able to accomplish her work by the simple process of reaching to the spiral scaffold. In that case, of course, the dotted line and arrows of Fig. 81 only represent in a general way the course of the body.

In ascending the orb, as well as in crossing from one side to another, the aranead must plod through all the course which has thus been imper-

Dropping. fectly indicated; but when she is on the downward course she is not compelled to stride along the radii and spiral scaffolding, and therefore simply drops from the point of attachment last made to the next radius. (Fig. 82.) This sheer descent of her web is made when those radii are reached which cross from the centre laterally to the circumference, when it is manifest (see R1, R2) that all required is that she should drop from the radius last intersected (R2) to the one next in order (R3). This is the usual course of the spider, and not until she makes the turn and again proceeds laterally across her orb is she required to renew the more tedious process described.

It is obvious that those Orbweavers which make vertical webs must, from necessity of the case, vary their mode of proceeding while spinning

Swinging the Circle. the spiral lines, according to the position which they may chance at the time to have upon their orbs. This fact may be illustrated at Fig. 83, which represents diagramatically the progress of the spider around an entire concentric. The web is represented with the radii, R, R, in place, and the spiral scaffold, S, located. The spider had already begun upon the viscid spirals, and had laid in one circular course of the series. Let us suppose that she starts at the point x on radius marked R1, to lay in her second spiral concentric. The ordinary course would be to stride along the radius to the spiral scaffolding (S) and so to the point x2, where she would fasten her new string. But it is obvious that such a course would be wasted time and energy, and that her purpose would be accomplished more readily by dropping directly from x on R1 to R2, and carrying her line to the point of junction x on the last named radius. This is precisely what the spider does, and this is her habitual method on all parts of her orb where such a direct drop is practicable.

Thus, to follow her course from R2 she would descend to the next radius, R3, by such a direct drop. When her string is attached to the **Varying Methods.** point x, on this radius, she will pursue the ordinary method and pass around to the spiral scaffold at its point of intersection (z) with the radius. Here now it is again possible for her to drop from z to x, on the radius marked 4. From this point onward, while proceeding across her orb, and during the ascent from R4 to R16, her habitual method is to swing around the radius to the spiral scaffold, and so down the next radius to the points of intersection, x. When she has

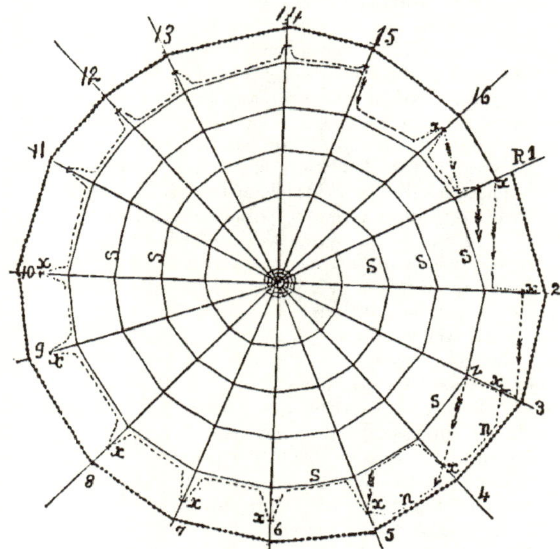

Fig. 83. Swinging around the circle.

reached radius No. 16 it is again possible for her to proceed by dropping directly from her last point of intersection to the radius next below.

It will be observed that an alternate course of progress is possible for the spider at certain sections of her orb. For example, between the radii 3 and 4, and 4 and 5, instead of moving from the point of intersection, x, along the radius to the spiral scaffolding, and dropping from the point **Walking Beaded Spirals.** z or swinging along the radius of the scaffold, she may pass from x3 directly along the line n, supporting herself by the beaded spiral last wrought in. This she sometimes undoubtedly does. Blackwall expressed the opinion that the last made viscid spiral line is also used as a support while spinning the next spiral in order, in cases where the spiral scaffold is not easily accessible.[1] I have occasionally observed this action, but cannot certainly confirm the observation as habitual. At all events, the diagram will show this alternate movement as it may be made between the radius 5 and radius 6, or again between radius 6 and radius 7.

From this point onward, while crossing laterally the lower portion of the orb, and again while ascending, the striding movements which have been described and illustrated by the previous figures become necessary.

Labor Saving. Usually, however, upon the downward course, she drops from one radius to another, and thus proves herself, like any human laborer in mechanics and architecture, both able and willing to make the best use of her time and strength by varying her ordinary habit, and availing herself of natural conditions. I have described what is the habitual course, as it may be seen by any careful observer. But there occur exceptions, and I have sometimes had occasion to note the fact that some spiders allow themselves to be so swayed by habit that they persist in crawling around the sides of all the sections, instead of relieving themselves by the direct drop after the manner of their congeners. I suppose that even in Spiderdom there is room for the ultra conservative constitution.

Mr. Blackwall thus describes the mode of spinning the spirals, which correctly summarizes the detailed account which I have given. From the circumference of the orb the spider passes along a radius to the outer line of the spiral scaffolding (having fixed a viscid thread to the end of the radius)—along which she goes to the adjoining radius, drawing out the thread, in her transit, with the claws of her hind leg nearest the circumference. She then transfers the thread to the claws of the other hind leg, and passing down the radius at which she has just arrived to the circumference, she places the foot of her hind leg previously employed in

Black-wall's Description. drawing out the threads on the point in the radius to which her filament is to be attached, and bringing her spinners to the spot there makes it secure. The precise place in each radius at which to fix the thread is always ascertained by the situation of the foot of the hind leg, and this is determined by touching with the feet of those legs nearest the circumference, the marginal line, or when the structure of the net is further advanced, the last formed circumvolution of the viscid spiral line.[1]

The spider advances, as we have seen, by a zigzag movement, partly striding, partly swinging, catching alternately upon the opposing foundation spirals and the next radius. Every radius crossed, at every crossing, is touched as above described and the spiral caused to adhere. In some orbs whose radii number forty or fifty, and the spirals as high as sixty, the number of attachments is very great 2500 or 3000, and they are

---

[1] "Nets of Geometric Spiders," page 183.

made with a rapidity which often prevents the eye from following the motions of the foot and spinnerets.

When the innermost spiral is reached the aranead swings or strides to the hub, takes up her position head downward and bites out the flossy guidon, which she takes within her mouth.[1] Whether or not it is finally rejected I cannot say, but it is certainly retained for some time, and I believe is dissolved within her mouth, and swallowed.

What becomes of the unbeaded scaffold lines which the spider uses for weaving in her system of beaded spirals? They are not seen among the concentries when the orb is finished, and the secret of their disappearance is only to be unfolded by watching the architect as she proceeds with her work. It will thus be found that as she spins her way from the outer margin toward the centre she bites off her scaffolding and permits it to drop away, rolling it up usually within her jaws. It has served her purpose by giving her footing while engaged in forming the essential part of her structure, and when she needs it no longer she removes it, precisely as the mason when "pointing" his stonework takes down his wooden scaffold as he works from the top toward the bottom of his wall. I have observed this process repeatedly, as others have done.[2] Mr. Emerton[3] speaks of "a few turns in the centre" apparently confounding what I have called the "notched zone" with the special scaffolding, as his figure also shows. The latter is not simply a continuation of the former, but is rather an independent and permanent part of the orb, having a wholly different use and is separately spun. Blackwall says that the "innermost circle" of the spiral scaffold is permitted to remain; but my observations, on the contrary, are that all the concentries are removed and the beaded spirals carried to the very margin of the free zone. Possibly the habit is not invariable in its details; and on the whole presents a good example of intelligent exercise of the spinning function.

Spiral Scaffold Removed. (marginal note)

II.

The efficiency of an orbweb for the capture of prey depends chiefly upon its viscidity and strength. The former quality pertains to the spiral lines which differ from the other parts of the web in being covered at close intervals with minute viscid beads. To these the value of the snare as an instrument is chiefly due, for they adhere to and melt upon the wings, limbs, and hairs on the bodies of insects that strike the web, and thus fatally entangle them. Rennie has

Spiral Beads. (marginal note)

---

[1] Kirby and Spence, Introduction to Entomology, page 413, are quite correct in their allusion to this fact, but the biting away of the cotton like tuft is not necessarily accompanied by the opening up of the hub. Blackwall suggested the probably true reason why the central space is without viscid beads.

[2] Blackwall, op. cit., page 183.

[3] Emerton, American Naturalist, ii., 478; Packard's Guide, page 616; Structure and Habits of Spiders, page 64.

certainly made a mistake in saying that the suspensory lines are as often studded with beads as the spirals.[1] The radii are often found more or less beaded, although this is a rather exceptional and incidental condition; but I cannot recall, among the vast number of orbwebs, a single instance of beads upon the suspensory or foundation lines. The dewdrops gather on those lines, however, and perhaps Rennie, like some other observers, was deceived by them.

Under the microscope the beads show as beautiful objects, not unlike pearls strung upon a cord. Indeed, were a jeweler to reproduce in exact form and suitable magnitude a geometric web, substituting pearls for beads, he would have a necklace of surpassing beauty. The beads vary in size according to the size of the orb and its maker;

Size of Beads.

they vary also upon the same orb and line. Some have a thickness little greater than the diameter of the line; others are several times greater, say in proportion of 6, 3, 4, and 2. The larger ones commonly alternate with the smaller, two or more of the latter succeeding the former, and this sequence is tolerably constant, but it is by no means absolute. Immediately after formation the beads are uniform in size, and the change in size is afterward caused probably by the interblending of two or more of the original beads. (See Fig. 84.)

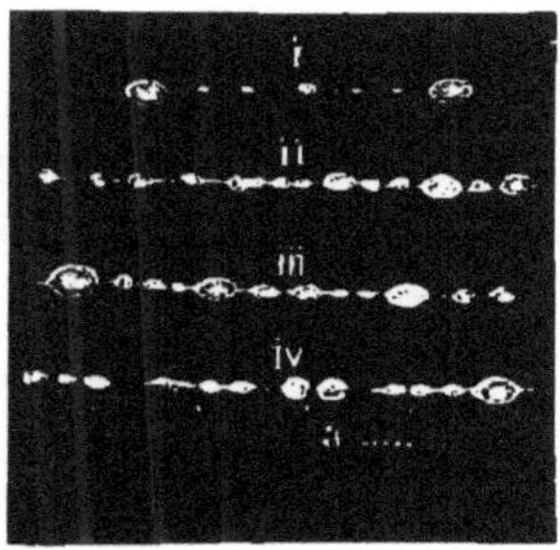

FIG. 84. Relative size and shapes of viscid beads. The space beaded at IV is shown at a, natural size.

They are for the most part semitransparent or translucent. Frequently there occur what appear to be opaque beads, showing quite black upon the line; these are simply particles of dust, around which a delicate coating of the spiral gum has gathered. Small spherical objects, grains of pollen and the like, also are seen, and the orb soon becomes well sprinkled over with minute extraneous particles, especially if the wind blows or the location is dusty. Under the microscope the beaded line shows through the substance of the globules, which is evidently aggregated around it. Indeed, one may scrape off the beads and leave the line intact. Fig. 84 shows a few of these viscid beads as they appear under a microscope. The sections I, II, III are from a snare of Cyclosa caudata examined afield. Section IV is drawn from a snare of Argiope argyraspis spun while in confinement. It shows the beading along a space of nearly five millimetres as marked off at a; and also indicated upon the magnified line. None of the beads upon this snare were longer than about one-tenth of a millimetre. In shape they were ovoid, more or less pointed at the poles; many were globular and some had

[1] Insect Architecture, page 313.

irregular forms. To the naked eye or under a common hand glass the beads often show as quite regularly arranged globules of two or three sizes. (Fig. 85.)

These two opinions are very deeply seated in the popular mind: first, that spiders are able to shoot out from their spinnerets lines or rays; second, that they are able to retract within the abdomen the lines **Elasticity** which they spin. In the former case the delicate filaments are **of Spiral** ejected from the spinning tubes as liquid silk, but the movement **Lines.** of the air is the means by which they are borne swiftly aloft or outward from the spinnerets. There is no ground in fact for the latter opinion, although it is not strange that casual observers should be deceived, as the optical illusion, for such it is, is very complete. The illusion is occasioned by two causes: the first is the action of the spider which in ascending a dropped line, for example, gathers up the thread under her jaws, as she goes, in a little flossy ball so delicate as to escape ordinary observation. The other cause is the extreme elasticity of the line, which may be extended greatly by the application of a slight force, and on its removal will contract proportionately. One who has carefully watched the movements of Orbweavers while laying in their spirals must have observed, what Blackwall has already noted,[1] that in passing from one radius to another the viscid line is usually drawn out to a much greater extent than is necessary to connect the two. Taking the last spiral cross line, after its formation, Fig. 80, iii—iii

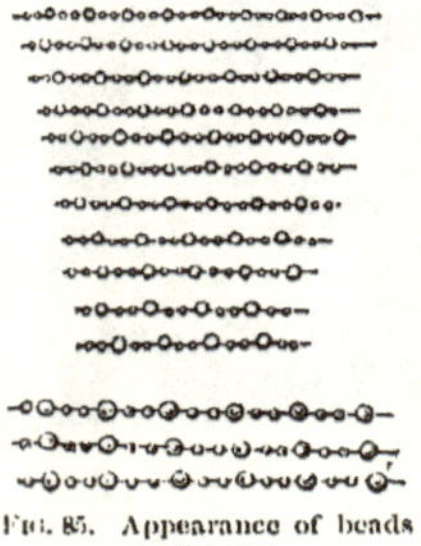

Fig. 85. Appearance of beads to the eye.

prolonged, as the base of a triangle, the line is actually drawn out before it becomes taut and is fastened as at iii—x, ab, occupying thus two sides of the triangle. I have seen the line thus stretched until it certainly was nearly if not quite twice the length finally assumed. This elasticity is of course of immense advantage in the preservation of the snare under the struggles of vigorous insects entrapped within it, as well as before the violence of wind, and beneath the weight of dew and rain. One may easily assure himself of this elasticity by touching some object to a single viscid string and drawing it out until it snaps. He will find that the united length of the two lines thus expanded will often be as much as four, six, or even eight times the length of the original line.

But there results from this elasticity another advantage which I believe has not heretofore been noted. It presents in part an explana-**Forma-** tion of the formation of the beads, a point which has been **tion of** much discussed and never yet fully explained. The spiral line as **Beads.** emitted from the spinnerets is covered with the viscid matter of which the beads are composed uniformly distributed over its surface.

[1] Spiders of Great Britain and Ireland, Intr., page 10.

When drawn out by the foot of the spider into the position of x-ab, Fig. 80, how is this viscid matter affected? In order to test the effect of expansion and sudden contraction upon viscid matter spread along a line, I covered thin bands of India rubber with mucilage, and then suddenly stretched them. The result was that invariably globules or beads were formed similar in shape to those upon the spiral of an orbweb. A twist of the band, by rolling it between the finger and thumb, caused the globules to mass equally around the band, a position which they would doubtless have kept permanently, as do the spider's beads, could the mucilage have hardened as rapidly as the viscid secretion from the spider does. This tendency would probably be greatly increased were the spider when emitting the viscid matter to give the line a sharp twist or even impart to it a vibratory motion. At all events, we know that an elastic line drawn out in the above manner and suddenly released is set into vibration, the mechanical effect of which would certainly be in the direction here indicated.

However, it is probable that a natural contraction or crystallization of the viscid matter itself would follow when exposed to the air, and thus

Natural Crystallization. produce the beads without any mechanical agitation, which nevertheless would undoubtedly assist the action of aggregation. Various experiments showed that an elastic line, or elastic band, when covered with mucilage and then stretched, soon becomes threaded with a series of beads not unlike those on the web of the geometric spider. The natural tendency of the material is evidently to gather into these minute globular masses. If we suppose this to represent a general tendency of viscid liquids, we have at once the reason why spiral lines covered with viscid secretion as they are emitted, should soon present the appearance of strings of beads.

Incidentally it may be said that the elasticity of the beaded spiral enables the spider to so graduate the interradials that they are all taut.

Equalizing Interradials. The fact that the radii converge upon the centre compels a great difference in length between a string drawn at the outer margin and one at the interior. Does it not imply a great degree of mathematical skill to pay out the requisite amount of line as the distances gradually and continuously diminish? I suppose that the whole matter is solved chiefly by the elasticity of the spiral thread. If the spider were to draw out an equal length of line in every case it would bridge the wider interspace at the circumference and the narrower one at the centre with equal facility.

What is the condition of the spiral thread as it escapes from the spinnerets? Does it show at once the appearance of viscid beads?

How Beads are Made. Or, is it smooth upon the surface, and do the nodules gradually form after emission? The difficulty of finding a spider at the exact point of spinning necessary for this observation is in itself considerable; to find a web so located as to allow study under a glass of sufficient power to separate the beads, is yet more difficult; and the excessive rapidity with which the spiral lines are spun forms the greatest obstacle of all to a successful observation.

However, I was able to obtain the required favorable conditions by colonizing a number of spiders of various species, especially the Basket Argiope, upon honeysuckle vines which cover a fence and arbor in my yard. I thus learned that the spiral thread issues apparently from the anterior spinnerets and that they issue as a pure white line, the whiteness being equally distributed over the thread, and presenting quite a contrast with the bluish whiteness of the lines which are used for the radii and foundation. Frequently I saw a minute globule of glistening liquid appear on the emitted thread at the space of four or five millimetres from the spinning tubes; but this was immediately spread along the line by the brushing movement of the fourth leg, or naturally distributed itself.

After various efforts to observe the character of the line as it issued from the spinning spools, in which I was only partially successful on account of the rapid movements of the spider, I fixed my attention upon a selected portion between two radii which had just been attached; and then upon the next and the next string toward the moving spider. By using a magnifying glass of moderate power I was enabled to see that in a short space, varying in different spiders, and indeed varying on the web spun by the same spider, the process of crystallization, as perhaps I **Breaking into Beads.** may call it, or aggregation, began. Here and there along the line there would first show points of roughening in the outline. From these several centres, on either side, the roughened condition would spread, presenting somewhat the appearance of the spiral threads of a screw. Gradually the detached points assumed figures more or less oval, and subsequently the globular or subglobular forms which are most common in the beads. By shifting the lens I could see this process going on all along the strings most recently spun. At one end of a string or interradial the beads would be forming, while at the extremity nearest the spider's spinnerets the line would be perfectly smooth.

Beyond the string under observation the parts spun a few moments earlier were covered with beads of normal shape. This observation was repeated a number of times, and these matters are now definitely settled: first, that the viscid material is placed upon the spiral thread contemporaneously with its emission; second, after a string has been placed between its two radii it naturally undergoes the process of aggregation common to viscid liquids in like position; and finally, it assumes with greater or less rapidity the forms of oval or globular beads gathered around the thread.[1]

---

[1] The two sorts of material are evidently secreted from two different glands, and perhaps also emitted through different spinning tubes.

Thus Fig. 86 will represent a section of a snare upon which an Orb-weaver is spinning in her spirals. She has finished her task along the beaded line, BL, and is working upon a line L. Just beyond it, immediately behind her, the string numbered 5 shows a white unbroken surface; No. 4 is slightly ruffled; in the string No. 3 a few points of segregation have begun to appear; at No. 2 the beads are nearly perfected on the part nearest the spider and quite finished on the further half. On string No. 1 the beads are completely formed. The figure, although sketched from nature as far as it is possible to draw such swiftly changing objects, is necessarily in part diagramatic. However, it accurately expresses the facts.

The beads when newly formed are of a white color, translucent and glistening. They are uniform in size, or nearly so, but there is a constant tendency in the first-formed minute beads to undergo a further process of aggregation, thus making larger beads. These large beads will often be found at the crossing of the lines.

The effect of rain upon the beads is to blend several into one until quite large globules are **Beads Dissolved by Rains.** formed, in good part mixed with water. If the rain be continued it dissolves the viscid material, and the

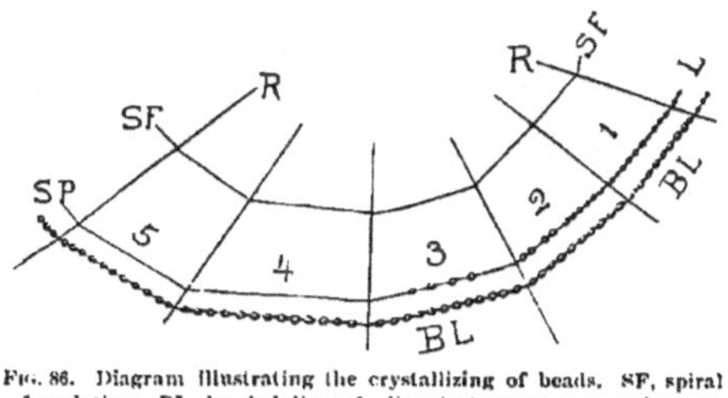

FIG. 86. Diagram illustrating the crystallizing of beads. SF, spiral foundation; BL, beaded line; L, line just spun; 2, 3, strings on which beads are forming; SP, the spider.

portions which do not drop off remain as large beads. These also soon pass away, leaving the snare without the ordinary armature for efficient service. I have frequently tested this matter during and after heavy or long continued rains; and neither by tongue, nor touch of finger, nor contact with other objects, nor by glass could the beads be discovered on many of the spirals; and often the whole web is disarmed. This accounts for the fact that spiders find it necessary to construct new snares after protracted rains. The rain also dissolves, but not quite so freely, the thick white shield and zigzag ribbon on the snares of Argiope.

In this connection I introduce the explanation of a phenomenon which long greatly puzzled me. While wandering in the woods of Delaware County, I observed on several separate occasions, always in the **A Peculiar Orb.** snare of the Orchard spider (Argyroepeira hortorum), a novel and striking variation in the arrangement of the spirals, which is represented at Fig. 87. It will be seen from this figure that the spiral space is divided into two distinct belts, of which the outer one contains about half the number of lines in the inner one. Of two specimens showing this appearance, the inner belt had sixteen and the outer eight, the difference

Fig. 87. Effect of rain upon an orb. The open marginal space was spun before, the remainder after, a shower.

being just two to one in both cases. This regularity of proportion added to my perplexity in seeking an explanation for the appearance. Why should the spider have made such a peculiar division in her spiral space? Was I on the track of some new and interesting departure from the fixed habit of this species? The snares were figured and described, and for a number of years I sought in vain for an explanation of the peculiarity, which, however, I saw but once again, and that in an Orchard spider's web.

At last I found the explanation. On the honeysuckle and ampelopsis vines growing in considerable profusion in my manse premises, I had colonized a number of Orbweavers, including several examples of Argiope cophinaria. One morning in September, just after a warm shower, while going the rounds of my colonists, I observed on several orbs that a series of spiral lines had been spun from the margin inward, covering about one-half the ordinary spiral space. No other beaded spirals appeared; and looking a little more carefully I observed that those upon the web were all greatly deluted and much more widely separated than usual. In fact, I came to the conclusion that the Argiopes had been engaged upon this part of their snare when overtaken by the shower; that

Effect of Rain.

they had abandoned their work, fled to their refuge, and in the meantime the beating raindrops had twisted the spiral lines already spun, until they presented the appearance described, and which is shown at Fig. 88.

An hour thereafter I left my study to reinspect the colonists upon the vines. The rain had ceased; the sun was shining pleasantly, and I was sur-

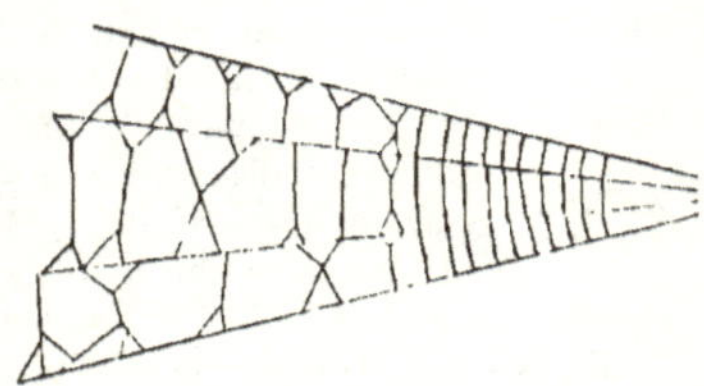

Fig. 88. Section of Argiope's orb interrupted by a shower.

prised to observe that the partly completed webs had now been finished. But instead of cutting away the portions originally wrought in, and which had been partially disabled by the rain, the spiders had taken up their spinningwork at the point where it was abandoned and finished it in the usual manner, so that the orb presented the appearance shown at Fig. 87. The spirals were not only greatly deltated by the action of the rain, the crossed lines being merged and twisted together at the middle part, but the beads upon them had been taken up by the raindrops, a number united into one, so that instead of the ordinary condition of a vast number of minute beads

Interrupted Beading Finished. spread entirely along the line there appeared a much smaller number of beads of larger size, that distinctly showed to the naked eye. Then the unexplained mystery of the Orchard spider's peculiar snare flashed upon my mind! At once the mystery was solved, and that in a most simple and natural way. The peculiar appearance of the orb was simply the result of the spiders resuming arrested work upon the spirals after the same had been abandoned on account of a shower, and which in the meantime had been twisted and deltated by the action of the elements, and the size and grouping of the beads changed. As the renewed work was spun in, in the ordinary way, both as to the position of the lines and the size of the beads, the contrast with the larger beads and the more widely separated spirals of the earlier belt was very great. It was not the first time that I learned the valuable lesson that natural phenomena are often to be explained by the simplest and ordinary causes, while we are vainly speculating and philosophizing over some supposed occult and mysterious reason.

III.

Mr. Blackwall remarks that "the estimate of the number of viscid globules distributed on an elastic spiral line in a net of Epeira apoclisa of a medium size will convey some idea of the elaborate operations of the Epeïroidæ in the construction of their snares."[1] This quotation evidently indicates that Blackwall supposed the viscid globules to be the result of "elaborate operations" on the part of the Orbweaver, in other words, that they are formed by direct and intentional action. This

Number of Beads.

An Error Corrected has been the well nigh universal belief. But in the light of the true mode above recorded, it is necessary to diminish by so much the credit heretofore bestowed upon this child of Arachne.

It would be an extremely laborious, if not impossible task, to ascertain the exact number of beads upon an orbweb, but I reached a near enough approximation by the following process: A sector of a snare was taken, that is, a complete section extending from the hub to the circumference between two

Numbering Beads. radii, and the number of beads thereon was carefully counted. This sector was then measured and the superficial area calculated. The superficial area of the entire beaded space having been obtained in like manner, the number of beads upon the whole web was readily calcu-

[1] Jour. Linn. Soc., 1829, Vol. XVI., page 477, and Ann. Mag. Nat. Hist., Vol. XV., page 239.

lated with approximate accuracy. The example chosen was a snare of Epeira sclopetaria five inches long by three inches wide, and the calculation showed a total of 140,800. This is an orb of only medium size; in many webs the number is certainly much larger, in some several times greater, although in others it is doubtless greatly less. Blackwall calculated that a net of Epeira apoclisa from fourteen to sixteen inches in diameter contained upwards of one hundred and twenty thousand viscid globules. "Yet it will complete its snare in about forty minutes if it meet with no interruption."[1]

That the viscidity of the spirals depends upon the beads, and that the latter are placed upon the former, is of course proved by the effect of rain, which separates the beads from the spiral line. But it may be also **Adhesiveness of Beads.** shown by scraping or rubbing off the globules with which the line is studded. This leaves an inadhesive line, apparently of the same constituency as the radii and other parts of the snare. An easy way to demonstrate the fact is to insert a bit of glass beneath the viscid portions of a web. The beads will adhere to the glass, if carefully handled, so as to show distinctly the spiral strings in their proper relations to the radii. By a little gentle manipulation with a camel hair brush or other small object, the beads will be separated from their strings and melt upon the glass, showing the string in the midst of the glutinous matter as a straight silken thread.

I feel well satisfied that the viscidity of the beads varies on webs of the same species at different times, and it is probable that the degree of viscidity is determined by the condition of the spider. When it is well fed the secretions are abundant, but after long periods of fasting the viscous quality of the secretion seems to be weaker, or the secretions being less in quantity the amount distributed upon the lines is greatly diminished, and hence the effectiveness of the spiral strings is decreased.

When exposed to the desiccating influence of the sun, and air briskly agitated, the nets of geometric spiders lose their adhesive property: but when formed in situations from which the light is excluded, and where the atmosphere is not liable to be perceptibly disturbed, they retain their viscidity for a long period. Blackwall says that upon a net of Epeira diademata constructed in a glass jar, which was placed in a dark closet, where the temperature was not subject to great or sudden fluctuations, the globules preserved their adhesive power almost unimpaired, and the last formed spiral line its elasticity for more than seven months.[2]

I placed a snare of Argiope argyraspis in my study October 3d, 1882. It was spun within a wooden breeding box, the front of which was covered by a sliding glass door, the back by wire cloth. It was thus exposed to light and air, in a well heated room. Examined as late as April 17th, 1883 (five and a half months after construction) the beads were found to

---

[1] Brit. Assoc. Reports, 1844, page 77. "Spiders of Great Britain," page 10, Introduction.
[2] Transactions Linn. Society, 1829, Vol. XVL, page 479.

retain perfectly their viscidity. They appeared to have thickened, and were of an amber color. At various angles or points of juncture between the radii and spirals, larger globules or masses of viscid matter had formed as though several beads had run together and settled there. I kept a snare of this Argiope until September, 1888, nearly six years, at which time the general form of the orb remained perfect, though of course all the viscidity had disappeared, and the web lines were covered with innumerable motes of dust, vegetable fibre, etc. On the contrary, a snare of Epeira thaddeus kept under precisely the same conditions as above, had in three months almost wholly lost the adhesive quality of the spirals and scarcely a trace of the characteristic beads could be observed.

Dr. Vinson[1] while hunting in a forest of Réunion (Africa) became entangled in the huge snare of a Nephila. While detaching from his lips **Medicinal Property.** the sticky threads pasted upon them, which he found to be bitter, he made the reflection that at some future day, no doubt, a medicine would be made from such threads, and formed into pills would serve as a substitute for sulphate of quinine in cases of intermittent fever. Spider webs have been frequently used in that way, although the medical uses of that substance are commonly thought to be limited to that suggested by the redoubtable Bottom in Shakespeare's play, viz., to stanch the flow of blood. The web which has been most commonly used in this country[2] for such purposes is that of a tubeweaver, Tegenaria medicinalis. A bolus of "Telen aranea," or spider web, used to be a not infrequent prescription in Philadelphia. Perhaps the somewhat revived interest in this old remedy may be profitably directed toward the Orbweavers' snares as well.

The gum of which the spiral beads are formed has a slightly acrid taste, and it probably is of an acid nature. An associate in the Philadel- **The Bead Gum Acid** phia Academy of Natural Sciences, Mr. Gavin W. Hart, said that on one occasion while hunting in the woods he was frequently arrested by the webs of a large Orbweaver. Wishing to avoid the unpleasant contact with the viscid material, he used his gun to strike down the web, pushing the barrel ahead of him as he passed among the trees. In doing this, of course, some of the threads adhered to the gun barrel. Three or four hours afterward he found that the barrel was quite gummy, and where the thread was thickest it had removed from the gun barrel the bluing, as it is called. Where the thread was thickest, the bluing was removed the most. Several friends, who accompanied Mr. Hart on this expedition, found that their guns were affected in the same way.

---

[1] Araneïdes des Isles Réunion, etc., page 22.
[2] See Dr. Chapman's " Elements of Materia Medica and Therapeutics," Philadelphia, 1825.

CHAPTER VI.

ARGIOPE AND HER RIBBONED ORB.

I.

In the United States the genus Argiope is represented by two species whose large size and beautiful markings have drawn to them the attention of most familiars of our autumn fields. They are the Basket **Full Orbs. Argiope.** Argiope (A. cophinaria Walckenaer), and the Banded Argiope (A. argyraspis Walck.) These resemble each other closely in their habits and spinningwork, but some striking differences will appear.

The Basket Argiope is the largest of our northern Orbweavers and is equaled in size by the genus Nephila alone, whose habitat is limited to the Gulf States and southern California. This species is widely distributed over the United States. I have examples extending from New England, through the Middle and Western States to Lincoln, Nebraska, the Rocky Mountains, and to the extreme southwestern point of our Pacific coast at San Diego, California. It is also distributed throughout the South, where Hentz saw it. Professor Wilder found it abundant on the seaboard of the Carolinas, and I collected specimens as far southwest as Austin, Texas.

Distribution and Habitat. Cophinaria is, therefore, a veritable "continental," and is able to adapt herself to the climatic extremes lying between our northern and southern borders without any apparent specific change. It is interesting to know that her habits remain uninfluenced by this distribution, as far as present information, variously collected, can determine. Her snare and cocoon everywhere bear the same characteristics, showing that the chief forms of her industry are unchanged by varying environment. The specific name which Hentz gave this spider (riparia) indicates that he considered the banks of streams favorite places for her snares. Certainly, I have often found her in such localities, but there seems to be no special fondness therefor, as is shown by her wide distribution over the prairies and plains. She builds in low bushes, tufts of grass, clumps of weeds, and like positions, and is fond of low and moist locations, but frequents lawns and fields, and, indeed, in the vicinity of Philadelphia, is quite commonly known as "the large garden spider," thus acquiring in America the popular title so long borne by the British cross spider, Epeira diademata. Her orbs are frequently very large, but in this are wholly regulated by site. A good figure of one of these orbs with details accurately drawn is given at Fig. 47.

The peculiarity which first strikes the observer is the oval shield of white silk tissue which quite covers the hub. This is thickest and closest in the centre, and grows thinner and more open towards **Central** the margin, where it gradually merges into the radii which **Shield** are attached to **and Band.** it. In the adult spider it is usually about two inches long by one and a half wide.[1] Attached to the shield above and below, and extending upward and downward between two radii, is a zigzag ribbon of white silk, an inch or more long and one-fourth of an inch or more wide. It traverses the whole central space and extends downward about two inches until it is lost in the spirals of the lower half of the orb.

These upper and lower ribbons vary in their degree of regularity; they are gen- **The Use** erally stretched **of the** between two ra- **Zigzag.** dii to which they are attached on either side; but sometimes they overspread three radii wholly or in part. Sometimes they are simply irregular patches or

Fig. 89. The orb of Argiope. The spider is represented at the right of the cut, the male near her.

strips and often are wanting above the shield; but the lower ribbon is rarely wanting. This variety in the character of the shield appears to be influenced more or less by age. The shield is generally less prominent in the young than in the adult spider; nevertheless, it appears often on the orbs of the very young. This is also the case with the zigzag ribbon, and I have seen a perfectly marked zigzag both above and

[1] The shield represented at Fig. 52 measured two inches long and one and a half wide; another example was one and three-fourths by one and one-half inches.

below the shield space upon the web of the spiderling Argiope, in the early part of June, when the little creature evidently had been but a few weeks, probably a few days, out of the cocoon.

The purpose of this zigzag is an interesting problem; it evidently has no special purpose in the daily life habits of the spider; at least, close and continuous observation of many species colonized upon my premises have uncovered nothing. I believe that it serves to strengthen the shield in its position at the hub, staying it by the broad bands which bind together and support the radii. The great weight of the spider is thus

FIG. 90. The central part and upper foundation lines of Argiope's snare.

distributed over a much larger part of the orb. It probably answers a similar purpose when the spider is engaged in swathing the large insects which often serve it for prey, the strong zigzag cord and central shield forming a secure attachment for the binding cords, thus keeping the net intact against the struggles of the victim.

This zigzag on the snares of Argiope is the nearest approach in nature to that "winding stair" up which the cunning old spider in the school-book rhymes of "The Spider and the Fly" dragged his "silly" victim "into his dismal den." Argiope certainly does pass over it to the lower part of her snare; but the ordinary open radii on other orbs are also thus used. However, in one snare noted, built within a lodge across the angle of two walls, the zigzag was prolonged into a series of lines like the rounds of a ladder, spun across the corner quite down to the floor. This was used as a gangway, by which on one occasion, at least, the occupant descended to the floor and thence escaped from the room.

The entire system of spinningwork thus described, shield and ribbons, is often five inches in length, and extends across the Free space, dividing it into two nearly equal parts. The spider hangs at the centre upon **Use of the Shield.** the shield which thus covers the lower part of her body. Her legs are well extended, but the corresponding pairs, the two fore legs and the two hind legs, are approximated so that these members are arranged somewhat X-shaped. The feet, however, are usually turned outward, the points of contact of the legs being at the tibia.

The main purpose of the shield I believe to be protective. It certainly may serve as a strong screen against attack of enemies from the under or

Fig. 91. Manner of spinning the sheeted hub. Spinnerets open and the conical mass of spinningwork drawn out. The abdomen lifted.

ventral side of the animal. As a rule that side of the shield which looks outward from the site is occupied by her; but at times the animal hangs also upon the opposite face, next the leaves or shrubbery. I have often seen an alarmed spider scurry through the open space from the outer to the inner face of the shield. Again, the spiders which on one day were found hanging to the inside of the shield, would be seen clinging to the outside

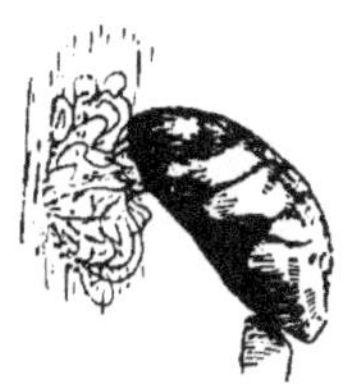

Fig. 92. The abdomen dropped, and the mass of lines gathered into loops.

on the next day; and, again, some on one side and some on the other. I have fully satisfied myself by experiment that a threatened danger will be avoided by placing the shield between herself and the apprehended peril. This is done by a dextrous movement, part swinging, part crawling, through the free zone.

The central shield and zigzag lines are not of slow growth, but are made immediately after the spinning of the web. The manner of spinning is as follows: When the orb is finished in the ordinary way, as heretofore described, the spider goes to the hub, cuts out the temporary central anchorages which she puts into her mouth, and proceeds to weave in the **Manner of Spinning Shield.** shield. She holds on with her feet to the lines of the notched zone, throws the abdomen upward and backward as far as convenient, the spinnerets being flared or extended to their utmost width instead of being closed upon each other. The threads, which issue from all the spinning tubes in streams of delicate filaments, are, of course, attached to the shield and drawn out by this motion and the action of the hind legs. (Fig. 91.) The abdomen is then dropped down against the shield space, a motion which causes the threads to rapidly contract and gather into a little ball of loops near the surface of the web. (Fig. 92.) The spider then swings her abdomen well to one side of this flossy hump of loops, as at Fig. 93, drawing after her a ray of milky filaments. Next, she draws back her abdomen, which is held close to the shield space, pulls the taut lines over the flossy mass (Fig. 94), and the spinnerets are then moved back and forth with a lateral motion like the spreading of mortar by a mason's trowel, thus pushing, beating, or spreading the loops against the cross lines of the hub. The spider repeats these motions, at the same time shifting her position occasionally, thus revolving herself by her feet around the circle of the shield. As the spinnerets, of course, revolve with the body, the weaving process is continually repeated, and the shield gradually formed. The movement of the spinnerets is from the centre of the hub outward, and it follows that as the greatest quantity and thickness of silk issue at the first expulsion and gradually diminish, the centre receives

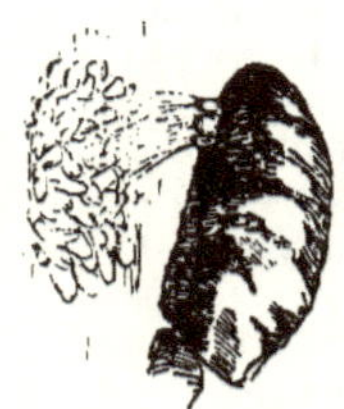

Fig. 93. A third position. The abdomen thrown to one side, drawing out a second ray of spinning lines.

the heaviest coating, and this decreases toward the margin. The fact that the shield is more closely woven in the centre is thus accounted for.

This describes the ordinary method by which Argiope's shield is spun, but there are other modes. One continually finds, in studying the new made webs of this species, that the zigzag ribbon entirely traverses the hub, in which there is no trace of the shield except a few straggling lines. In this case the ribbon has evidently been spun first. Again, one sees the same extended ribbon, and, in addition, on either side are woven one or more zigzag bands, arranged in arcs of circles, which occupy the space usually taken by the shield. In the course of time these would be overspun, so that the hub would be occupied by the thick shield which is common to the species.

When the hub is covered over, the spider proceeds to insert her zigzag ribbon. She moves downward to a point a little below the shield. Dropping her spinnerets to one of the radii, she attaches all the numerous filaments at once, say at the point 1, Fig. 95. She then raises her abdomen and begins to ascend, moving slowly, and dragging after her a band of silk. As she mounts, she swings her spinnerets across to the opposite radius, drops them at the point 2, and attaches her ribboned dragline thereto. Of course, the upward movement of the spider and the simultaneous lateral motion of her spinnerets give to the ribbon a diagonal course, so that the second point of attachment, 2, will be higher than the first point, 1. So also when the abdomen is swung back again, the spider meanwhile still climbing, the third point, 3, will be higher than the

Insertion of Zigzag.

Fig. 94. Fourth position; the abdomen returned to the looped masses, which the spinnerets are beating and squeezing down.

preceding attachment. The figure represents the species in the act of ascending the line and swinging her abdomen from the point 3. The natural uplift of her body, combined with the crosswise motion of the abdomen, will cause the direction to be along the dotted line towards the point 4, where the next attachment will be made. After that attachment the abdomen, still manipulated in the same way, will be carried across and upward to the point, 5, and so on until the band is completed. As the spinning is thus repeated alternately from side to side, and the ribband first fastened to one radius and then to its opposite, there naturally results the peculiar zigzag formation known to all observers of this web.[1]

The habit of spinning the white shield and zigzag ribbons is deeply imbedded in the species. One sees it continually in very young spiders, and at all the ages of the aranead until its death. It is extremely persistent, and it is rare to find any individual under normal conditions that does not make the whole or a considerable part of this characteristic spinningwork.

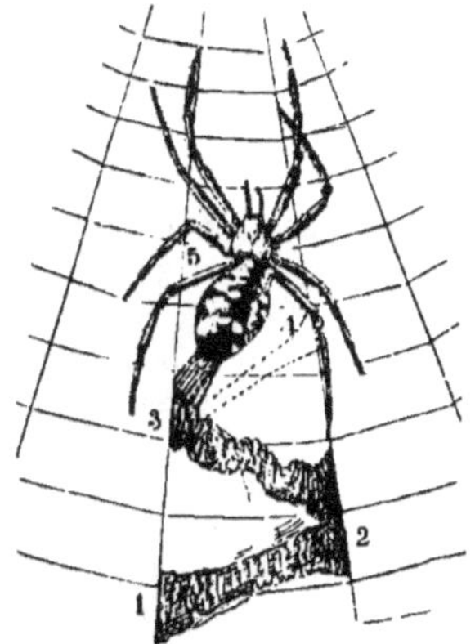

Fig. 95. Manner of spinning the zigzag ribbon. The spider is represented as having spun the bands 1-2 and 2-3, and has just started to make 3-4, swinging the abdomen across from 3 to 4 while she climbs the radial lines.

I venture to give some extracts from notes of observations upon the daily movements of Cophinaria. They were made at my request, by a gentleman, Mr. Benj. H. Hunt, resident in Frankford, one of the outer wards of Philadelphia.[2] Since this journal was made I have been able to follow the life of this species through long periods, even up to her death, by means of colonized individuals. But at that time I was not so situated as to make such consecutive observations, and I insert these notes of a "lay observer" because they are not only accurate and piquant, but vary the point of view and thus add value to the study.

A Spider Diary.

The spider was reported as first observed on August 30th. I will take up the journal at a little later date. The spider was at the time fully mature

---

[1] This description is the result of a number of observations. It was several years after I had described before the Philadelphia Academy of Natural Sciences the manner in which this spinning was done ere I was able to see the actual operation. It was pleasant to find that I had anticipated the mode with absolute accuracy, and thus again shown that the naturalist can at times truly "predict."

[2] Mr. Hunt became interested in one of these spiders observed on his premises, reported the fact to me, and following my instructions was able to place in my hands several new facts. Many persons living in rural parts and suburbs could render valuable service to natural history by thus taking up one creature and following its behavior closely and continually, taking care to record everything seen, with such rough drawings as might be possible.

and was doubtless a female. "September 7th.—The web is of the ordinary form, consisting of irregular concentric polygons, suspended from a strong breastwork of thick thread which forms the base of a triangle, the other two sides consisting of the two garden fences. A diary of the spider's movements would be rather monotonous. Nearly all the time she would seem to sit quietly in the centre of the web. One morning she was absent for an hour or two, and I supposed she had fallen a victim to some of her enemies, either the 'thick or thin billed birds that gladly eat them,' or a solitary toad which has lately appeared about the place. But the next time I visited the web she was in the centre again.

"The rain seemed to be her greatest enemy. After a violent shower which took place a few mornings ago, about three or four o'clock, I found that the bit of zigzag lace had entirely disappeared. In the course of the morning she began to repair it, and when I found her at the work she rapidly ran off to the extreme end of the breastwork. However, before two o'clock, she had entirely replaced her bit of lace, though it was less straight and symmetrical than before. Since then she seems hardly to have moved from her position. I had supposed that the violence of the rain had swept the bit of lace away, but I now think that the rain acts chemically upon it and dissolves it. This morning it rained gently for a couple of hours before five o'clock. Directly after that hour I went to see the spider, and found that half of the lace strip above the centre of the web, and also above the spider, had disappeared entirely at the top, and nearly disappeared close to the spider's abdomen, which is always uppermost. Below, the parallels and zigzag were but little impaired. She also seemed uncomfortable from the wet and was scraping her legs and body, somewhat as a fly does, until at least one drop of water fell. There are no wasps about the place, and if the sparrows had been inclined to eat the spider they would have done it before now. She hangs too high for the toad, fights between whom and spiders I think are oftener read of than seen.

"Monday morning, September 11th, 1876.—The spider has replaced the zigzag strip for the sixth time, four times after rains, and twice on mornings when no rain had fallen over night. In the latter cases little cottonlike tufts were left, which seemed to form her bed (shield). Possibly, the strip, on these two occasions, had been destroyed by the dew, though it was by no means heavy. Each renewal of the strip is more imperfect than its predecessor. This morning it is very slight indeed, of inferior architecture, and not three inches long. She always forms it very rapidly, not by drawing out single threads, as in making the web, but by producing little bands, one-sixteenth of an inch wide. The difference between the threads and the bands is similar to that between the 'roping' and the yarn turned out by the old fashioned hand cotton spinning wheel in use fifty odd years ago. The 'roping,' it will be remembered, was formed of the cotton rolled together and twisted a little, the rolls being too short to be spun into yarn without the intermediate roping process. The use of the strip I cannot see. Not a fly has been caught in it, while the web catches a few flies and many mosquitoes and gnats, which two latter insects I do not perceive that the spider notices. Yesterday I saw a fly struggling in a part of the web, distant from the centre; the spider did not move towards it while I was looking, but a few minutes afterward I found her devouring it. She replaces her strips, on an average, in less than five minutes.

"Wednesday, September 13th.—Something, apparently a cat, jumped through the lower half of the spider's web yesterday morning, of course carrying away the meshes and part of the zigzag strip, deranging the rest. The spider did nothing all day, seeming to be discouraged; and I found her still sitting on the remains of her rumpled bed[1] (shield) early this morning. But during my absence for some fifteen minutes she had removed these rumpled remains as rubbish, and had begun to repair damages. She was replacing her bed by bringing forth congeries of very minute fibres, and kicking[2] them into place with her foot. This work was very soon finished. There is nothing architectural, so to speak, about the bed; it is a mere tuft.

"She then let herself down about two inches and a half below the bed, fixing a thread to the web as she proceeded, and then turning about began to crawl up again, arranging behind her as she went her zigzag strip. **The Zigzag Strip.** This is not confined, as I first thought, between parallel threads (radii), but is attached on one side to the thread made in descending, and on the other side, to the general mesh.[3] The strip is irregular in width, just as all the late ones have been, and when the spider had brought it up and attached it to the lower part of her bed she did not, as heretofore, continue its reconstruction above the bed, but, turning round, settled herself quietly into her old position, head downwards, possibly somewhat exhausted by the late demands on her spinning resources. I omitted to say that since five o'clock yesterday afternoon she has replaced a portion of the web carried away by the cat. The long strong thread from which the whole depends, and which was broken by the cat, she has not replaced, but only mended, and it is now a little out of line.

"Thursday, 14th.—A cat again jumped through the web last night, damaging it badly, breaking the main beam, which throws the web quite off its balance. I found the spider, early this morning, prospecting among

---

[1] I have several times seen the crumpled remnants of an old shield left, like a rude boss, on the outside of a new one, which had been woven underneath it. This is probably the "rumpled bed" alluded to.

[2] The rapid motion of the hind leg to and from the spinnerets in seizing and pulling out the thread, has certainly the appearance of "kicking."

[3] This is sometimes, but not always, the case.

the morning glory leaves which cover the board pile, apparently for the purpose of making fast to something in order to place her main beam. But she soon gave over and went back to her bed, seeming discouraged. Towards noon I found her with a miller or moth in her clutches, wrapped in what seemed to me a scrap of her bedding. As I looked, a fly became entangled about three inches from her. She directly went towards it, but

Swathing Insects. in no great haste, no doubt because sure of her prey, and when near enough she reached out, hauled it into close quarters, and before I could see how, the fly also was wrapped in a bit of white gauze.[1] She took it to her bed, and I suppose fed on it and the miller.

"In the afternoon I found her on her bed on the inside of the web, exactly opposite to her old place on the outside, and there she remains this evening. Perhaps she thinks the inside the safer place of the two in the dilapidated state of her dwelling. This spider is certainly subjected to great trials.

"Friday morning, September 15th.—There was a heavy rain last night, with wind, and the spider has disappeared. I have shaken the convolvulus leaves roundabout, but find no sign of her, and the wreck of the web has the appearance of being utterly deserted."

The journal here ended, and I heard nothing more of the creature whose life and trials had been followed with so much interest and intelligence by my Frankford correspondent. The above quotations throw some interesting side lights upon the humble daily life of this representative of the spider world.

It may interest the reader to know what caused the sudden disappearance of the Argiope at this point. The date (September 15th) is the cocooning season; and no doubt Cophinaria had retired to some shaded nook among the leaves or adjacent lumber, to spend the last forces of life in weaving the beautiful basket shaped cocoon of the species, within which the young are reared.

The Central Space of the Basket Argiope's snare consists of the hub and its adjuncts, as described, and several (there are four in Fig. 89) un-

Notched Zone. beaded spirals. These are more widely separated as they approach the beaded spirals, and they occupy nearly the entire space, so that there is little or no Free Zone. Some of the notched spirals are nearly always covered by the shield, and when the spinningwork thereon is light they may be seen beneath it. The fact that they are without viscid beads explains Mr. Hunt's wonder that no insects were entangled in this part of the web.

The architecture of the entire snare is shown at Figs. 47, 89, 90.

An interesting feature in the construction of Cophinaria's snare is that which I have called "protective wings" or fenders. These are outlying

[1] The swathing of the insect is often done rapidly, by one outgush of silken filaments from the spinners, and a quick motion of the feet revolving the captive.

lines spun on either side or in front of the orb at the distance of one or more inches from it. In certain positions these wings are thrown on either

Fenders or Protective Wings. side of the orb, as represented at Fig. 96, where the web is hung within a conical or pyramidal mass of cross lines, a retitelarian web, in fact. In this snare both the upper and lower sections of the orb were attached to strong foundation lines set within this mass, which was itself attached to the surrounding foliage. This structure appears to be common as to the upper half of the orb, but the lower part is frequently fastened directly to the foliage or other objects of the site. Such an arrangement adds to the elasticity of

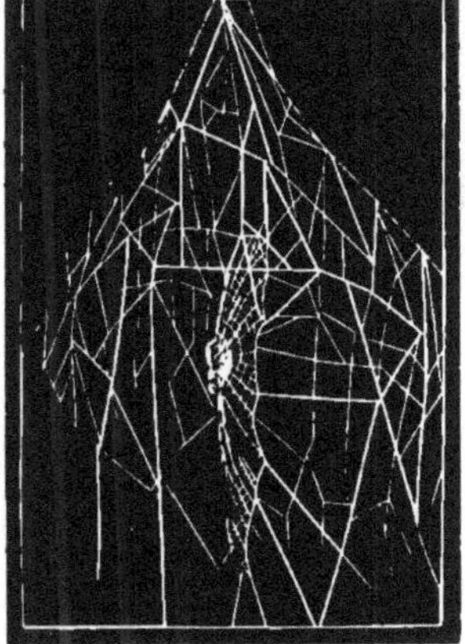

Fig. 96. Protective wings or fenders of Argiope's snare. (Side view.)

the snare, and must materially contribute to its powers of resistance. When the webs of Argiope are spun in such a position as to expose the spider from either side, the wings are thrown out on both sides, as in the figure. But in a great number of cases only one side is thus defended, and it will be found in such cases that the other side is protected by the foliage against which the orb is spun. These fenders or wings are by no means universal. Indeed, I have examined scores of snares on the same day and for several successive weeks without noticing one example. The Banded Argiope makes the same kind of protective wings, and I have found several half grown individuals of this species on the seashore of Cape Ann, Massachusetts, whose webs were all thus characterized. Sometimes the fenders are wholly separated from the spinningwork of the orb itself, and are thrown out well upon the flank, and attached to projecting parts of the foliage. They then commonly consist of very strong thick lines resembling those spun for the foundation of the snare.

The purpose of this outlying spinningwork is probably protective. The scaffolding of crossed lines is thrown over both faces of the orb like wings, chiefly over the middle and upper parts, thus covering the point where the spider domiciles. The wings are several inches distant from

Uses of Wings. the orb. Any large hostile insect or other enemy hovering around the web must first touch the outlying wings, whose agitation telegraphs a warning to the occupant. The detention resulting, trifling as it would be, might yet allow sufficient time, in many cases, for the occupant to escape. The protective wings might even happen to ward off wholly some assailants. On such provisions as this often hangs the

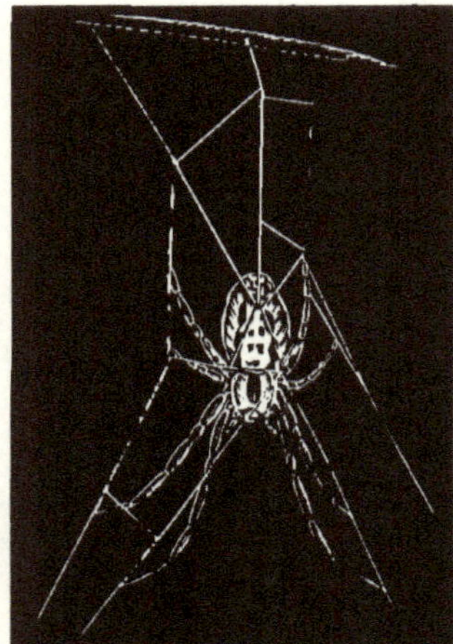

Fig. 97. Rudimentary web of female Argiope.

preservation in nature of the individual and even the species. The wings do not appear to impair the efficacy of the orb as a snare for trapping the natural prey of the spider. Such insects break upon and through the web with an elan bred of unconsciousness of danger quite different from the perceptible caution and hesitation which mark the conscious approach of a hymenopterous foe.

In the snare figured above (Fig. 89), the number of radii was twenty-five. The number of spirals in the lower part of the orb was twenty-six; in the upper part it did not exceed nine. The hub was thus placed well above the geometrical centre of the orb. This snare was spun by a female colonized upon a young tree. After the ordinary preliminary prospecting, she spun a rudimentary web, Fig. 97, consisting of a few perpendicular lines looped and crossed, upon which she hung in the natural posture. She remained thus until evening and then spun her characteristic orb. This manner of resting upon a few straggling ratlins is quite habitual. The male of Cophinaria appears very small by the side of his adult mate. He is not very active in his predatory habits after maturity; at least the snares upon which I have always found him appear to be poorly adapted to the capture of insects, although I have occasionally seen a fly entangled in one of them.

The drawing of one of these rudimentary webs, given at Fig. 98, was made from a pencil sketch kindly furnished **Webs of the Male.** me several years ago by Mr. Emerton, and is a fair representation of the ordinary character of the web upon which I have found the male Cophinaria. It may be noticed that the snare quite closely resembles the meshed hub spun by the female before the shield is made, and which is characteristic in most orbs of the genus Epeira. However, there is a good deal of variety in the form of the male webs, and some of them are much

Fig. 98. Male of Argiope cophinaria on a rudimentary web.

more elaborate than that shown at Fig. 98, having well defined radii and a spiral system at least in the lower part; but I have never seen one that extended beyond the bounds of what in a perfect orb is the central space. The zigzag ribbon is present, but scant and ill defined. The habits of the male and another drawing of his snare will be found in a subsequent chapter.

The following are measurements of several webs of Cophinaria: No. 1. Radii, 35; notched spirals, 13; beaded spirals, 24. Specimen half grown. No. 2. Radii, 26; notched spirals, 13; beaded spirals, not counted. No. 3. Radii, 30; beaded spirals, 16 above the hub, 31 below; the orb 12 inches in length, 10 inches wide. Shield and ribbon 5 inches long. A strong fender placed three inches from the spider. Eight notched spirals partly covered by the shield. The ribbon entirely traverses the shield space. No. 4. Radii, 35, 18 on one side of the ribbon, 17 on the other, including the radii inclosing the ribbon.

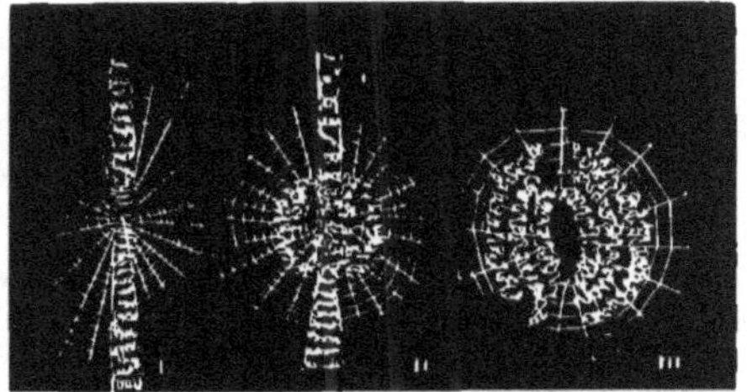

Fig. 99. Central decorations on orbs of Argyraspis.

Notched spirals 13, nearly filling the open space. Beaded spirals 24. Width of orb, 8 inches. Zigzag ribbon, 3 inches, including the shield, which is about five-eighths inch.

II.

The Banded Argiope (A. argyraspis) is an abundant species, at least in Pennsylvania and the adjacent States to the south and east. The female is generally somewhat shorter in body length than the Basket Argiope, and otherwise smaller. The abdomen tapers gradually **Banded Argiope.** from the middle part toward the apex. The spider is of a general whitish gray color; her abdomen is covered above with a bright silver gloss, and is crossed longitudinally by two pretty yellow bands, and laterally by a number (thirteen or more) of black lines unbroken, alternated with interrupted ones.[1]

Argyraspis is seen most frequently in the later summer, from July until November, nested upon hedges, shrubs, bushes, and in tall grasses and weeds. Her snare is substantially the same as that of Cophinaria, see Fig.

[1] Argiope argyraspis is closely related to the well-known Arg. fasciata Fabr. of Europe. See Koch's "Die Arachniden," pages 159, 160, and Tab. ccxciv., Fig. 951. It is not strange that Hentz should have supposed it to be the same or near thereto. It is distributed generally throughout Central and Southern Europe and Northern Africa. A quite full synonymy may be found in the works of Walckenaer and Simon.

47, but I have usually been able to determine it, when found without an occupant, by the following features: The sheeted hub is not as large and the tissue is not as thick, indeed it is sometimes expressed by only a faint puff, or simply by a serrated or nodulated cord, as at Fig. 99, i. In short, a well defined shield seems to be a permanent characteristic of the Basket Argiope's orb, while Banded Argiope rather inclines to omit it or express it by zigzag cords. These cords are often thrown in arcs around the hub as at Fig. 99, ii and iii, and give a pretty and striking effect to the web. However, I must confess that my confidence in these distinctions is not very great; and to the untrained observer the differences between the two webs would hardly be apparent.

It is significant, as illustrating the community and persistence of habit in a genus, however widely separated, that a spider (Epeira mauritia Walck.) closely allied to our Argiope argyraspis is found in the islands of Mauritia, Réunion, and Madagascar (Africa), with precisely the same habits. Vinson[1] describes the snare of this aranead with its peculiar zigzag decorations, with the X-like position of the legs as she hangs upon her snare, and the cocoon in its site, in language which might be used with equal propriety of Argyraspis. With slight change the figure of the African Argiope as given by Vinson might stand for a drawing of our American species.

An African Congener.

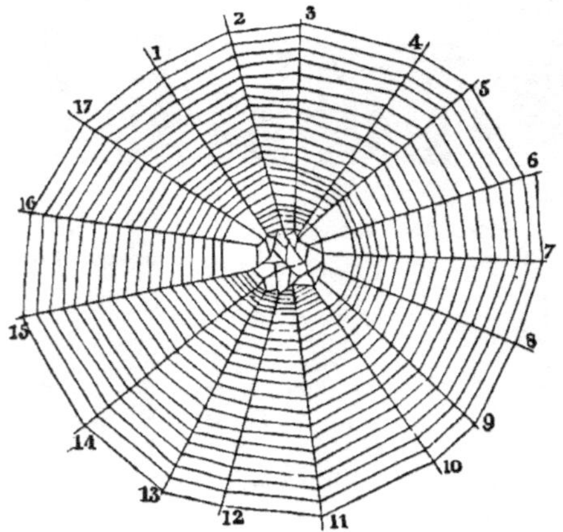

Fig. 100. A snare of Argiope argenteola.

Argiope argentata.

A third species of Argiope, which appears to be the Argiope argentata[2] of Koch, is found abundantly in the extreme Southwest of the United States. I have many specimens from Southern California, where it abounds, spinning its large, beautiful webs everywhere in the neighborhood of San Diego. It extends southward through Mexico, is widely distributed thoughout the states of South Amer-

[1] Araneides des Isles Réunion, &c., page XIII., 198, and Plate VIII., Fig. 2.

[2] Argiope argentatus, Koch, "Die Arachniden," t. 5, page 58, pl. 154, Fig. 360. Also A. fenestrinus, id., Fig. 155. The Epeira argentie (E. argentata) of Walckenaer, figured Pl. 18, Fig. 3, Atlas, Aptères, is with little doubt the same spider or a close variety thereof. Vol. II., Aptères, page 115. I first introduced this species to the Philadelphia Acad. Nat. Sci. as new under the name of Argiope argenteola. It is possible that the spider will be found specifically different from A. argenta when specimens can be had for comparison.

ica,[1] at least in the northern tier. Eastward it has been located in Texas and at Tampa Bay and Key West, Florida, and is found scattered throughout the West Indies[2] and the Caribbean Sea Islands.[3] Mrs. Eigenmann, from whom I have notes and specimens, describes the snare of Argentata as about one foot and a half in diameter. The foundation lines are very strong; the centre irregularly meshed and the notched spirals eight in number, the three outermost of the series being about twice as far apart as the others. The spider rests at the hub of the orb in the position characteristic of the genus as above described. The snare is decorated with zigzag lines and other thickened lines like those of Cophinaria and Argyraspis.

One of the specimens sent me, a mature female, survived shipment through the mail and spun three successive webs for me in a trying box or jar. In these the hub was sparsely meshed and the orb other-

Argentata's Orbs. wise of the usual Epeira character, with one remarkable exception, which, as it occurred in every one of the three snares spun, appears to suggest that it may be a permanent characteristic. In ordinary orbs, it will be remembered, there is an open space or free zone between the spiral space and the notched zone: but in these orbs of Argentata sections of the spiral space immediately above and below the hub were continued through the free zone to the hub. Thus between radii 1–5, Fig. 100, the spiral lines were prolonged to the hub; and similarly between radii 10–15 in a position nearly opposite, at the lower part of the orb, the spirals were prolonged upward. Is this a new form of orbweb? Were the three successive examples simply abnormal modes of working in the notched zone, caused by the unnatural conditions under which the web was made? These questions can be answered only by those who may be able to study the spider in its natural home. The open section thus peculiarly intercrossed composed substantially the part over which the legs of the spider were spread as she hung upon her orb. Her abdomen hung free from the hub, to which it was attached by a thread from one-fourth to three-fourths inch long. The spider's hind legs clasped successively the radii 1 and 4; the third pair held by a little pyramidal pull up between radii 1–17 on the side, and 6–7 on the other; the two fore feet on one side grasped radius 9, and the two other side radii, 13 and 14 respectively, extending well down the spiral space.

[1] Specimens received from Venezuela through the kindness of Professor Peckham.
[2] Specimens received from the late Mr. William Gabb.
[3] Specimens received from Mr. Charles H. Thompson, Swan Island.

CHAPTER VII.

EPEIRA AND THE WEAVERS OF ROUND VERTICAL WEBS.

I.

THE orbwebs most frequently seen in the Middle, Northern, and Atlantic States are made by a group of spiders closely related in structure and almost identical in economy. Among the most abundant of these are the Furrow spider (Epeira strix), the gray Cross spider (E. sclopetaria), Epeira patagiata, the Domicile spider of Hentz (E. benjamina Walck.), and Epeira trivittata. Next to these, perhaps, are Epeira insularis,[1] and more rarely the Shamrock spider (E. trifolium). There is little or no difference in the character of the snare made by these araneads, but Insularis and Trifolium invariably, and frequently Domiciliorum, are found in leafy nests with a trapline attachment to the hub of the snare. Strix and Sclopetaria and sometimes Domiciliorum nest in rolled leaves, but do not maintain as decided a trapline attachment.

Epeira Meshed Hubs.

In the typical orb of these species, represented at Fig. 101,[2] the hub is commonly meshed. This is not always so, but in spite of the occasional exceptions, I regard the meshed hub as a characteristic. One will rarely fail to identify unoccupied orbs of the type figured as belonging to one of this group.

The notched zone has from four to six concentries, rarely more; the number of radii and spirals varies, but has a pretty strong tendency to keep about twenty-one.[3] They are found in all manner of sites where insects abound.

The Furrow spider is one of the most numerously and widely distributed of our indigenous Orbweavers. I have taken it as far north as Montreal and the Thousand Islands on the St. Lawrence, and as far to the

---

[1] The Epeira insularis of Hentz and Ep. conspicellata of Walckenaer. I have Prof. Thorell's authority (to whom I sent specimens) that the species is quite identical with the European Ep. marmorea. I have, however, in the absence of specimens of the European species, concluded to continue the name of Hentz at least in the two volumes on Habits and Industry. For the same reason I retain Hentz's name Epeira domiciliorum, for what seems to me without much doubt to be Walckenaer's E. benjamina.

[2] For the original photograph from which this engraving was made I am indebted to Mr. Horace P. Chandler, of Boston.

[3] The average of 11 snares counted was 21¼, the lowest number was 18 radii, the highest 28 radii, and 25 spirals.

southwest as Texas. It abounds along the Atlantic seaboard from Maine southward at least to Delaware and Maryland; and Hentz found it in Alabama; he named it from the scalloped or furrow like markings on the dorsum of the abdomen. In appearance and habits it resembles Epeira cornuta of Europe, and is not improbably a variety of that species.[1] If this be so the species has a vast distribution, and retains its peculiarities in all countries, latitudes, and conditions with undisturbed persistence.

The Furrow Spider.

Fig. 101. Typical orb of Epeira. Half tone engraving made from a photograph.

None of our Orbweavers more habitually shuns the light. She is rarely, except when very young, found upon her snare during the day; but occupies a neighboring crevice, tubular tent, or rolled leaf, concealed within

[1] I have compared with the habits of E. cornuta as described by Menge in his Prussian Spiders. The spinning, nesting, and cocooning and general habits of the two well agree.

which she remains until nightfall. She thus shuns the hymenopterous enemies who hunt in the sunshine, and is in position to capture the night

Nocturnal Activity.

flying insects, among which chiefly she finds her prey. So persistent is this habit that Strix will rarely leave her hiding place by day even to take the insects that become entangled in the snare.

When the night begins to fall she may be seen swinging in the air against the darkening sky, laying in the foundations of her net and spinning her orb. It is surprising how many of these creatures start into activity in sites where their presence is not suspected. The skipper of a yacht on the St. Lawrence River, during a fishing trip, complained to me that the spiders were a great nuisance to him; that he brushed away numbers of cobwebs every day, but that in the morning he was sure to find the vessel again fringed and laced with their webs. He could never make out where they all came from, or how they got aboard the ship.

I was able to solve the man's perplexity. A few days before, while coming down the river in the passenger steamer about twilight, I had noticed my aranead friends dangling from various parts of the boat, engaged in their tentative efforts at web building. Thereupon I examined the under parts of the railing and the cornices of projecting parts of the deck, and discovered a large number of Orbweavers, principally Epeira strix, young

Spider Stowaways.

and old, male and female, curled up against the woodwork or domiciled in silken nests. I called our skipper's attention to similar localities on his own boat, which were occupied in like manner, and his wonder at once ceased. He had innocently thought that clearing away the webs had disposed of the weavers. He never imagined what a colony of unbidden passengers or "stowaways" he was carrying, who kept to their dens by day, and at night, when the yacht was laid up, turned out, spun their webs, and were back to their retreats before the good sailor men were astir the next morning.

This example illustrates and explains a mystery in spider manners that has puzzled many housekeepers, viz., " Where do the cobwebs come from ?" The query should be, rather, " Whither do their spinners go ?"

When the snare is spun the Orbweaver takes position at the hub with her head downward. The artists do, indeed, persist in putting her upon

Position at the Hub.

the web with head upward, but facts are against them. The Orbweaver never assumes that position except when she turns to run to her nest or to take prey, in which cases she may remain stationary for a few minutes, but will soon resume her inverted posture. As the nest or retreat of the Epeïroid is usually above the median horizontal line of the orb, one would think that the head upward position would be the safer one as affording an easier approach to her refuge in case of danger. But on the contrary the naturalness of the inverted posture appears from the fact that when the spider is within her tent, as she generally is except at night, the head is then turned downward toward the web. The posture at the hub, therefore, is the natural one taken when, upon disturbance of the snare, the aranead runs down the trapline to the centre. Convenience and habit combine to fix the posture as we find it.

Moreover, the majority of vertical orbwebs have the longer part of the spiral surface available for capture of insects below the median horizontal line, a fact caused, as has been seen (Chapter V.) by the corner loops that stretch downward beyond the concentrics. **Head Downward Natural.** Thus the habitual posture of the spider really gives the widest command of the snare, being the best posture from which to sally forth against entangled insects.

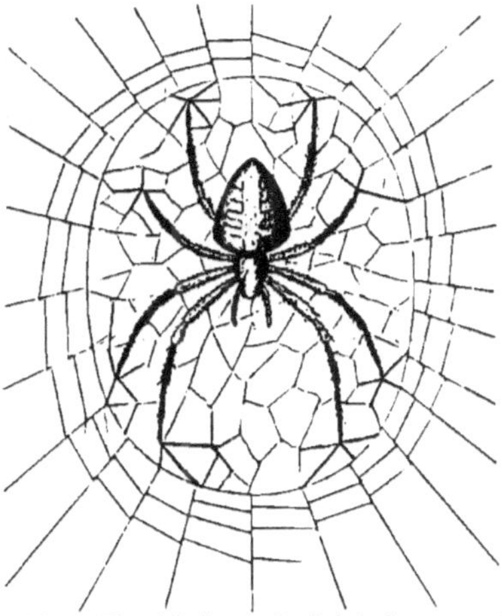

Still further it may be said, that the nest does not necessarily afford the readiest or even safest retreat in case of assault by enemies. It is much easier for the spider to fling herself from the web and drop to the ground than to mount to her nest. Not only is this movement executed with marvelous dispatch, but, as I can well testify from my experience in collecting specimens, the concealment afforded by the grass, leaves, etc., at the surface is very complete, especially as the animal instantly curls herself into a ball and lies in the foliage with the rigidity and stillness

Fig. 102. Position of Epeira upon her hub, to show command of the snare.

of death. On the whole the inverted posture of the Orbweaver, however unnatural it may seem to us, is precisely the one which nature has made most advantageous to the spider.

The legs of the Orbweaver are rarely, never habitually, I think I may say, spread out equally over the hub. The two fore feet on each side are approximated, and spread out from the body at an angle **Feet Command the Snare.** more or less acute. (See Fig. 102.) The two hind pairs of legs are similarly placed, although the short third pair is more likely to be extended directly from the body. The approximation is sometimes so close that the legs are arranged X-shape. If the claws be closely examined as the spider thus hangs, they will be seen very generally to clasp the lines of the hub at or near the points where several radii unite, or to hold on by little pyramidal clusters of threads whose basal extremities touch the united radii, the apical ends being converged within the claw. (Figs. 102, 103.) Thus the agitation made at any point of the snare is communicated through the radii to the feet, made extremely sensitive by the numerous delicate hairs and spines which clothe them. The eight claws of the spider, each one of which is in communication with three, four or more converged radii, together command the whole number of radii, and through them also the interwoven spirals. By this arrangement Madam Arachne, like a good housewife, may be said to have the whole of her household establishment literally "under her thumb."

Under Her Thumb.

The Orbweaver while thus in waiting is chiefly supported by the claws, and apparently by those of the hind feet. But the spinnerets also aid in maintaining the weight, by means of a thread or threads which may be seen issuing from them and attached to the hub beneath by a minute white dot of silk. The frequent formation of these attachments, as Menge has observed of Epeira diademata, on the return from her various excursions after insects or on housekeeping duties, sometimes causes the hub to be dotted over by white specks, especially in the region underneath the spinnerets. This is especially apparent on a thinly sheeted hub of Argiope.

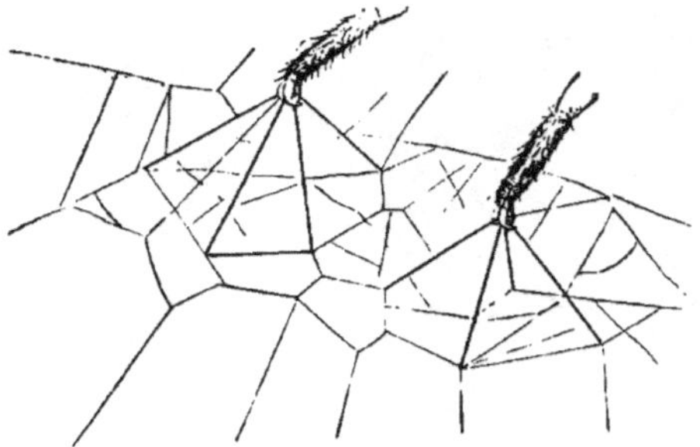

Fig. 103. Feet of Orbweaver while in position at the hub, to show the radiating footlines.

The Furrow spiders, like others of their genus, are found near running streams and still water, where the congregations of insects are usually largest. I have seen multitudes of them upon the railings of the old Gray's Ferry Bridge over the Schuylkill before the restless innovations of human creatures had set up the new structure; and on the famous Long Bridge over the Potomac at Washington they were domiciled in legions. This species will often be found upon the shrubbery and trees of yards, lawns, and orchards, and in such locations frequently selects a site for her snare which forms for it a beautiful background of leaves, tendrils, and flowers. Such an example is Fig. 104, snares spun among lilies and sprigs of coxcomb in a flower garden in Eastern Ohio. But more than some others of the especial group to which she belongs Strix is a wood spider. I have often found her in forests, groves, and fields, building upon the branches and nesting among the foliage. In color Strix varies much; the young specimens are often found quite black; in maturity the prevailing color is yellowish, with reddish

Natural Sites of Snares.

rings upon the legs, and bands upon the cephalothorax. I have some adults with whitish abdomens.

Epeira sclopetaria (Ep. vulgaris Hentz), the gray Cross spider, I have not found abundant in wooded spots, but more frequently near bodies of water. Immense colonies are domiciled near and upon the boathouses, taverns, and outhouses at the inlets and boat landings of **Epeira sclopetaria.** Atlantic City and Cape May, N. J. They grow to great size, feeding upon the swarms of green head flies and other insects that frequent those places. The cellars, open and latticed spaces under the porches, stables, and outhouses of the cottages and hotels of these watering places are also favorite resorts. The proprietors would do well to encourage their presence and propagation as at least some check upon the flies and mosquitoes.

In South Carolina, where Hentz first observed the species, she is seldom found far from the gardens. This partiality to human homes he supposed due to the additional safety thus afforded from the terrible Sphex, though on what ground I cannot conceive. In South Carolina she is subject to such variations in color and markings that it is quite difficult to distinguish between these and several other species. Hentz once

FIG. 104. Snare of Epeira strix among the lilies.

found in the nest of a mud dauber (wasp) seventeen variations of this species, each differing more or less from the others. In this latitude (Philadelphia) I find no such difference as to color, which is a quite uniform gray; but there is some tendency to variations in the markings of the abdomen especially among the young. The species is distributed[1] from South Carolina northward to Maine, and westward through New York and Pennsylvania to Wisconsin, including Canada, at least along the St. Lawrence River.

[1] Of course in all these allusions to geographical distribution, etc., the reference is to that known by the author to date.

Closely related to Selopetaria is the well known species Epeira patagiata. It is distributed throughout Europe, and is one of the common species of **Epeira patagiata** Syria. Its round snares must have been familiar objects to the ancient Palestinian prophets, and are as likely as any other to have suggested the several Scriptural metaphors drawn from the spider's web. It is an abundant species in parts of the United States, especially in New England along the seashore, and in the Adirondacks and northern sections of New York. I have studied its habits and spinningwork in those parts, and find that they differ in no respect from those of Selopetaria. I have little doubt that the two spiders are one species, and indeed one finds it difficult to separate them into even two well defined varieties.

Epeira benjamina Walck., the Domicile Spider (Epeira domiciliorum, of Hentz), has a very wide dis-**The Domicile Spider.** tribution. Hentz found it in Alabama; Emerton in New England; I have collected it in Massachusetts, Pennsylvania, Canada, New York, Ohio, New Jersey; and Mr. Peckham in Wisconsin. Dr. Marx has specimens extending northward and westward from Rhode Island, through Minnesota, Nebraska, Colorado, to Spring Lake, Utah; and southwest as far as Fort Graham, Texas. It thus has been traced over the entire United States to the Rocky Mountains. In Colorado it has a vertical distribution of 12,000 feet. In the South, Hentz says that she is often found in dark places, and even spins her web in dark apartments not much frequented. I never found the species, though abundant in this latitude, in any such sites—but usually upon bushes and trees, in yards and woods, commonly bright and sunny places. In one case I found several adult females hanging upon their large webs, which were spread against a frame house, in the full blaze of a September sun. They kept the position throughout the entire day. Such a difference in habit is certainly noteworthy. After a heavy summer shower I once found two webs of this species temporarily marked by what is a quite fixed characteristic of the webs of **Tempo-rary Ribbon Decora-tions.** Argiope. (Fig. 105.) Below the hub the notched zone was crossed by a disk of thick, sheeted silk which extended downward between two of the radii, uniting them. A similar band united two of the radii above the hub. I conjectured that these had been thrown out from the spinnerets to strengthen the web against the weight of the rain: or as a protection, a sort of umbrella, between the spider hanging on the side toward the bush and the shower driving from the opposite quarter. Several specimens of Epeira

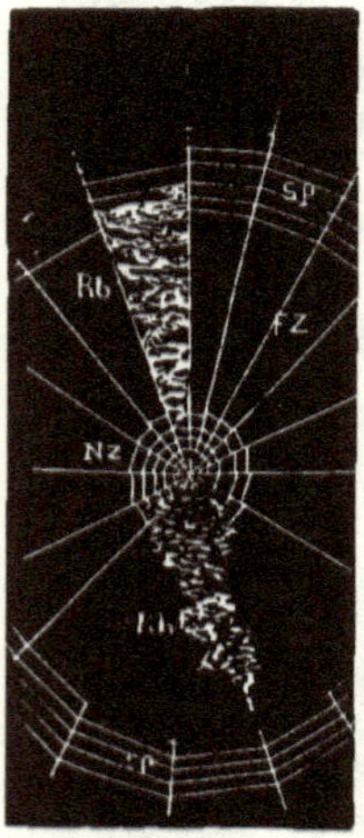

Fig. 105. Temporary ribbon central of Epeira domiciliorum.

trivittata were found with a like peculiarity in Connecticut. Yet, I cannot regard it as other than incidental.

One might indulge the conjecture that this accidental feature of a snare of Epeira offers a clue to the reason for the permanent features of a like character upon the webs of Argiope, Acrosoma, and Uloborus. The difference or differences which have caused the characteristics to become fixed in the last named genera are at present unknown. I venture only to suggest that my observation shows that these genera quite habitually remain upon their orbs continually, whereas the Domicile spider and her congeners usually retire from their orbs in day time, and have nests or dens to which they can resort in foul weather or in case of attack. I have frequently found Domicile in a leafy tent, but oftener without one; her habit in this respect seems to connect Scolope-taria whom I have never seen in such an abode,

FIG. 106. Nest and snare of Epeira insularis.

and Insularis who is always so found. On one occasion while driving along a New Jersey road, I observed an orbweb spun upon the tall grass beneath a young tree. The foundation lines and supports reached upwards to the lowest branch, about twelve feet above the surface. Having climbed out upon the branch I observed a spider nested within a curled leaf and holding to a trapline that extended entirely to the orb beneath, the longest trapline I remember ever to have seen. The nest was collected and the occupant proved to be Domiciliorum. Closely related to the Domicile Spider is Epeira trivittata. The two are very similar in general appearance and markings, the latter, however, being somewhat smaller. Their webs and general habits are the same.

Epeira trivittata.

In the group of Epeïras with hub meshed snares, the most remarkable in appearance is Epeira insularis. The bright yellow markings upon the back of the abdomen, and the orange legs with their brown rings distinguish her as one of the most beautiful of her genus. She attains even greater size than Strix and Sclopetaria, and in the late summer and fall, when the female is full of eggs, appears quite formidable. Hentz named her from the fact that he discovered her upon an island of the Tennessee River. She is however widely distributed, having been traced as far south as Georgia and South Carolina, through the great Middle-Western and Middle States, as far to the northwest as Wisconsin, and throughout New England. She is very abundant in Ohio, Pennsylvania, and New Jersey, in woods, groves, and out grounds, and invariably domiciles upon shrubs, bushes, and bushy trees, commonly choosing a well elevated site, within seven or eight feet from the ground. If we admit the identity of this spider with the European Epeira marmorea, the distribution is vastly widened, and this fine species must be enrolled among those which probably inhabit the entire northern hemisphere.

The snare of the adult is a large orb of the type heretofore described; several measurements of which are as follows (in inches): 13 x 11, 14 x 14, 20 x 14, 14 x 14, 8 x 6. That which especially distinguishes Insularis from the foregoing group is the well nigh unvarying habit of living in a nest of rolled leaves situated above the orb, and attached thereto by a trapline. This varies in length according to the size and situation of the snare; it will frequently be found about seven inches long. At one end it is held by the spider's outstretched claws as she sits within her tent; at the other end it is fastened to or near the margin of the hub, or notched zone, by a little delta of diverging termini. These slightly pull up the centre of the web and thus tighten the radii; the trapline itself being held quite taut, the motions of struggling insects are readily communicated to the vigilant watcher within her leafy sentry box. Just beneath the nest, and serving to brace it, may often be found a wide and irregular netting of lines, communicating with surrounding objects but rarely extending far downward toward the snare.

The Shamrock spider, Epeira trifolium, received its name from the trifoil or clover like markings upon the back of the abdomen, which is a whitish, whitish gray, or purplish color. The legs in the typical form are ringed with black, and most species are so marked, but I have taken specimens in which the legs were a uniform orange color. The abdomen of the adult female becomes strongly marked, especially along the sides, with bright red. One individual was collected whose abdomen was quite white, but after a period of confinement gradually turned to a dull brown. Another was well marked with black patterns, but also finally came out with shades of red and yellow. The Shamrock spider is somewhat more robust in form than her above named congeners, i. e., the abdomen more nearly approaches a globular shape. In Massachusetts I found one specimen with a white abdomen; two with yellow abdomens; one with bright strawberry or burnt sienna marks; one Trifolium that was blackish, the markings on the abdomen being white or silvery. These were all found in nests of several leaves, fastened together in the ordinary ways. A similar variety in coloring characterized specimens found in huckleberry patches and wooded hillsides just back of the bay, at Niantic, Connecticut.

In habit and spinning-work Trifolium resembles Insularis, living in a curled leaf with a trapline attachment to her snare.[1] Hentz in his description, based upon a specimen from Maine, says that the spider is found in houses and near dwellings. Mrs. Mary Treat reports the same characteristic of the individuals seen by her in New Hampshire. On the contrary I have rarely found a specimen except in the open fields or among shrubbery and often quite remote from human habitations.

A summer (1888) spent on Cape Ann, Massachusetts, gave me an admirable opportunity to observe the habits of this species. Those who are

Fig. 107. Orb and nest of the Shamrock spider, Epeira trifolium.

Tents in Hedge Rows. familiar with New England hedge rows know how they are formed; granite boulders and blocks, brought from the meadow or elsewhere, are piled along the boundaries between field and road into low stone walls or fences. On either side of these walls grow in unchecked profusion the native plants and wild flowers of New England. There are shrubs of various sorts, golden rod, great ferns,

[1] Fig. 107. measurements: Orb, 14 x 14 inches; hub, 1 inch; notched zone, $\frac{1}{4}$ x $\frac{1}{2}$ inch, irregularly placed; 4 notches below; central space nearly 3 inches. Vineland, N. J., on the bank of a run.

red raspberries, countless bushes of wild roses in full bloom, elder with its white blossoms or purple fruit clusters, and many other flowering plants, intermingled with weeds and grasses. This interesting bit of tangled plant life is a favorite camping ground for innumerable spiders, among which I found in August many of the leafy domiciles of Trifolium.

This species lives from Maine southward; I have found it in Massachusetts, New Jersey, Pennsylvania, and Ohio; and have specimens as far to the northwest as Wisconsin. Dr. Marx's specimens carry her range to Bismarck (Dakota), Minnesota, Colorado, and Wyoming. Its distribution is probably coterminous with that of Insularis although possibly more limited southward. Trifolium closely resembles the European Epeira quadrata both in appearance and habit. It is not at all unlikely that they may be regarded by future students as simply varieties of one species. There is indeed a very close relation between these two species and Epeira marmorea, and the entire trio might without violence be classified as varieties of Epeira quadrata Clerck.

Among various species sent me from California is one which I have heretofore described as Epeira vertebrata.[1] It is evidently a very common species on the Pacific coast, judging by the number of representatives always found among collections from that quarter. A few notes as to its habits were sent to me by Mrs. Eigenmann; but a fortunate event enabled me to study the species on my own premises. Mrs. Smith sent me from San Diego, in the month of May, 1888, a number of cocoons from which hatched out a vast colony of young. These I placed in an arbor in the manse yard, hoping that they might there become domesticated.

Epeira vertebrata.

I was surprised to see how slow they were in leaving the home nest, clinging fast to the cocoon, and then in little clusters above it for more than a month. I left my home for a summer vacation on the 8th of July, at which time the young Vertebratæ were still hanging in clusters and apparently had not grown a particle. I returned September 1st, and found five full grown specimens, all females, comfortably domiciled in different parts of the yard on honeysuckle and ampelopsis vines. Three of them were quite near each other, within a few feet of the spot where the cocoons hung. Other individuals may have migrated into adjoining premises, but these five remained with me and gave me quite full knowledge of their spinningwork. The following year a number of young appeared, and it is not improbable that the species may become permanently fixed in this section.

Its snares are identical with those of the Domicile spider, and in its general habit it differs little from that species. It occupies a leafy nest for much of the time, but not so persistently as Insularis and Tri-

---

[1] Proceedings Academy Natural Sciences, Philadelphia, 1887, page 312.

folium. The nests, moreover, were not as carefully formed as with those species. Vertebrata makes its orb early in the evening, and thereafter hangs to it pretty closely, unless disturbed. The traplines by which the webs are connected with the nests are much deflated at the point of union with the hub, and diverge at the point where they are united with the nest. So that the spider, instead of clasping a single line as is usual with Trifolium, really has its feet upon several lines. I have seen this peculiarity in traplines of Domicile spiders that had spun on iron fences. Vertebrata appears to be a very diligent weaver, working with steadiness and energy at the daily renewal of her snare, until early October. She then begins to show less activity; the sluggishness increases rapidly, the webs are rarely renewed, and soon the spiders disappear within the leaves and die.

Epeira displicata is an interesting little spider which makes a round web, usually

Epeira displicata. somewhat inclined. I have found it in New England, woven against a leaf whose edges were curled up and formed the support for the foundation lines. I know little of its general habits, but it is distributed quite extensively throughout the United States.

Among the most interesting of our spider fauna is that group of the genus

Diadem or Cross Spider. Epeira which may properly be termed the Angulata group. The individuals are distinguished by two processes, more or less decided and pointed, upon the base or front part of the dorsum of the abdomen. They

Fig. 108. Snare of Epeira displicata. From a sketch by Mr. Emerton.

are situated near the margin and overhang the sides and the cephalothorax. They are not hard or leathery like the spinous processes upon Acrosoma and Gasteracantha, but have nearly the consistency of the abdominal integument. To this group belongs the Diadem Spider, Epeira diademata, so familiar in European landscapes, and known popularly as the Cross Spider or Garden Spider. I have specimens of this species collected in the United States, one as far to the north and west as Minnesota. The spider undoubtedly has found lodging upon our shores, probably as an importation by immigrants from Europe, but is very rare as yet.

Others of this group are Epeira gemma, a fine large species, which inhabits the Pacific slope, and as far eastward at least as Utah; also Epeira cinerea, a large gray species, in many respects resembling E. gemma, which ranges the Northern Atlantic slope and the Adirondack Mountains.[1] To the same group belong Emerton's Epeira sylvatica, and my E. bicentennaria. The species are closely related to each other and to the European Epeira angulata and E. bicornis. Systematists may hereafter unite them all into two or three species. The habits of the entire group, as judged by the species which I have studied, are like those of Insularis and Trifolium as above described. They dwell in silken tents or nests of rolled leaves, and spin webs of the type shown at Figs. 101 and 107.

Angulata Group.

Epeira stellata is remarkable for the formation of its abdomen. Around the sides are inserted a number of spines, one of which projects prominently over the cephalothorax, which gives the creature a striking and weird appearance. I have taken it, especially the young, in Pennsylvania, New Jersey, and Connecticut. In the last named State numbers of the species were seen occupying orbicular snares, which were spun low upon grass, ferns, and golden rods on the margin of a meadow near a stone fence. They were of the general type of that group of which Epeira strix is a representative. The spiders hung at the centre with legs bunched up against the body, the half grown individuals looking like seeds of certain plants. The dull grays and grayish browns of its color helped to make it inconspicuous against the background of the browning foliage on which their snares were spun. At the least disturbance the spider dropped suddenly to the ground, or ran for refuge to the foliage at one end of the web.[2]

Fig. 109. Figure of Gasteracantha, female.

Among the Orbweavers constructing full vertical orbs is Gasteracantha, a spider whose remarkable shape has attracted the attention of many observers. Fig. 109. I have received numerous specimens of Gasteracantha cancer, and perhaps several varieties of the same, from Mrs. Rosa Smith Eigenmann, which were collected in the neighborhood of San Diego, California. On the Mesa land near the Mussel Beds, and also along the bay shore in that vicinity, a great number of specimens were found. The orbs of the spider were usually spread at a considerable angle, occasionally nearly horizontal, and sometimes almost

Gasteracantha.

---

[1] It was first made known by me in the Acad. Nat. Sci. Phila., under the name Epeira harrisonae, after the lady from whom Mrs. Mary Treat (who sent me specimens) received it. Emerton subsequently gave a detailed description and obtained priority.

[2] The measurements of one snare of an individual about half grown are given as follows: Orb, 6¼ x 6¾ inches in dimensions. Central space, 1½ x 1½. Notched zone and hub, ¾ inch in diameter, of which the hub itself was ⁵⁄₁₆ inch. The notched zone contained 8 spirals. The hub was slightly meshed. From the notched zone to the spiral space the distance was ¼ inch. The interspaces between the last 3 spirals of the notched zone were much larger than those of the rest of the series, being ¹⁄₈ inch. The spiral space itself covered from 3 to 3½ inches. The radii numbered 35. The spirals were 26 below, 20 above, and 21 at the sides of the hub. Another web was 5 inches in diameter, and was nearly round in shape; had 18 radii and 18 to 19 spirals.

perpendicular. The heavy spider hanging on the under side of the close-meshed hub pulled the net down at its centre as the snares were swayed by the wind. The upper foundation lines were quite strong and usually of great length, being from three to five feet, and in one case twelve feet long. The orb itself is often about eighteen inches in diameter, and is conspicuous object to one driving by it upon the road. The concentric spirals are numerous and placed in with great beauty and regularity. They extend entirely around the snare, giving it a more circular appear-ance than is common with those webs which have looped spirals below the hub, thus giving the orb an elongated form. For the most part the hub is closely meshed, but in one case was found open.

My own observation of the snare of Gasteracantha is limited to a single indi-vidual seen in Texas in the neighborhood of Aus-tin. This web was spun within a triangular space of two feet or more in length from top to bottom. This space was marked off by foundation lines, which were decorated in a pecu-liar manner, as represented in Fig. 110. This decora-tion consisted of tufts of flossy white silk from one-eighth to one-fourth inch long. They were spread

Fig. 110. Snare of Gasteracantha, to show the flossy spirals.

along the outer foundation lines throughout nearly their entire length. Several were also placed on the two inner supports of the orb. Two radii, one above and another below the centre, were similarly decorated, and several tufts were grouped around the hub, which was open. The number of these flossy tufts on one foundation line was twenty-one; on the other fifteen. The spider being at the centre of her web, which was vertical, and consisted of twenty-three radii regularly crossed by spirals, many of which presented the deflected appearance usually produced by the capture of insects. The figure given is drawn simply to indicate the exact position of the flossy

Flossy Tufts on Webs.

and of the orb within the triangular foundation lines.   The other details are only approximately accurate.

My notes do not show the complete form of the web, but Mrs. Eigenmann's observations abundantly establish the fact that the orb of Gasteracantha has the notched zone and free space as is the case with the webs of Epeira, which it closely resembles. None of the California webs, however, had anything like the tufted decorations which I observed in the Texas individual. Whether or not other examples in the same vicinity exhibit the peculiarity which I have described I am not able to say.[1]

The interest in the problem here presented is much increased, although the problem itself is brought little nearer solution, by facts concerning the snares of this genus recorded by M. Vinson.[2] He observed the same characteristic noticed by me in the Texas example, in the webs of Gasteracantha bourbonica of certain African islands.

African Species Tufted.

This spider spins a vertical web a metre or more in diameter. The snare is often suspended across the path in forests. The threads are different from those of other spiders; they show little cottony tufts (renflements cottoneux) distributed at intervals, but quite nearly approached. The spider hangs at the centre. She is active when she moves; but when one touches her she throws herself from her place, holding on by her thread, by the aid of which she is able to replace herself upon her snare.

In another part of his book M. Vinson records the same observation in this language: The Gasteracanthae of the Isle of Réunion introduce into the variously stretched lines [foundation lines], in the midst of which they establish their regular nets, a finishing-up ("confection") altogether special. As these lines are isolated, quite separated one from another, they are differently wrought from those of the interior net, and show at short intervals little cottony puffs ("renflements") which cause them to appear as though interrupted from point to point. These puffs give the web, of necessity, very great strength and elasticity.[3]

The same author, however, introduces another observation upon this species, which brings us face to face with the same curious diversity, if not divergence, in the habit which I have shown in the Gasteracanthae of our country. M. Vinson declares that the Gasteracanthae of Madagascar, which are both larger and more numerous than those of Réunion, do not follow the custom of

Webs Without Tufts.

decorating their webs with cottony tufts as do those of the last named island, but spin their vertical snares in a manner altogether similar to those of the common Epeïra.

---

[1] As I was at the time intent upon the study of the natural history of the agricultural ants, I was compelled, often at great sacrifice of my feelings, to resist the attractions everywhere around me to observe and seek out the habits of the spider fauna.

[2] Aranéides de la Réunion, Maurice, et Madagascar, page 238.

[3] Op. cit., Introduction, page xvii.

How shall we reconcile or explain these strange unities and diversities? It might be said, in view of the numerous observations made by Mrs. Eigenmann in California, that my own description of the Texas species, which was based upon observation of a single web, was that of an abnormal act, a freak, an accident, an individual peculiarity. When, however, we see spiders of the same genus, so widely separated in their habitat, presenting in both America and Africa on the one hand the same curious habit of web decoration, and on the other the same adherence to the nor-

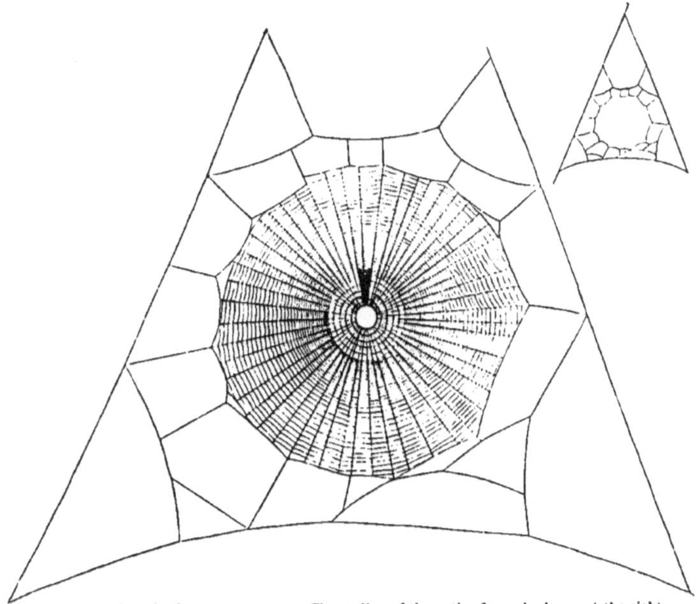

Fig. 111. The orb of Acrosoma rugosa. The outline of the entire frame is shown at the right.

mal type of snare, it seems impossible to account for the web observed by me on the ground of a freak or individual peculiarity. At present I can only record the facts, without venturing to suggest a theory to explain them. I am not even able to say what differences, if any, may exist between the species which spin the several webs. The difference is certainly not very great. A future observer will doubtless find a simple explanation of the phenomenon; and whatever it may be it will probably be found similar to that which causes individuals of Argiope and Acrosoma to twist and string ribbon decorations around the central parts of their orbs.

11.

The third group of Orbweavers making vertical webs is composed of those which retain the open hub. Among these are our indigenous species of the genus Acrosoma. These are found in the neighborhood of **Orbs with Open Hubs.** Philadelphia, and are distributed very generally throughout the Middle, Northern-Middle, and Southern States, east of the Rocky Mountains. The favorite site for their snares is a large open space between two bushes or trees, or between the diverging branches of the same. I have most frequently found them in the margins of an open grove, wood, or forest. As a rule they swing their nets at a considerable height, so that one's face comes in contact with them while passing through the woods. The foundation lines are frequently of considerable length, four or five feet, or even more. The delicate orb swung between them is a very pretty sight as one sees it outlined against the sky, showing through the vista of the opening trees. (Fig. 111.)

The three species common to our neighborhood are Acrosoma rugosa, spinea, and mitrata.[1] They are all characterized by abdomens which present **Favorite Sites.** upon the dorsal surface spines of greater or less length and hardness. These spines are more decidedly developed upon the first two named species. In the last named species, the Mitred spider, the spinous processes are small, and the integument is not so tough.

All the three species make substantially, and I might say almost precisely, the same sort of web. The shape of the snare is usually quite orbicular, nearly always approaching a circle more nearly than that of most species of Orbweavers. The number of radii is very great, amounting at **Character of Orb.** times to as many as eighty, and the number of spirals is correspondingly large. The orb itself is not very large, generally being within six inches in diameter rather than above. It results, therefore, that the spiral space presents a remarkably close texture of checkered openings between the cross lines. The free zone, which in the typical Epeira net contains no lines crossing the radii, is always occupied in this genus by the lines of the notched zone, which wind in three or four comparatively widely separated concentrics through the entire free zone. These take the place of the notched zone of the Epeira orb, whose concentrics are wound close up to the hub.

The hub, as has been stated, is always open, and within it the spider is usually found hanging with its legs outstretched, grasping the marginal circumference of the hub. Spinea and Mitrata hang in a position closely resembling that of the ordinary Epeira, that is to say, with the head

---

[1] As I have heretofore shown (Proceed. Acad. Nat. Sci. Philada., 1888, page 5), the names of these species as given by Walckenaer are entitled to priority. They will probably be known respectively as Acrosoma gracilis (rugosa), A. saggittata (spinea), and A. recluviana (mitrata).

downward and sustained by the feet, the difference being, as already noted, that the Epeira clasps with her feet the meshed terminations of the radii within the hub, while Acrosoma supports herself by the margin of the open hub. In the case of Rugosa, the method is the same but the position of the spider a little different. The two hindermost legs are clasped to the upper margin or to the bit of ribboned lace that frequently runs upward from the hub of the spiral space. The back or dorsum of her abdomen thus hangs towards the ground. The spinnerets are turned upwards and assist to support the spider by a little dragline. The head in this position is of course depressed, and at an angle say of forty-five degrees, more or less. She supports this part of her body not only by the first and second pair, but

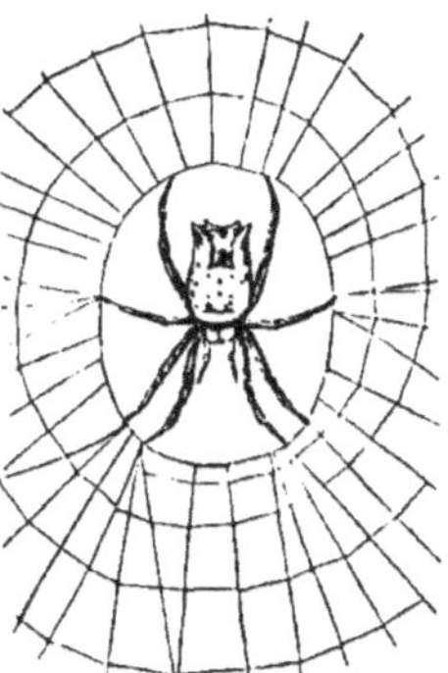

Fig. 112. Acrosoma mitrata suspended at the hub of her orb.

Position of Third Legs. also by the third pair of legs, which, contrary to the custom of Orbweavers generally, are thrown forward on either side of the face. Generally the third pair of legs is correlated with the fourth pair, and the second with the first, but here the third is associated with the first two.

Long Fourth Legs. The fact is doubtless in some way connected with the peculiar character of the fourth legs, which in the genus Acrosoma are as long as or longer than the first legs. The length of the fourth pair is an evident convenience to the spider when walking; for the ventral part of the abdomen is an inverted pyramid or cone, at the apex of which the spinnerets are placed. The additional length of the fourth legs thus serves to raise these organs above the ground as the spider moves. The same reason, viz., the length of the fourth legs, together with the open hub, influences the position of the third legs. These organs are not long enough to clasp the marginal ring of the hub near the feet of the fourth legs, and as there are no cross lines in the hub to grasp as in the case of Epeïra, they must necessarily seek the nearest place of rest, and thus are stretched straight out from the body to the side of the hub, as is common with Mitrata (Fig. 112)

Fig. 113. Acrosoma spinea in position at the hub of her orb.

and occasionally with Spinea; or else are bent forward in the direction of the first and second pairs, and grasp the circumference of the hub, as does Rugosa habitually and Spinea frequently. (Fig. 113.)

In the same group with Acrosoma, among the spiders having an open hub and vertical snare, may be placed Cyclosa caudata or the "Tailed Spider," and her closely related congener of Florida, Cyclosa bifurca. The snares of this species are never very large. They are hung, as a rule, within a system of secondary foundation lines, as represented in Fig. 111, thus giving them, as with Acrosoma, a considerable degree of elasticity. The spirals of the notched zone, instead of clustering close around the hub, wind through the free space, and the number of radii and beaded spirals is usually very large. The hub in the normal condition is open, and the spider may be found hanging therein with its feet attached to a ribboned string which extends upward through the free zone. The ribbon runs below the hub as well as above it, and the two bands are frequently connected by an irregular strip of spinningwork, thus giving the hub the appearance of being meshed or even sheeted. It is, however, properly placed with the group with open hubs, to which I have here assigned it.

A striking peculiarity of the Tailed spider is to attach her cocoons to a line extending upward from the hub to the circumference of the orb. In accomplishing this the surrounding spiral lines and sometimes one **Peculiar Habits.** or two of the radii are cut away, giving to the snare the appearance of the sectoral orb made by Zilla. This, however, is simply an accident of the cocooning habit. The species has also the custom of hanging flossy pellets of silk upon her orb at various points; and these are often to be found mingled with the remains of devoured insects. This habit is common among very young specimens of Caudata. In the mature spiders the detritus of insect remains is attached to the cocoon. This habit is considered at length in Vol. II. in connection with Maternal Instincts and Industry. I have occasionally seen similar nodules placed upon the snare of Acrosoma rugosa, but the habit does not appear to be fixed in that species, but in Caudata it is permanently established.

The genus Meta has its chief representative in the geographical district of Philadelphia, and indeed throughout the Eastern United States, in the species **Meta menardi.** Meta menardi. The snare of Meta does not differ from the full orb webs of Epeira. Meta segmentata of Europe, according to Cambridge[1] invariably spins her orbicular snare at an inclination to the plane of the earth; he had never found one extended perpendicularly. The hub of the orb is open, in this respect approximating the snares of the spiders which make horizontal webs. Like Tetragnatha extensa, it has the habit of extending the first and second pairs of legs in a line with the body. This species is quite catholic in the selection of its orb site, as there is scarcely a conceivable situation among herbage, bushes, heather, on heaths and commons, where it may not be found.

[1] "Spiders of Dorset." Vol. II., page 241.

Another European species, Meta meriannæ, approaches in the general trend of its habits our Meta menardi. This spider is found in the corners and windows of outhouses, verandas, and greenhouses, also under overhanging banks and rocks, and in other damp, dark situations. This quite accurately describes the habit of our Meta menardi. I have found the webs at the foot of the Allegheny Mountains in Central Pennsylvania, quite generally in dark and shady positions. Indeed, I collected quite a number of species within Sinking Spring Cave. These had established their snares **Snares in** from one to two hundred feet from the opening of the cavern, **Caves.** and had swung them against the face of the rocky sides. From the point at which I collected the spiders, I could see the mouth of the cave, which is not large, and beyond it the dim light of the ravine through which it is approached. But no light penetrated to the spot, at least not enough to make it possible for me to collect specimens or examine the snares. My observations were made by the light of a torch. I found a few specimens in sheltered positions outside the mouth of the cave. It is probable that the spiders drifted within the cavern when they were young, or may have floated within it upon the waters of the stream that enters it. But it is evident that a location within such a darkened domicile is agreeable to this aranead, and a tendency to this habit is manifestly a characteristic of the genus Meta.

According to Emerton Meta menardi lives in caves and other damp and shady places in New England, and he reports specimens obtained from **Loving** caves in Kentucky and Virginia.[1] It is thus manifest that through **Darkness.** a wide extent of territory, the habits of the species preserve the same characteristics.

Blackwall describes the species under Walckenaer's name, Epeira fusca.[2] Emerton, following Thorell, accepts the specific name menardi of Latreille.[3] If, therefore, we accept the American and European species as substantially the same, we shall find that this tendency to seek obscure places characterizes both the American and the European species. Blackwall says that in North Wales the principal haunts of the species are caves, cellars, overhanging banks, and other obscure places.[4]

[1] "New England Epeïridæ," Transactions Connecticut Academy of Arts and Sciences. Vol. VI., page 328.
[2] Hist. Nat. des Insect. Apt. Vol. II., page 84.
[3] Gen. Crust. et Insect. Vol. I., page 108.
[4] Spiders of Great Britain, page 259.

CHAPTER VIII.

COMPOSITE SNARES AND SECTORAL ORBS.

I.

In the following chapter I have placed the spinningwork of two groups of Orbweavers that appear to me, in spite of some marked differences, to have many points in common, namely, those which habitually make a composite snare and those which spin an orbweb, lacking one sector. Composite snares combine the round web of Orbweavers with the netted maze of lines which marks the typical Retitelarian. Two spiders which most prominently associate with their own snare that of the Lineweavers are Epeira labyrinthea and E. triaranea. Of these two, the habit is most permanently fixed in the former, which is rarely, if ever, without its maze, while with the latter it is sometimes very scant.

The Labyrinth Spider.

Triaranea's orb is habitually sectoral, Labyrinthea's snare inclines to the orbicular, but, as will be presently shown, appears to be a transition form between the orbicular and sectoral. In the methods on which it is constructed it properly is grouped with the sectoral orbmakers.

The web of the Labyrinth spider is perhaps the most remarkable example of the composite snare. Its orb is spun at one side of a mass of variously crossed lines, designated as the maze or labyrinth, from which it is separated by a small but quite distinct space usually of about an inch. To the centre of the orb is attached the trapline, a ray of several threads which

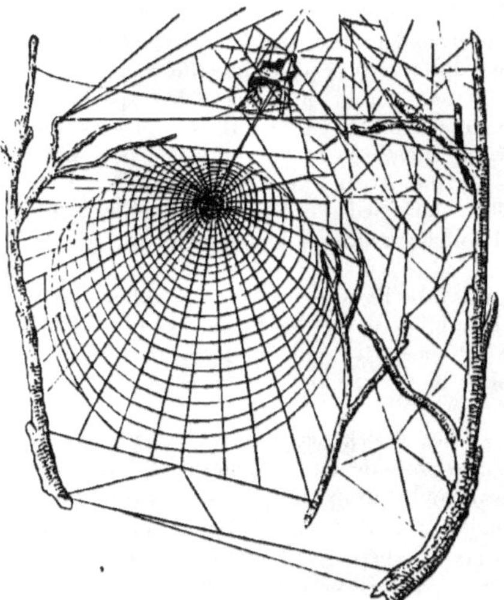

Fig. 111. Snare of the Labyrinth spider, seen from behind. The leaf tent is shown in the maze.

slants upward into the labyrinth to the point where the spider is domiciled. The domicile is a small, bell shaped, silken tent, which is usually protected above by a withered leaf; or is simply a slight silken canopy spun within or against the lower end of the leaf. In the cocooning season this shelter tent is sometimes spun against the lowest one of the

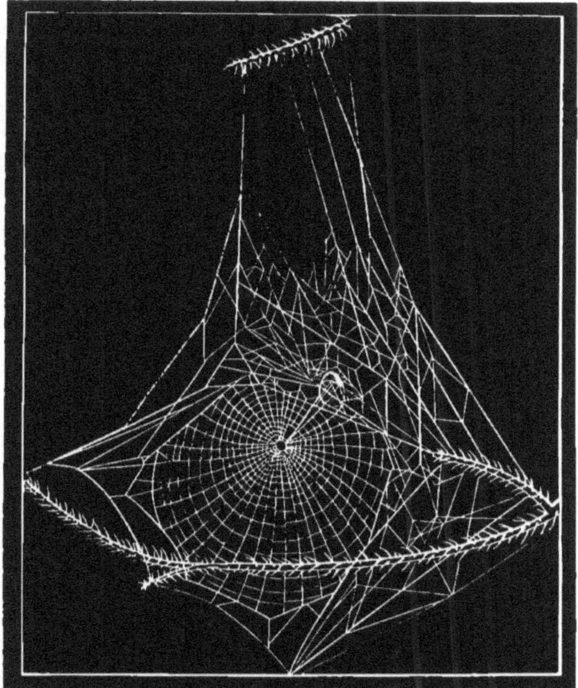

Fig. 115. Labyrinth spider's snare, to show the maze of intersecting lines above the orb.

several cocoons which the spider habitually makes. (Fig. 114.) The retitelarian snare or maze of netted lines, which happily suggested Hentz's specific name, labyrinthea, is situated above and to one side of the orb, which it somewhat overlaps. It is irregular in shape, but often rudely pyramidal, sometimes making a bulk of spinningwork from ten to twelve inches wide and high, and six to eight inches deep. For example, Fig. 115, a snare spun in a fir tree measured

The Labyrinth of Lines.

twelve inches wide, twelve inches high, seven inches deep. The shape and size are of course modified, as with all webs, by the particular features of the site.

There is a decided space between the labyrinth and the orb, except that the orb is, with rare exceptions, attached above by its foundation lines to the labyrinth. This is seen in the side view shown at Fig. 116. The spider is there nested under one of her cocoons. The side attachment of the orb is apt to be upon some of the long guy lines by which the labyrinth is held in form. It generally extends downward as far as the middle, or a little below the middle point of the orb.

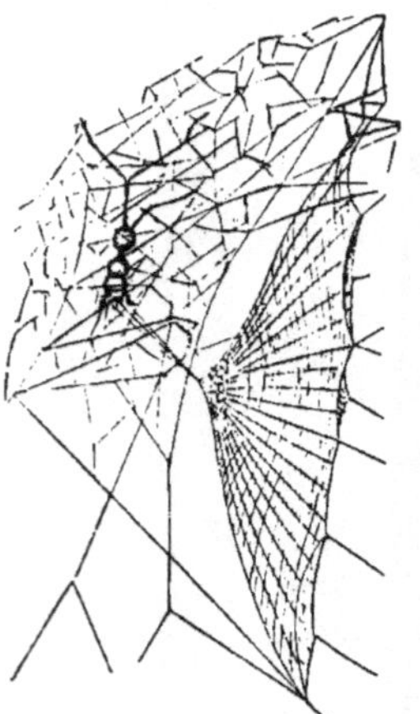

Fig. 116 Side view of Labyrinthea's snare, to show the space between orb and snare.

The maze serves its little proprietor and factor the following uses: First, it is environment and support for her tent; second, it gives convenient points of suspension for her orb; third, it provides a safe and convenient nursery within which to hang her cocoons: and, fourth, proves an admirable field upon which the young can find exercise and forage. I have seen the little fellows, late in the season, scrambling up and down among the interlacing lines, picking out here and there minute entangled insects. Fifth, the labyrinth serves as a true snare as well as domicile for the adult spider, for I have seen her capturing small insects that had been caught within the maze, cutting through the lines for that purpose. Her chief dependence for food is, however, upon the orb. Moreover, sixth, the labyrinth must have value as a protective environment for the occupant against raiding mud dauber wasps and other enemies, and

Uses of Labyrinth.

for her cocoons against various parasitizing foes, since the tangle of crossed lines certainly raises a formidable barrier against approach of winged insects. It might be added, seventh, that in the pairing season the males appropriate the labyrinth for purposes of temporary rest in their gradual approach when courting the female. They pull down the lines by their feet as they hang back downward until they form the ribs of a sort of araneal groined arch. I have seen three males hanging upon one web at the same time. Labyrinthea rarely makes great changes in this portion of her snare, although the orb, as is usual with Epeïroids, requires frequent renewal. Indeed, the maze has greater natural strength than the orb, for I have observed that winds and showers which had completely beaten down and dissolved the latter did not affect the former, and in such cases the occupant abode within her retitelarian bounds for a day or two without reproducing the orbweb.[1]

Strength of the Labyrinth.

[1] On this point see further in the chapter on Engineering Skill.

The Orb Described

The orb of Labyrinthea is a delicate and beautiful structure. It is not large in size, usually measuring six or seven inches at the longitudinal axis and five or six at the lateral. The largest web I ever saw was twelve inches in diameter.[1] Within this space are disposed a large number of finely spun radii and spirals, the former sometimes numbering as high as seventy-five, the latter exceeding eighty. The spirals, as is common in orbwebs, are more numerous below than above the hub, but this difference is very marked in the web of Labyrinthea, sometimes being as great as three to one, and even six or seven to one.[2] The spirals in the lower part of the orb are not complete circles, but are looped in, the lines terminating at the sides. This feature is sometimes seen in full orbwebs, and is habitual in sectoral orbs. (See Fig. 121.)

Construction Central Space

The diminished number of spirals at the top of the orb is in part due to a peculiar feature of the snare, which at least suggests that combination of characteristics of full orb and sectoral orb already alluded to. This feature results, first, from the position of the spider's domicile behind the orb, making it necessary that the trapline should penetrate the snare in order to give the spider admission to its outer surface; and, second, from the slanting direction of the trapline which compels a larger opening than would otherwise be required. This is illustrated at Fig. 117, which shows the centre of the orb from behind and above with a special view to the connection of the trapline with the hub, and its relations to the spirals.[3] It will be seen that the unbeaded spirals of the notched zone are cut off above, leaving a triangular open space somewhat like the free radius of a sectoral orb. This opening is larger or less according

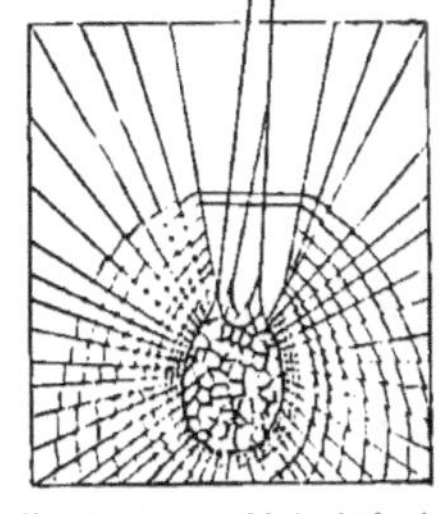

Fig. 117. Centre of Labyrinthea's orb, showing arched opening.

to circumstances; it may be increased by the trapline impinging upon the spiral space, thus leaving but a few continuous spirals at the top of the orb. The spider when seeking prey runs through this opening, underneath the overspun arch of spiral lines, to the outer face of the orb upon which the insects are ensnared. It returns along the same path to the tent with the captured insect.

[1] The following measurements in inches show ordinary sizes: 7 inches long by 6 wide; 6 x 5; 6 x 6; 9 x 7; 6 x 4½; 12 x 12.

[2] The following counts will illustrate this: No. 1, radii, 55; spirals, 31 above, 82 below. No. 2, spirals, 8 above, 55 below, 17 at the sides. No. 3, radii, 75; spirals, 80.

[3] Measurements of Fig. 117, orb 9 in. long by 7 wide; hub ¾ in. long, ¼ wide; centre of hub 2½ in. (about one-third the length of the orb) from the top margin of the orb. The hub is meshed, oval, narrowed at the top. The notched spirals fill the free space, three being close to the hub, the others widening as they wind. Traplines about 2½ in. long.

The trapline of the Labyrinth spider differs from that of Trifolium and Insularis in being composed of several threads instead of a single **Trapline and Hub.** line. Fig. 118. These threads usually diverge at the nest, with which they are united, and again sometimes at their attachment to the hub. Most frequently the trapline is a ray of threads converging upon the hub. The hub is characteristically meshed (Fig. 117), the sides of the meshes being in part the ends of the radii as continued within the hub, where they are of course greatly contorted. This feature is also observable in the notched zone, where the lines of the radii are often broken or zigzagged, and much bent out of their course, as may be seen at Fig. 119.

I have observed the Labyrinth spider in the act of spinning her maze. The process appears to be a simple one to the observer, although it is difficult to describe and yet more difficult to figure. The strong foundation lines are first spun, and these lines, after having been once made, will be pre-

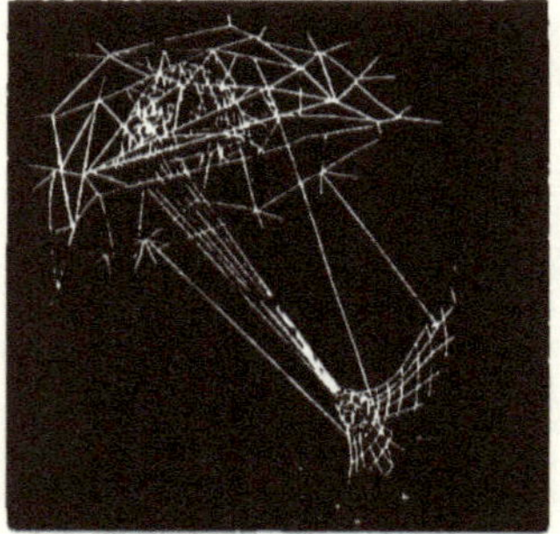

Fig. 118. Multiplex trapline of Labyrinthea.

Fig. 119. Bent radii in the notched zone of Epeira labyrinthea.

Spinning the Labyrinth. served carefully for a long period of time. Indeed, unless broken by external violence, a spider might preserve this sort of household property through an entire season. From these lines, by dropping and carrying draglines, by crawling around upon the foliage, by establishing here and there central intersecting cables, and then by dropping and striding from one to another, the labyrinthian maze of crossed lines is in the end evolved.

However, the complete condition of the maze is a matter of growth through a longer or shorter period. When a comparatively few lines have been spun, the spider will take her place at the central part therein. She begins here to spin out a few short lines, which in the course of a few moments present rudely the appearance of the dome of Linyphia. By **Framing the Tent.** pushing her body and her spinnerets against the top and sides of this domelike framework, she gets it into a somewhat consistent shape. This is the foundation or scaffold upon which eventually is built her silken tent, which acquires consistency of tissue as the threads are gradually spun up against it. Here now she establishes herself, and from this point stretches out her traplines and proceeds to spin her orb, swinging it upon the strong cables or foundation lines of her retitelarian system. Her method, as far as I have been able to judge, is precisely the method of Theridium and other true Lineweavers, and, indeed, may be described as the method which Agalena also uses when spinning the retitelarian supports of her long sheeted snare.

The peculiar snare of Labyrinthea and other spiders making a composite web appears to be a larger development of a habit which is seen to a greater or less degree in the genus Argiope. In considering the particular **A Developed Habit.** spinningwork of this genus I have already called attention to the fact that both Cophinaria and Argyraspis suspend the upper foundation lines of their orbs to a series of intersecting straight lines which are spun with more or less consistency to the overhanging and surrounding foliage. This system of crossed lines is very frequently carried downward to one side of the orb and sometimes upon both sides, so that it forms what I have called the protective wings or fenders. If the reader will compare the more perfect and permanent spinning habit of Labyrinthea and Triaranea with that which is described and figured as the work of Argiope, he will see the close resemblance between the two. One may therefore say that what appears as a rudimentary habit, or a habit more or less developed in the case of Argiope has appeared as a perfectly developed and fixed habit in the spinning behavior of Labyrinthea. There is a marked peculiarity in the **Favorite Sites.** favorite site that Labyrinthea chooses for her snare. This is noticeably a dead and leafless bush, or a leafless part of a tree or dead branch. The habit is quite persistent, and I have seen it in every well established habitat of the species. It is true that she will spin her snare among leaves, but her preference is for a locality not so obstructed. In such sites she is often seen in little groups or colonies. In one such colony at Radnor, Pennsylvania, I counted thirty adult spiders, whose snares were spun upon a dry brush heap within a space six feet long, six wide, and five high. To this "clearing" every individual settler had no doubt been attracted by the same favorable conditions for an unobstructed habitation. Perhaps the instinct which induces this choice is under the same influence as that which urges many Theridioid species to seek similar sites for their retitelarian snares, which exactly resemble the maze of Labyrinthea's web. Certainly, it is interesting and curious to find these two

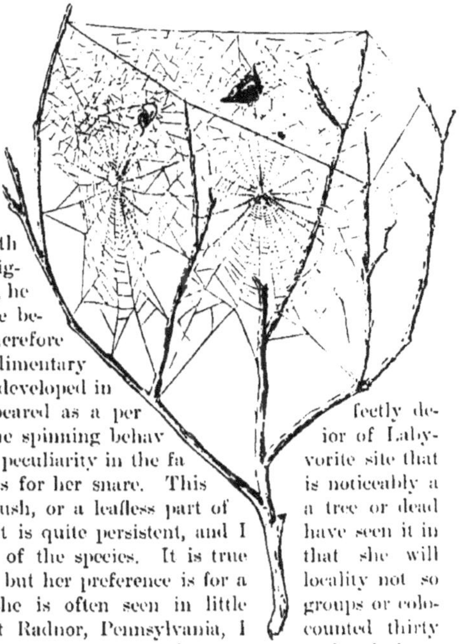

Fig. 120. Coöperative housekeeping by two Labyrinth spiders.

habits existing side by side in the Lineweavers and an Orbweaver which affects a lineweaving spinningwork.

On one leafless bush I found two individuals established whose several premises had been merged into one by the blending of the two labyrinths. (Fig. 120.) It was quite a case of coöperative housekeeping; or, to make a closer analogy, it suggested the double houses one often sees in city architecture, with united party wall and common porch separated by a rail. The cross lines of the two mazes completely blended; one spider was domiciled under a leafy roof, the other under a woven tent; one orb faced toward the front, the other toward the side of the united labyrinth.

Coöperative Housekeeping.

The Labyrinth Spider has a very wide distribution through the United States, and will probably be found to inhabit our entire territory. It has been traced from New England south and westward to Colorado and California, and I have specimens from several States of South America. These last, like numerous examples from Southern California, differ from the more northern fauna in being larger and somewhat more brightly marked. Their cocoons are also larger, and probably their snares are more formidable; otherwise, they are substantially the same species. It, therefore, must be added to that class of our aranead fauna whose physical elasticity enables them to occupy with equal facility a far northern and far southern home. However, in questions of geographical distribution, the factor of vertical distribution ought not to be forgotten. A far southern species may have a practically boreal habitat by elevation upon a mountain range. I cannot speak positively as to this point concerning South American Labyrintheas, but the specimens from Southern California were taken from the seashore and the ordinary level of San Diego.

Geographical Distribution.

II.

One of the most abundant of the small group of spiders that weave sectoral orbs is Epeira triaranea, so called because of its composite snare, which combines with that of the Orbweaver a decided retitelarian web, and a quite good approximation to that of the tubeweaver.[1]

I have found the orbs of this species, from June 1st throughout the summer, on bushes, shrubs, trees, hedges, on and between fences, and in

Epeira triaranea.

---

[1] This spider was first noticed by me under this name in Proceedings Academy of Natural Sciences, Philadelphia, 1876, page 201. Subsequently, in the same journal, 1878, page 127, I gave a full description of the animal and its spinningwork, with figures, under the name of Epeira globosa, a spider closely resembling my species, which had been described by Keyserling, Verhand. d. zool.-bot. Ver., XX., 1865, page 820. I had the name changed at that time in the page proofs of my paper, but being now less certain as to the identity of Keyserling's species I follow Mr. Emerton in returning to my original name. It is not improbable that Keyserling's name will be finally given priority.

great numbers on the lattice work and open slats of the corn cribs and other outhouses of farms. In the last named site very many young spiders were seen in the first week of June, having but recently issued from the cocoon. They were distributed along the lattice work for several yards, forming a goodly colony. As late as June 21st a similar colony was found in like position, the spiders being from one-half to two-thirds grown. In July and August I found many individuals located within the interstices of a stone fence near the seashore, at Cape Ann, Massachusetts.

Triaranea persistently makes a web with an open sector and **Free Radius.** free radius, that is, a prolonged line not crossed by viscid beads, which, although it may occupy the position of a radius, is free from the general radial system. Examples occasionally occur, particularly among adult webs, in which the spirals entirely cover the orb space, but the general habit is otherwise. Among young Triaraneas I have very rarely noticed such an exception. For example, in the colony just alluded to I counted consecutively fifty-two snares, every one of which had the free radius. The same fact was true of the colony of June 6th. In these young webs the radius was always entirely free, with four exceptions, in three of which there was one thread stretched across the opening near the top of the web, and in the other case there were two lines so placed.

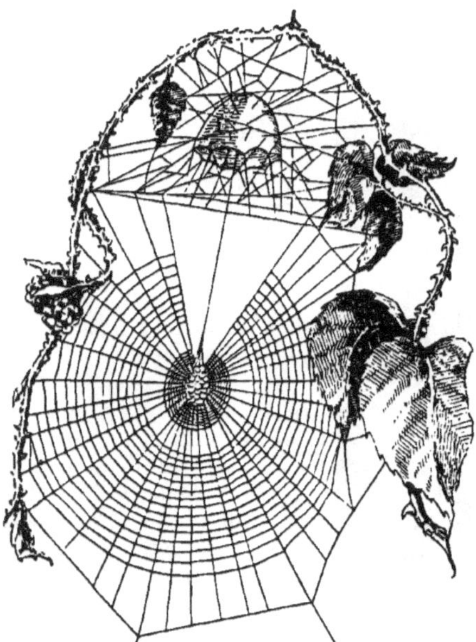

Fig. 121. Tent and sectoral orb of Epeira triaranea.

Fig. 122. Epeira triaranea (globosa).

Occasionally I have found a colony in which the tendency to a full orb was much stronger than usual. One such was noticed at Niantic, Connecticut. In the interstices of a stone wall bordering the beach of Niantic Bay, on the country seat of one of my brothers, many Triaraneas are established. Their tents are woven against the upper surfaces of the round rocks and their snares fill the openings. In a number of these, made by adults (August), the proportion of full round orbs was much greater than sectoral orbs. I am not able to account for this remarkable difference, as nothing in the site gave a clue. It would almost seem that the species is in a state of transition from the one habit to the other; the habit of weaving a sectoral orb being now in the ascendant, but the power to spin full orbicular snares remaining intact and sometimes becoming dominant.

The wedge like open space always occupies the upper semicircle of the snare, but has no fixed position therein. I conceived the idea that the orientation of the open sector and trapline might have some special relation to the economy of the spider, or even to its structure. But, after making an immense number of notes and sketches of webs, I concluded that the matter is largely dependent upon the convenience of a site for pitching the shelter tent. Sometimes the sector opens directly upward as in the typical snare at Fig. 123, sometimes to the left, or again to the right. Much the greater number of openings noted by me were on the right side of the web (facing the object), and next to that the favorite position was at the middle. The sectoral opening usually occupied about the space of one-eighth of the surface of the orb. I have measured sectors covering respectively about one-fifth, one-sixth, one-eighth, one-tenth, and one-fourteenth of the same. Or, the proportions may be yet better understood by these measurements. Let ab (Fig. 124) represent the diameter of several orbs and cd the width of the sector at the circumference. In No. 1, ab = two and a half inches, cd = six-eighths inch, three-tenths the orb space; No. 2 (Fig. 124), ab = two and a half inches, cd = one inch, two-fifths the orb space; No. 3, ab = two and a half inches, cd = one-half inch, one-fifth; No. 4 (Fig. 125), ab = two inches, cd = three-eighths inch, over one-fifth; No. 5, ab = two inches, cd = three-eighths inch, one-fifth orb space; No. 6, ab = two inches, cd =

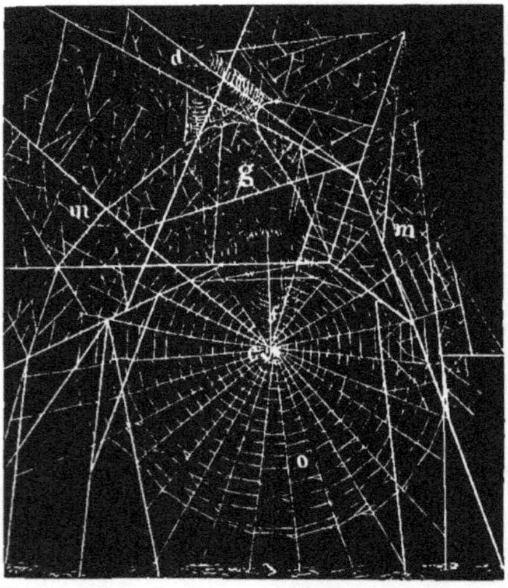

Fig. 123. Triaranea's snare. o, orb; m, the maze; g, guy lines supporting orb; d, den or tent; f, free radius; c, central.

three-eighths inch, one-fifth the orb space. These were all webs of young spiders. It will thus be seen that there is no fixed rule by which Triaranea is guided in this outlay of her web, and that she allows herself a wide range of variation, although the greater number of orbs show a sector of about one-fifth the orb space.

Through the open sector passes the free radius or trapline, for such

FIG. 124.

FIG. 125.

Illustrations of the orientation of the trapline, and width of the open sector.

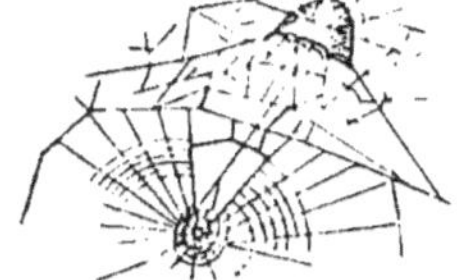

FIG. 126. Bell shaped tent in which the trapline terminates.

it is, its use being precisely that of the trapline in full orb making spiders. Near the point of attachment to the hub this is deltated, diverging into several lines that **Trapline.** are fastened at various points to the meshes of the hub. The other end of the trapline enters a little bell shaped silken tent swung amid a retitelarian maze, where it is held by the spider. (Fig. 126).

Sometimes several spiral lines will cross the upper part of the open sector (Fig. 127); again one may see the variation shown at Fig. 128, where two radii (dr dr) detached from the hub (H) are lifted out from the plane of the orb, leaving an open space (O) through which the trapline (T) passes. Another variation differs from this in having but a single detached radius (dr) to which cross loops (cl) pass from the marginal radii R, R. (Fig. 129.) When weaving in the spirals this spider does not pass entirely around the orb, as is the case with the full orb makers in the major part of their snare, but moves back and forth between the radial borders (Fig. 125, c and d) of the open sector, spinning her spirals in successive horseshoe loops. This **Spirals in Loops.** is the method observed

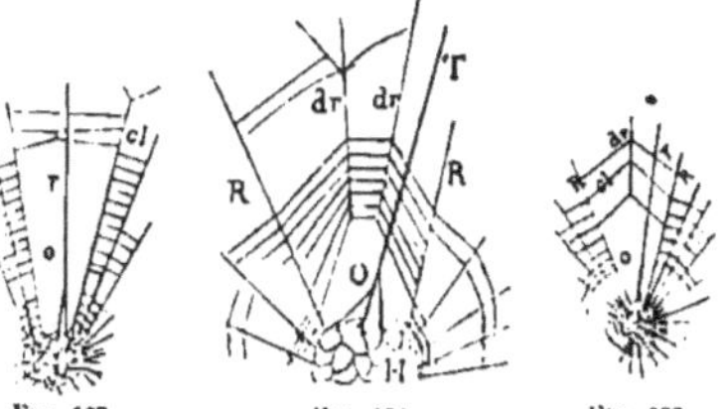

FIG. 127.   FIG. 128.   FIG. 129.

Variations in the open sector; detached radii.

by Zilla, and all sectoral orb makers in fact. The necessity for it is at once apparent. Of course, in this case the term "spiral" has only a technical application to these lines. (Fig. 130.)

The number of both spirals and radii varies greatly. The latter are more numerous, often far more numerous below than above the hub, which frequently is situated well above the geometric centre of the orb. Thus, in an orb six inches wide by seven long the spirals in the upper part of the snare numbered nineteen, in the lower thirty-two. The lower spirals were thus drawn in shorter loops with much less curve, and the centre of the hub was well toward the top, two inches therefrom. In another adult web the orb measured eleven inches long by eight wide, the number of radii was forty-one, of spirals forty-five, of notched concentrics nine. The centre of the hub was five inches from the topmost spiral.

The following measurements give some idea of the size of Triaranea's orb: Web No. 1, about four inches diameter; radii forty-three; spirals thirty-five. No. 2, radii twenty; spirals twenty. No. 3, diameter six and a half inches; radii thirty-five; spirals thirty-five. No. 4, seven inches long by six wide. No. 5, six and a half long by five and a half wide. Radii forty; spirals, forty-eight below, twelve above. No. 6, forty-one radii; forty-five spirals. No. 7, two and a half by two and a half. No. 8, eleven by eight inches, central five inches from top, three and one-fourth from side; radii forty-one, spirals forty-five, notched zone nine.

Web Measurements.

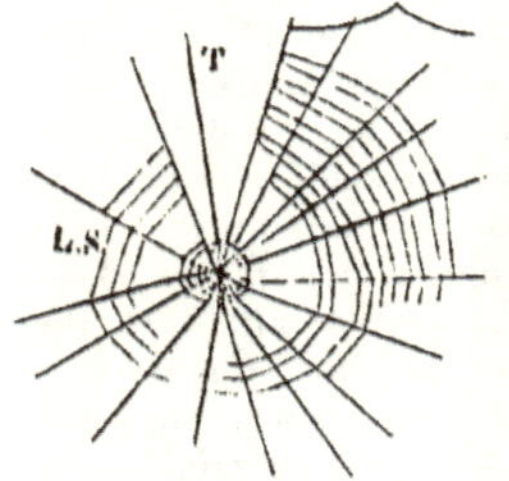

Fig. 130. The looped spirals, L.S., in Zilla's orb.

Triaranea is frequently found in the neighborhood of human habitations, around barns and various outbuildings of farms, but also loves the field, and is frequently found therein. It does not appear to have in so marked a degree as Labyrinthea a preference for nest sites naked of foliage, when such can be conveniently procured.

The maze or snare of netted lines in the web of Triaranea is, on the whole, not quite so prominent as that of Labyrinthea, but in some cases it is very heavy, and generally is decidedly marked in the adult spider. The variation in this portion of the snare may be seen from the following extract from my note book, made during one day: No. 1, retitelarian lines not heavy; No. 2, little or no retitelarian lines: No. 3, slight retitelarian lines above; No. 4, retitelarian lines quite abundant in a protecting wall behind and above but not before the orb.

Retitelarian Maze.

These, like other differences in webs, may often be accounted for simply by the fact that they exhibit different stages of completion. Spiders do not invariably finish secondary parts of their web at the same time that they spin the primary one. The nest or tent, for example, will sometimes be a matter of growth, and it is probably the case that the netted cross lines of composite snares are developed in the same way. Young spiders also differ from adults in the degree of attention which they pay to the secondary parts of their snare. The principal part, however, the orb in the case of Orbweavers, is invariably completed, if circumstances will permit it, before the spider settles herself to the pursuit of prey.

Cause of Differences.

It is certainly interesting to find these Orbweavers possessing in so marked a degree the spinning habit of the tribe most closely related to themselves in general structural characteristics, although it may

Affinities. not be possible to trace a close relation between the community of habit and the com munity of structure. The affinity of these snares and their weav ers with the spinningwork and the weavers of the Retitelarian tribe will be more fully traced hereafter when I come to con sider the Domed orbweb of the Basilica spider; but it may be here remarked that they both possess very de- cidedly the Epeïroid character- istics.

In the meantime, there is another interesting peculiarity of Triaranea's web which needs to be noted, namely, the bell shaped den or tent of white silk hung amidst the maze (Fig. 131), and connect- ed with the trapline. A struct- ure of this kind, within which the spider constantly dwells, is not confined to this species. Many Orbweavers have a sim- ilar tent or some flossy uphol- stered crevice, hole, or leafy nest, within which they con- ceal themselves frequently or habitually. Triaranea often 'shows a remarkable addition to this ordinary bell shaped tent. There is an open and quite distinct tube attached to the mouth of the

Tube- weaving Tendency tent, from which it to the centre of the free radius is fasten runs through or along the floor ally kept taut, and is clasped fore feet of the spider. This feet, shortened, or even whol ly found as in Fig. 132. In

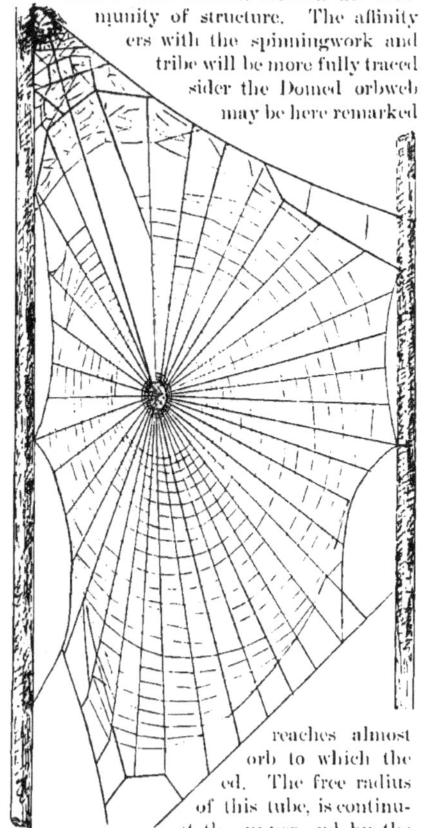

Fig. 131. A snare of Epeira triaranea, showing the looped spirals and elongated lower part of the orb.

reaches almost orb to which the ed. The free radius of this tube, is continu- at the upper end by the gangway is at times imper- ly omitted, but is frequent- this bell shaped den and

connecting tube one may see a germ or modification or suggestion of the typical snare of the tribe of Tubeweavers. We thus see that our spider represents in her spinningwork three separate tribes of spiders, namely, the Orbweavers, to which she herself belongs; the Lineweavers, whose spinningwork she imitates in her netted maze of crossed lines; and the Tubeweavers, whose snare is represented by the structure just described. See also Fig. 123, g.

Distribution. The distribution of Epeira triaranea has not been very satisfactorily determined; but it probably inhabits all the northern, central, and northern-southern portions of our continent between the two oceans. It has been located by collection in New England, the Middle and Western States, Utah, and Santa Cruz, California.

Epeira thaddeus. Among the spinners of sectoral orbs is Epeira thaddeus Hentz. In size and habit it closely resembles Triaranea and weaves a similar orb. As far as my observations extend it affects wooded locations more persistently than Triaranea, or at least shuns the neighborhood of human habitations. It is inclined to screen itself beneath a curled leaf or within a leafy tent, and in such sites spins a strong silken tubular nest within which it dwells, holding to the trapline of its snare. The maze of right lines in the midst of which Triaranea hangs her bell shaped nest is wanting from the web of Thaddeus. These are the chief variations in general habit and spinningwork between the two spiders.

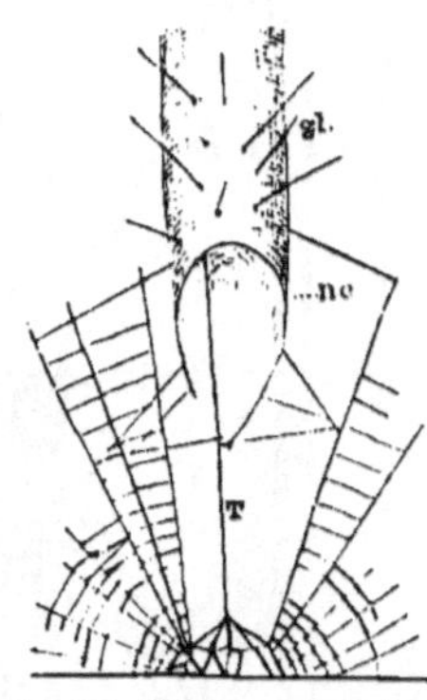

FIG. 132. Tubular gangway (n.c) between the tent and orb of Triaranea. g.l., guy lines supporting tube.

Distribution. Thaddeus is widely distributed, its southern locations being Alabama, South Carolina, as far as to Enterprise, Florida; northward it has been found in New England, Wisconsin; and in the Middle States at least to the prairies. It probably has range over the entire Atlantic slope and Mississippi Valley.

III.

During the winter of 1882–3 Mrs. Rosa Smith Eigenmann sent me from San Diego, in the extreme southern part of California, a few spiders, among which were several of a species which proved to be Zilla x-notata. **The Snares of Zilla.** In subsequent correspondence I ascertained that the snare of this aranead was distinguished by a free sector, and several cocoons were forwarded, from which I succeeded in raising fine broods of younglings. These I located upon plants and various elevated objects within a warm room, and as they freely spun their characteristic orbs I soon had a number for study, of which an example is figured. Fig. 133 was spun underneath the handle of a small basket, and is drawn natural size. The spirals were carried around in loops, quite as represented; the hub was meshed and surrounded by a notched zone. A bit of cotton cord that clung to the handle had been utilized as a support for the foundation line on one side (on the right of the cut), and within a scant series of cross-lines at the top a slight nest had been woven in which the little Zilla rested. Her feet clasped a trapline attached to the hub by a deltated

Fig. 133. Sectoral orb of young Zilla x-notata, woven under a basket handle. Natural size.

terminus. The free space was decidedly marked, as it was in most of the orbs made.

My first opportunity to study Zilla in a natural site (uncolonized) happened to be upon the grounds of Mr. F. M. Campbell, at Hoddesdon, Hartz, England. Later I noted the snares of great numbers of the genus in the highlands of Scotland, particularly in the neighborhood of Loch Achray and Loch Katrine. One especially interesting colony was located at the sluices which regulate the flow of water from Loch Katrine. A footwalk crosses the stream, along which are short iron posts and an iron rail. Vast numbers of Zilla had settled along the cornices and panels of these posts, and from their nesting places had

A Scotch Colony.

stretched their characteristic webs diagonally across to the hand rail. It thus happened that as many as a dozen or fifteen snares would be built out from the same cornice or moulding, their upper foundations occupying the same horizontal plane, but diminishing in length as they approached the angle made by the post and the hand rail. The wedge shaped space thus defined was almost completely filled with spinningwork, the orbs varying a good deal in size, but being alike in structure.

The position was a good one for trapping insects, which fly in vast numbers over the surface of the streams, but I could not but wonder whether some of the spiders occupying the interior snares were not sore put to it to pick up an honest living, and might not have been constrained to resort to cannibalism. However, I saw no raids "ower the border," notwithstanding the traditions of the Scottish site, but all the aranead clans seemed to be dwelling in peace.

I had a fine opportunity one summer of studying the spinning habit of Zilla atrica at Annisquam, Massachusetts. Many of this species were colonized upon the spacious grounds and surroundings of the place where I was lodged. They were domiciled upon the chicken coops and outbuildings, upon the shrubbery, and in considerable numbers upon the boat house on the very verge of the inlet. In the latter position their snares were swung just above the point of high tide, and they were very busy capturing the insects that flew around and above the water, and defending themselves from vigorous colonies of Epeira patagiata domiciled in the same site.

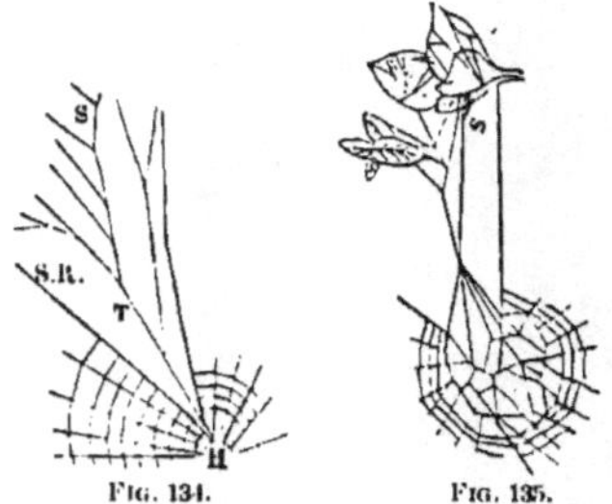

FIGS. 134, 135. Complex or branched traplines of Zilla. S, the spider; S.R., sectoral radius.

Zilla atrica.

I noticed an occasional tendency among these Zillas to spin a full round orb. For example, in one colony of fourteen, all the nests were sectoral except one. In another of fifteen, fourteen were sectoral, and one had a complete orb. I could observe no obvious reason from the nature of the location why this difference should appear. It evidently is characteristic of the genus. Zilla callophyla, a European species, can usually be recognized among the British Orbweavers by the open sector, which characterizes its web. This peculiarity, however, does not always exist, as webs formed by young individuals, probably of the same brood, are occasionally found within a short distance of each other, some with the characteristic free radii, others constructed after the usual Epeira type.[1] There appears, thus, in both hemispheres to be a tendency in this genus to revert to the typical round

Exceptional Round Webs.

[1] Staveley, "British Spiders." page 247.

web of the Orbitelariæ; or, shall we say, a tendency to run tangent from its own typical form into that of the established type of Epeira? On one small bush, where perhaps a dozen Zilla atricas were domiciled, I found no less than four orbs with completely rounded webs. In one of these, a very rare circumstance indeed, I found that the trapline occupied a sector below the median line of the web. In this interblending of spinning habit Zilla shows the peculiarity already noted in the closely related species of the genus Epeira, Epeira triaranea.

This colony afforded some very interesting illustrations of the strong tendency to variation in the manner of forming the trapline. Ordinarily, as has been shown, the trapline of orbwebs consists of a single cord, which connects the hub of the orb with the feet of the spider lodged **Trapline Variations.** in her retreat above and at the side of her snare. As a rule, the end which is attached to the hub divides into several branches, obviously giving greater facility in the way of telegraphy. Sometimes one or more branches will be observed near the feet of the spider, where she clasps the trapline. But generally one fore foot reaches out and holds the single line within the claws. In the case of the Labyrinth spider, the trap line consists of a number of threads which diverge near the point where they are clasped by the foot, and converge toward the hub, and thus reverse the ordinary rule in the genus Epeira. The single trapline is probably the one most commonly used by Zilla, but the series of drawings presented will show how widely she can depart from this habit. Fig. 134, for example, shows the trapline with a number of diverging lines toward the foot of the spider at S, the whole system forking about the middle of the line, T, and being supported by another Y-shaped line still nearer to the hub. At Fig. 135 the trapline has

Fig. 136. Branched trapline system of Zilla.

assumed the rude outline of an hour glass. Five or six deltations grasp the meshed hub, and these lines converge about the middle of the trapline system, from which point they diverge toward the spider's nest and the surrounding leaves, upon which the snare is supported. The feet of the spider at S are extended beyond the leafy nest, and grasp at least two lines of the system. Fig. 136 shows still further divergence from the original type. Here the hour glass, if I may continue the figure, appears to have been cut into two, and the ends well separated by a bent line, in the midst of which is a triangular patch swung to adjoining leaves. The two fore feet of the proprietor are thrust from her tubular nest and grasp the principal diverging lines of her system.

I have observed similar arrangements in the trapline system of Epeira domiciliorum whose orbs were swung upon a barbed wire fence inclosing the grounds of Woodland Cemetery. The question, of course, naturally arose, what has caused this divergence from the typical single line? I am rather inclined to think that it is accidental, resulting probably from the breakage and pulling out into irregular forms of the original thread, and the efforts of the spider to repair it without reconstructing her snare. Its telegraphic efficiency is probably thereby impaired.

IV.

Nephila plumipes[1] is the largest of our indigenous Orbweavers, and is, perhaps, our most decided representative of tropical spider fauna. Some examples of the genus Nephila in the collection of the Academy of Natural Sciences of Philadelphia, from Africa,[2] have reached an immense size. **Distribution of Nephila plumipes.** Their webs are formidable impediments when stretched across paths and among forest trees, even to human passengers. I know of but one species in the United States, and for much of our knowledge of this we are indebted to the intelligent studies of Professor Bert Wilder, M. D. While stationed on the Southern Atlantic coast as an army surgeon during the war of the Rebellion, he became especially interested in this creature, and published various papers descriptive of his observations. The chief habitat of Nephila, as Prof. Wilder found,[3] is Long Island, a low, narrow uninhabited strip of land about five miles southwest of Charleston, South Carolina, covered with palmetto and pine trees, surrounded on all sides by creeks, and in the midst of a great salt marsh. During a two years' stay on the coast and in the interior of South Carolina and Florida he never met with any traces of Nephila elsewhere than near this island, except a specimen found upon Folly Island, and a cocoon found in a tree on James Island. He had not observed it

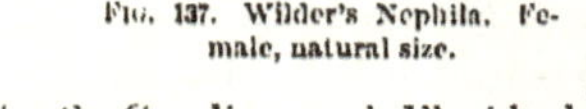

Fig. 137. Wilder's Nephila. Female, natural size.

[1] Prof. Thorell expressed the opinion, on the strength of specimens sent to him, that our American Nephila is a different species from N. plumipes. I propose for it the name of N. wilderi, in recognition of the gentleman who has made its habits so well known, should the suggestion prove to be well founded.

[2] Collected in Zululand by Rev. Mr. Grout; some also from Liberia.

[3] Proceedings Boston Natural History Society, Vol. X., page 205, 1865.

on any of the adjoining islands, although there appears no physical reason why the species should not occur all along the seaboard.[1]

The female is a beautiful, as well as large, spider. The body is over an inch long and the longitudinal spread of the legs is nearly four inches. The cephalothorax is jet black above, but covered, except in spots, with silver colored hairs. The abdomen is not oval but cylindrical in shape, the length much greater than the width. In color it is olive brown, a light yellow above, and variously marked with yellow and white spots and stripes. The legs are yellow, with dull red annuli and feet. The first two and the fourth pairs have at the tips of the femur and tibia strong hair brushes or feathery tufts to which the best known species of the genus owes its name—plumipes, featherfoot, or plumefoot. The male, like that of Argiope, is very small in comparison with his mate, who is four or five times larger than he. He is not more than a quarter of an inch long and is of uniform dull brown color.

Prof. Wilder found the spiders in forests spinning their webs between trees and **Nephila's Snare.** shrubs, sometimes within reach, but oftener ten or fifteen feet or even more from the ground where the sunlight could strike them. The orb varies from one foot to three or four feet in diameter, as large as a wagon wheel. It is composed of two kinds of silk, of which one is white or silver gray, inelastic and perfectly dry. To this belong the

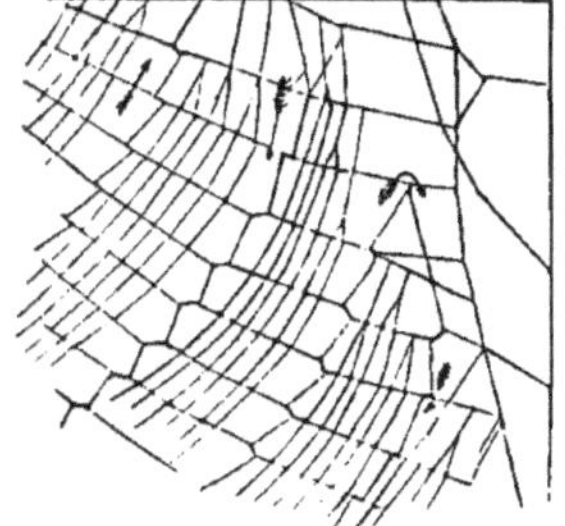
Fig. 138. Section of the orb of Nephila. (After Wilder.)

radii, foundation lines and retitelarian supports. The spirals, on the contrary, are a bright yellow or golden hue and very elastic. This **Golden Strands.** is a remarkable peculiarity, which I have never seen but once, in an exceptional case of the web of the Furrow spider woven in captivity. This had a bright, golden yellow color, which continued throughout several months, during which I preserved the web. I attribute this phenomenal appearance to some abnormal condition of the spinning organs, by which the glands that furnish the flossy, yellowish silk used for blanketing the cocoon and for winter covering, had been required to secrete material for snare weaving. But with Nephila the yellow secretion appears to be habitually used for the viscid spirals. This color marks the webs of the genus generally, as described by Vinson (of African spiders) and others.

The spiral scaffolding, however, is spun of white silk, and is not removed after the completion of the spirals, an exception to the habit of

[1] I have had specimens from Florida.

Orbweavers. Each concentric of the scaffolding, which is marked by the arrows in the figure (Fig. 138), makes a marked division between the intermediary spirals, which are thus divided into groups or bands, adding much to the peculiar form of the snare.

Wilder states [1] that the free sector or space uncovered by beaded spirals in the snare of Nephila, in natural site is equal on an average to about one-sixth the surface of the orb. He, however, gives a drawing of a web made by a spider in captivity upon a circular wire frame, which has a free sector equal to two-thirds of the orb.[2] (Fig. 139.) No doubt this abnormal form was due to the artificial conditions under which the spider plied her industry. Prof. Wilder is sufficiently explicit in his

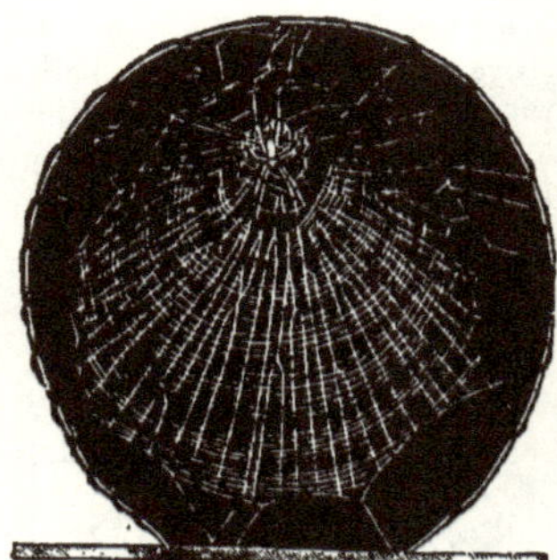

Fig. 139. Snare of Nephila, woven on a wire hoop. (After Wilder.)

description to allow us to present the diagramatic or restored web, Fig. 140, as approaching the characteristic form in natural site.[3] It thus closely approximates that of Epeira triaranea and Zilla. The spirals do not form complete circles, but are looped across the radii, in a manner already described, and in spinning them the spider does not move around the web, but returns upon her course from one side to a corresponding point on the other. The web thus made is strong enough to support a light straw hat when hung upon it.

Gosse speaks of the immense snares of Nephila as one of the obstructions to free travel in the woods of Jamaica. These, he says, are infested with the great long bodied spider with brush tufted

Jamaica Nephila: Gosse.

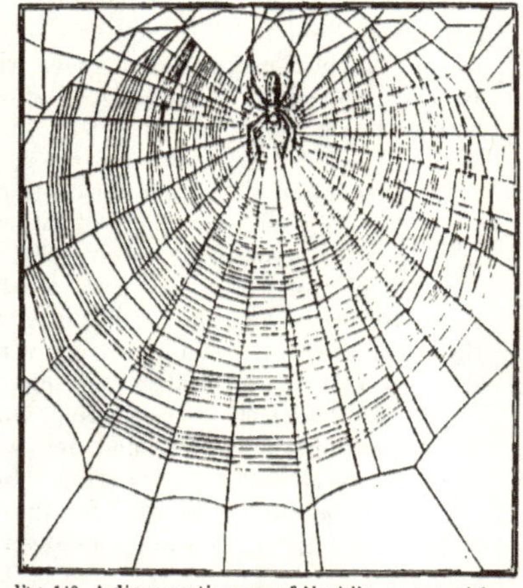

Fig. 140. A diagramatic snare of Nephila, composed from the descriptions and sketches of Prof. Wilder.

---

[1] Proceedings American Association, 1873, page 265.

[2] This has led Emerton, Structure and Habits of Spiders, page 66, to the erroneous statement that her snare "consists of loops running round about quarter of a circle."

[3] Prof. Wilder, in his paper, Proceedings American Association, 1873, page 272; also Galaxy, page 111, 1869, and on the Triangle Spider, Popular Science Monthly, page 653, 1875, gives an outline cut of Plumefoot's orb, which corresponds with that of Fig. 140.

feet, Nephila clavipes. If one succeeds in pushing his way with much difficulty through the briers, his face is pretty sure to come into contact with the strong threads of these spiders, which are spread over the bushes and between trees along the roadside. The web is perpendicular, the part on which the spider sits, head downward, is geometric, but this is surrounded on all sides by a vast array of irregular lines, the frame of which consists of compound threads, stretching from the surrounding trees and shrubs. Some of these threads are twelve feet long, of a yellow color, and nearly as thick as sewing silk; Mr. Gosse found them able to resist a great pressure without breaking; but thought it utterly improbable that the rapid and powerful flight of even the most minute hummingbird could be for a moment arrested by the web of this or any other spider.[1]

[1] P. H. Gosse, "Naturalist's Sojourn in Jamaica," page 240.

CHAPTER IX.

HORIZONTAL SNARES AND DOMED ORBS.

I.

Hortorum and Gibberosa. The Orbwebs heretofore considered all belong to the general division described as vertical orbwebs. The snares to be considered in this chapter are known as horizontal orbs. The horizontal orbweb in all essential particulars is woven like the vertical orb and differs chiefly in the fact that it is usually hung wholly or partly in a horizontal position.

In the species making vertical webs, the habit is so firmly fixed that the spiders rarely deviate therefrom, and never, except under circumstances which constrain a departure. Nevertheless, it is interesting to remark that sometimes they do spin orbs that more or less approximate the horizontal. Occasionally these orbs are entirely horizontal. For example, I have known a brood of young Epeira sclopetaria, freshly escaped from the cocoon, to spin upon the same object minute orbs, some of which were vertical, while others were as truly horizontal as though they had been made by a species that habitually weaves an orb of that sort. Fig. 141. It was not difficult for me to determine that these individuals were influenced to an abnormal act by the conditions under which they wrought. It was comparatively easy for them to get foundation lines so placed that a horizontal web almost inevitably resulted; while, on the other hand, the frames for a vertical web could not have been obtained except with the greatest difficulty. Yet, in the case of a few of the same brood nearly as great difficulties were overcome, and a vertical web was made. For example, the little fellows in the cut (Fig. 141) found it easy to weave an orb horizontally around the metal frame that supports the lamp chimney, and this they did. But others followed the specific habit and sent down lines to the table, making a triangular frame and a vertical orb within it.

Variations in the Orb Plane.

So, too, it may be said that spiders which make horizontal snares are sometimes constrained by difficulties of the site chosen to deviate more or less from the horizontal plane. Indeed, I have seen the orb of Tetragnatha inclined at almost every angle, and occasionally have found it spun in an absolutely vertical position.

Such are the facts in the case. Whether this accidental tendency on both sides to vary the habitual position of the snare may have laid the foundation upon which has been developed the permanent habit which we are now to consider, is a point which others, perhaps, may be able to settle, to their own satisfaction at least. To my mind, the difficulties of originating a fixed habit from such an accidental variation are so formidable that they seem practically insurmountable. In addition to these is the difficulty of explaining why the same accidental variation, appearing with equal frequency in many species, should have succeeded in fixing itself upon a few species alone?

Development.

In the United States the spiders which habitually are found upon horizontal snares are Argyroepeira hortorum, Epeira gibberosa, and the various species of the genus Tetragnatha, and the several species of Uloborus. For reasons which will hereafter be explained I do not include the last named species within the group to be described in this chapter.

Argyroepeira hortorum, or the Orchard spider of Hentz,[1] is one of the most beautiful of our indigenous species, presenting in its varied green, yellow, and metallic silver colors all the characteristics of some of the brightest tropical species.

Orchard Spider.

It is widely distributed, probably throughout the entire United States, and is thus equally at home in the cold climate of New England and the winterless regions of the South. Its web is usually found in low

FIG. 111. Varied orbs of a colony of spiderlings.

---

[1] Epeira hortorum Hentz, "Spiders of the United States;" Argyroepeira hortorum Emerton, "New England Epeiridae," page 333.

situations, spun upon branches and stalks of tall weeds and grasses, or in the lower branches of shrubs, bushes, and trees. The orb is frequently quite round, indeed is habitually round when spun in open spaces where the spider's action is unfettered. An adult spider's orb has an average diameter of from eight to nine inches. The spirals and radii are closely placed and average in number about thirty. The hub is open and the spider has its position just beneath, clinging back downward to the margin of the hub or to the notched zone immediately surrounding it. The abdomen is often turned upward almost at right angles to the cephalothorax, and is stayed by a line attached to the orb above. Fig. 142.

From the foundation lines of the orb downward there usually extends a mass of crossed lines, which may be called the apron. These are thick-est upon two sides, although sometimes they extend entirely

Protect- ive Apron.

around, giving the whole mass of spinningwork the appearance of a hemisphere with the circular plane upwards, or of an inverted cone. The purpose of this apron is evidently protective, as it must shield the spider from assaults of enemies that would be inclined to strike her as she hangs beneath her orb. Spiders occupying vertical orbs which for the most part are swung upon foliage and other objects which form a background, are tolerably secure against attack from that quarter at least.

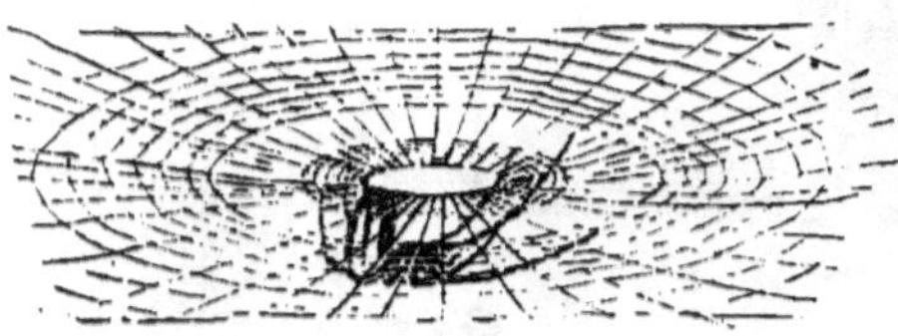

Fig. 142. Position of Orchard spider on its orb.

But the weavers of horizontal orbs have no such natural local protection. Hence it is the more needful that they should manufacture one for themselves. The apron may also stay the foundation lines that support the delicate work of the orb itself, and perhaps protects it from the approach of insects who would break through without giving the spider an opportunity to catch them. It doubtless also serves for the arrest of insects, as I have found flies entangled upon the threads. It may thus, as in the case of the Labyrinth spider, be of some benefit to the occupant in the way of providing food. But for this the principal reliance is of course upon the orb, and the chief supply is from those insects that strike it as they fly downward. The outside foundation lines, to which the horizontal orb is hung, are sometimes of considerable length; I have found them thirty-six inches long. Fig. 143 is an accurate representation of the foundation system of the Orchard spider, and also a section of the snare showing the spiral system as well as the central space. The lines are drawn vertically, but, of course, the reader will understand that they are to be considered as spun horizontally as they were in nature. A little better view of the central space is shown at Fig. 144 where the delicate arrangement of the unbeaded and notched spirals one is represented. If one will imagine a web thus constituted throughout the entire orbicular space, and hung in a pretty site among meadow plants or wild flowers, he will have a true conception of the delicate beauty of this work of aranead art.

In appearance the orb resembles that of Acrosoma. **Orb Characteristics.** The open hub, the numerous spirals, and the numerous and delicately spun radii and beaded spirals are characteristic of Hortorum, as they are of Acrosoma. But I have never seen in Hortorum any of the ribboned decorations which mark the spinning-work of Acrosoma. The free space also is decided in Hortorum, but small or lacking in Acrosoma. When disturbed the spider usually runs along the dragline to which she hangs underneath

Fig. 113.   Section of foundation lines and orb of the Orchard spider.   Natural size.

the hub, to the remotest part of her foundation lines, with which the dragline is generally connected. She remains stationary at her point of refuge, or hides beneath a leaf, or sometimes drops to the earth.

I have never seen the snare of Hortorum in a vertical position, and have rarely noticed it inclined in any degree from the horizontal; but have record of one web that inclined about forty-five degrees. In this orb the foundation lines were attached to the leaves of a plant eighteen inches high,

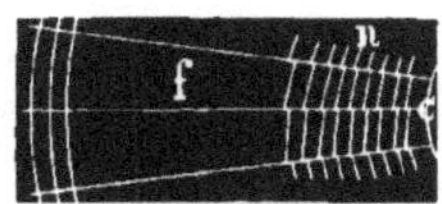

Fig. 114.   Central section of Orchard spider's orb. f, free space; n, notched zone; c, open hub.

upon which the snare was hung. From these, retitelarian lines were carried downward to an adjoining tree, making a rude appearance of an inverted pyramid. This apron was not carried up close to the orb, but separated from it about the distance of five or six inches. This is the ordinary position of the apron, and in this respect is quite analogous to the corresponding situation of orb and labyrinth in the snare of Epeira labyrinthea. Indeed, it may be said as a general fact that in all orbweaving species which make a composite web, either habitually or occasionally, the mass of crossed lines is separated by a little space from the orbicular part of the snare. This is the case with the protective wings of Argiope, which are always so placed as to leave free action for the spider as she moves back and forward between the orb and the retitelarian lines on either side.

Epeira gibberosa, the Hunchback spider, closely resembles Hortorum in the sites selected for her snare. Like Hortorum the species is probably dis-**Epeira gibberosa** tributed throughout the entire United States. I have collected it in Florida, in the border and Middle States, and in New England, and have specimens from Wisconsin, but none further to the west or northwest. Its snare rarely diverges from the horizontal plane, and is like the Orchard spider's in every respect, except that I have never found it with the apron or protecting maze of crossed lines. Instead of this, however, the spider has the habit of making for herself a netted hammock of lines stretched between leaves of the plant up on or near which her orb is spun. (Fig. 145.) This hammock is sometimes woven between the pulled up edges of one leaf, as may be seen figured in the chapter upon Nesting Habits. Underneath this hammock the Hunchback hangs back downward, holding to a trapline which is attached, at the opposite end, to the central part of her snare. In this respect her habit is related to that of the Shamrock and Insular spiders and others of that

Fig. 145. The hammock nest of the Hunchback spider.

group. Sometimes she forsakes this position and hangs like Hortorum underneath her orb, and sometimes I have found her thereon **Her Ham-mock.** without any such associated hammock nest. Gibberosa appears to be less timid in disposition than Hortorum. At least, when touched by my pencil, the Orchard spider would invariably swing away from her position or crawl off to the outlying foundation lines. The Hunchback, on the contrary, instead of forsaking her position, would only turn around, shake her body, or jerk her trapline in a nervous manner. Gibberosa lacks the bright silver markings of Hortorum, but keeps the general green hue of legs and body, the color, however, being somewhat darker.

II.

The genus Tetragnatha furnishes some of the most familiar and interesting species of spiders making a horizontal snare. Our two most common species in the Eastern United States, and probably throughout the whole continent, are Tetragnatha extensa and T. grallator. The former species has been supposed to be an importation from Europe. It is impossible, of

Tetragnatha. course, to determine whether this is so or not, for the species is so widely distributed, over the greater part of the continent in fact, that the probabilities are that its life in North America antedates the period of European communication. My collections and specimens range from Canada, Connecticut, and Massachusetts to Florida, on the eastern shore; to Texas on the south and southwest; and on the Pacific coast as far northward as Vancouver Island, and southward to San Diego, at the extreme border of California. Emerton has collected it on the White Mountains of New England and

Fig. 146. Tetragnatha extended on a twig.

along the seaboard, and Dr. Marx has specimens ranging from Fort Simms,

Distribution. Labrador, to Florida, and westward and northwest through Kansas, Alaska, and the Aleutian Islands. As the species is widely distributed throughout the continent of Europe, and is probably found in Asia as well, it is easy to see that it might have been transported without the aid of human ships, simply by the agency of the winds, either from America to Europe, or from Europe to America. The original centre of the species, if one is to suppose an original centre at all, cannot, therefore, be positively determined. It is a spider of delicate greenish and yellow colors, and appears to be rather delicately organized, notwithstanding the formidable jaws which characterize it in common with its congeners, and to which its generic name is due. (Fig. 147.) Nevertheless, it has

Fig. 147. The jaws and mouth parts of Tetragnatha.

been able to find and hold a habitat amid the most diverse climatic extremes, and in establishing itself has crossed continents, lofty mountain ranges, and oceans.

Tetragnatha extensa is a spider which when once seen cannot easily be mistaken for another. It well deserves its name of "extensa," or the extended spider, for its abdomen is in the shape of a rather narrow cylinder, is greatly extended, as compared with the cephalothorax, and it has the habit of stretching its front legs forward, its hind legs backward until, together with the long body, the entire spider is drawn out into a straight band and forms a peculiar vision, which the observer is apt to bear in mind. The colors of Extensa vary a good deal, but for the most part the cephalothorax is pale white and yellowish. The abdomen is delicate yellow, tinted with shades of green, and has a fine branching black line running down the middle of the dorsum. The sides are finely reticulated, and the under part has a dark band down the middle with green on each side.

It loves the neighborhood of water, but is found distributed widely throughout the meadows and in the foliage of bushes and low trees. Its snare is of a delicate texture, finely spun, as a rule, but oftentimes short and straggling. It is placed either in a vertical, horizontal, or inclined position, but its general habit is horizontal, and with this class of Orb-makers I have placed it. It is armed with a pair of formidable jaws, whose immense teeth and long fangs would appear to give it a great advantage in its conflicts with enemies and efforts to secure food.

In construction the orb of Tetragnatha extensa, as well as all other species of the genus, corresponds very closely with that of the Orchard spider. The hub is open, and a series of notched concentrics follows; then comes the free space; then the spiral space, the foundation space, and the foundation lines.[1]

The position of Tetragnatha is underneath the central part of her snare. Her body is usually stretched across the open hub. The legs do not radiate from the body at open angles, but are drawn very close to the cephalothorax at the fore part, and to the abdomen at the hinder part of the body. The fore feet clasp the radii at or beyond the notched zone, or one foot holds fast to a line which is stretched to the under part of the web and bows downward to the foot. The abdomen, as in the case of the Orchard spider, is hitched by a similar line to the orb. In this position the spider sometimes swings almost free from direct contact with her snare. The fore legs touch or approximate near the middle, and the feet are curved outward. In spite of its somewhat awkward appearance, Tetragnatha is remarkably lively in its movements.

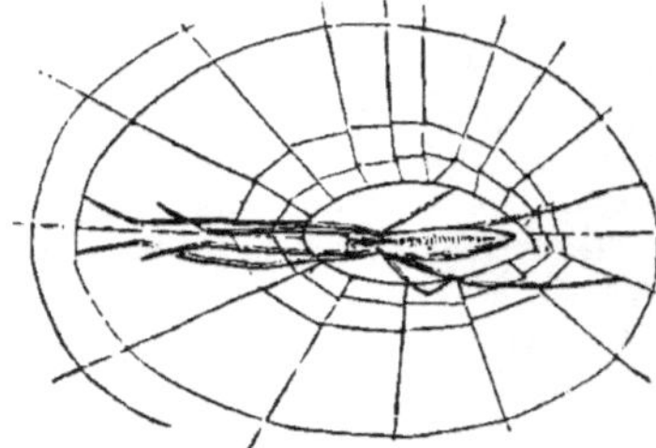

Fig. 118. Tetragnatha outstretched beneath the hub of her snare.

Position on the Orb.

When alarmed, Extensa runs down into the weeds or grass, and stretches herself along the stem on which she has found refuge. Her legs hug her body closely, even more closely than when suspended to her web as just described. As her entire body is of a greenish yellow color, not greatly different from that of the plant, it is somewhat difficult to distinguish her from the stem on which she rests. This peculiarity is well known among observers of the species wherever it is found, and is cited as one of the examples of protective form mimicry.

[1] *Description of Orbs.* No. 1. Vertical; 5 x 4 in.; n. z., ¼ x ¼ in.; f. z., ⅜ x ⅜ in.; hub irregular meshed work. No. 2. 5 x 5 about; f. z., ½ to ¾ in.; hub open, with few irregular threads. No. 3. Nearly vertical; 3 n. sp.; r. 16; sp. 21 below, 15 above. No. 4. Horizontal; 4½ x 5 in.; r. 22, sp. 13 and less above; n. z., ¼ x ½; f. z., ¼ x ⅞; open hub. Nos. 5, 6, 7. Orb inclined about 45°; small, 3 to 5 in. in diam. Several orbs 2 in. diam.

The next most common species of Tetragnatha is the Stilt spider,
Tetragnatha grallator Hentz.[1] In color the adult is not so brilliant as
The Stilt Spider. Extensa, being a dull gray; but in its general form, habits, and
the structure of its web it corresponds with Extensa, but is
larger, darker, and less attractive in appearance when adult. It
differs, also, in its greater fondness for a location near or over water. Its
webs are frequently seen stretched above the surface of running streams.
In pools, in the quiet nooks of brooklets and creeks, where branches droop
down from the banks and overhang the water, I often find a colony of

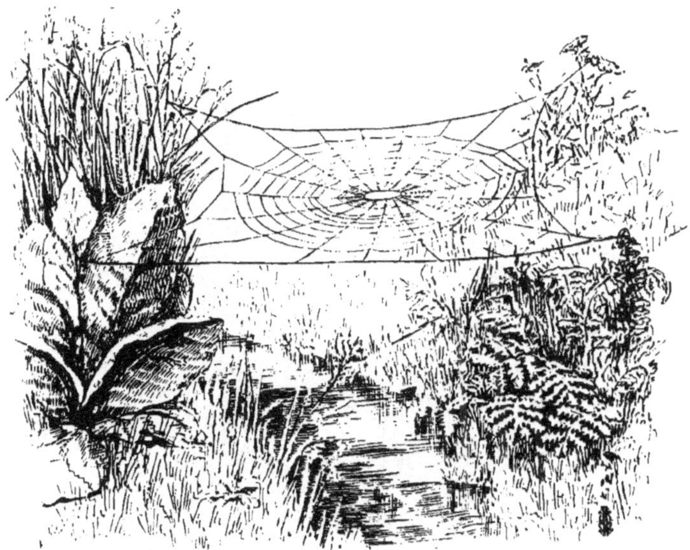

Fig. 149. Horizontal orb of the Stilt spider, stretched above a brooklet (Doe's Run).

Stilt spiders that have spun their horizontal orbs upon the leaves and
twigs close down to the water's face. As the wind moves the branches
to and fro the webs almost dip into the stream beneath. Here the creatures hang and prey upon the insects that always frequent such sites in
great numbers and hover over the stream. (Fig. 149.)

Another favorite position is underneath the boards and cross logs of

[1] T. elongata Walck., Nat. Hist. d. Ins. Apt., ii., page 211. Dr. Thorell has little doubt
that Hentz's species T. grallator is identical with Walckenaer's T. elongata. See "Araneæ
of Colorado," Bulletin U. S. Geolog. Surv., 1877, page 479.

mill races. I recall one such site at Bellwood in the Allegheny Mountains, where very many Stilt spiders were thus located, and had found it so admirable a feeding ground that they had grown to large proportions. Some of the orbs were fourteen inches in diameter. (Fig. 150.)

With this fondness for the water are associated some most interesting habits which especially adapt the Stilt spider for its favorite site. One of these was observed in individuals of the Bellwood colony above **Walking the Water.** mentioned. The webs were stretched between boards laid on narrow beams as a gangway across the mill race near the sluice gate, and also from these boards to the sides of the race itself. While studying them I was often compelled to disturb the spiders. They

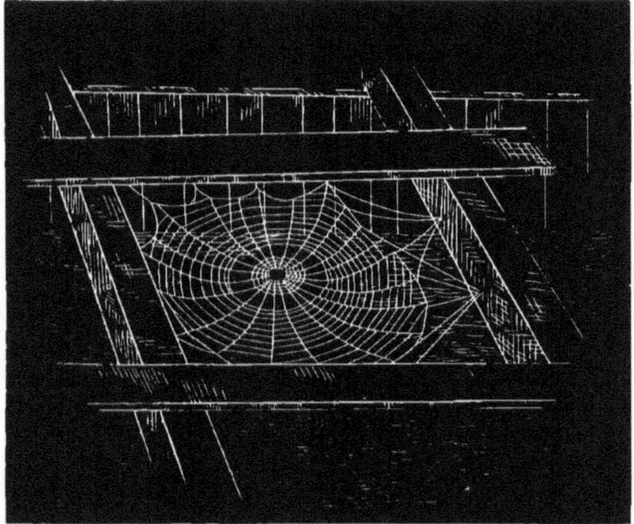

Fig. 150. The Stilt spider's web beneath logs.

ran from the centre of their large orbs and took shelter on the sides of the cross beams or underneath the boards. If still further disturbed, they would sometimes drop by a dragline from the lower surface of the plank and hang with their legs stretched out straight, fore and aft, in the characteristic position already described as assumed by them when resting along a branch or other surface. In this posture they would hang motionless for some time. (See Fig. 151, left hand of cut.)

On one occasion, while attempting to seize one of these individuals, she dropped downward suddenly for several feet. I was not surprised at this motion, for it is the one resorted to by alarmed Orbweavers when they precipitate themselves from their snares to the ground. I prepared to draw my specimen upward by her dragline, feeling sure that I would certainly capture her, when, to my amazement, she threw herself upon the surface of the water, a distance of eight or ten feet. I looked to see her drown, or at least to be swept away through the open sluice gate by the fast rushing stream. Neither of these things happened. The moment our Stilt spider struck the water she reached upward one hind leg, clasped the dragline in her claw, and began to scurry over the mill race toward the shore.

A Spider Sailor.

I watched the movement with exceeding interest, and was delighted to see the adventurer reach her destination. (See Fig. 151, right hand figure.) The dragline, partly by its natural elasticity, but also because the spider probably reeled out thread as she traveled, continued to stretch as the spider moved toward the shore. It thus held her firmly anchored to the surface of the plank to which her dragline was attached, so that the force of the current, thus counteracted, did not sweep her through the open sluice over the shoot. In the meantime her feet were kept in motion, and she appeared to me to be walking the water in the manner of certain so-called " water spiders," belonging to the genera Dolomedes and Lycosa of the Citigrades. It certainly is an interesting fact in the natural history of an orbweaving spider, that it possesses a habit so closely resembling one characteristic of a tribe widely separated from it in nearly every other respect.

Fig. 151. Tetragnatha hanging extended, and running on water.

The outspun filaments that serve the spider for navigating the air are also utilized for propulsion over the water. In one case they serve as a balloon, in the other as a sail. This discovery was made on a pleasant October day while walking along the shore of Deal Lake, Asbury Park, New Jersey.[1] I stopped before a clump of tall grass that grew upon a little tongue of land that jutted into the lake, in order to shake down from the foliage any spiders who might for the time be domiciled thereon. The especial object of my search was water frequenting species, particularly the common Dolomede (Dolomedes sexpunctatus), whose mode of run-

Navigating Water

[1] October 21st, 1881. I believe that I have the honor to be the first person who observed, or at least announced, this interesting behavior. See a note published in "The Continent," Philadelphia, August 2d, 1882.

ning over water, and behavior when cast upon water, I wished to observe. The beaten marsh grass yielded me no Dolomedes, but instead several half grown Tetragnatha vermiformis, Emerton, dropped upon the surface. To my surprise they seemed not the least disconcerted, but immediately recovered themselves and with one exception ran to the shore precisely as do the Lycosids. The excepted individual had been thrown out from the bank farther than its comrades. For a moment it paused, its body bowed and held upward upon the eight legs which were spread out so that the feet marked the outline of a rude circle upon the surface. Then it started rapidly across the mouth of a tiny baylet between a tongue of the land and the main shore, traversed the intervening space, and pulled itself to the land by the overhanging grass. My attention was attracted by the remarkable fact that during this transit there was no appreciable movement of the legs. That an Orbweaver should be able to glide so rapidly and gracefully over water was a fact in itself sufficiently new to me; but that one should do this without any physical exertion whatever amazed me. Could the action of the air upon the body have been the impelling force?

I addressed myself eagerly to the solution of this mystery. A second clump of grasses was beaten, and a Tetragnatha fell upon the lake. She ran over the water to the shore, using apparently her fore legs as paddles. Before she climbed into the grasses I thrust my cane under her body, gently lifted her up, and reaching outward as far as I could, gradually sunk the tip of the stick into the water without causing any ruffling of the surface. The spider was thus eased off the stick and placed upon

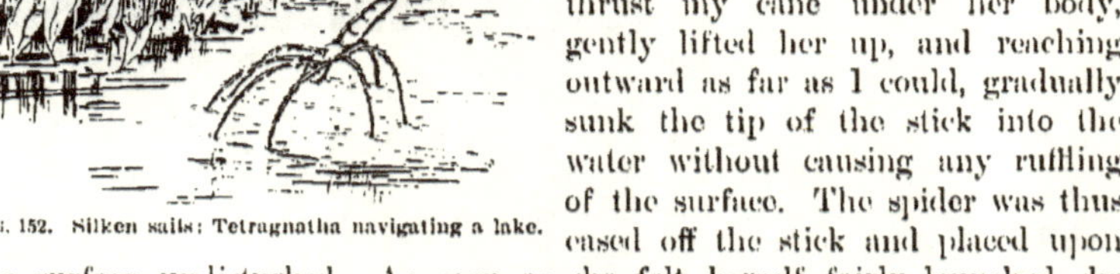

Fig. 152. Silken sails: Tetragnatha navigating a lake.

the surface undisturbed. As soon as she felt herself fairly launched she made a few strokes with her fore feet, then suddenly paused and thrust the apex of her abdomen down to the surface. Directly, the abdomen was raised from the water and turned up until it made an angle of about 60° with the surface. Next a long streamer of silk filaments was emitted from the spinnerets, precisely as in the case of aeronautic spiders when about to ascend, and immediately the spider began to scud at a great rate over the water. The mysterious motor was thus revealed--the silken threads served as sails upon which the wind played, propelling the vital craft across the water.

The discovery into which I was thus accidentally led was so interesting that I devoted the remainder of my day to the full investigation of the habit of navigation by means of filament sails. The first experiment was repeated a number of times with various details upon several spiders, and always with the same result. The gossamer thread was undoubt-

Sails of Silk Filaments. edly used as a sail, and the action of the wind bore the little navigator to the shore. I frequently blew the tiny craft out to sea, either with my breath or by fanning with my hat. My stick could at any time arrest the thread by placing it a foot or more above the spider, and having entangled it, I could draw her thereby in any direction. The filament was plainly seen floating above the spider, waving to and fro, generally bending above her back.

The legs during motion were raised upward and bowed, thus holding the body well up from the surface, exactly in the attitude of a spider about to take aeronautic flight. They were kept quite rigid and motionless. The feet were spread out, describing the outline of an irregular octagon. I fancied that they were united by threads and that thus the spider sat upon a delicate raft of silk. Before spreading her sails the first act of the spider was to drop the abdomen to the surface, at which moment, I inferred, an attachment to the legs was made. I can hardly bring myself to believe that the threads were attached to the water, although it may so have been.

While the spider was un-

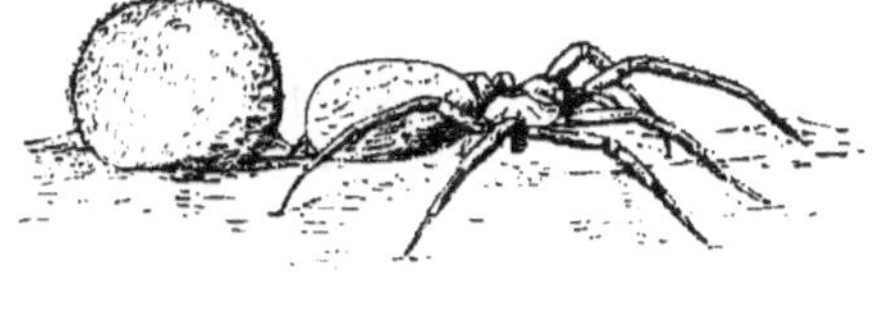

Fig. 153. Epeira using her cocoon as a float.

der sail the feet made a very noticeable ripple of wavelets as they were hurried along. She could accomplish short distances from the shore by running, without spreading sail, but when put well out she always resorted to the latter mode. However, any floating object which she met during the voyage was pretty sure to be taken advantage of as convenient harborage. A downy seed which fell upon the water and drifted within reach of one of my aranead sailors was immediately seized by the creature's fore feet, the spinnerets were set in motion, and the seed was overspun with a delicate floss, which converted it into a sort of float.

In this connection I record an incident which may throw some light upon the development among Orbweavers of this interesting water habit. A large

Epeira and Her Float. female Epeira sclopetaria was collected, along with an abandoned cocoon, behind which it had spent the winter, at Atlantic City. The spider was accidentally dropped into the Inlet, together with the flossy ball of the cocoon. She immediately threw out threads around the ball (Fig. 153), to which she remained attached as to a buoy, and thus the two drifted along safely under the floor of a boat house and so out of sight. One associates such an action with the water walking and navigating of Tetragnatha, and wonders whether Epeira could ever, under favorable environment, develop like behavior. Moreover, the query arises, whether from some such accidental occasions, often repeated, may not have sprung such a perfect navigating habit as that attributed to Dolomedes fimbriatus, who makes for herself a raft of leaves united by threads of silk, and so navigates the fens of Northumberland, England, in search of prey.

Distribution. Like her congener Extensa, the Stilt spider has a wide distribution over the United States. It is dispersed throughout the entire belt of Eastern and Middle States; and the collections of Dr. Marx locate it in Empire City, Colorado; Fort Bridger, Wyoming; Kanayah, Aleutian Isles; Sitka, Alaska, and as far to the northeast as Unga Bay, Labrador.

III.

Distribution, Form, and Habit The remarkably extended geographical distribution of these species of Tetragnatha, and especially of T. extensa, necessarily raises the question as to the effect of environment upon structure and habits. Throughout the wide area alluded to, the habits of Extensa, as far as I have been able to learn, are absolutely identical. I have studied the spider at widely separated points in the United States, and have made some observations of its habits in Great Britain. I have also compared my observations with all recorded by European observers to which I could have access. There is no essential variation in the testimony. The structure of the animal herself remains unchanged. The character of her web is everywhere the same. Her cocooning habit, her pairing habit, and in short all her life economy appear to be wholly unaffected by change of climate, food, site, and elevation. It must be allowed, indeed, that much remains to be done in the way of carefully noting the habits of the species in the various localities at which it has been collected; but the spider has been known for more than a century, and, in Europe particularly, has been studied by all arachnologists, and has had as much attention given to her as to any other species, with the exception, perhaps, of Epeira diademata. The above conclusion, therefore, may reasonably be regarded as accurate.

Other Examples In this respect, Tetragnatha extensa is not alone. I have shown that in the case of our large representatives of the genus Argiope (A. cophinaria and A. argyraspis) precisely the same facts obtain. (See Chapter VI.) From the rugged winters of New England to the perpetual summer of Southern California, throughout the mountain regions of Pennsylvania, and on the broad stretches of the American plains, these spiders have been traced, and are found everywhere the same in structure and habit.

To these may be added a large group of the genus Epeira, all of which are distributed over Europe, North America, portions of Asia, and probably throughout a great part of the northern hemisphere. The spiders of the southern temperate regions have not yet been sufficiently studied to enable us to decide whether or not this group is represented there. It certainly would be a valuable addition to our knowledge could it be known whether they are as widely distributed in the southern hemisphere as in the northern; and especially if it could also be determined whether or not the peculiar conditions of the torrid zone have prevented distribution of these species across that area. No doubt this would throw light, as far as spiders are concerned, upon the power of certain species to originate and maintain life independently in certain natural geographical areas.

Among this group of Epeiroids may be named Epeira insularis or E. marmorea, Epeira cornuta or E. strix, E. diademata, E. quadrata or E. trifolium, E. sclopetaria, and E. patagiata. In the case of some of these species the records do not show quite as great extremes of climate and **Power to Resist Environment.** elevation in their distribution. But the facts concerning them all contribute to the general conclusion that certain araneads have an immense power of resisting the external influences of their environment; possess a remarkable elasticity of temperament, which allows them to adapt themselves to widely different conditions of life. In the midst of all this, so thoroughly fixed are their habits that they resist all those centrifugal influences of varying surroundings which are supposed to be so potent to overcome the conservative tendencies of natural behavior.

Environment does influence the distribution of some species. The spider fauna of the tropical regions when placed alongside of those of the temperate zones show marked individuality. There are certain groups that have found lodging along the warm regions of our Gulf States, throughout Texas and Southern California, but have never been able to push their **Climate Limits Distribution.** way farther to the north. The genus Nephila, for example, is limited to the southern belt of States; and although in geological time, as early at least as the oligocene or the tertiary, the genus was established as far north as Colorado, in the region of Florissant and South Park, it is not now found above the parallel of Charleston, which in a general way indicates the limit of its northern distribution. What are the influences that prevent it from breaking through this barrier? One must hesitate to answer; but they are probably climatic, inasmuch as the genus has immense development in various species throughout tropical regions.

Another example is the genus Gasteracantha or Crab spider, distin**Gasteracantha.** guished by its round or circular abdomen, upon the margins of which are fixed various spinous processes. (See Chapter VII.) In this most striking characteristic, namely, the presence of spines upon a leathery abdomen, Gasteracantha certainly resembles the genus Acrosoma; yet that genus has several representatives in our northern spider fauna, while Gasteracantha has never been found farther north than the southern areas of our Gulf States. Both these genera, like Nephila, appear to be more especially characteristic of the tropical spider fauna, among which they also have a great variety of prolific and peculiar species.

One's curiosity is sorely puzzled to know why our three northern representatives of Acrosoma have been able to find and hold a place among the fauna, not only of the temperate, but of the more northern areas, while other species, and the genus Gasteracantha in all species, have ceased their northward march at the line already indicated. Or has the progress been in the reverse direction—from the north towards the south? And are our indigenous species of Acrosoma the survivors of a fauna that once held sway throughout the region stretching from New England to the Pacific?

IV.

Closely associated with spiders making a horizontal snare is the Basilica spider, the sole known representative of species that spin what I have called a Domed orb. The history of this species, which I have heretofore recorded, is as follows:[1] In the month of June, 1877, I was encamped upon the hills of the Colorado River of Texas, a few miles southwest of Austin, studying the habits of the agricultural and cutting ants.[2] A limited portion of my time was given to observing spiders, in the course of which the object of this sketch was discovered. Her snare was hung about two feet from the ground, upon a bush which stood in the midst of a grove of young live oaks. This

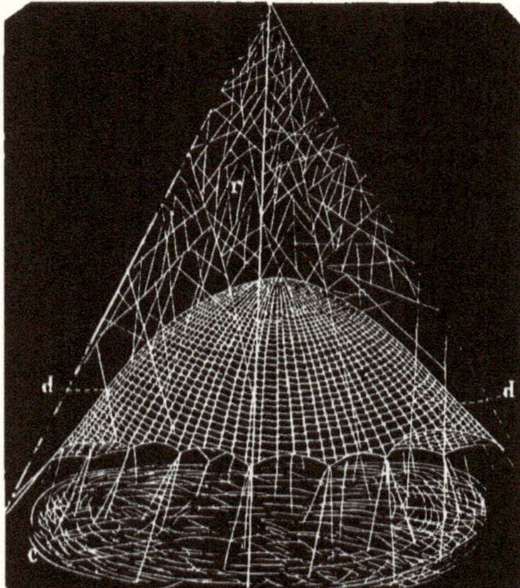

Fig. 154. The dome-shaped snare of the Basilica spider. r, the retitelarian snare; d, the dome.

Domed
Orbs,
Epeira
basilica.

[1] Proceedings Academy of Natural Sciences of Philadelphia, 1878, pages 124-132.

[2] Observations upon the former species are recorded in a volume entitled "The Agricultural Ant of Texas." J. B. Lippincott Company, Philadelphia. For some account of the Cutting Ants see "Proceedings Acad. Nat. Sci. Phila.," 1879, page 33, and Chapters XIII. and XIV. in my popular work entitled "The Tenants of an Old Farm."

snare had the composite structure imperfectly represented in Fig. 154. The general form of the snare was that of a pyramid the upper part of which, r, was a mass of right lines, knotted and looped and crossed in all directions. Within this mass was suspended an open silken dome, d d, constructed of a vast number of radii crossed at regular intervals by concentrics after the manner of the common orbweaving spider. The radii were about one-sixteenth inch apart at the bottom or circumference of the

The Dome. dome. The concentrics extended entirely and with equal regularity to the summit. They did not cross the radii in circular lines, but presented that notched appearance which characterizes the notched zone in the ordinary webs of Orbitelariæ. The meshes formed by the radii and spirals had thus much the shape of the meshes in a fisherman's net. The diameter of the dome was from seven to eight inches at the base, and the height nearly the same. It was suspended in the midst of the retitelarian lines by silken guys of like character, which thoroughly steadied the delicate structure, and perfectly preserved its form.

Beneath the dome, from two to three inches removed, was a light sheet of cobweb, e, irregularly meshed by waving and straight lines. **The Curtained Floor.** It had a decided convexity upward, and was supported, like the dome above it, and of which it seemed to be a protecting curtain, by silken threads or guys, so stretched as exactly to meet this purpose. This curtain may have been simply the collapsed remnant of an old web, which had been stripped downward, or abandoned in order to construct a fresh snare above

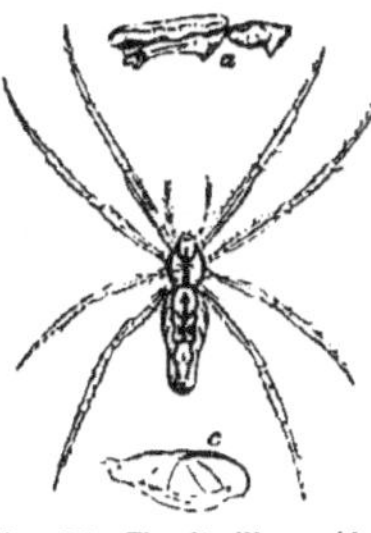

FIG. 155. The Basilica spider. a, side view of body; c, cephalothorax enlarged.

it. But it presented the appearance of a special structure, intended to serve a special purpose.

Of the many specimens of spinningwork which I have studied, I have never seen one quite so beautiful as this. It was with real regret that such a rare piece of spider architecture was destroyed, after it had been sketched, in order that the architect, herself one of the most beautiful of her kind, might be collected for the cabinet. The species was named Epeira basilica.

It would be an interesting study to the architect of human habitations, to uncover the principles upon which this silken basilica was reared. He **Architecture.** would doubtless find admirable adaptation of means to ends; he would be likely to meet methods quite familiar to himself; and perhaps to stumble upon some of which he is yet ignorant. He certainly would have occasion to marvel that a structure so stable could be wrought out of such fragile material as spider silk, and that the delicate dome could be so poised in the midst and by the help of silken threads as to preserve its perfect form.   Perhaps he would rise from the study with a higher appreciation of the quality and character of despised Arachne.

Nor would he find the creature herself unworthy of admiration as she hangs inverted within and just below the summit of the dome.   The term

The Architect. beautiful is rarely associated with individuals of her order, but it may properly be used in this case.   There is a combination of crimson, various shades of green, yellow, snow white, and black colors, which might prevent the most fastidious lady from raising the cry of "horrid spider!" against a creature bearing such delicate hues and dwelling in such a fairylike domicile.   However, the main point of interest in the Basilica spider is neither its architectural skill nor its fair colors. Its chief importance to the arachnologist is that it seems to form a perfect connecting link between the orbweaving and lineweaving spiders, in the characteristic spinningwork of the two tribes.

In order to perceive this statement it is necessary to recall what has been written in the last chapter about certain Orbweavers

A Connecting Link. that make composite snares, as for example, Epeira labyrinthea and E. triaranea.   These species, it will be remembered, not only spin the typical orbweb of the tribe to which they belong, but combine therewith a mass of right lines intersecting one another in different planes and at various angles, the whole combination forming at once the home and snare of the animal. The maze is an exact retitelarian snare, as has already been shown, and will be readily

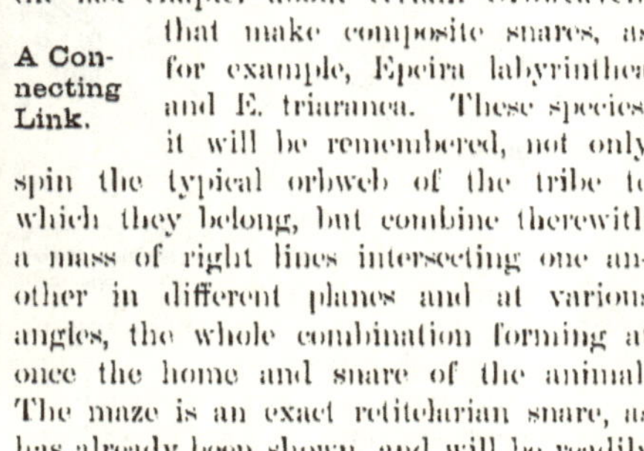
FIG. 156.   The bowl shaped web of Linyphia communis.

recognized by any ordinary observer of the cobwebs, for the most part made by Theridioids, which form the bulk of those infesting the angles of the walls of our stables and outbuildings.   Thus our first connecting link between the spinningwork of Orbweavers and Lineweavers is established at the typical web of the latter, as shown in the snares of the family Theridioidae.

The second link, which itself constitutes in the web of the Basilica spider a complete interblending of the groups, is seen at the snares of the Linyphioidae.   The genus Linyphia is one of the largest and most impor-

Linked to Linyphia. tant among the Lineweaving genera.   In order to show the steps by which the two groups approach each other in habits, some explanation of the spinningwork of the Linyphians is necessary.   Their web differs from that of the Theridioids substantially in the addition of a sheetlike web to the web of intersecting lines.   Indeed, the lines take a subordinate or subsidiary place, and the sheet appears to be the real snare.   There are three common variations of the form: First, a plain sheet of thin silk attached to the under part of leaves or suspended between branches as in the webs of Linyphia costata. Second, the snare of L. communis, represented at Fig. 156. It has a mass of right lines, r, to which is suspended a bowl like sheet, b, beneath which again is a dish shaped sheet, d, of more open spinningwork with the concavity upward, as in the bowl. The snare from which this figure was drawn had a total height of from twelve to fourteen inches. The diameter of the bowl was from six to seven inches, its depth one and a half to two inches.

Linyphia communis hangs inverted to the lower surface of her bowl, and is thus protected from assaults by the underlying floor or dish or curtain, d.

A third variation is that of the beautiful snare of Linyphia marginata (L. marmorata of Hentz), which is in form precisely like that just described except that the bowl becomes therein a dome. That is to say, the sheet, b, has the concavity downward instead of upward, and the dish or curtain undergoes a similar change. In other words, the web of Marginata has the exact form of Basilica's web, except that in the latter the dome, d (Fig. 154), is constructed of open regular meshes formed by the intersection of radiating ribs of silk with notched concentrics, while Marginata's dome is woven of irregularly placed threads into

Fig. 157. The snare of Linyphia marginata.

a thin sheeted web. The lower curtains, and the upper retitelarian web are substantially the same in both. In other words, the typical character of an Orbweaver's snare, namely, regular radiating lines regularly crossed by spiral concentrics, appears in the web of Basilica without any other change from a fixed generic Linyphian web. In the figure (157) the three netted domes were apparently made successively by one spider, and abandoned for some undiscovered reason. The ordinary web contains only one dome. It is probable that the curtain usually found beneath this is the compressed remains of a former dome, above which a new tent is reared. Something of the same habit may be seen in certain Orbweavers, who, however, push the rejected material to the outer margins instead of beneath the web.

We may trace this interesting analogy from another point in the group of Orbweavers, and find yet further coincidence. The typical orb of the

Orbitelariæ is vertical, but the corresponding section of the web of the Basilica spider, Fig. 13, d d, might be properly described as horizontal, or rather as a blending of the horizontal with the vertical. In other **Linked with Hortorum.** words, if a horizontal orb attached at the circumference in the usual way were to be lifted up by a thread fastened in the centre, it would assume the shape of the dome in the web of the Basilica spider. In point of fact, this effect might be produced from the characteristic snares of those species which have been described in the opening of this chapter. If, for example, one were to fasten a thread to the central point of the orb of Tetragnatha or the Orchard spider, and gradually lift it until the orb should assume the dome shape, he would have a snare very strongly resembling that of Basilica. The principal difference would be that the apron of intersecting lines beneath the dome of the Orchard spider appears in Basilica's web as the underlying curtain; and in addition thereto a similar mass of spinningwork appears above the orb. Another difference is that the spiral concentrics all have the notched appearance of the few central concentrics which compose what I have named the notched zone.

Several years after I had observed and published the description of Basilica's web and its relations, substantially as described above, I was greatly **Observations Confirmed.** delighted to have my study confirmed by the observations of Dr. George Marx, of Washington, D. C. He had received my account with much skepticism, as indeed did other arachnologists.

Unfortunately, my description of this entirely new form of orbweb, and the remarkable deduction therefrom, were based upon observations of a single example both of spinningwork and spider making it. I had no doubt of the accuracy of my notes and sketches, which were made with care and painstaking, for at the first glance I apprehended the importance of the discovery. Nevertheless, I greatly desired to find other examples, but searched in vain in the neighborhood of my camp.[1]

It was, therefore, with unusual satisfaction that I learned from Dr. Marx that he had observed several specimens of Basilica in the shrubbery on the beautiful parked grounds surrounding the Agricultural Department and other public buildings of the national capital. He confirmed my description of the character of the web, and added thereto an obser- **Building the Dome.** vation of the manner in which the dome is reared. The hypothetical case, given in my original paper, of the manner in which the domed orb of Basilica might be (substantially) erected out of the horizontal orb of the Orchard spider, proved to be a fortunate anticipation of the exact method of the spider. Dr. Marx says that the orb is at first a

---

[1] I had gone to Texas with a special purpose, namely, the study of the Agricultural Ants; and it was absolutely necessary, in order to follow my line of study and experiments, that I should limit the time given to other observations. I have often regretted that I could not have spent a day or two in searching the surrounding district for other examples of Basilica.

horizontal one; and that it is lifted up gradually by attaching lines at various points upon the upper surface and drawing them taut, one after another, until the whole is lifted up into the domed structure represented in Fig. 154. I may add that Dr. Marx was also able to collect cocoons of the species, and describe the manner in which they are hung in the neighborhood of the web.[1]

The manner in which this change is wrought was determined by Dr. Marx, and he has kindly placed at my disposal his notes upon the same. When first observed by him (at 8.30 A. M.), the snare lay in a horizontal plane, as shown at Fig. 158, and had more than fifty radii. It was hung between the tips of the branches of a bush. At 12 M. the borders of the snare were bent downward, causing it to assume the form of a shallow dome. At 4 P. M. the transformation had so far progressed as to bring the web to the structure represented at Fig. 159. The work was carried on in this wise: At the marginal edges were outgoing lines, as c b, Fig. 158, used to support or brace the snare, as is usual with horizontal orbs. On

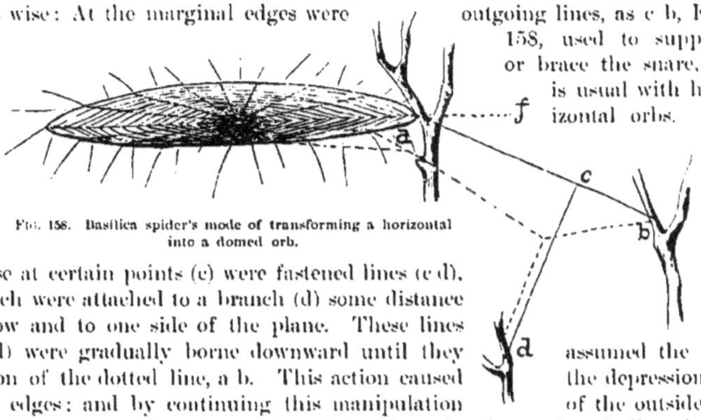

Fig. 158. Basilica spider's mode of transforming a horizontal into a domed orb.

these at certain points (c) were fastened lines (c d), which were attached to a branch (d) some distance below and to one side of the plane. These lines (c d) were gradually borne downward until they assumed the position of the dotted line, a b. This action caused the depression of the edges; and by continuing this manipulation of the outside or foundation lines, the orb was forced first into the shape of a shallow dome flattened at the pole, and then into the form of the typical web as above described. (Fig. 159.) This action was seen "repeated over a dozen times."

But it was manifest that some other method had been brought to bear than that already explained. The position of the snare in its original horizontal form had been exactly located by a fork (f, Fig. 158), in the branch to which the stay lines were attached, which was on a level with the horizontal axis of the orb. Now, however, the edges of the web were not only drawn below the level of the fork, but the central part was raised at least three-fourths of an inch above the fork. (Compare f, Fig. 158, with f, Fig. 159.) The manner in which this had been done was readily seen by a glance at the various lines, perpendicular and inclined, which

<hr>

[1] See Vol. II., Chapter on Maternal Industry.

extended upward from the exterior of the dome to the inclosing and supporting labyrinth of crossed lines. Evidently the little engineer had completed the work, so well begun in the depression of the edges of her orb, by elevating the central part through the same method of applying force, but in an opposite direction. So well had the power been graduated that the proportions of the dome were beautifully preserved.

We have thus traced the analogy between the spinningwork of this species of Orbweavers and that of Lineweavers in these several particulars:

Spinningwork Analogies. First, in the dome shaped snare and dwelling place, which corresponds with that made by a species of the Retitelarian genus Linyphia. Second, in the mass of intersecting lines placed around and above the dome, which is the characteristic web of the Retitelarian genus Theridium and of many other genera. Third, in the sheet like curtain beneath the dome, which in form resembles the thinly

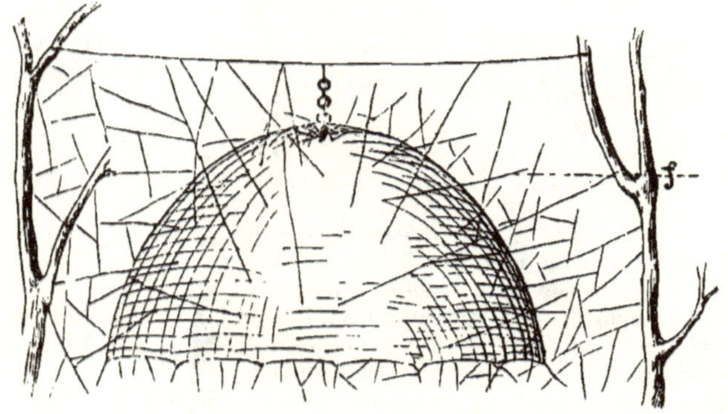

FIG. 159. Position of Basilica's web after the horizontal orb has been transformed. The meshed structure is only indicated. The original plane of the orb is shown at f.

sheeted web of many species of Linyphia, as, for example, L. costata; and which in both position and form corresponds with the underlying curtain or dish of L. communis and L. marginata.

Thus, Epeira basilica is seen to possess all the leading characteristics of the principal families of the Retitelariæ, namely, (1) the maze of crossed lines, and (2) the sheeted web in exact detail, and (3) the dome shaped web in outline. It also possesses the chief characteristic of the Orbitelariæ, namely, the geometric web, or radiating lines regularly crossed by concentrics. Moreover, it combines in its dome structure the vertical and horizontal forms which are the prevailing ones in the orb of its congeners. The Basilica spider may, therefore, be regarded as well nigh, if not completely, bridging the space between the spinning economy of these two great tribes of the Araneæ.

In this connection it should be remembered that there is a general resemblance in structure between the Orbweavers and Lineweavers; and it may be stated, moreover, that this resemblance is more marked in the case of the genus to which Basilica is closely related, Meta; and also in some of those species which have the habit of making a composite snare. This is so striking in Koch's genera Meta and Zilla that they have been classed with both sections. On this point Dr. T. Thorell has remarked, "As Zilla shows an analogy with Steatoda of the Lineweavers, so does Meta form a transition to Linyphia of the same tribe."[1] These relations may be more fully considered in the systematic part of this work, but in the meantime we are justified in saying that in the case of the above named species, we find the tribes of Orbitelariæ and Retitelariæ approaching each other in structure as well as in the interblending of their spinning habit.

[1] "On European Spiders," page 61.

CHAPTER X.

THE FEATHERFOOT SPIDER, ULOBORUS PLUMIPES.

I.

THE remarkable genus Uloborus is represented by at least two species in the United States, namely, Uloborus mammeatus Hentz, and Uloborus plumipes Lucas (Phillyra riparia Hentz). These spiders closely resemble each other in structure and, as far as I know, have no difference in habit. The genus, in both its species, is widely distributed over the United States, probably covering the entire area. I have traced its distribution from New England, in the States of Massachusetts, Connecticut, and Rhode Island, southward to New Jersey, through the District of Columbia, to Florida. Moving westward, along the Gulf States, it was found by Hentz in Alabama, and by myself in Texas. Specimens have been sent me from Wisconsin, where the Peckhams have observed it, and I have collected it at various points in Eastern and Central Pennsylvania. This record of distribution would indicate that the spider probably occupies the whole area of the United States, with the possible exception of the Pacific coast; and I have no doubt that it will be found there also. Plumipes is found in Europe, as are other species of the genus. Uloborus is not of modern origin, as the family, at least, is represented among the fossil spiders of the amber.

My studies of Featherfoot's local habitat show some decided preferences for moist, low, and well shaded sites, but indicate a quite miscellaneous taste. In Connecticut I found its snares in the decayed hollows of old stumps or cavities beneath their roots, and spun near the ground upon the low underbrush of thickets. One very large colony of young spiders was found on laurel bushes at the foot of Brush Mountain, Pennsylvania, above one of the branches of the Juniata River. Their snares were swung at the height of four feet and less above the surface. In the neighborhood of Philadelphia I have found them quite low down, swung between the stalks of a blackberry thicket, and once only within a shallow cavity among the stones of an abandoned mill dam. I have always happened to observe them in moist places near running streams. In Texas I found Uloborus, probably Mammeatus, in bushes on the uplands south of Austin, above the deep gorge of Barton Creek.

Hentz observed the species on limestone rocks on the banks of Cyprus Creek, and in moist places in North Alabama. Its congener, U. mammeatus, he found dwelling most frequently in cavities, among large logs, and in hollow trunks of trees.[1] Emerton found Plumipes between loose stones or low bushes in New England. Mrs. Peckham almost invariably found this species building in dead branches, six out of seven being thus located.[2] She gives an apt abstract of its habits. In form and color it resembles a scrap of bark; its body is truncated and diversified with small lumps, while its first legs are very uneven, bearing heavy fringes of hair on the tibia, and having the terminal joints slender. Its color is a soft wood

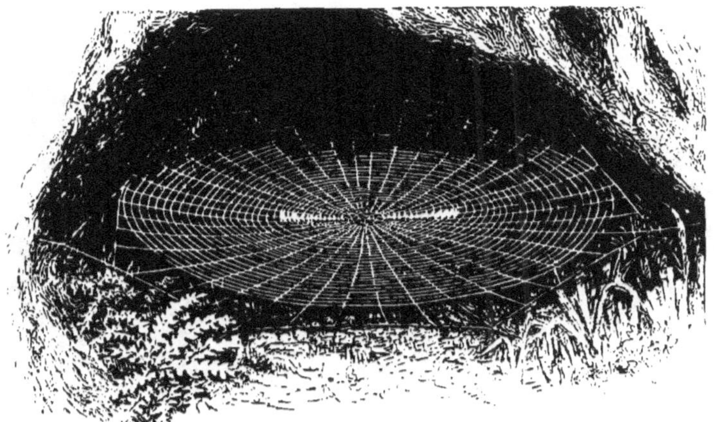

Fig. 160. Orbweb of Uloborus, spun in the opening of a hollow stump.

brown or gray, mottled with white. It has the habit of hanging motionless in the web for hours at a time, swaying in the wind like an inanimate object. The strands of its web are rough and inelastic, so that they are frequently broken, and this gives it the appearance of one of those dilapidated and deserted webs in which bits of windblown rubbish are frequently entangled.

Baron Walckenaer says that the closely related European species, Uloborus Walckenaerius Dugès, generally spins its horizontal snare between the stems of rushes in dry and warm places, which resembles that of Epeira in form, but of looser tissue.[3] Hahn found the species in the

Phillyra mammeata. "Spiders of the United States." page 129.

"Protective Resemblances in Spiders." Occasional Papers of the Natural History Society of Wisconsin, Vol. I., 1889, page 77. By George W. & Elizabeth G. Peckham.

Aptères, Suites a Buffon, Vol. II., page 229.

neighborhood of Nuremberg on the edge of forests, building its snare between young pines. Simon says that the species lives upon dry brambles or in the cavities of old walls, that it is always found stretched **Uloborus Walck-enaerius.** lengthwise beneath its snare, and is readily confounded with adjoining objects.[1]   Uloborus Walckenaerius is one of the spiders inhabiting Palestine, being among those listed from Syria by Mr. Cambridge.

I have never seen the orbs in any other than a horizontal position. They measure from three to four and five and a half inches in diameter.

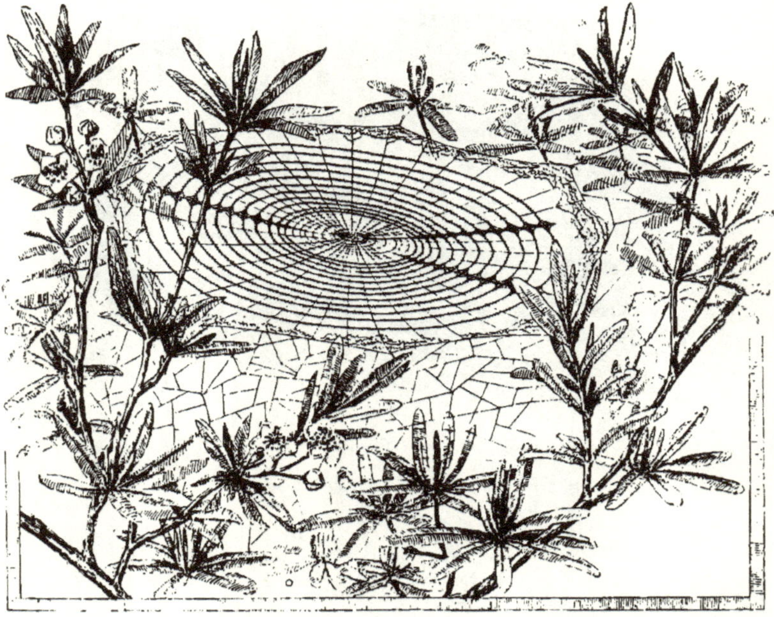

Fig. 161. The orb of Uloborus on a laurel bush. The curled spiral thread is represented, and the remnants of a former web pushed back to the margin.

The hub is generally closely and beautifully meshed, like the snare of the Labyrinth spider, and the central space is entirely filled up by concentrics, corresponding with those composing the notched zone in the or- **Charac-ters of Snares.** dinary webs of Orbweavers. The radii diverge in the ordinary way, but seem to be of a rather delicate material. In the Juniata colony above named many of the webs were surrounded by what appeared to be the collapsed remains of a former snare. The spiders

<hr>

[1] "Arachnides de France," Vol. II., page 169.   [2] Proc. Zool. Soc., 1872, Part I., page 279.

appeared to have cleared away and pushed back the old broken webs so as to make space for new ones, and the fragments occupied the margin of the orb space close up to the points at which the foundation lines were attached to the adjacent foliage. (See Fig. 161.) On one of these webs I counted thirty-six radii and twelve spirals, not including among the latter the concentrics which fill up the central space. The hub measured a quarter inch in diameter, and the distance between the concentrics was one thirty-second of an inch. Beneath the orb there extended **Web Measurements.** a mass of retitelarian lines, somewhat after the manner of the Orchard spider, but not so abundant. The central spirals gradually opened as they approached the true spiral space, and were separated by distances ranging from one-eighth to one-fourth inch. A notched ribbon about an inch long was spun on each side of the hub, gradually terminating in a point. The central spirals crossed the ribbon at the points of its angular scallops. The hub was one-fourth inch wide.

Snares of Uloborus found upon the banks of Bride's Run, at the outlet of Bride's Pond, near Niantic, Connecticut, were spun in the cavities of old stumps, or upon the ferns and grasses near the banks of the stream. The hub was checkered or meshed somewhat like the notched zone of Epeiroids. The notched or central spirals seized the points of the little ribbon that extended centrally through the horizontal orb. The spirals of one orb were twenty-two in number, the radii thirtynine and forty. The spirals continued close up to the margin of the notched zone, without any interspace, and the web was about four and a half inches in diameter. (See Fig. 160.)

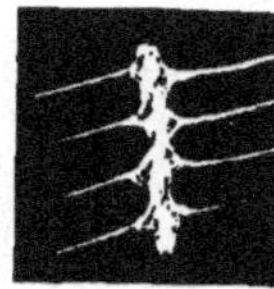

Fig. 162. Piece of the scalloped ribbon on the orb of Uloborus.

A striking peculiarity of the orbs of this species is the ribbon decorations which are quite characteristic, and unite the spinningwork of the genus with that of such genera as Argiope and Acrosoma. Perhaps **Ribbon Decorations.** the most frequent form of decoration is a scalloped band about one thirty-second inch in width, which crosses the central part of the orb, being scarcely perceptible at the hub, and gradually diminishing towards the circumference of the orb. Where the spirals cross, this ribboned spinningwork is pulled into points, thus giving the band the toothed or scalloped appearance represented at Fig. 162. The distance between the spirals was from one-fourth to one-eighth of an inch; the distance across the band from point to point about one thirty-second of an inch.

Another form of decoration shows simply the addition on one side of the hub of a second ribbon, which makes an angle with the first. In this snare the spider hung beneath the hub, with its fore and hind legs respectively attached to the points where the ribbon joins the hub.

The most remarkable decorations of this sort I found upon the orbs of

Uloborus mammeatus in Texas. They formed interesting and beautiful examples of this character of spinningwork, which is more easily illustrated than described. Fig. 163 represents one web. The upper ribbons, traversing nearly the entire area of the hub, were very much the same as the last described, except that on one side the spinningwork was greatly thickened at the termination, giving a club shaped appearance. On each of the other sides of the hub were thrown two parallel semicircular bands slightly separated from each other. In another snare, represented very imperfectly, indeed, at Fig. 164, the longitudinal bands were lacking, but instead of them a series of four or five circular bands encompassed the hub. My sketches, taken upon the spot, do not show that these bands were concentries, though I have been inclined to think that such might have been the case. At one side of this orb was stretched a ladder like structure leading from the hub to the outer foundation lines. This was a very peculiar

Fig. 163. Decorated orb of Uloborus mammeatus.

formation, and reminded me somewhat of the zigzag band characteristic of Argiope cophinaria, but the rounds were not continuous as with that spider.

The purpose of these ribbons I have never been able to determine satisfactorily. I have called them decorative, not because I imagine that the purpose of the spider in placing them upon her web is in anywise analogous to the human sentiment expressed by that word, but simply as a convenient term to indicate the character of the spinningwork as it presented itself to my own mind. Certainly it did greatly enhance the beauty of the delicate structure. It is probable that these decorative ribbons or bands serve to protect the spider herself, and may also be of service in strengthening the web. But I have sufficiently expressed my opinion on this subject when treating of the snare of Argiope. (Chapter VI.)

No one who has studied with any care the spinningwork of the Orbitelariae can doubt that the web of Uloborus is that of a genuine Orbweaver. In its round shape; in the arrangement of lines radiating from the centre; in the structure of the hub; in the preliminary spiral scaffold; in the central concentrics, which correspond with the notched zone; in the form and distribution of the spirals; in the character of the ribbon decorations; in the manner in which the snare is swung to foundation lines in whatever site it may be placed; in the position of the spider underneath the web;—in all these points the spinningwork of Uloborus is analogous to that of Orbweavers, especially Tetragnatha, or of the Orchard and Hunchback spiders.

A Genuine Orbweaver.

There is, however, one important difference. The spiral concentrics, instead of being composed of single lines covered with viscid beads, as in typical snares of the Orbitelariæ, are composed for the most part of several very delicate filaments, although in certain parts the thread is single. To threads and filaments alike are often attached a number of minute objects, opaque, and for the most part amorphous; but many of them being very small globes of a yellow color, per-

No Viscid Beads.

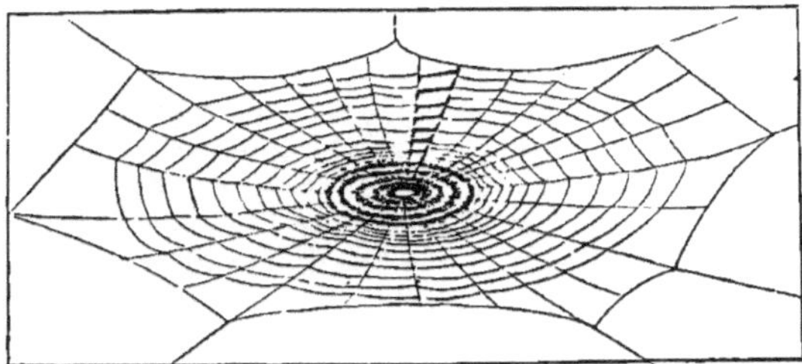

Fig. 161.　Circular ribboned decorations on the snare of Uloborus.

haps the pollen of flowers. They adhere to the single threads, but more fully to the portions containing several distinct filaments. These opaque objects have so much the appearance of beads that a careless observer is likely to be deceived by them; at least, I was thus led astray in my first studies of the Uloborus snare. There are, however, no viscid beads upon any of the lines, although the thread is certainly very adhesive, chiefly I suppose by reason of the delicacy and flocculence of the fibre. The smooth point of a pencil touched to it does not adhere; but when my finger was laid upon a spiral it adhered as in the case of a beaded web.

In this respect the snare of Uloborus resembles that of the Triangle spider, Hyptiotes cavatus, and also certain species of the Clubionidæ, such as Dictyna philoteichus and other species of that genus. This flocculent web was discovered and described by Blackwall, and is produced by special organs known as the cribellum and calamistrum. The calamistrum is located upon the metatarsus of the hind pairs of legs. It resembles somewhat in form the flyers upon

Relations of Flocculent Spirals.

an old fashioned spinning wheel, and is apparently used to separate into a flossy mass the threads of silk as they issue from the spinning glands. Bertkau, in an article on the cribellum and calamistrum, has shown certain secreting glands at the ends of the fine tubes which have their outlets in the former organ. It is not improbable, in view of this discovery, that the viscidity of the flocculent spirals of Uloborus and other spiders possessing this organ is caused in some measure by a slight secretion from these glands.

It is the possession of cribellum and calamistrum by Uloborus and Hyptiotes which has led various arachnologists to separate these two genera from the Orbweavers. Emerton, for example, following Blackwall, Keyserling, and Bertkau, assigns them to the Clubionidæ. Without entering at length into the reasons, based upon structure, for dissenting from this opinion, I have felt constrained, on the grounds of their spinningwork

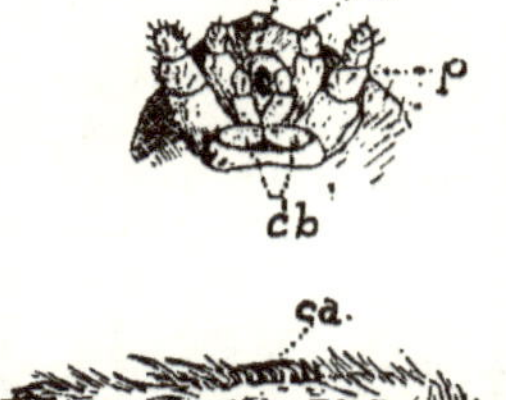

Fig. 165. Spinning organs of Clubiona, showing the cribellum, cb. P, posterior; m, middle; a, anterior spinnerets; ca, calamistrum. (After Blackwall.)

Calamistrum and Cribellum

alone, to place both these genera among the Orbitelariæ, where indeed such a distinguished systematic arachnologist as Professor Thorell has already placed them, and continues to keep them, notwithstanding all the objections that have been advanced by the able naturalists who have espoused the other view.

Mr. Emerton has made some studies of the web of Uloborus Walckenaerius, the common species of Northern Europe. I reproduce his figure (Fig. 167), which represents an unfinished web of this species seen in France. It shows the central part still occupied by the preliminary spirals or scaffolding, while the outer part is covered with curled threads, and the smooth spirals cut away (or not yet inserted), leaving thickened spots or ribbons on the rays. In the finished web most of the spirals pass regularly around, but the outer ones are often more or less irregular, as in Epeira webs, according to the shape of the space in which the web is made.

European Species.

According to this author, Uloborus, after inclosing her eggs in the cocoon, becomes careless about her web, and repairs it only enough to keep the cocoons in place, so that many imperfect and irregular webs are found at the cocooning season. The only web of Uloborus plumipes seen by Emerton

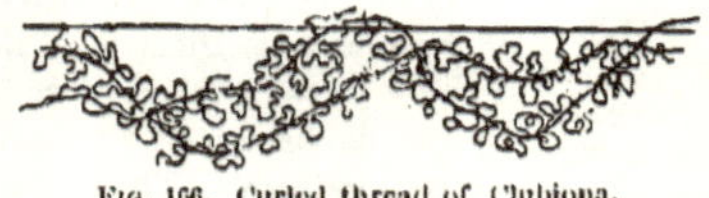

Fig. 166. Curled thread of Clubiona. (After Staveley.)

was imperfect from the above cause, but was evidently the remains of a nearly round web, the rays meeting somewhat nearer the upper than the lower edge.

The same author says that the spiral lines of Hyptiotes and Uloborus have a strong, smooth thread through the centre. That of Hyptiotes, which he examined fresh, had the finer

Spiral Thread. part arranged in regular leaves or scallops, in which the separate fibres could not be distinguished. The thread of Uloborus, at least when old and dried, had the loops longer and less regular, and he had not been able to distinguish the separate fibres except at the edges of the band. To my eye the spiral seemed to be a single continuous flocculent filament without any supporting thread, thus differing from Hyptiotes. But of this I am not confident. Under a common hand lens it has a milky or filmy hue.

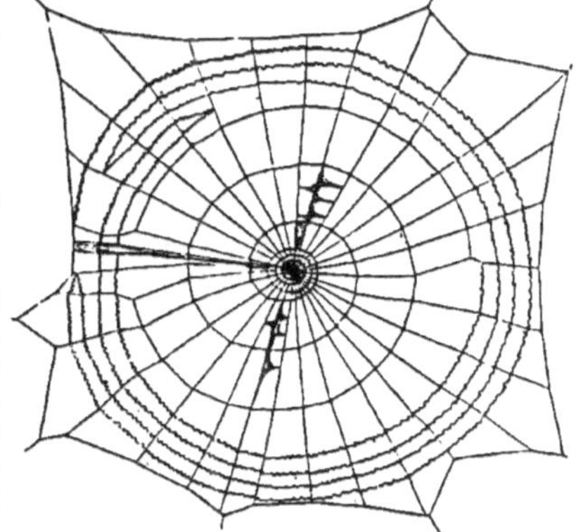

Fig. 167. Unfinished web of Uloborus Walckenaerius. (After Emerton.)

The position of the spider upon her snare is very much like that of Tetragnatha. I have found her stretched out underneath the hub, with

Position on Snare. the legs extended fore and aft almost in a straight line with the ribboned decorations to which the feet clung. Sometimes, however, she turned and hung beneath the hub at a position at right angles with the ribbon.

One young specimen, captured upon her snare, I saw repairing the broken margins of her web. It was done line after line, one

Repairing Snare. radius and one spiral at a time, precisely in the manner common to other Orbweavers. The broken lines were cut out, and new ones substituted, or were picked up by the spider's feet, spliced, and stretched into position. She worked very deftly and rapidly. I saw her capturing a small insect, a gnat. The two hind legs were used for rapidly pulling out the enswathing thread, while the second and third legs revolved the insect and held it to the web. According to Hentz, Uloborus

Fig. 168. Uloborus hanging beneath her orb.

has the habit of violently shaking her web when threatened. But when at rest he always found it in an inverted position underneath its orb, with its hind legs extended in parallel lines like Tetragnatha. This record of habits, imperfect as it is, indubitably places Uloborus among the weavers of orbwebs.

CHAPTER XI.

THE TRIANGLE SPIDER: THE ORB SECTOR.

I.

The snare of Hyptiotes cavatus, the Triangle spider, has awakened deep interest among naturalists on account of its peculiar construction and manner of operation. The little spinner is equally interesting to the systematist, because of its relation to other individuals of its tribe; and indeed because of the question, which has divided arachnologists, as to what tribe in the order Araneæ it truly belongs.

I have no hesitation in assigning it to the Orbitelariæ, where it seems to me that its spinningwork undoubtedly requires it to be placed. On the **Systematic Place** grounds of structure, also, I follow Dr. Thorell and give it the same position,[1] although it must be allowed that the authorities are well worthy of consideration who place it among the Clubionidæ. As in the case of Uloborus, this is done almost exclusively upon the grounds that Hyptiotes possesses the cribellum, a special organ for the exudation of spinning material, and the calamistrum, by which such material is manipulated or hackled until it presents the appearance which will be further described hereafter.

The snare is a sector of a circle, including about forty-five degrees of the area, and with a radius varying from twelve to twenty inches or less. **The Snare.** It is thus, as to shape, in strong contrast with the typical orb of Epeïra, which is a full circle, and with the sectoral orb of Zilla, which is a circle lacking its upper sextant, while the net of Hyptiotes is just about a sextant or sixth of a circle. In the language of Professor Wilder, who has pointed out these relations, to use a more homely comparison, the net of Epeira is an entire pie; that of Zilla or Nephila is a pie with a piece cut out; while that of Hyptiotes represents the missing piece. In algebraic language, Zilla $+$ Hyptiotes $=$ Epeïra.[2] (See Fig. 170.)

The snare is habitually spun in a vertical plane, although it is subject to some variation, and I have occasionally found it more or less horizontal. It is hung in all sorts of positions between the branches of trees and bushes, but its most favorite habitat appears to be pine woods. I have

[1] On European Spiders, page 68.

[2] Professor Burt G. Wilder, Triangle Spider, "Popular Science Monthly," 1875, page 653.

found it abundant among the mountain pines of Central Pennsylvania, as well as among the flat, sandy, pine barrens of New Jersey, and in pine groves on the seashore at Ipswich Bay, Massachusetts. But **The Site.** I have frequently seen it in other positions, among shrubs and evergreens on the lawns of country residences; in groves of deciduous trees in Connecticut; in the underbrush of Woodland Cemetery, Philadelphia; on the banks of the Schuylkill, and in shady ravines in Fairmount Park. Mrs. Mary Treat found it in New Jersey dwelling among flowering peas, having its snare attached to the dry sticks upon which the vines were sup-

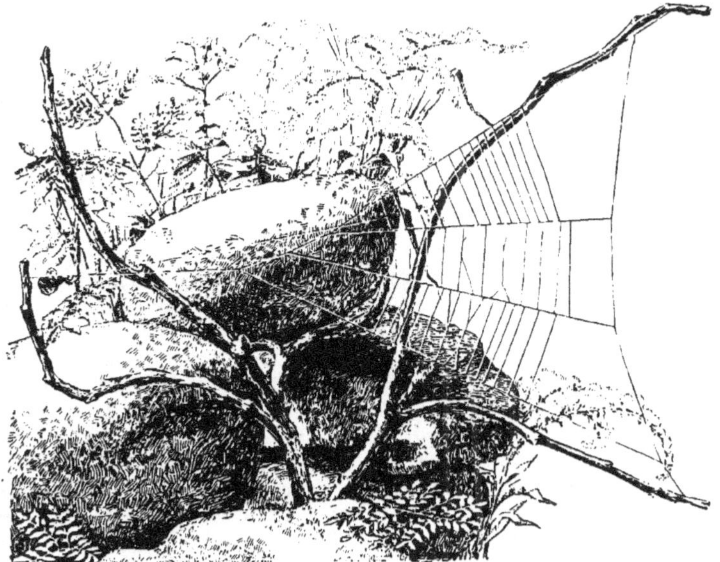

Fig. 169. The snare of a Triangle spider, spun on a dry bush by a New England stone fence. One-half natural size.

ported. While Hyptiotes thus shows a disposition to domicile on any sort of bushes or foliage, its favorite location may be said to be groves of pine. In this respect it corresponds with its European con- **Favorite Net Site.** gener, Hyptiotes paradoxus, which Professor Thorell found in the neighborhood of Stockholm during July, August, and September, principally in woods of trees of the fir kind, especially in pine woods.

Our Triangle spider, like Paradoxus, seems to choose most freely the dry bare branches of the pine or other trees; but this is by no means a

universal preference, for I frequently find the snare spread among the
green needles of the pine boughs and stretched amidst the green foliage
of other plants.   The nest site is generally low down.   I have rarely
noted it more than three or four feet above the surface of the earth.
As the lower branches of pine trees are always dry, it would follow as
a necessity, without any special preference on the part of the spider, that
her habit of swinging her net low down would compel her in such
positions to spin between dry limbs.

The spider is probably distributed over a wide geographical area.   I have
traced it from New England on the northeast, from Maine to Massachu-
Distribu-
tion.
setts, through New York, New Jersey, as far south as the District
of Columbia and Alabama.   I have also taken it in Ohio, and
as far to the southwest as Texas.   It thus shows a considerable
range of climatic extremes.   It will probably be found wherever forests
of fir and pine flourish.

Hyptiotes is very small, being little over an eighth of an inch in body
length, with rather short, stout legs.   It is a dull grayish brown color,
with occasional brighter tints of red intermixed.   It thus strongly resembles the color of the branches
to which its snare is oftenest
hung.   This identity of color
makes it difficult sometimes
to find the animal; but I can
hardly think that it presents
a case of protective mimicry,

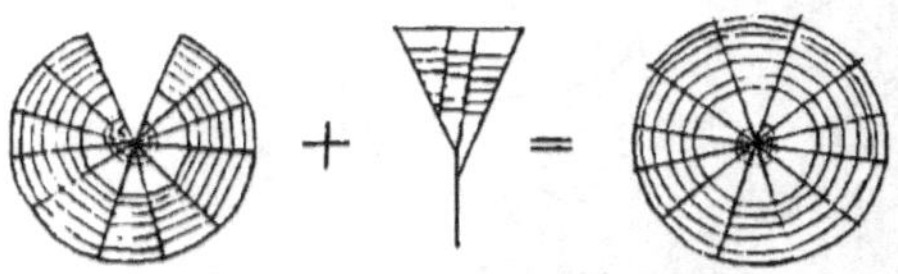

Fig. 170. Zilla plus Hyptiotes equals Epeira.

as does Mrs. Treat, who also concludes that Hyptiotes recognizes color,
and that its habitual resting place is a matter of intelligent choice.[1]   On
General
Appear-
ance.
the contrary, as I have just stated, it is supposable that the
position is simply a matter of convenience, as it gives the best
attachment for the trapline of its peculiar web; and, moreover,
since the spider domiciles in all sorts and parts of shrubs, living
and dead, it is certainly reasonable to think that a bright green would
have been as great a protection to it as the dull brown and gray which
prevails.

The appearance which the snare presents to the observer is that of a
circular sector, attached at the open or outer end to surrounding objects,
Construc-
tion of
Web.
and at the apex to a straight line of varying length, similarly
anchored.   The number of radii is always four, never more nor
less, and in this number, of course, is included the two outside
rays.   The two central radii are crossed by lines which may be
regarded as the equivalent of the spiral lines which intersect the radii in
ordinary orbwebs.   The manner in which these several parts of the snare
are constructed will now be pointed out.

[1] "My Garden Pets."

The mode of spinning the foundation lines or frame has never been observed, as far as I know, by any naturalist. A careful study of a number of webs, however, has led me to conclude that it is spun as follows: In the first place, the spider stretches between two points a single line, which we may represent by the dotted line, PB, in Fig. 171. She then proceeds to attach to this line, say at the point A, another thread, which is carried along the original line, PB, to the place of attachment, B.

Making the Frame.

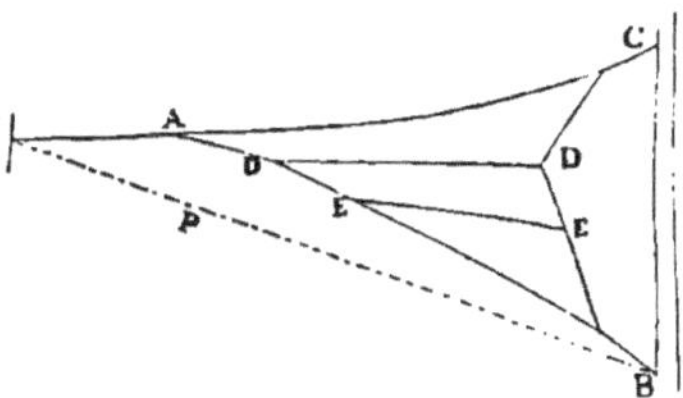

Fig. 171. Making the frame of the Triangle spider's snare.

Thence up the branch or other object to C, where the carried line is drawn taut and fastened. There is thus produced the line AC, and the original foundation line having been drawn upward by pulling upon AC, has assumed the curved form of AB. The two outer radii of the snare are thus in place. Now the spider drops from the point CB, carrying with her a thread, which is attached at B, and becomes thus the base line of the triangle CABC. Proceeding along the line BA, carrying with her a thread as before, she makes another attachment at E, returns upon her course to B, and thence upward to E, on the base line where the carried thread is straightened, fastened, and the third radius, EE, completed. In a similar way the fourth radius, DD, is stretched. This, of course, does not express the exact order in every case, but the general method.

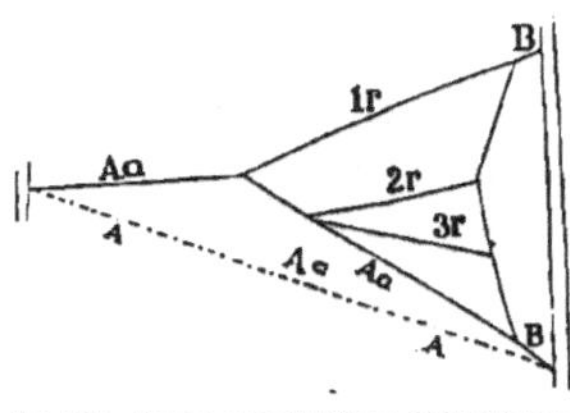

Fig. 172. Frame or radial lines of Hyptiotes' snare, as in nature.

It will be observed that these radial lines do not meet in a common point. This is indeed contrary to most published descriptions of the appearance of the snare. For example, Thorell speaks of these threads in the net of Hyptiotes paradoxus as forming "equal angles with the original thread, and each other."[1] Emerton speaks of the apex as "the point where the rays meet."[2] He again

Have Radii a Common Point?

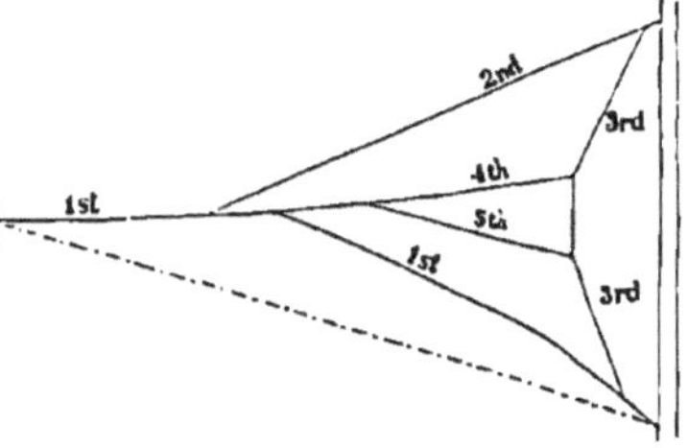

Fig. 173. Natural arrangement of radii, to show the order in which they are spun.

speaks of the four branches as radiating from the extremity of the sector.[1] Fig. 171, with the exception of the dotted line, is drawn from nature; so also are Figs. 172 and 173. These show, better than any worded description, that the interradials are attached in the manner which I have represented, and are not drawn out from a common apex or point.

According to my view, the position of the first line spun is indicated by the dotted line (AA, Fig. 172). Afterward the first radius (1r) was formed by attaching that line to AA, thus drawing it up until it assumed the position of Aa, Aa. To this again were successively fastened the lines 2r and 3r, which completed the radial framework, ready for inserting the spirals. So also, at Fig. 173, one sees the same order of progress as shown by the numbered lines, viz., the dotted original line drawn up to make the trapline and first radius (1st) by the attached thread, which constitutes the second radius (2d). The base line (3d) comes next in order, and thereafter the two additional radii (4th, 5th) in their order.

No doubt, the radial lines may be at times found meeting at or near the same point; I have certainly so found them, but I believe that this is not characteristic of the spinningwork, but is simply an accident thereof. In other words, the spider having made her first main line, attaches the three succeeding shorter ones to a convenient point thereon without much regard to whether they meet in a common angle or not, but in fact ordinarily places them at different points along the line.

The framework being thus prepared, the spider proceeds to place in her spirals. For the manner in which this is done we are indebted to Professor Wilder. His account is based upon two personal observations of the mode of spinning. He says: "Let us suppose that the framework of the net is completed, and that the first or longest interradial line (Fig. 174, I[1]) has also been made. Instead of beginning the second interradial at S[4] she begins at 4; and instead of climbing up the interradial or the strong and convenient base line (BB), she runs to a point (2) on the lowest radius near the apex, crosses the two intermediate radii from 2 to 3, and passes along the upper radius to the attachment of the first interradial (S[1]). On reaching this, she turns and moves for about her own length toward the apex. Contrary to the usual habit of spiders, during this roundabout passage from 1 to 4 she spins no thread. She now spreads her spinnerets a little, and presses them upon the radius, keeping them so while she advances again about her own length. This forms the attachment of the second interradial (I[2]). The spider then lets her abdomen fall somewhat, supporting her body and advancing upon the line by means of her first, second, and third pairs of legs. The fourth pair are applied together to the spinnerets with great rapidity, at least five times in a second, or

Mode of Spinning Spirals.

Rapid Spinning.

[1] Structure and Habits of Spiders, page 76.

three hundred times in a minute, and in so doing they draw out a double line.

"The spider moves slowly along the radius until she reaches a point (5) where she can step across to the next radius. While so doing, she ceases to draw out the double line, and carefully keeps it from contact with either of the radii. She then reverses her course and moves along the second radius to a point (6) nearly under that whence she started. The double line has shortened itself considerably; any slack she draws in, and then turning about, with her head toward the apex, she makes a second attachment with her spinnerets close pressed against the radius. This done, she again hangs from the radius, draws out the spiral line, and advances toward the apex, crosses at 7 to the third radius, returns thereon to 8, and makes a third attachment. She then repeats the same process upon the third radius, and in Fig. 7 is represented (at 9) as having finished about one-half of the line."

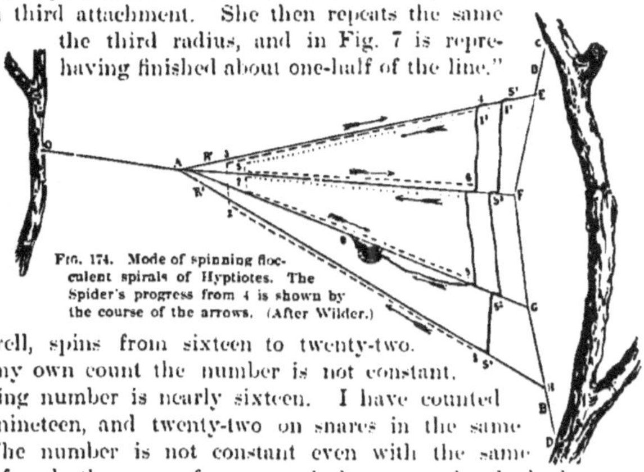

The number of crossed lines when the work is completed varies, according to Wilder, from six to sixteen. The European Paradoxus, according to Thorell, spins from sixteen to twenty-two. According to my own count the number is not constant, but the prevailing number is nearly sixteen. I have counted five, fourteen, nineteen, and twenty-two on snares in the same general site. The number is not constant even with the same individual. A female that spun fourteen spirals on one day had nineteen the next; and like differences showed in the other parts of the snare. Evidently there is no mechanical necessity in the constitution of the aranead that compels it to a machine regularity of product.

Fig. 174. Mode of spinning flocculent spirals of Hyptiotes. The Spider's progress from 4 is shown by the course of the arrows. (After Wilder.)

These lines are not single threads, covered with viscid beads, as in the case of most Orbweavers, but resemble those of Uloborus, as heretofore described. That is to say, as they exude from the spinnerets and cribellum, they are teased, or to borrow a word from the flax manufacturer, "hackled," by the calamistrum into a somewhat irregularly widened flocculent mass.

Wilder speaks of the spiral thread as simply double lines, the two strands being from one five-hundredth to one two-thousandth of an inch apart.[1] Emerton says that it "has a strong smooth thread through the

------

centre," and "has the finer part arranged in regular loops or scallops (see Fig. 176, a, b[1]) in which separate fibres cannot be distinguished."

Fig. 175. Calamistrum of Hyptiotes. (After Wilder.) a, tarsus and metatarsus of fourth leg; b, the claws, open; c, cross section of the metatarsus, showing its cavity in which lie the muscles; also a single curved bristle upon the side, a part of the calamistrum; e, a similar calamistrum bristle still more enlarged; d, f, two feathered bristles from near the joints.

The spiral lines, according to my own studies, when examined under an ordinary hand lens, present a milky appearance, as though composed of very thinly spun material. With a little higher power the supporting spiral thread is seen passing through this milky mass. Placed under a microscope, the line is seen to consist of three strands, namely, the central spiral thread, and two curled lines, which alternately cross and recross each other above and below the centre, forming the loops as represented at Fig. 177. In this respect Mr. Emerton has correctly represented the spiral line of Hyptiotes. The two curled lines seemed to me to be sometimes composed of a flocculent instead of a smooth thread, and it is this which, seen by the eye, or by a lens of low power, gives the milky appearance described. The above results I obtained from freshly spun webs, whose clean silk was unmarred by use.

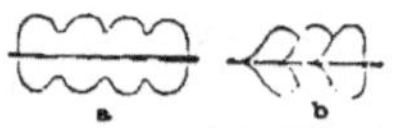

Other studies of this cross line, made from older snares, showed that it consists of one, two, or three separate threads, around or between which the fine flocculent material was twisted or fastened somewhat as in Fig. 178. The latter presented a milky appearance, and was spread out so fine that often no traces of independent filaments were observed. In short, it was a very delicate, cottony mass, much wider at some parts than at others, presenting in miniature something like the appearance of the woolen rolls which, as a boy, I used to watch with intense interest as they passed into the flyers of an old fashioned spinning wheel.

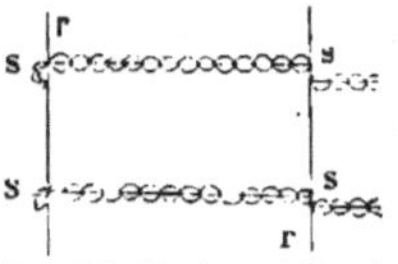

Flocculent Thread.

Fig. 176. Thread of Hyptiotes, showing opposite sides. (After Emerton.)

In this cottony mass one frequently observes a number of particles of dust, pollen, and various minute amorphous objects, which have been caught upon the sticky material as they drifted before the wind. As in the case of the web of Uloborus, they present to the casual observer, even when looked at by a common magnifying lens, the appearance of beads upon the ordinary thread of Epeira. It is not strange, therefore, that many have been deceived and led to suppose that the Triangle spider makes a beaded web. The true

Bead like Appendages.

Fig. 177. Section of Hyptiotes' snare, to show the arrangement of the flocculent thread. Greatly magnified.

[1] Cobwebs of Uloborus. Am. Jour. Sci., 1883, page 205. Also New England Spiders of the Family Ciniflonidae, Pl. XI.

character of the spiral can only be satisfactorily determined by taking it upon a suitable frame and observing it under the microscope.

The spiral lines, where they cross the two interlying radii, are not contingent to the radius at one and the same point, but present precisely the appearance of the concentrics in the notched zone of a common full orbed snare. The entire snare of Hyptiotes is thus notched, and in this respect it corresponds with the domed orb of the Basilica spider as I have described it.

The length of the snare proper varies a good deal. I have measured one five and a half inches in length, another two and a half, and another thirteen inches, measuring from the apex to the base line. The **Dimensions.** spiral space itself will measure two and a half inches, three and three-fourths inches, rarely more, often less. The length of the base line, which represents the width of the snare at the open or widest part of the triangle, also varies much. I have measured one twenty-six inches in length, the longest of which I have any note. The radii are not separated from each other by equal spaces at their points of attachment to the base line. For example, one snare measured two inches in the upper space, between the first and second radii; in the middle space, one and one-fourth inch; in the lower space, one and one-fourth inch. At the point nearest the apex,

Fig. 178. Hyptiotes' spiral armature, greatly magnified. The regular curls of the flocculent thread are broken up and hang irregularly.

where the spiral lines terminated, the width across the snare between the two outer radii was three-fourths of an inch.

The distance from the apex of the triangle to the point where the original line is attached I have called the trapline, and this also varies in length. I have the following measurements: One and one-fourth inch, one and one-half inch, one and six-eighths inch, two and one-half, five, and thirteen inches. The snare drawn at Fig. 169 gave the following measurements: trapline, two and a quarter inches; number of spirals, fourteen, separated from each other by distances varying from one-eighth to one-fourth of an inch; the spiral space, two and a half inches long; distance across the web at the origin of the spirals (the point nearest the trapline), two inches; distance across the web at the termination of the spiral system, four and one-half inches. The three radial openings measured at the base line respectively, two, one and a half, and one and three-fourths inches.

A fine large snare spun by a male Hyptiotes gave the following measurements: number of spirals, twenty-three and twenty-two; the spiral space occupied three and three-fourths inches in length; the distance across the snare at origin of the spiral space, one inch and five-eighths; distance straight across a, the end of spiral space, five and one-half inches. From the point of the triangle to the origin of the spiral space was two inches. There was a quite long trapline, about thirteen inches. The base line of

the radii was also very large. The space between the several radii, measured at the termination of the spiral space, was about equal in all to one
and seven-eighths inches. Across
the snare at the beginning of the
spiral space the distance was one-
half inch in all.

When the web is completed,
the spider takes a position upon
the trapline, sometimes
very close to the apex,
but more frequently
removed from it by a varying
space. Sometimes she is close
to the apex, at other times well
removed therefrom; sometimes

Position of Spider

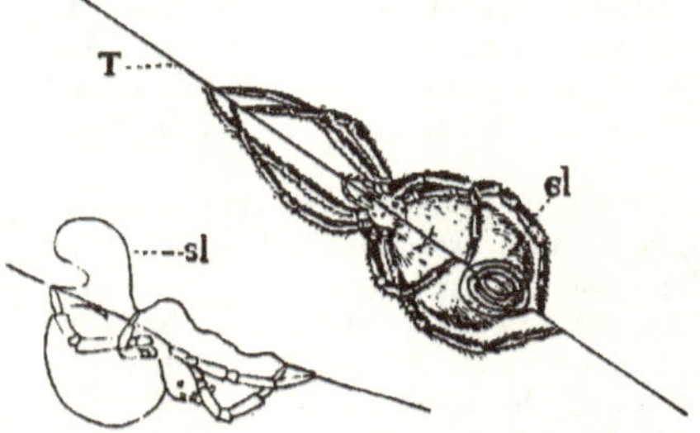

Fig. 179. Position of Hyptiotes on her trapline, T. The coil,
cl, is shown in the upper figure, and at sl in the lower.

she hangs upon the line between the apex and the branch to which the
line is suspended, and again is found close up to the branch, even resting her abdomen against it.

II.

The position of the spider upon her trapline is very peculiar, and
worthy of careful study, for it gives a clue to the curious phenomenon
which is now to be described. Her face and fore feet are
towards her triangular snare. The trapline is held within the
first two pairs of claws, which are placed near each other (see
Fig. 179, upper figure), and is drawn so tightly that every portion of the wedge shaped
web is perfectly taut, as represented in Fig. 180. Upon
applying the lens to the
spider as she thus hangs
with back downward, it will
be seen that between the
second pair of legs and the
third pair of legs, the line
is also taut. This is its
condition according to most
of my observations, but it
seems that sometimes it is
slightly slackened, as shown

Using the Spring Net.

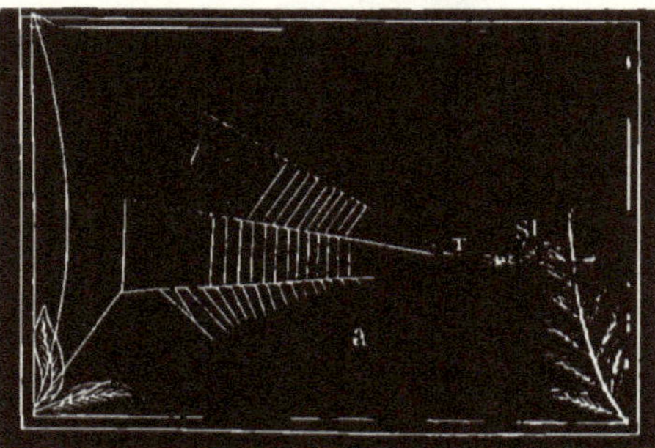

Fig. 180. Hyptiotes' snare drawn taut.

in the lower figure in the cut. (Fig. 179.) Carrying the lens along to
the short third pair of legs we see that they are bent at the knee, and the
claws approach each other at the trapline, which they firmly clasp. Glanc-
ing at the fourth or hind pair of legs, it is observed that these are stretched

backward, and also clasp the trapline in the approximated claws. But between the third and fourth pairs of legs the trapline presents a peculiar

Coil of Slack Line. form. Instead of being drawn taut or held loosely, it has the appearance of a coil, and this in fact it is. About three-fourths of an inch of the trapline, or a portion equal to four times the entire length of the spider, is rolled up above the spinnerets and the hinder part of the abdomen, between the third and fourth pairs of legs. (Fig. 179, cl.) Behind the spider the trapline is in the same taut condition that it presents in front of the spider.

The net is now in perfect condition for operation. The whole front part of it, which includes the snare proper, is drawn taut in every cord and fibre. (See Fig. 180.) The trapline behind the spider is in

Springing the Snare. the same tense condition. The only portion that is relaxed is the bit of coil between the last two pairs of legs, and occasion-

ally (perhaps) the short stretch between the front legs and the third pair. We will now suppose that an insect strikes the snare, although the same effect can be produced by touching the spider herself or by tickling the fibres of her web in a manner to imitate the movement of a fly. She is not, however, easily deceived by the latter trick; at least, I have rarely been success-

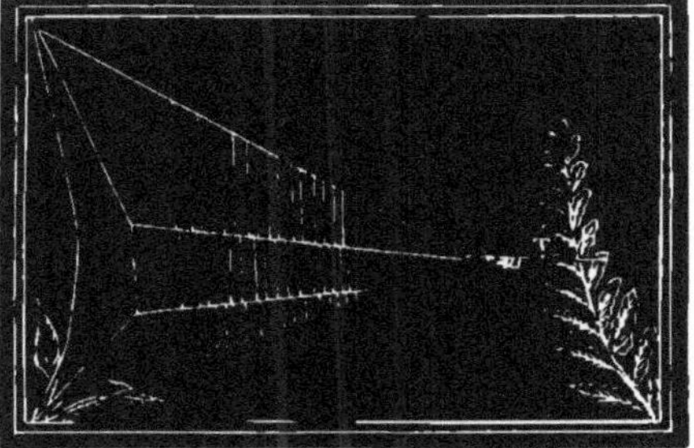

FIG. 181. A relaxed snare of Hyptiotes, after the snap.

ful enough to compel her to spring her net by mimicking the movements of an insect, and when I desired to make the observation, was compelled to touch her gently with a pencil. As soon as the spider perceives that her prey is trapped, she unclasps simultaneously all the fore feet holding upon the trapline, and those of the third pair of legs which keep relaxed the coil of slack line. Instantly the entire snare shoots forward (Fig. 181), and by a principle of inertia which needs no explanation, the spiral lines are thrown forward around the insect (Fig. 182), whose entanglement is thus secured. With a rapidity so great that the eye is not able to follow the details of the movement, the snare is tightened; the spider momentarily assumes the previous position of expectancy, and again springs her net. This may be repeated several times, Wilder having observed six successive springings of the net.

In this movement the spider appears to shoot forward with her snare, but in point of fact she has remained stationary, or at least has advanced but a trifle. But now, crawling to the apex of her snare, she seems to ascertain the exact location of the fly by pulling upon the radii. Having satisfactorily decided this, she runs along the loosened radius and some-

Securing the Prey. times, when the prey is small or hopelessly entangled, contents herself by pulling it up by means of the lines about it, and carries it to her accustomed station, to be eaten at leisure. More frequently she moves along the trapline, and almost entirely destroys the triangular section which forms the web. This action is thus correctly described by Professor Wilder:—

Before reaching the apex the spider cuts with her jaws the apex line, but as she maintains her hold in front of the cut by her first and second pairs of feet, and has a communication in the rear through the line which most spiders always attach to a point behind them, she does not fall, neither is the net loosened beyond a certain limit; it usually seems to recoil about an inch; this recoil tends to entangle the prey like the original snap of the net. The spider again advances, gathers the radii together and cuts them all, still keeping the line drawn out behind; again the net recoils and collapses. Again she advances and cuts the radii; the net is now hardly

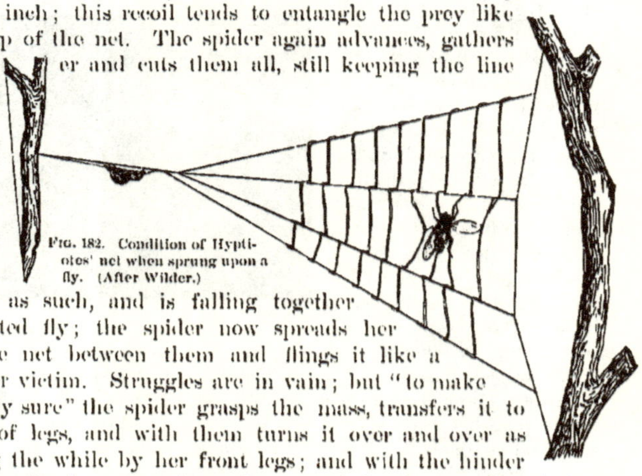

Fig. 182. Condition of Hyptiotes' net when sprung upon a fly. (After Wilder.)

distinguishable as such, and is falling together about the devoted fly; the spider now spreads her legs, gathers the net between them and flings it like a blanket over her victim. Struggles are in vain; but "to make assurance doubly sure" the spider grasps the mass, transfers it to her third pair of legs, and with them turns it over and over as a ball, hanging the while by her front legs; and with the hinder pair, used alternately, draws out from the expanded spinnerets broad sheets of silk which, relatively to the power of the fly, are like steel bands upon a man.

Having in this way reduced the prey to a rounded ball, in which its limbs are hardly distinguishable, the spider takes it in her jaws and mounts to her place. A single fly of ordinary size seems to occupy a whole day in the eating. When finished, the remains are cast down as a pellet, so perfectly deprived of moisture that it is probable that this species, like Nephila and perhaps all Epeïridae, sucks out the gum of its old net and reëlaborates it for use in making a new one.[1]

My observations of the feeding habits of Hyptiotes correspond with those of Professor Wilder. She is very deliberate in her mode of proceed-

____
[1] Op. cit., page 651.

ing; slowly rolls the insect in swathing thread until it assumes the appearance of a round flossy ball. One female that I observed was a

Feeding Habits. long time in thus preparing for her banquet. The spirals of her web had been broken in the capture, a single thread alone remaining. In another example observed the entire interradial system was obliterated.

This, however, is not, as Wilder supposes, a peculiar habit. I have frequently noticed Epeïroids doing precisely the same thing. The only difference is that in the case of the latter a space consisting of two, three, or four

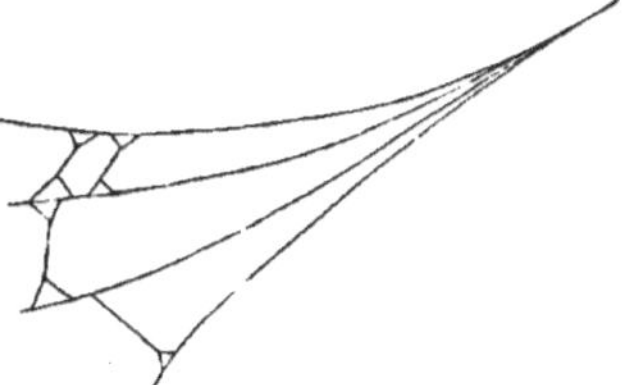

Fig. 183. Outlines of a relaxed net after service.

radii would be cut out, leaving thus a large circle or wedge shaped gap in the snare. This gap corresponds almost precisely to the appearance of the Triangle spider's net after she has cut out the entangled fly and completed the enswathment preparatory to feeding. Of course, however, as Hyptiotes makes only a sector of a circle, she has nothing left of her snare after the insect is thus prepared; whereas spiders making circular webs have a goodly portion of their orbs intact and ready for service after one sextant is destroyed. Substantially, then, we may say that the same thing occurs with the snare of Hyptiotes and the snare of Epeira when the entangled insect is captured, cut out, and enswathed.

I noticed what seemed to me a remarkable peculiarity in the manner of swathing and feeding upon a gnat taken by one of these spiders. Hyptiotes hung to her trapline by the two fore feet, which were stretched out quite at length from either side, as represented in Fig. 184. Her jaws and palpi appeared to me (although I could not quite make this out) to be supported upon the trapline. At least they overreached that line and grasped the partly enswathed insect, which lay over the line on the side opposite the spider's body. The palps reaching upward from one side and the third feet reaching beneath from the other side revolved the insect,

Fig. 184. The Triangle spider swathing a fly.

while the hind legs paid out the silk and manipulated the swathing as represented at Fig. 184. The attitude was an extremely odd one, and had the savor of that grotesqueness which seems to me always to mark the appearance and behavior of this aranead.

When the fly was sufficiently secured it was carried back to the trapline, whereupon Hyptiotes rolled herself over beneath her line in the ordinary posture, laid hold of the trapline by the two hind pairs of legs, and gathered up between them the ordinary coil of silk thread. Then she stretched forward the two fore legs upon one side of her body and grasped the trapline just in front of her face, and bent the other two fore pairs of legs around toward the ball within which the insect was swathed and which was held well elevated within the mouth. The two bent fore legs evidently assisted in manipulating the food while the spider made a meal. This seemed as odd a posture as that assumed during the swathing of the fly. (See Fig. 185.)

When the snare has been sprung and the spider wishes to tighten it, she does so by apparently first drawing upon the trapline with the fore **Use of the Feet.** feet, accomplishing the movement after the manner of Epeïroids by placing one claw before the other, as a sailor ascends a rope hand over hand. At the same time, or immediately thereafter, she executes a similar movement with the two hind feet, only reversing the direction. It should be said that during the process of snapping the net, the hind pair of feet hold to the trapline and never let go until the spider abandons her position to visit the snare in search of prey. The third pair are also held in position, so that when the hind feet begin to

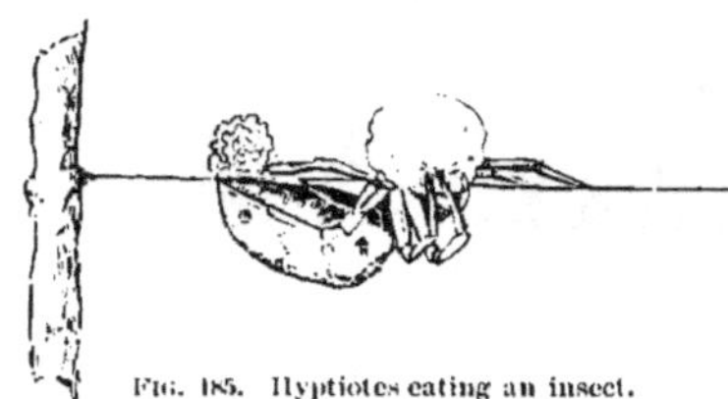

FIG. 185.   Hyptiotes eating an insect.

pull backward, shoving hand over hand, so to speak, under the trapline towards the point of attachment, an amount of slack is formed between these feet and those of the third pair, which very soon rolls up into the coil of slack line which has just been described. It is thus quite prepared for another spring of the snare.

I have observed the same peculiar use of the hind legs when the spider had occasion to raise herself from beneath upwards. Epeïroids **Backing up Cables** ascend a dropline head uppermost, pulling themselves hand over hand, and allowing a coil of thread to accumulate between the palps and the jaws. Hyptiotes, instead of turning and ascending head foremost, mounts tail foremost, keeping her claws attached to the trapline and drawing herself up hand over hand, following the method by which she draws herself backward in order to tighten her snare. It presents a very odd appearance to see her ascending a dropline in this position, literally "backing" up it, although one is not so much struck with the oddity of it when he sees her recovering after snapping her snare.

The Triangle spider has the habit of violently oscillating her web, just as do many of the Orbweavers; that is to say, she not only draws it back and forward by snapping her trapline, but shakes it up and down or to and fro.

According to Professor Thorell, the males of Hyptiotes are extremely rare, although the females are pretty common during the summer months. Mrs. Treat found the males of our Triangle spider at home with the females during two seasons. They were not in webs of their **Males.** own, but always in the upper corners of the nets of females where the foundation lines are fastened to the trees. They were thus opposite their mates, who were waiting beyond the apex, and apparently were watching all their movements with great interest. This is the custom with males of most Orbweavers during the pairing season. It is a mistake, however, to suppose that the males do not spin snares. I have frequently found them upon webs of the same construction and operated in the same way as those of females. At one time, I found in a fir tree a group of ten males, with their snares spun close together.

A curious behavior was noticed in a Triangle spider observed in a pine wood in the Allegheny Mountains. Numbers of snares were there found on hemlock trunks and dead standing saplings. I cut the trap-**Muscular** line of one of these webs to see how it would affect the spider. **Rigidity.** She was hanging at the time with her hind legs quite near the trunk of a tree. Instead of dropping downward when the support of the fore part of her body was broken, she simply settled backward a little so that the end of her abdomen rested against the tree. In this position her body extended straight out from the trunk in a line at right angles thereto. The fore legs were slightly bent and held but a remnant of the trapline, which was greatly ruffled in the manner of a taut string when suddenly untwisted. Both pairs of hind legs in the meantime were holding tightly to two short cords, one in each pair of claws, which were attached to the tree by little conical clusters of threads firmly glued to the bark. The spider in this attitude presented an odd figure, the like of which I have never

Fig. 186. Muscular rigidity of Hyptiotes.

·observed in any other species. (See Fig. 186.) Her body was perfectly rigid, although there was nothing to maintain it in position except the bracing which resulted from the hold upon the lines above described. I watched her for a long time, and she showed no signs of wearying or relaxing her attitude.

The amount of muscular vigor displayed by the spider in maintaining this position must have been very great, but certainly not greater than required to preserve the attitude which she assumes when holding her snare ready for prey. This attitude she will maintain, without the slightest appearance of muscular tremor or weariness, for a long period of time. I have never had patience to see how long she would thus hold out if not interrupted by insects striking her snare; but I can readily believe that her patience will endure not only for a day but probably for more than a day.

We thus have a tolerably full natural history of this interesting species. There are few animals whose habits better repay the student; but one who wishes to know the secrets of Hyptiotes' daily life must be content to bear patiently many disappointments, endure many discomforts, and attend, through days of tedious waiting, with unruffled temper and unflagging zeal, upon the slow unfolding of the record. The spider is one to be looked after, not stumbled upon; its form is so inconspicuous, and its home in such obscure sites, that the naturalist will need to seek for it. No doubt much yet remains to learn of its behavior; its cocooning habit, for example, is wholly unknown, and the cocoon which Professor Wilder supposes to be hers is by no means well identified. The little mother has persistently denied me, in spite of numerous endeavors, the pleasure of settling this question. I cordially wish some of my readers better success in unraveling this and other unwound threads of the Triangle spider's life.

CHAPTER XII.

THE RAY SPIDER AND HER SNARE: ACTINIC ORB.

I.

In the vicinity of Philadelphia, June 14th, 1881, I found a number of spiders grouped not far from each other on orbicular webs, which proved to be of a type previously unknown, and which I called the Actinic or Ray formed orbweb. At the time of my discovery **Name and Position.** I considered the spider new to science, and gave it the name of Epeira radiosa in a paper containing a careful and detailed description of its spinning habit.[1] I then intimated that it would probably be assigned to a new genus, and subsequently in a verbal communication proposed for it the name Actis radiosa. Emerton, in his monograph of the New England Epeiridæ, created for the spider the genus Microepeira.[2]

Subsequent investigation led me to believe that the spider belongs to Cambridge's genus Theridiosoma,[3] and probably is identical with the European form Theridiosoma gemmosum of L. Koch.[4] This genus has marked resemblances to Epeira, as Cambridge himself allows; and on the ground of structure appears to be at least equally related to the Epeïroids. Count Keyserling, however, in his extended and admirable monograph of the American spiders,[5] retains the species among the Retitelariæ, where it had previously been placed.

But the spinningwork shows conclusively that it must be placed with the Orbitelariæ. To that position, therefore, I have assigned it,[6] and it becomes necessary to transfer the genus Theridiosoma from the Retitelariæ to the Orbitelariæ, and to make for it a new family, for which I have proposed the name Actinæ.[7] The systematic position and relations of the

---

[1] Proceedings Academy Natural Sciences of Philadelphia, 1881, pages 163–175.

[2] Trans. Conn. Acad., Vol. VI., 1884, page 320.

[3] Rev. O. Pickard-Cambridge. Theridiosoma argenteolum: Annals and Magazine of Natural History, 1879, page 193.

[4] Theridium gemmosum: Verzeichniss der bei Nurnberg beob. Arten, page 69.

[5] Die Spinnen Amerikas: Theridiidæ, von Graf E. Keyserling, Zweiter Band, page 218.

[6] Proceed. Acad. Nat. Sci., Phila., 1889, page 180. "Note on the True Systematic Position of the Ray Spider."

[7] Actis, ἀκτίς, a ray.

Fig. 187. The Ray spider seated on her snare, just before drawing the trapline.

species will be considered more fully in the appropriate part of this work.[1] At present we may devote our attention to the remarkable and most interesting character of the web.

The locations in which I first discovered the snares, and where afterward I found them to be quite abundant, had been for several years a familiar and favorite hunting ground for spiders. It illustrates the fact that some of the most interesting discoveries that await future observers may be found near their own well known haunts, and upon ground that has been often searched by other workers, or even by themselves.

The first examples of the species collected by me attracted little attention so far as the snare was concerned, because they seemed to be simply a new species, or the young of an old species of Orbweaver, hanging upon the remnants of webs greatly broken by ordinary wear and tear in capturing insects. But the repetition of the form, particularly the peculiar character of the open central, struck me as strange. How could the nets of several spiders possibly happen to be twisted into the same shape, and that shape so strikingly odd as that which I observed? This caused me to make a

Discovery.

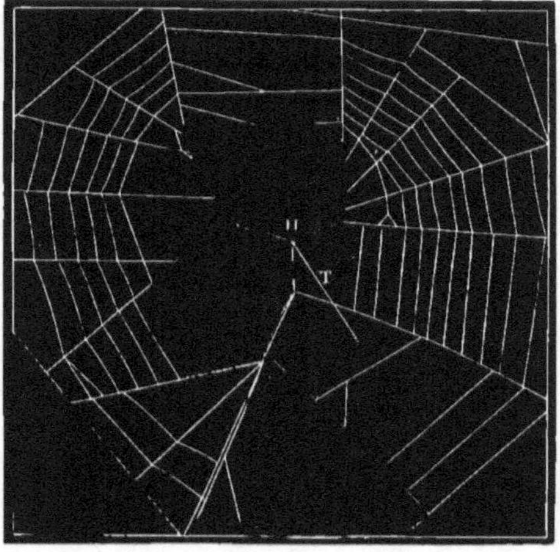

Fig. 188. Interblending of rays upon one axis. H, hub, or central point; T, trapline.

<hr>

[1] Dr. Thorell, to whom I sent specimens, has recently written me that he considers my Radiosa quite identical with Theridiosoma gemmosum (L. Koch), and agrees with me that on structural grounds alone it may be well ranked with the Orbitelariae.

more careful examination of the spinningwork of these little strangers. As the snares were hung invariably within the interstices of rocks forming the remains of a ruined dam, or in cavities underneath roots of old stumps of trees, or in recesses of the overhanging banks of a little brook or run, everywhere shadowed by shrubbery and thick foliage, it is not strange that the peculiarity failed to attract attention, and was only developed by more careful research.

On account of the continually changing form of the snare, it will be necessary to present it from various points of view, and as seen in different **Snare Described** stages of its diurnal changes. Fig. 187 presents a view of the snare in a partially relaxed condition. The spider is seen seated in the centre of a series of rays, i, ii, iii, iv, v, which are grasped by the third and fourth pairs of legs. There is no hub, properly speaking,

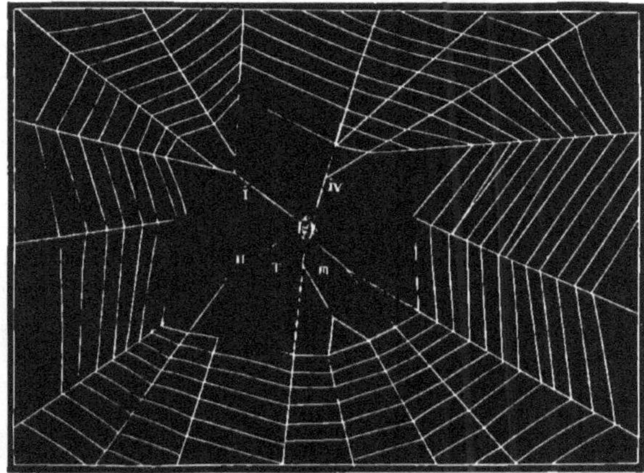

Fig. 189. View from front. Web taut. Perspective not shown. Central opening exact.

but the axes of the rays may be seen at times united upon a central point, as at H, Fig. 188. The general tendency is to four or five main divisions or rays, as may be seen by studying the figures presented. But there is more or less variation, and in the course of the day's usage in capturing prey two sections will become interblended upon one axis, as appears to be the case in Fig. 188 and also in Fig. 191.

The central space is a large, irregular opening, constituting about one-third of the entire snare, whose diameter is usually from three to five inches, as at Fig. 189, which is drawn natural size. The central circle, meshes, and notched spirals which so generally characterize orbwebs are thus wholly wanting in the Actinic snare.

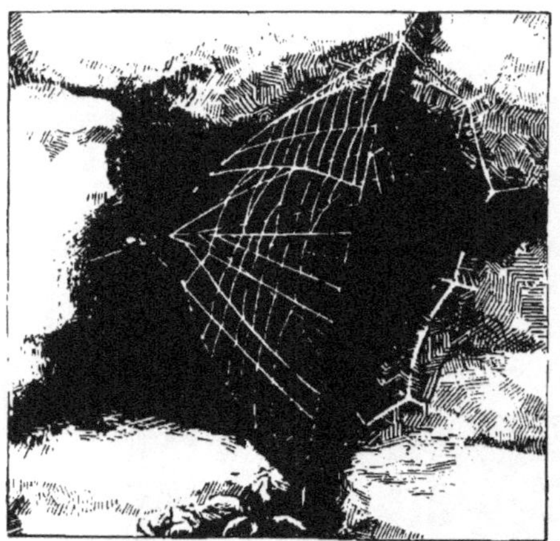

Fig. 190. Side view of Ray spider's snare when drawn taut or bowed. Seen within a cavity.

The orb may be said to be composed of a series of independent rays or sectors, each ray consisting of several spirally crossed radii, and the whole series united into an orb by cross lines or spirals like those which unite the radii. In the shifting of the section lines above referred to, this separation of the orb into independent rays is always quite evident. The spirals are covered with viscid beads, as in most orbwebs. The radii do not all pass to the hub or centre, as do those of orbwebs generally, but converge for the most part upon the axes of the rays as represented at Figs. 187, 188, 189. Thus at Fig 189 the various radii of the several sectors converge consecutively upon the axes i, ii, iii, iv. These axes themselves converge upon a single strong thread or trapline, T, which is attached to some part of the surrounding surface of rock, earth, or plant. When the snare is flat or relaxed, as was the case with the one drawn at Fig. 188, and as appears in Fig. 187, the trapline is often about perpendicular to the plane of the orb, having the relative position of the handle to the rays of an open Japanese umbrella. This, however, depends somewhat upon the environment ; a convenient point for the attachment of the trapline will cause the animal to divert the thread more or less from the perpendicular.

We may now suppose the spider placed as in

Fig. 191. Ray spider's snare when bowed. Viewed from behind.

Figs. 187 and 189, at the point where the rays converge, grasping the axes with the four hind feet. She has the posterior part of her abdomen toward her snare, thus reversing the attitude of all her tribe. Moreover, her back is turned upward. The two front feet seize the trapline and draw it taut. Then, precisely as a sailor pulls upon a rope, "hand over hand," the little arachnid's feet move along the trapline, one over another. As she moves, going, of course, away from her net, the axes of the rays, **Bowing the Snare.** held firmly in the hind feet, follow her; the centre of the snare bears inward, the other parts are stretched taut, and the web at last has taken the form of a cone or funnel as at Figs. 190, 191. In this position the snares continually suggested an umbrella with ribs reversed by the wind and the covering stripped loose from the top of the handle. Fig. 190 gives a side view of the web when thus bowed or drawn taut; another snare is shown at Fig. 191, as seen from behind. These snares were located within cavities formed by the dropping away of stones from the ruined dam breast in which they were first discovered.

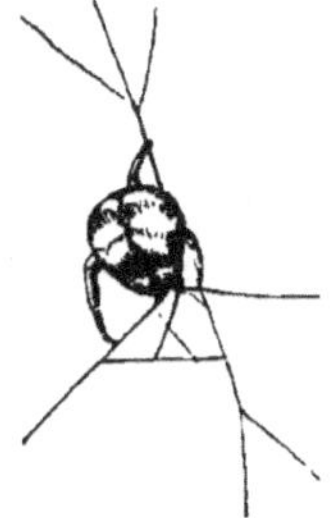

Fig. 192. Ray spider seated upon her foot basket, back upward.

In the example shown at Fig. 191 the spider has moved quite down the trapline to the surface of the little twig projecting into the cavity to which it is attached. It will thus be seen that the snare is more or less a plane surface, or more or less conical, according to the position of the animal upon the trapline and the degree of tension thereof.

II.

When an insect strikes the snare, the spider has two modes of operating. The first somewhat resembles that of the ordinary Orbweaver, in that the insect is simply permitted to entangle itself, and is then taken, swathed, re-**Operating the Snare.** turned to the centre, and eaten. There is, however, this difference: before the spider goes to the insect, the axes of the snare are twisted or knotted by a rotary action of her body and movement of the legs, so that the parts of the orb unbroken by the captive remain taut. Fig. 188 represents a snare thus "locked," or, perhaps I might more properly say, "keyed." The trapline is now relaxed, although its elasticity is such that the change can scarcely be noticed. The spider then moves upon her victim, quite habitually cutting out the spirals with her mandibles as she goes. When the insect is ensnared well towards the circumference of the web, and indeed, for the most part, in other cases also, it results that the ray or sector

Fig. 193. Position on foot basket with head bent downward.

upon which the entanglement had occurred is quite cut away. The spider thereupon proceeds to operate the remaining parts of her snare, which, in time, is thus destroyed by sections, as will be fully illustrated hereafter.

The second mode of operation resembles that of the Triangle spider, Hyptiotes cavatus (Hentz). It is at this point that the habit of our Ray spider becomes particularly interesting. The Triangle spider makes a tri-

Resemblance to Hyptiotes. angular web, which is in fact an orb sector, composed with unvarying regularity of four spirally crossed radii converging approximately upon a single line. Upon this line the spider hangs back downward, grasping it with all her feet, and having a portion of the line rolled up slack between her two hind pairs of feet. Thus the forward and back parts of the trapline are taut, while the intermediate part is slack. The spiral parts of the snare are also taut. When

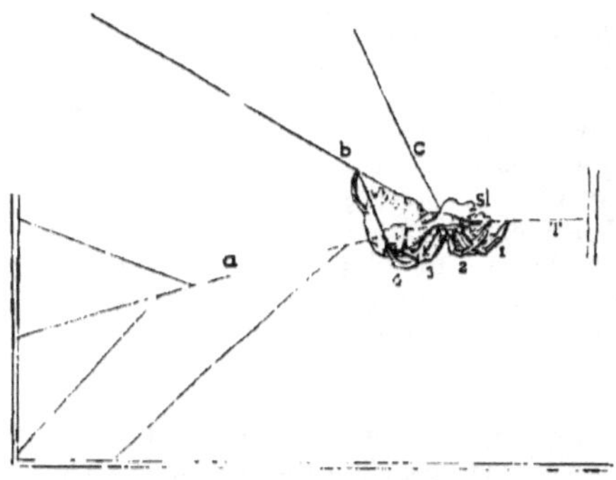

Fig. 191. Ray spider (greatly enlarged) in position, back downward, on a taut snare. To show the slack line coil, Sl. The positions of the feet on the foot basket are marked by numerals; a, b, c, the axes of several rays.

the web is struck by an insect, the spider suddenly releases her hind feet, the slack line sharply uncoils, the spider shoots forward, the whole web relaxes, and the spiral lines are thrown around the insect. This is repeated several times before the prey is seized. (See description and cuts in Chapter XI.)

Precisely the same action characterizes the Ray spider. Her ordinary position, or at least the one in which I most frequently observed her, is a sitting posture, back upward, as shown at Fig. 187. The axes of the rays are held in the third and fourth pairs of legs, the fourth commanding the upper, the third the lower

Posture on the Snare. series, quite habitually, as it appeared to me. A sort of "basket," or system of connecting lines, shown at Figs. 187, 195, unites all the feet, seeming to converge toward the fore feet (perhaps, upon the second pair), where they grasp the trapline. It is upon this foot basket that the spider sits when her net is bowed.

This, however, is not the invariable posture; in the reconstruction of the rays and shifting of the axes, as the day's work tells upon the snare, the spider will vary her posture to that of Fig. 191. The trapline generally has a direction downward rather than upward, so that the head and fore feet tend to be depressed below the abdomen, Figs. 192, 193, and this depression may gradually result in the complete inversion of the animal, so that she assumes the natural position of Orbweavers. I have even seen individuals with the back turned downward, Fig. 194, as is the habit with the Triangle spider and with all those species who make a dome or horizontal orbweb, as the Basilica spider and the Orchard spider. (See Chapter IX.)

If now the feet of the spider be carefully examined with a good glass, a coil of slack line will be seen, precisely as in the case of the Triangle spider. This is illustrated at Fig. 194, where a, b, c, are the axes of several rays, grasped in the third (3) and fourth (4) pairs of legs, and Sl is the coil or slack line curled up between these and the fore pairs (1 and 2), or simply between the pair of fore legs; that is, between the two first and the two second feet. As the spider does not exceed one-eighth of an inch in body length, and the position of the snare is within cavities and interstices of rocks, where the light does not bring out the delicate tracery of the fine webs, the observation of these and other points of like character, is a matter of some difficulty. But, although the exact relations of the coil to the feet were sometimes in doubt, and indeed seemed to vary somewhat, the existence of the coil and its general relations were determined beyond doubt. It is also certain that the slack line sharply uncoils and straightens when the spider releases her grasp upon the trapline, and that the web unbends and shoots quickly forward. It is instantly changed from the bowed or conical form of Figs. 190 and 191 to the circular plane of Figs. 187 and 188.

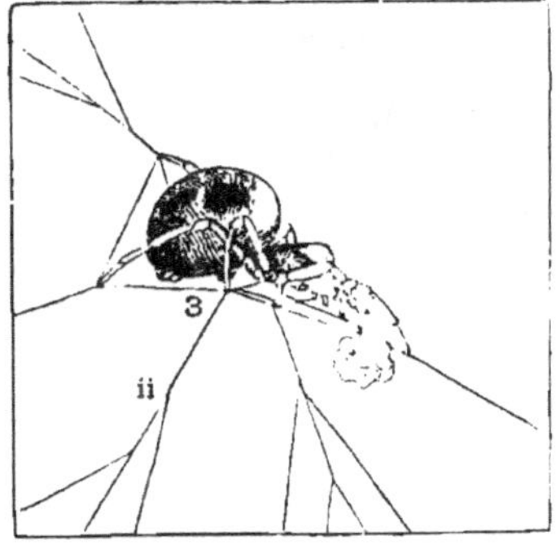

FIG. 195. Ray spider in position, back upward, showing slack coil and foot basket, ii; axis of a ray grasped by third foot, 3; trapline grasped by fore feet.

The following points, however, long evaded my observation, before webs were found which presented the conditions for successful study. But at last I was well satisfied. The "springing" of the snare is **Springing the Snare.** caused by the sudden releasing of the trapline from the fore feet, instead of the hind feet, as with the Triangle spider. The polarity of the two arachnids relative to their webs is reversed, Hyptiotes having her fore feet, but Theridiosoma her hind feet towards the snare. The slack line is therefore coiled between the two fore feet or between the fore and hind feet of Theridiosoma, but between the two hind pairs (as a rule) of Hyptiotes.

I have already explained the manner in which Hyptiotes is affected when her two hind feet are released from the trapline. The coil straightens, and the whole body of the spider shoots forward. If now we turn to

Theridiosoma, as represented at Fig. 194, or again, as shown at Fig. 195, we observe that if the fore feet, 1, 2 (Fig. 194) are released suddenly from the trapline, T, the whole body shoots backward, although still toward the snare, as with Hyptiotes. This was the action which I observed.

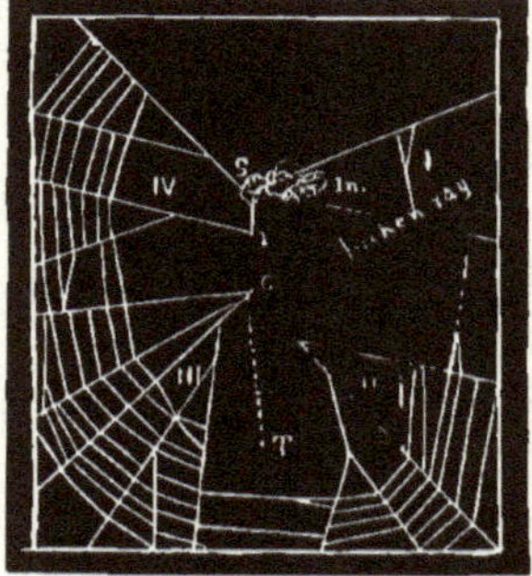

Fig. 196. Ray spider. Action when an insect is taken. S, spider; In, insect.

The determination was finally accomplished by first carefully sketching the arrangement of the basket stretched between the feet (2, 3, 3, 4, 4, Fig. 195). With this chart in one hand, and in the other hand a magnifying glass focused upon the feet, I watched until favored with several successive and unsuccessful springings of the net. As the spider only leaves her seat when she thinks that an insect is well entangled, and again bows her net by pulling on the trapline if no prey be ensnared, the above conditions enabled me to compare my chart of the basket, with the basket itself as seen under the glass. I found that the outlines on the paper and the lines under the animal's feet exactly corresponded. There had therefore been no change in the relative positions of the hind feet, mandibles, and palps, and perhaps also of the second pair (2) of feet. There had been an actual (not seeming) motion of the body with and in the direction of the snare, and this had been caused by releasing the first pair of legs (1) from the trapline. The only actual motion, therefore, was the slight hitch forward produced by the elasticity of the axes of the rays and other parts of the snare behind the aranead.

The importance of this determination seems greater from the fact that I had at first concluded that the Ray spider actually operated her snare by sections. That is, instead of springing the whole orb at once, as above described, she simply sprung the ray struck by an insect, by unclasping the foot holding the axis of that ray. Thus, ray ii, Fig. 195, would be sprung by releasing the axis of ii from the third foot, No. 3. This is probably not done when the snare is in complete form (as at Figs. 187, 189, 190), but I believe that it is done when the web has been partially destroyed, and is reduced to two rays or sectors, as at Fig. 197.

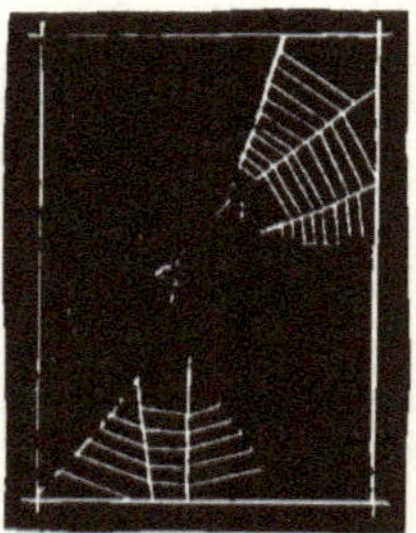

Fig. 197. Ray spider's snare after usage in taking prey. The spider is at the centre, holding the rays "locked."

The fragmentary condition of the Ray spider's web after contact with insects has already been referred to. The snare is gradually obliterated, a conclusion to which the spider herself very curiously contributes. When an insect strikes the snare, as at Fig. 196, ray I (broken ray), Theridiosoma first "keys" the snare by twisting together the foot basket and the parts adjoining (C), including the end of the trapline. This **Gradual Obliteration of Web.** maintains the compact condition of the snare after the spider has left the central point at which she has held all parts together in the manner heretofore described. Then the insect is sought.

Creeping along the axis of the ray upon which the prey is entangled, she cuts away the cross lines as she goes, leaving the bare skeleton of radii, as shown, Fig. 196, I, marked "broken ray." The insect is then brought back to a point (D) near the centre, but (in this case at least) above it, where it is eaten. While the feast goes on, not unmindful of future supplies, the spider (S) clasps the adjoining axis and (C D) the connecting lines, which appear to be in condition for operating somewhat in the usual way. When the former position is resumed, the insect is eaten, the trapline clasped, and the net bowed and tight ened.

After a morning's trapping, if the game has been plenty, and generally towards the middle of the afternoon, the snare will be found reduced to one or two rays or fragments of rays. I have seen it reduced to a bare skeleton. In Fig. 197, one ray (I), and two fragments of two others, are united into a new ray, and these are placed in opposite parts of the orb. Again, one-half of the orb may be eliminated (Fig. 198), leaving two radii (i, ii) to operate with. The Ray spider was also observed to construct or adopt a new trapline, thus changing, so to speak, her base of operations.

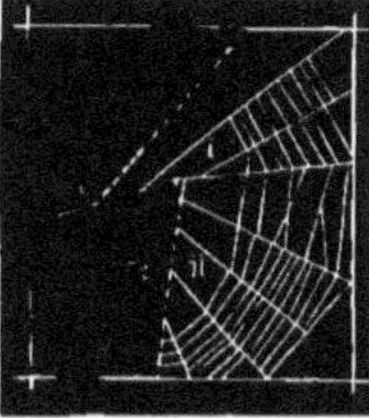

Fig. 198. Ray spider. Half of orb eliminated and a new trapline, Th, formed. Ta, position of old trapline; i, ii, remaining rays.

This action is illustrated at Fig. 198, where Ta is the original, and Tb the new trapline. This is not a frequent occurrence, as the necessity for changing the original line does not appear to arise very often.

III.

Not the least interesting and valuable feature of the Ray spider's industry is that it constitutes a connecting link between two forms of snare **Affinities.** which stand at the very opposite poles of the spinningwork of the Orbweavers. At the one extreme is the familiar circular snare or full orb of the ordinary garden spider. At the other is the orb sector of the Triangle spider. A glance at these will show how far they are apart in structure. The same separation appears in the habits of the two araneads. As opposed to Hyptiotes, the spiders of which Epeira is a type hang head downward in the centre of the orb, with their feet grasping small groups of the radii; or sit in a silken den, or crevice, holding to a taut trapline which is connected with the centre. There is no slack coil, and no springing of the net as with the Triangle spider.

The industry of Theridiosoma is united to that of the full orb makers, on the one extreme, by its orbicular character and its beaded spirals; but with that of Hyptiotes, on the other extreme, by the independent character of the rays, the nature of the trapline, and the entire mode of operating the snare. The facts necessary to trace these affinities I have already given.

Some of the striking differences I have also recorded, and they may thus be summarized. The web of Hyptiotes is a single sector; that of Theridiosoma has four or more sectors united. Hyptiotes commands one line with her feet, the trapline and its continuation; Theridiosoma commands several axes, which are connected with, but not continuous of, the trapline. Hyptiotes has her head, Theridiosoma her abdomen towards her snare. Hyptiotes habitually hangs to the trapline, back downward; Theridiosoma generally sits upon a foot basket of lines, back upward. Hyptiotes shoots forward when her net is sprung; Theridiosoma shoots backward; but both spiders move toward their webs. Hyptiotes holds her slack coil between the two hind feet; Theridiosoma between the fore feet. In these differences, the points wherein Theridiosoma varies from Hyptiotes show a quite apparent approach to the behavior of the full orb makers. Thus the distance which heretofore had separated between the far away extremes of the spinningwork of the Orbitelariæ, has been bridged over by the industry of our little indigenous aranead—the Ray spider. It is to be remarked that while structurally the Triangle spider is as widely removed from Epeira as economically, the Ray spider is more closely allied structurally to the latter than the former.

In correspondence with arachnologists, concerning the true position of the Ray spider, the question was raised as to the accuracy of the statement, in my paper of 1881, that the interradial lines of Theridiosoma are covered with viscid beads. The question is certainly one of great importance. Mr. Cambridge, in establishing the genus, which he regarded as a connecting link between Theridium and Epeira, alludes to the fact that Dr. Koch describes the snare as consisting simply of a few lines spun from plant to plant. "This habit," he declares, "together with some structural considerations, exclude it from the Epeïrides." Thus, it would seem that the spinning habit of the creature bore quite as strongly as its structure in determining its systematic position. Had Mr. Cambridge then been familiar with the real spinningwork of the species he might have had no hesitation in relegating it to the Orbitelariæ.

The question was raised, whether the spiral lines of my Ray spider might not have been covered with flocculent strings, somewhat after the manner of the snares of Hyptiotes and Uloborus. As the spider is desti-

tute of the calamistrum and cribellum, which are always associated with
this character of spinningwork, it was hardly possible that the spiral armature could have been of this sort. However, I was not able to testify on
the subject with that assurance which seemed to me desirable. It is certainly possible for one to be deceived by even an ordinarily careful examination. The webs of Theridiosoma are so habitually placed in
Grounds for Doubt. dark cavities and shaded locations, and in positions that often
extremely embarrass the observer, that on this ground alone one
would be liable to mistake. Again, I have often noticed that even the
simple lines of Theridium will be found covered with particles of dust
and the spherical grains of pollen, which at a casual glance present very
much the appearance of beads. More than once I have been drawn into
a second and third examination by this deceiving resemblance. Moreover,
I had limited my original examination to the use of a hand lens, and had
not made the more careful microscopic test which would have placed the
matter beyond doubt. I therefore resolved to reëxamine the subject before
a final expression of opinion.

An opportunity to do so did not present until the 8th of July, 1889.
In the vicinity of Wallingford, Pennsylvania, in a shaded ravine covered
with a wild growth of natural
plants that overhang a stream of
clear running spring water (Doe's
Run), I found a number of this
species, and made a thorough
study of the point in question. I
took with me apparatus by which
portions of the web could be separated and placed under the microscope.

Fig. 199. Beaded spirals on the snare of Theridiosoma
genimosum. (Magnified.)

Thus tested, in three separate snares, I was able to determine beyond doubt that the spiral line of Theridiosoma is precisely like that of
Epeira. The beads upon several strings, that is, the several portions between two radii, were counted, in one case numbering sixty-four. I was
able to make satisfactory drawings of these beads, Fig. 199.

The behavior of the web upon the frames and glass cups was precisely like that of Epeira, the beads melting upon the surface of the
glass, and the string remaining as a simple line in the midst of
The Spir-als are Viscid. the viscid mass. The beads reflected light; in appearance exactly resembled those of Epeira, and in some cases the cord upon
which they were attached was distinctly seen running through
them. Further, I examined portions of the snare upon which small insects
had been caught, and these showed in every respect the manner of entanglement which I have so frequently observed with the true Orbweavers.
(Fig. 200.) Previous to removing the sections from the webs, I tested
them with the tip of a blade of grass, to which the lines adhered very

closely; indeed, the viscidity of the beads was not only equal to that of Epeira, but greater than that of some species, as, for example, that of Labyrinthea.

In order to have separate and independent testimony to this fact, I requested my private secretary, Mr. Edwin S. Gault, to examine the various points submitted, and give an impartial report upon the same; first, as to the snapping of the snare; second, as to the recovery of the trapline by pulling upon it; third, as to the character of the web itself, whether it was a round web, resembling the Orbweavers'; fourth, as to the character of the spiral, whether it was beaded or unbeaded; fifth, as to **The Conclusion.** the manner in which insects were entangled upon the web, namely, whether they presented the appearance of having been caught in ordinary beaded snares of Epeira. In all these points Mr. Gault entirely corroborated my investigations.

It may therefore be considered as established beyond doubt that the snare of Theridiosoma gemmosum (or radiosum) as it appears in America is not only an orb of the character above de**Theridiosoma an Orbweaver.** scribed, but is armed with viscid beaded spirals. This fact alone, in view of the known relations between spinningwork and structure, would compel us to place it with the Orbweavers. But when we find that the indications of structure are quite sufficiently in harmony with those of habit to justify such a decision, we can no longer hesitate. I may venture the prediction that a careful study of the spinning habit of the European species will show that it entirely conforms to that of its American congener. It is greatly to be desired that such a study be made.

Fig. 200. Insect entangled upon snare of the Ray spider. (Magnified.)

IV.

The first specimens of the Ray spider taken by me were hung in large openings left between the breastwork stones of a ruined mill dam. The **Natural Habitat.** wall had crumbled and quite fallen away in places, leaving large cavities, within whose moist, cool shelter, among ferns and mosses, this species had domiciled. The brook poured over the middle part of the wall, making a pretty waterfall; briers, bushes, ferns, and various wood plants grew out of the wall and stretched over a deep pool twelve or fifteen feet in diameter, into which the water dropped. On the lower bushes and branches above the stream, and continually agitated by the splashing of the water, was a colony of Stilt spiders, Tetragnatha grallator, stretching their long legs along their round webs, and dancing with the motion of the waves; the beautiful nets of the Featherfoot Uloborus (Uloborus plumipes), nets of Tegenaria persica, Linyphia communis, Linyphia neophyta,

Epeira hortorum, and of one or two species of Theridioids, were in close neighborhood. The whole pretty scene was embowered in a grove of young trees. A more charming habitat could not well have been found.

Another colony, not far away, was established within the cavities formed underneath the roots of a large fallen tree, and beneath the ledges of some rocks over which the roots turned. In several similar positions were found the same snares, and also among the rocks in a wild ravine through which ran the stream, Lownes' Run.

Further explorations of the surrounding country showed that the spider was largely distributed, and in similar conditions. I found numbers in ravines, on the broad leaves of the skunk cabbage,[1] whose snares were stretched above the brooklet, and beneath the shelving banks. They were also found among the rocks of Crum Creek over the beautiful drive to Howard Lewis' mill. Subsequently I collected the same spider in Eastern Ohio (New Lisbon, Columbiana County), where it was domiciled in a deep, cool ravine, Mineral Spring Glen. A runlet that cuts across the escapement of a hill on its way to Little Beaver Creek, has worn out the rocks into a series of descending steplike platforms, over which the stream flows, forming one or two waterfalls of some height. On each side of the stream, and particularly under the ledges of the rock platforms, the snares of Theridiosoma were placed. The habitat of the Ray spider may therefore be described as moist, cool, shaded cavities and recesses among rocks and roots, beneath banks and foliage, over or near running water. I have compared my specimens with some of Mr. Emerton's collections, made in various parts of New England, and find them identical. A specimen sent by Dr. Koch to Count Keyserling had been collected by Dr. Brendel in Peoria, Illinois.

The distribution of the Ray spider is thus greatly enlarged, and no doubt it will be found in many other parts of America. One might venture the opinion, based upon its peculiar habitat, that the species will also be found in Canada. Accepting the species as identical **Distribution.** with Theridiosoma gemmosum, of which I have no doubt, we are able to place this interesting aranead also among those American species that have an intercontinental and possibly a cosmopolitan distribution.

[1] Symplocarpus (or Ichtodes) foetidus.

CHAPTER XIII.

ENGINEERING SKILL OF SPIDERS.

I.

It is a generally received opinion, even among well informed naturalists, and is certainly a fixed popular tradition, that Orbweaving spiders construct a web that is perfectly true in its geometric arrangement. This has highly redounded to the praise of the little weaver, particularly as she may spin by the sense of touch without the aid of sight.[1] It seems a pity to destroy any notion that may throw around despised Arachne a greater measure of respect in the popular mind, in which her standing is, as a rule, anything but favorable. However, in the interests of truth it must be said that concerning this point the popular opinion is only true in a general sense. There is much irregularity in the execution of many geometric webs.

The radii are not laid out with absolute mathematical accuracy, but are separated from each other by distances varying considerably. If, for example, one carries the eye around the circumference of this large orb, he will find here two radii terminating upon their marginal foundation lines at points half an inch apart, and there two others three-fourths of an inch apart, and in yet another place two others separated by one and a half inches. It is true that all orbs are not laid out as irregularly as this from whose measurements I have quoted, but more or less irregularity will be found on almost every web, particularly upon those spun by adult spiders. Again, the radii will be found blending with one another at various points instead of converging regularly upon a central point; and more or less departures of a like kind from mathematical accuracy characterize the spiral concentrics. However that may be, the actual facts in the case are sufficiently striking, and the general regularity of plan and the frequent close approach to geometric accuracy in special orbs are remarkable enough without resorting to exaggerations. In fact, it may well be doubted that absolute regularity, in the sense of symmetry, would be the most desirable for the uses of a web. The departures from mathematical accuracy may mark, and I have reason to believe do mark, a higher measure of utility, and

Imperfect Geometric Arrangement.

Symmetry not Essential.

---

[1] See Wood's "Homes without Hands," page 321.

show a continuous power to adapt the spinningwork to its environment. This seems to be done almost unconsciously. If this view be true the lack of mathematical symmetry may prove the presence of a higher skill rather than the reverse.

The query was started in my mind whether spiders dwelling along the seashore or in wind swept heights might not have developed some special habit of resisting the extraordinary danger to their snares by some extraordinary protection. But I have not found evidence favoring such a suggestion. I have only one example that looks at all in that direction.

FIG. 201. Orbweb (A) among rocks, braced against sea wind. B, braces; C, C, connecting line or trapline to the den, D.

Among the rocks around the lighthouse at Annisquam on Ipswich Bay, Massachusetts, I found a large orb of Epeira sclopetaria spun within a few feet of the surf, and stayed in the peculiar manner which is represented in Fig. 201. The snare was in a sort of gully or canal between the granite boulders on the shore, through which the wind blew **A Wind Swept Snare.** strongly as through a funnel. Across this little gully and exposed to the full force and suction of the wind the orbweb was built and stayed upon the side of one of the rocks, as at A. Farther along, a few lines were stretched across the opening, fastened to rocks on either side as at B, and upon this a line, CC, was suspended, attached at one extremity to the centre of the orb, and at the other to a cavity in the rocks, D, at which the aranead had her den. The line CC undoubtedly served as a trapline and a sort of bridge along which the spider moved from her snare to her nest. But its general appearance and structure suggested the idea that it was braced by the line BB, and acted as a stay to the orb itself.

I was inclined to think that this peculiar spinningwork showed an effort of the spider to brace a snare peculiarly exposed to winds. It may be, however, that the line B was an abandoned foundation line, or was one of those tentative threads which spiders are often spinning, and that its connection with the trapline was either an accident or afterthought. Perhaps, indeed, it might have been intended to increase the communicating power of the trapline.

The fact is, one is very apt, by an unconscious anthropomorphism, to attribute to the humblest creatures of the fields methods of reasoning and principles of action which have no existence in the inferior ani- **Anthro-pomorph-ism.** mals, and are simply the reflections of a higher intellect upon the works of a lower one. The naturalist must continually be on his guard against thus attributing to the creatures whose habits he is studying methods which in like circumstances would have been suggested to his own mind.

An illustration of this is quite in point. I have at various times met suggestions that especial engineering skill is shown by spiders in protecting their snares from the effects of wind or other violence of the natural elements, by the use of sundry objects as counterpoises. Although I had little faith in the theory, it seemed to me entitled to careful examination.

Once while walking along a graveled path bordered on either side by shrubbery, I saw what exactly corresponded with reports of so called engineering spinningwork. A large orbweb blocked the entire pathway before me. The foundation lines were strung across the walk and supported upon the bordering shrubbery, but a large pebble hung to the bottom of the web. It was nearly two inches above the surface of the ground, and my first thought was, here now is a case that confirms the opin- **A Case of Counter-poise.** ion that spiders support their orbicular snares with weights in order to balance them against the wind! Kneeling upon the ground, I made a careful survey of the premises, and came to the conclusion that there was no special intention in the case at all, but that the uplifting of the pebble was a matter of accident. The spider had run down her supporting lines to the ground, as is her invariable custom when spinning in a similar site; but, not having a tuft of grass or like material whereon to fasten the lines, she stuck them upon one of the pebbles scattered over the walk beneath.

Now the pebble lay but loosely in its artificial matrix, and when the wind rose and played upon the orbweb, bellying it somewhat, and when in addition the spider began to run up and down her snare, the pebble was simply lifted up by the tightening of the upper lines of the snare. This result was probably assisted by the natural contraction of the elastic threads, and by the pulling of the shrubbery under the force of the wind. My conclusion was, therefore, that the spider had balanced her orb in the usual way, but discovered that, although it was "founded upon a rock," her house was rendered insecure by the simple fact that the rock was not able to keep its place against the strain.

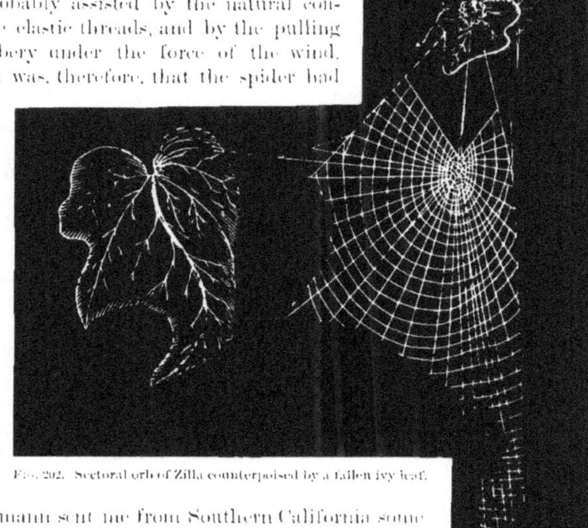

Fig. 202. Sectoral orb of Zilla counterpoised by a fallen ivy leaf.

Mrs. Eigenmann sent me from Southern California some cocoons of Zilla x-notata, from which I succeeded in raising a number of broodlings, who domiciled in my library. Many tiny snares were woven upon a potted ivy plant, and one of these gave an example of ready adaptation. The stay lines of the orb were attached to sundry leaves, and the upper and side attachments proved secure. But the leaf to which the whole lower system of supports was fastened fell off and stretched them downward, giving the snare a peculiar, elongated shape, which I have never seen quite approached. (Fig. 202.) This swinging pedestal amply served the purpose of the wee architect, whose frail web (drawn here natural size) was well balanced even by so light a weight. The weaving went on upon this new basis, radii were spun down into the elongation, and when the spiral loops were put in, that part was not omitted. Thus, the net space available for business was a good deal enlarged, and what was lost by the free sector at the top was quite made up by the netted

Zilla's Leaf Counterpoise.

prolongation at the bottom. The free space exscinded about one-fifth of the orb. The trapline branched at the hub end, and was held at the other end by the spiderling, which was backed against the axil of the leaf, surrounded by a tiny open booth of delicate cross lines. This leaf was braced to one behind it by various cords.

The late Rev. J. C. Wood, a good observer in many things, indorses the current opinion that if spiders find that the wind stretches their nets to a dangerous extent, they hang pieces of wood, stone, or other substance to them, so as to obtain the needful steadiness. He declares that he had seen a piece of wood which had been thus used by a Garden spider, and which was some two inches in length and thicker than an ordinary drawing pencil. The spider hauled it to a height of nearly five feet, and when the suspending thread was accidentally broken the little creature immediately lowered itself to the ground, attached a fresh thread, ascended again to the web and hauled the piece of wood after it. It brought this balance weight a distance of five feet along the ground before reaching the spot below the web. There were eight or ten similar webs in the veranda, but only in this single instance was the net steadied by a weight.[1] I cannot pretend, in view of the indefinite nature of the record, to explain on more natural principles the action of this spider. Had the stick been attached to the bottom of the web, I could have more readily drawn the inference that the purpose was to stay the orb against the violence of the wind; but I cannot imagine what use it could have been at the top, where it ought to have had a contrary effect. However, the inference which the ingenious and interesting popular writer has drawn from the incident is in any case entirely too sweeping.

Mr. Wood's incident does not stand alone. In " Hardwicke's Science Gossip," an admirable repository for general observations made by naturalists and nature loving persons in Great Britain, I find several records of a similar character, which I here note.

A large Diadem spider had begun a web by fastening threads to the eaves of a corridor roof about seven feet high. The extreme points of the outer stay lines were about four feet apart, and these were united at a distance of about three feet from the roof, thus forming a triangle. From the point thereof a single strand was carried down to within two or three inches of the ground. To the end of this strand was suspended a small triangular stone about half an inch across and one-fourth of an inch thick. It is evident, says the observer, that the stone must have been fastened to the glutinous web as it lay upon the earth, and was subsequently drawn up. As the wind caught the web it caused the stone to vibrate gently, and the motion thus communicated

Epeira's Wooden Anchor.

A Stone Anchor.

---

[1] Wood, " Homes Without Hands," page 319.

to the geometrical part of the web was scarcely perceptible.[1] The fact is not questioned, but the inference here made that the spider purposely drew up the stone as a counterpoise is wholly gratuitous.

Another correspondent[2] contributes a similar case observed by a lady in Scotland. She was walking through a wood when she suddenly noticed at some distance from the ground a small stone apparently poised in midair, but which, on closer examination, was seen to be suspended by a long thread from a spider's web, built between two trees.

A Scotch Case.

Yet another fact is recorded in the same journal, although it is quoted from an American magazine.[3] A gentleman, while passing along one of his garden walks in Brooklyn, saw, upon a cherry tree, a spider's web which was spun within foundation lines that stretched from the trunk to fastenings that ran out upon a large limb. The web rose at an angle of perhaps thirty degrees from the earth. The spider had by some means formed a corner downwards and suspended from it a little stone about half an inch long, three-eighths wide, and one-eighth thick. This was well secured, and hung some eight or ten inches below. This weight kept the web taut, and swung slightly as the wind affected it, and there it remained for several days.

An American Example.

Still another correspondent declares that, like many other persons, he has observed a small stone suspended from a spider's web, but expresses his doubt as to the suspension being an intentional act of the spider, and gives what I regard to be the true explanation, namely, that by the shrinking of the threads, or some change in the position of the web supports, the stone had been raised from the ground.[4] In all the above cases it will be observed that the evidence for intentional engineering is simply the fact of the stone's position, which is equally explained as above.

A Doubter.

Professor Pavesi has recorded a similar experience in his "Spiders of the Canton Ticino."[5] His attention was first called to the fact by a friend, and he was at the outset incredulous, but had confirmed his original observation. He begins with a statement which I can corroborate, viz., that when Epeira makes a web in the path of a garden or other sites between trees, it is her custom to drop a thread from the lower angles of the polygonal foundation lines of her net, which lines converge upon this single cord. Further, he declares (which is contrary to my experience) that upon this cord the spider ties a counter-

Prof. Pavesi's Case.

<hr>

[1] John Hepworth, "Science Gossip," November, 1868. page 262.

[2] J. F. D., id., page 283.

[3] J. R. S. Clifford, "Science Gossip," April, 1869, page 94. Quoted from the "New York Gardener's Magazine," 1841.

[4] George Guyon, id., page 118.

[5] Ragni del Canton Ticino: Annali Mus. Civ. Di Genova, Ser. 1, IV., 1873, page 39.

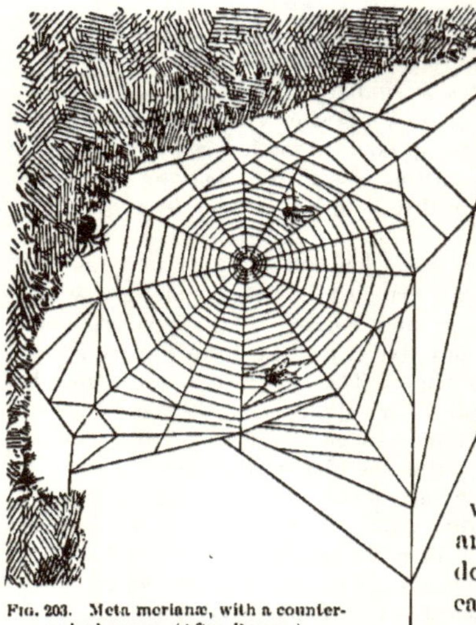

Fig. 203. Meta merianæ, with a counterpoised snare. (After Parona.)

found lifted above the ground
inally been in the same po
been raised by the elasticity
the wind, the motion of the

Another observation has
aly, and recently communi
ity in the Habits

**Meta's
Counter-
poise.**
he observed in a
of Meta merianae,
ficial gallery exca
customary with nets woven
of lateral lines, which were
vault, and were prolonged
was about sixteen inches
posed to the sweep of the
outer margin to the ground
seven centimetres) in length.
fragment of soil identical
large as a seed of Indian
soil was compact and heavy,
poise, holding the web fully

poise, which may be
a dry leaf, a little
piece of wood or oth-
er like material, but
commonly is a small
pebble or gravel from the
path. In one such case,
when he had taken away
the counterpoise, he saw
the spider descend by the vertical thread to ascertain what
had happened, and, having arrived at the ground, she fastened
the line to another pebble.

It will be observed in this case
that the pebble to which the thread
was fastened lay upon the ground,
and this fact itself compels me to
doubt Professor Pavesi's conclusion. I
cannot resist the thought that in this,
as in other cases where the pebble was
and acting as a counterpoise, it had orig-
sition upon the garden path, and had
of the thread, the mechanical action of
spider, and the swaying of the trees.
been made by Professor Parona of It-
cated in a paper entitled, "A Peculiar-
of Meta merianae."[1] In October, 1886,
villa at Baccione, on Lake Orta, a web
spun in the entrance of a short arti-
vated in solid earth. The orb, as is
in like positions, was stayed by a series
suspended upward against the arching
downward toward the walk. The snare
wide (forty centimetres), and was ex-
wind. The thread prolonged from the
was about twenty-seven inches (sixty-
At the end of this line was hung a
with that of the vault, and about as
corn (di grano turco). (Fig. 203.) The
and the pellet acted as a counter-
extended, so that it was sufficiently

[1] Particolarita nei Costumi della Meta merianae, Scop. del Prof. Corrado Parona. Annali
del Museo Civico di Stor. Nat. Di Genova, Ser. 2, Vol. VII., 1880, pages 250-5, Tav. VI.

taut to capture prey, as indicated by the number of victims entangled in its meshes. It was so firmly implanted, and so opportunely repaired, that Prof. Parona was able to observe it continuously for eight days. The interest of the observer was so much enlisted in what seemed to be an interesting and novel fact, that he made various inquiries and researches as to previous records.

Among others, he communicated his observation to the veteran arachnologist, Professor Thorell, requesting his opinion thereupon. The question was submitted by Professor Thorell to myself, as lying within the line of my special studies of life habits, and I returned for answer substantially some of the facts which have been recorded in this chapter. Nevertheless, Professor Parona has done well to place his observation upon record, and he has fortified it by like observations from other authors. Among these is the experience of Professor Pavesi, in part as above. He quotes a second observation in the same line made by Ninni, on the web of Epeira umbratica, as recorded in the Acts of the Society of Natural History of Veneto-Trentina.[1] This spider wove her snare under the roof of a beehive, and gave it stability by carrying down a thread to the soil and wrapping it around a pebble which was raised to the height of about seven inches (about eighteen centimetres) from the ground. Desiring to know if such ingenious work were confined to that case, the author destroyed the web and waited to see how the spider would behave in the face of the difficulty that it had previously overcome. Three days afterward he saw the web built in the same manner as before, but more perfectly finished. As though conscious that without another point of attachment the construction of her snare would be impossible, the spider carried down a thread which was maintained in a taut condition, not with one pebble as before, but with two pebbles and a straw. From this line, as an initial foundation line, she constructed the framework of her orb in the shape of an isosceles triangle, within which the orb was spun, in a position well sheltered from wind and rain. In order further to test the matter, the author destroyed this second web, but awaited the spinning of a third one in vain, as Umbratica abandoned the site.

It is to be observed that in this case also the testimony is defective, in that the observer did not see the spider actually using the pebble as a counterpoise; that is to say, in the act of suspending it upon the line. In point of fact, what possible benefit could have been obtained from staying the orb by a pebble hanging above the ground, when an attachment to the solid earth below in the usual manner, or to

Professor Parona.

Epeira umbratica.

Cui bono?

[1] Sopra la tela dell' Epeira umbratica: Atti Soc. Veneto-Trentina di Sc. Nat. Padova: 1876; Vol. 3, pages 204-5; Tav. VI. e VII. I regret that the particular number of this journal in which the reference is made does not happen to be in the library of our Academy of Natural Sciences, and I have not, therefore, been able to consult the original.

a pebble fixed therein, would have been more advantageous to the spider? This is equally true of all known cases of counterpoise.

After having cited my opinion, as communicated in my letter to Dr. Thorell, Professor Parona expresses, though with some reserve, his belief

Fig. 201. Swinging nest of the Shamrock spider, Epeira trifolium.

that the act recorded by him was an intentional one on the part of Meta. The counterpoise could not have been lifted up from the garden path, **Parona's View.** as no such material entered into the composition thereof. It had evidently come from the vault above, as it was of the same material, and retained living tufts of a moss that grew upon the overhanging vault. Moreover, if I correctly understand Professor Parona, the distance of the web (counterpoise?) from the ground was about a metre and a half, which would seem to preclude the theory that it had been raised up from the ground by the elasticity of the web, or the mechanical impact of the wind.

Nevertheless, I am constrained to believe that in this case also the explanation of intentional engineering must be dismissed. The pellet had evidently been separated from the vault by the erosion of the atmosphere, and had either been lifted up from the ground, where it had fallen, in the manner I have described, or, which is more probable, it had entangled within the web as it fell; had been prevented by the foundation cords from dropping entirely to the ground; had been held above the surface by the viscidity and natural elasticity of the threads; and while thus hanging, accidentally poised, it was made use of by the spider as a point from which to re-attach her foundation line. As long as it remained in poise, undisturbed by the wind or passing objects, it would be available for the purpose of staying her web; and in this position it was the fortune of Professor Parona to see it.

The Author's View.

However this theory may accord with the facts, I am perfectly assured that the spider could not have cut off from the vault a particle of soil so large, and then have transferred it to the position where it was seen. Such action is so wholly foreign from all that I have observed of the habits of Orbweavers, that I cannot possibly allow myself to admit it as a reasonable explanation. On the whole, my judgment is that none of the instances heretofore observed, in the form at least in which they are recorded, afford sufficient testimony to permit us to believe that Orbweavers have the engineering ability to counterpoise their webs against the action of wind and the natural shrinkage of the web material, by means of pebbles or other objects attached to marginal lines.

Indeed, if such action were really proved, it would seem to me an unwise and not a cunning exception to the general habit in like web sites, which is to carry the principal supporting line quite down to the firm earth. Nothing could be gained, and much would be lost, by exchanging this for an unstable counterpoise. Would the spider be apt to pause within an inch or two of the ground, which was thus clearly within its reach, to make so unprofitable an exchange? The only special wisdom that can be allowed the spider in the case is that which accepts an undesirable situation as at least available, and adapts her spinningwork thereto; and that is certainly to be recognized, and it is sufficiently remarkable.

Counter-poising Useless.

II.

It is not to be doubted that spiders do show considerable powers of adaptation in adjusting their spinningwork both to peculiar situations and special exigencies. Most of the above examples and perhaps all are illustrations of this. Another case in point was furnished by a Shamrock spider, Epeira trifolium, that exhibited a remarkable ability to adapt her domicile to very peculiar circumstances. She had placed her nest in the curled leaf of a grape vine, which becoming detached from the stem fell and entangled within the lines of the orb beneath. Whereupon the occupant, in nowise disconcerted, adjusted her tent, stayed it above and at the sides with guy lines, braced it beneath,

Special Adaptation.

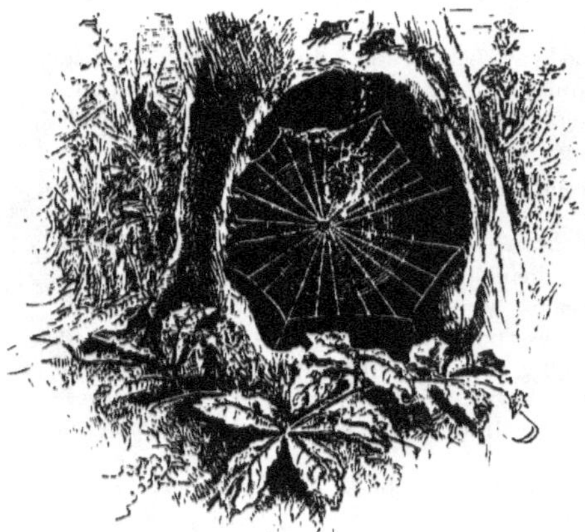

FIG. 205. Furrow spider's extemporized den of sawdust.

and proceeded to spin her snare directly below the opening. She attached her trapline to the hub, and thus in her hanging home continued to wait for prey.[1] (Fig. 204, page 216.)

Another somewhat similar case of adaptation in nest making was due to an accident in the environment of the web. A half-grown Epeira strix had woven a snare in the hollow of a tree (at New Lisbon, Ohio), within two feet of the ground. A colony of Pennsylvania carpenter ants (Camponotus Pennsylvanicus) had quarters in the tree, and a squad of black workers were busy excavating their wooden galleries. These dumped their chippings from openings just above the spider's orb, whose viscid spirals retained a goodly quantity of the brown sawdust. In course of time a ball of chippings as big as a walnut had accumulated,

A Sawdust Nest.

FIG. 206. A blockaded path.

---

[1] The incident occurred at Vineland, New Jersey, and notes and measurements for the figure were furnished me by Mrs. Treat. The incident is also recorded in that author's "My Garden Pets."

or, perhaps, had been purposely massed by the spider. However that may be, the ball was utilized as a nest; its centre had been pierced, a spherical cavity formed by silk lining the interior, which was entered by a circular door bound around the edge by spinningwork. This quaint domicile was pendent from one of the strong upper foundation lines, and herein Strix rested, while the emmet carpenters worked away above her, continually dropping chips over the roof of her nest and the orb beneath, until one side of the snare was quite covered with them. In this case the position of the nest, as well as its form, was exceptional,

Fig. 207. A meadow orbweb braced to an overhanging branch of a tree.

as the nest site of Strix is well nigh invariably beyond the limits of the web, sometimes, indeed, several feet. In these points the spider was evidently led to an intelligent variation of her nest building by circumstances. (Fig. 205.) A series of interesting illustrations of the same elasticity of habit in the nesting industry of the Furrow spider may be found in the subsequent chapter on Nesting Habits, and might, with almost equal propriety, have been introduced here.

Another case of adaptation may be cited, without impropriety, as a good example of Epeiroid engineering. While walking through the pine woods at the head of Deal Lake, New Jersey, I found a narrow path blocked by a structure which is represented at Fig. 206. It is easy to explain the mode of forming this remarkable framework, if we suppose that the spider was

From Treetop to Path. perched upon the twig, a, and emitted from her spinnerets a thread which was carried out and upward by the wind, and entangled at b, thus forming the prime foundation line, ab.

Thence she could have moved to the point between d and a, whence she would have dropped to the ground, a distance of ten feet, and hitched a second line to a tuft of grass. A third line might readily have been secured by dropping from the point d, the natural swaying of the spider, increased by a breeze, carrying her to e. This line, de, could easily have been pulled in by the cross lines above and below the orb. A convenient frame being thus obtained, the spinning of the orb would be a simple mat-ter. The entanglement to the side shrubbery at e, e, may also have been made by aid of the breeze in part.

If, in the absence of direct observation, one were to deny the use of air currents, then it must be supposed that the spider carried its line along the tree to the tip of the branch, b, which was twenty-five feet above the ground; and after that it would be difficult to conjecture

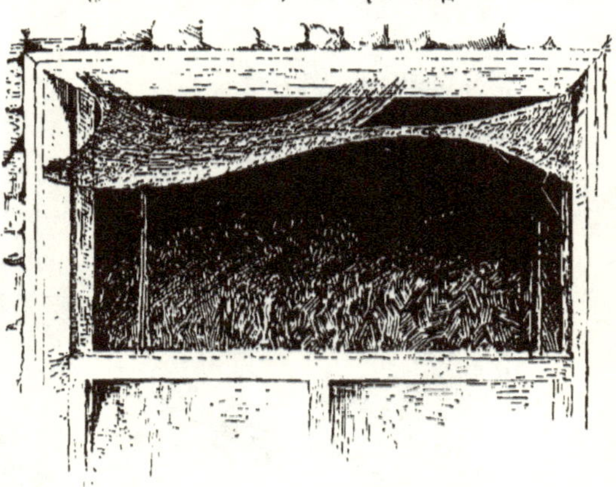

Fig. 208. Trusses on a fractured snare of Agalena naevia.

how she could have proceeded. In fact, in this case the "carrying around" theory alluded to in a foregoing chapter appears to me quite incredible. If we admit that the moving breeze materially aided the spider in her work of construction, and that she was thus in part dependent upon chance, yet there remains a pretty wide field for intelligent selection and adaptation. One would suppose that it required a really nimble witted creature to seize an unexpected opportunity like the above and turn it to such good account.

Nor is this an exceptional or even rare example. One often meets, in his walks through our fields and woods, the snares of Orbweavers woven upon the grasses or bushes bordering a meadow path (Fig. 207), or the low undergrowth of an open wood or grove, while the nesting tent and the upper supporting lines are attached ten or fifteen feet aloft upon a branch or dead limb of a tree. It would be as idle to suppose

that a wire suspension bridge is swung across a valley or stream without
engineering skill, as to think such spinningwork structures are wholly
without handicraftmanship of some sort.

The Speckled Tubeweaver (Agalena nœvia), which is probably the
most abundant familiar spider of our fauna, affords admirable illustrations of this facility. In a stable at Almora, Wallingford, the
following form of a sheeted web of this species was observed.
The upper sash of the stable window had been lowered for purposes of ventilation, thus probably rending the original snare. But in one
of the upper corners of the window frame and within the space thus left
open, Nævia had renewed her web. (Fig. 208.) The tube was in the corner, and of rather feeble character, but the pouch was doubled up some-

Agalena's Trestles.

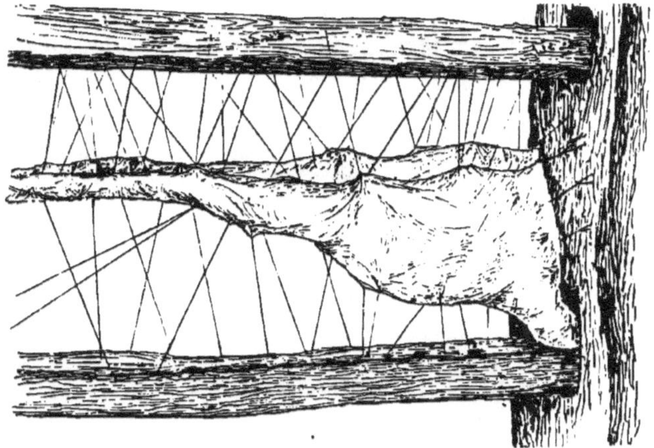

FIG. 209. Agalena's web with suspension lines and trestles between the bars of a fence.

thing like a roll, and extended entirely across the window. For about two-
thirds of the way it was an ordinary sheeted snare. Then it flared upward
and was attached to the upper part of the window frame, and was continued to the opposite side of the window with rather straggling lines. As
though to support this structure at either end, a series of strong and very
straight taut brace lines was extended downward from either end as shown
in the figure. No conclusion is possible except that this was done for the
purpose of staying the drooping pouch of the snare, and this, of course,
implies intelligent engineering.

The example cited is only one of many which might be presented
from my somewhat extended and varied studies of the Speckled Tube-

weaver. Her snares are found in all sorts of positions and locations. In the angles of houses and walls, among leaves of trees, in shrubs and grasses, in old stumps, and caves and holes in the ground, wherever a **Trestling Her Floor.** footing can be had and a spinneret can be laid, this universal occupant of outhouses and grounds proceeds to weave her snare. Under all circumstances she shows rare ability to adapt it to the particular site where chance has fixed her abode. If bracing is required from above she sends upward a series of lines which support her sheeted snare. If bracing is required from below, as we have seen (Fig. 208), she sends out a series of trestle lines, which keep the sheet in poise, and suggest the methods of carpenters when scaffolding a platform or floor, or trestling a bridge. If bracing be needed both above and below, as in the pouched snare (Fig. 209) woven between the bars of a farm

Fig. 210.   Tubular work of Dysdera bicolor.

fence, the lines are sent out in the very positions to give the required support. In fact, a civil engineer would decide, upon examination, that his profession could have suggested no better arrangement under the circumstances.

In the lawns and grounds around Philadelphia, and indeed almost everywhere in the United States, Agalena's snare will often be seen spread like a broad white sheet upon the upper surface of hedges and thick set plants, such as arbor vitæ, boxwood, and honeysuckle. Into these she works a silk lined cylindrical tunnel, which extends to the very heart of the plant, and often to the ground beneath. She manages, in some way, so to lash back the stems and twigs that, in spite of the natural elasticity and growth force of the plant, the tubular den or home is held quite in **Tubular Bridges.** place. Not only so, but the sheeted web will be stayed and held in position by a series of lines that seem to display no little skill in adjustment. She thus places a tubular bridge between her foraging ground and her retreat.

Once while visiting a brother, the late Commander Rhoderick Sheldon McCook, U. S. N., at his home in Vineland, N. J., my attention was called by him to one of these snares of Agalena built upon an evergreen bush planted in his yard. The comments of the sailor were striking and characteristic, and I regret that I cannot accurately recall them now. But I well remember the amazement which he expressed as he pointed to this point and that in the structure of the snare, and compared it to the shrouds and other portions of a ship, and showed how the right lines seemed always to have been placed in the needed position. This aranead is so common that any one who chooses to test my descriptions and observe independent examples can easily do so for himself. (See Fig. 215.)

This is not the only Tubeweaver that shows an engineering skill that challenges the admiration of human observers. Fig. 210 represents the **Dysdera's Skill.** ordinary tubular snare of Dysdera bicolor, which was spun within a paper box in which I had captured the spider, and of course in absolute darkness. In the morning I found a circular snare placed against the curved edge of the box, and stayed to the sides and bottom in a way that I have attempted with indifferent success merely to suggest in the figure. As I looked at it, and set to myself the problem of how to weave a mass of silken threads into the corner of a room, for example, in such a cylindrical shape that it would stand out stark and smooth, my admiration for the cunning skill of my aranead friend was much increased. At all events, the art that can build and stay such a work out of such flimsy material as the silken lines emitted from a spider's spin ning spools, is entitled to a high place, at least in animal engineering.

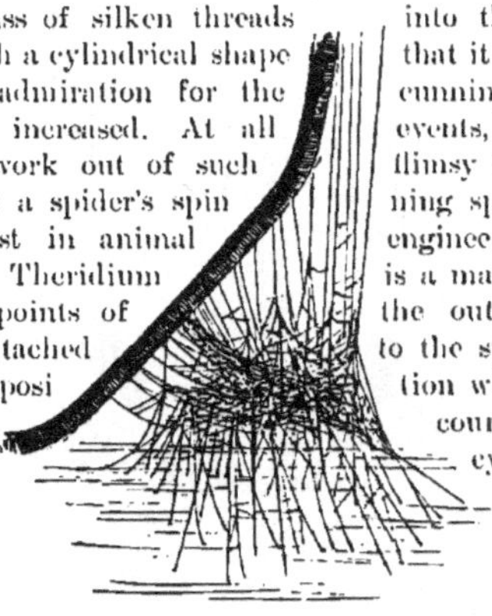

The snare of Theridium is a mass of intersecting lines suspended at all points of the outer margins by con- verging threads attached to the surrounding site. The spider takes her posi tion within the centre of this mass, and in the course of time there is a very strong tenden ey in the spinningwork to assume the shape of a nest. The lines become thickened in the centre, and may occasionally be found so approxi- mated that they pre sent the appearance of a net, not un like the snare of

Fig. 211. **Trestlework snare of a young Theridium.**

Linyphia, but not so closely textured as that of Agalena. Beneath this thickened centre a series of lines will often be found stretched downward and attached at the basal extremity. (See Fig. 211.) A web suspended **Therid- ium's Trestles.** between the joists of an old barn, the slats of a lattice work screen, or within a box, or other like situations which will allow these supporting lines to be formed with some degree of regu- larity, presents a striking resemblance to the trestlework of a wooden railroad bridge. I have observed this especially in Theridium tepidariorum, and some very beautiful and remarkable examples in the web of the long legged Cellar spider, Pholcus phalgioides. When such a web is formed, the spider is found suspended to the under part of the thickened portion, which thus becomes to her a sort of nesting place.

Fig. 212 was sketched from the snare of a female Theridium differens woven upon a wire frame fastened with staples upon a wooden block.

The block was laid upon a rough plastered cellar window (in my church cellar) much frequented by spiders, and was overspun as indicated in the figure. The ridge of the pyramidal structure drooped between the tips of the wire hoop, quite like the main cable of a wire suspension bridge. From this numerous diverging lines stretched on either side to the edge of the block and the window ledge beyond. Below the ridge cable and within the side guy lines a maze of thickened netted lines was spread, from which supporting trestle like lines dropped down perpendicularly to the surface of the block. The spider herself, with several white globular flossy cocoons and a bevy of younglings besides, was domiciled within a series of lines that extended from one of the wire tips (left hand of the cut) to the stone window frame. The resemblance of this structure to the wire bridges or wooden trestlework of human engineers is apparent at a glance.

At times, when the situation will allow, the spinningwork of Theridium assumes even

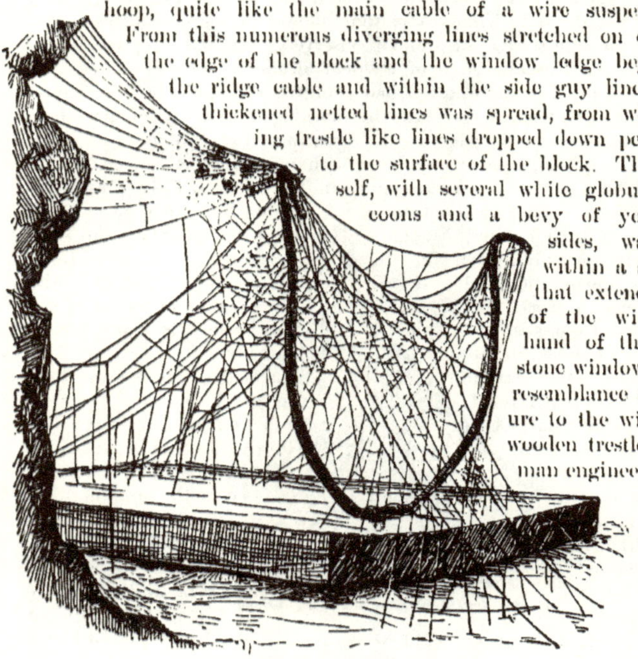

Fig. 212. Theridium's silk suspension bridge.

more decidedly the form of a nest. For example, in the horse stables of "Almora," the country seat of a gentleman resident at Wallingford, the windows are protected by a wide meshed wire frame. Within the meshes and around the window frame a vast number of spiderlings of Theridium tepidariorum had colonized. The scant lines which formed the original snares had gradually been thickened around the margins, from which stay lines were thrown out in all directions. In the course of time the snare assumed the globular shape which is indicated in the cut. (Fig. 213.) Within the centre, which was more scantily woven and more open than elsewhere, the spider was established. This condition of the central part was quite the reverse of what one usually sees, viz., the thickening of the web near the spider's habitat. The variation appears to have been caused by the necessity of strengthening the points at which the guy lines and

Globular Structures of Theridium.

radiating supports seized the margins. These structures, modified as they doubtless were by their environment and in a measure thus compelled to their final form, evidently show considerable skill in adapting spinningwork to circumstances.

There is no doubt that in the ordinary operations of snare making and nest building, the Labyrinth spider continually brings into play certain **Labyrinth Spider's Snare.** principles of operation which may be properly designated by the term engineering. For example, in looking at Labyrinthea working up the maze of crossed lines in which her domicile is hung, one is continually impressed with the fact that she so balances and adjusts the lines as they are successively spun out, that the whole spinningwork is as well suited to its purposes as is the complex scaffolding used by human carpenters in building a house. I cannot conceive in what manner the spider perceives the various inequalities, on this side or that, which require special treatment in the way of staying, tightening, adding, etc. Perhaps her sense of touch is so delicate that her perception of these

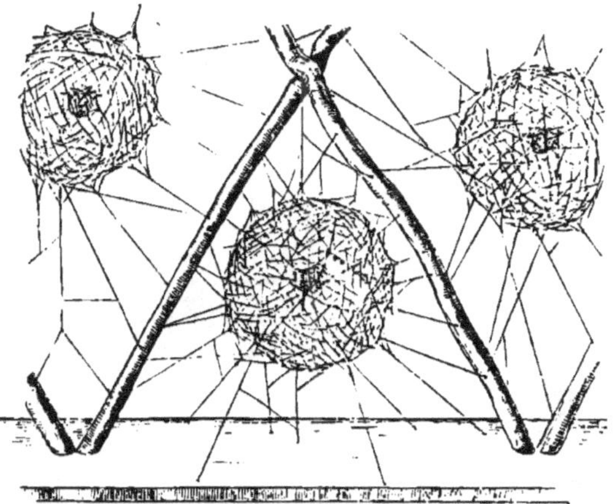

FIG. 213. Globular structure of young Theridium tepidariorum.

necessities is accurate enough to enable her to construct her intricate snare so as to attain precisely the same results as would have been reached had she been guided by an engineering intention from the very first.

Again, Labyrinthea is in the habit of roofing her silken tent with a leaf. Sometimes the leaf is used in lieu of the tent, and again the tent **Roofing.** is woven inside of the concavity of the leaf. In order to observe the mode of treatment I once dropped a curled leaf into a newly made snare of this spider. She at once perceived its presence by the agitation of the maze, ran to it, and appeared immediately to perceive its value. She fastened to it here and there a line, as though to preserve it from falling farther and thus damaging her snare. She then ran to the stem, attached a strong thread to it, and clambered out upon her silken trestle for the distance of two inches, and then fastened her line, leaving the leaf stayed in a most admirable way. She then took her position underneath the roof, apparently satisfied with her new shelter. The only thing which it seemed to me she might have done better was to turn the leaf. It had fallen with the cavernous part upward, and the spider so left it, although that part was the one best fitted for a den. I watched for awhile to see if this point would be observed and remedied by the little architect, but saw nothing. During the night there was a heavy storm of rain and wind, and in the morning I found the orb destroyed and the maze much damaged; but the leaf remained, and the spider was nestled against it. It had manifestly been her refuge against the storm.

Pitching a Leaf Tent.

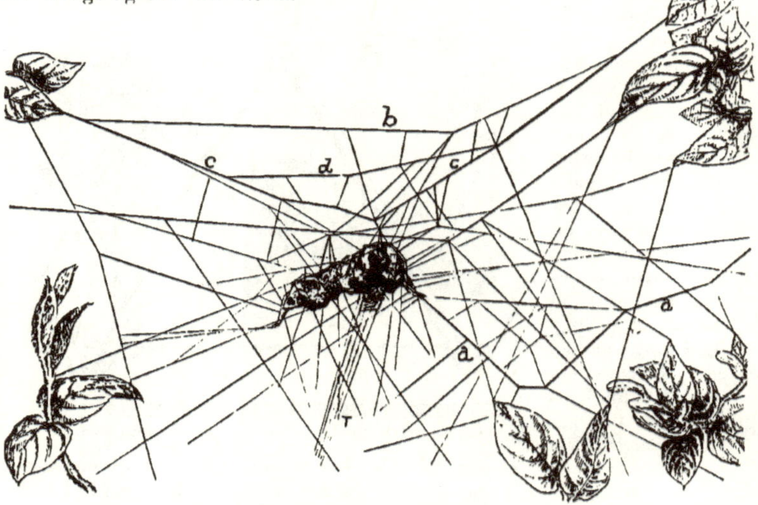

FIG. 214. How a Labyrinth spider swings and stays a leaf.

The day cleared, and next morning a new and beautiful snare had been spun. However, a site had been chosen six or eight inches removed from the original one. To this point the leaf had been shifted; and now I noticed that it had been turned over so that the concave part was downward, as at first I had thought it ought to be. This could hardly have been the result of accident. The whole leaf was now so arranged as to make the best shelter possible, and it was stayed within its position in the maze in an admirable manner. Fig. 214.

To the point of the stem was fastened a very strong, thick, white line (a, a) similar to that with which Labyrinthea suspends her string of cocoons. This extended through the labyrinth in a somewhat waving course for a distance of eight inches. This line was braced throughout its course by various threads fastened upon the intersecting lines of the maze. From a little corner in the upper part of the leaf a similar line, b, was stretched,

Laby-rinthea's Cables. braced by two interior lines of a like character cc and dd, which like the stem cable were also held in place by numerous slighter cords extending through the maze. A careful study of these main supporting cables, and indeed of all the lines used for upholding the leaf, convinced me that, whether or not the spider was conscious of any principles of engineering, she had in her results proved herself an admirable engineer. I kept this leaf under observation for a number of days of varied weather, and it never lost its poise, or was

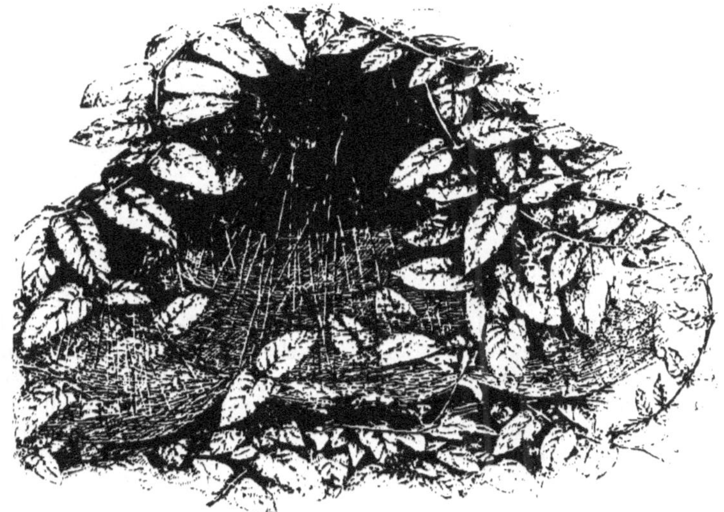

Fig. 215. The snare and stay lines of Agalena nævia in a honeysuckle vine.

moved from its place within the labyrinth. It endured well the strain of one of the most severe downpours of rain that I ever saw. It thus stood the test of actual use as well as careful observation.

In accounting for such acts as this, one is compelled to suppose the exercise of reasoning powers of some kind by the spider. Whether the reasoning may have been accomplished by the processes known to man and more highly organized animals, or whether the behavior of the spider was the result of sensations produced by her delicate sense of touch, and a perception of irregularities of weight and tension, which passes human experience, one need not stop to discuss. In point of fact, judging these phenomena as one would decide upon the behavior of his fellow man, one is not astray in attributing to the spider a rude sort of intentional engineering skill. Is it any less worthy of this title because exercised with seeming unconsciousness and without a moment's hesitation or apparent reflection of any sort?

In the same direction look the facts which I have recorded in the chapter on the construction of webs (Chapter IV.), under the head of alternate apposition of the radii. Indeed, it may be said truly, that in the entire work of laying out the foundations of an orb and placing in the radii, regard is had continually to the proper adjustment of the various parts, with view to their counterpoise and adequate support beneath the weight of the operative. One side is balanced against another side, one line is stayed by its opposite, and so from part to part the spider moves, evidently to keep her orb entirely balanced until it is completed.

Alternate Apposition of Radii.

The manner in which the ends of the radii, which terminate upon the hub, are wrapped round about and braced by the notched zone; the manner in which the wide nonviscid spiral scaffold lines are woven in order to give vantage ground from which to place in the close lying and permanent viscid spirals, upon which the usefulness of the orb depends—all these, to mention no other points, seem to indicate a very delicate perception of those modes (shall I also say principles?) of construction which are continually recognized in the art of the builder, the architect, and the engineer. The examples of various orders of spinningwork which I have given above have been grouped in this chapter to give the force of assembled and consecutive illustration to the inquiry as to the intellectual quality of araneal architecture. In point of fact, the special industries detailed in the various chapters, and notably the two on Nesting Habits, will furnish illustrations of equal aptitude and force.

Spider Intellect.

CHAPTER XIV

MECHANICAL STRENGTH OF WEBS AND PHYSICAL POWER OF SPIDERS.

I.

THE size of orbwebs varies generally with the size of the builders. But location, the condition of the wind, and contiguity of other webs have much to do in determining the matter.

The abundance of insect food may be a factor modifying both form and size. An example of this was seen in the colony of Epeiroids referred to, Chapter III., as stretching their nets across the water between the boat houses at Atlantic City. (Fig. 61.) There the flies swarmed in such myriads that the difficulty of obtaining food was reduced almost to the minimum. As a consequence most of the spiders hung in the merest rudiments of webs, as shown at Fig. 216. In some cases these may have been the remains of more or less perfect snares, which had become reduced to remnants by struggles of insects; but many of them showed no traces of any other architecture than that here represented, and I inferred that the spiders had discovered that the building of complete orbs was a useless waste of labor and material, and had spun no more than the central space.

Food Supply Modifies.

Fig. 216. A rudimentary snare of Epeira.

A Furrow spider taken from the railings of a bridge, where its space was circumscribed by location and by numerous webs of its fellows, when placed in a roomy cell spun an orb eleven and a half inches long by eight inches wide, hung upon a foundation line sixteen inches long. The same aranead, when placed in a glass jar three inches wide, wove a small characteristic web, or an apology for one, not unlike the rudimentary snare at Fig. 216. Argiope cophinaria often makes a very small web, and is quite sure to do so when the arboreal spaces surrounding it are straitened. But when domiciled where her lines could be carried long distances I have known her to make an orb more than two feet in diameter.

Modified by Site.

Again, it is obvious that in cases where an Orbweaver is dependent upon the wind to carry her foundation lines from the starting point to a point of attachment, the length of that line will necessarily be determined by circumstances. The cord may float off a goodly distance before striking an object, or may entangle soon. In the latter case, as the foundation line will be limited, the snare will be diminished accordingly. I have known a Furrow spider to make a web a foot wide one night, and the next night, when becalmed and prevented from stretching a foundation in her old site, spin an orb four inches in diameter.

Modified by Wind.

Young spiders make small webs, and invariably very perfect ones. The irregular, abridged, or patched snares which one sometimes sees, when not

Fig. 217. Typical orbwebs, Epeira strix.

the result of wear and tear, are those of adults; never, I believe, of young Orbweavers.

The following are a few measurements of the orbs of some of our common species. Epeira insularis: inches, six by six; thirteen by eleven; fourteen by fourteen; twenty by fourteen; fourteen by fourteen. Epeira strix: two by one and one-half; twelve by eight; nine and seven-eighths by nine and one-half. These are measurements of the orb alone, not including the foundation spaces. It will be seen that only a part of the above orbs are nearly circular; more frequently, perhaps, they are somewhat elliptical, the vertical diameter being the longer. The central space occupies about one-third or from one-third to one-fourth of the orb, the spiral space on either side about equaling it in width. The hub approximates the geographical centre when the web is quite round, but otherwise is elevated above the centre; sometimes is placed well to one side. (Fig. 217.) Its width, though subject to variation, may be said approximately to equal one-third of the central space.

The frailty of a spider's web has passed into a proverb. Yet, comparatively, the silken line of an Orbweaver is very strong. According to Schafenberger [1] it requires ninety spinning threads of an Epeira to yield one thread of the thickness of a caterpillar's thread; and, according to Leeuwenhoek, it requires eighteen thousand spider lines to make the thickness of a hair of the beard. These comparisons are suggestive, although in a measure deceptive, since there are vast differences in the size of the threads woven by Epeiroids. It is probable that the extraordinary strength of the thread is due to the superposition of a large number of extremely minute threads. However, after the thread is woven, Meckel could not recognize it as consisting of more than eight to ten strands. A geometric snare, whether vertical or horizontal, must be strong enough to sustain the weight of a spider of considerable size, such as Argiope cophinaria or Epeira insularis, particularly when the female is heavy with eggs.

Blackwall thus determined by experiment the strength of a line by which a female Epeira diademata, weighing ten grains, had sustained itself from a twig. He attached to the extremity of the line a small piece of muslin with the corners nearly drawn together, so as to form a minute sack, into which he carefully introduced sixty-one grains weight in succession, being more than six times the weight of the spider. On the addition of one-half grain more the line broke. [2]

Not only must an orb sustain the weight and movements of its maker, but it must also have sufficient strength to hold the various insects which strike upon it. Bees and wasps are sometimes able to break **Supports Insects and Dews** through the spiral meshes of a large snare, but generally the threads are strong enough to hold them, in spite of their struggles, until the proprietor can enswathe them. Moreover, the orbweb must be able to sustain the weight of evening dews. One who has seen such snares in the early morning, when every viscid bead appears to have attracted to itself an encasing armor of silvery dew, and has noticed how the spiral strings are bagged down under the weight of the same (Fig. 218), must have inferred that the snare was able to support a comparatively heavy burden. The same is true concerning summer showers, which must fall very heavily and be driven before a pretty strong wind in order to batter down a well constructed orbweb.

Indeed, I have often wondered at the capacity of these fragile structures to resist the force of winds. Here, for example, are webs of Epeira strix

[1] As quoted by Meckel.
[2] Transactions Linnaean Society, Vol. XVIII., 1841, page 321.

and Epeira triaranea in the full sweep of a strong gale, blowing over a near by bay of the sea, and are scarcely damaged. Sometimes, it is true,

Resists Wind.
the webs are blown away or lashed into threads wholly or in part; but frequently they will stand all the ordinary high winds and even some of the extraordinary ones which blow off the ocean. This is true even when they are spun quite near the beach, and have little protection under the lee of surrounding objects.

An illustration of the remarkable strength and elasticity of the foundation lines of orbwebs appears in a biographical notice of the distinguished astronomer, the late Gen. Ormsby M. Mitchell, printed with an edition of his lectures.[1] Prof. Mitchell directed his great ingenuity

Strength of Foundation Lines.

to the problem of causing a clock to record its beats telegraphically, and at the same time perfectly perform the work of a timekeeper. The required makes and breaks in the battery were effected by means of a cross of delicate wire and a mercury cup. Many obstacles having been overcome, there arose the great difficulty of procuring a fibre

Prof. Ormsby Mitchell.

sufficiently minute and elastic to constitute the physical union between the top stem of the cross and the clock pendulum. Various materials were tried, among others a delicate human hair, the very

Fig. 218. Section of a dew laden orbweb. (Magnified.)

finest that could be obtained, but this was too coarse and stiff. Its want of pliancy and elasticity gave to the minute "wire cross" an irregular motion, and caused it to rebound from the globule of mercury into which it should have plunged. "After many fruitless attempts," says Prof. Mitchell, "an appeal was made to an artisan of wonderful dexterity; the assistance of the spider was invoked; his web, perfectly elastic

[1] The Astronomy of the Bible, page 35.

and perfectly pliable, was furnished, and this material connection between the wire cross and the clock pendulum proved to be exactly the thing required. In proof of this remark I need only state the fact that one single spider's web has fulfilled the delicate duty of moving the wire cross, lifting it and again permitting it to dip into the mercury every second of time for a period of more than three years! How much longer it might have faithfully performed the same service I know not, as it then became necessary to break this admirable bond, to make some changes in the clock. Here it will be seen that the same web was expanded and contracted each second during the whole period, and yet never, so far as could be observed, lost any portion of its elasticity."

De Laet,[1] in his Novus Orbus, as early as A. D. 1633 speaks of certain beautiful spiders, elegantly marked by various colors, which build nets strong enough to entrap small birds. Of others, or perhaps the same species, he says that their webs are so tough that they can scarcely be broken.[2]

Sir Hans Sloane[3] describes a West Indies spider, which he calls the "Great Yellowish Wood Spider," and which is undoubtedly a species of Nephila, perhaps N. clavipes or N. plumipes, as making a web **Strength of the Snares.** strong enough to ensnare birds. "They have," he says, "an almost spiral large Web made of Yellow Spider's Thread, like Silk, glutinous or viscid, with which it will stop not only small Birds, but even wild Pigeons; they are so strong as to give a Man inveigled in them Trouble for some Time with their viscid sticking Quality." He also cites "Smith of Bermudas" (page 172) as describing "certain spiders of a large size, not dangerous, but making a sort of raw silk, catching birds bigger than blackbirds and like snipes, in their nets."

Wallace, speaking of the spiders of the Aru Islands, in the Malay Archipelago, says that the web spinning species were a great annoyance, stretching their nets across the footpaths just about the height of his face; the threads composing which were so strong and glutinous as to require much trouble to free one's self from them.[4] Mr. Mosely, the **Webs Entrap Birds.** naturalist of the "Challenger," says that at Little Ke Island, one of the same group, "Von Willemos Suhm actually found a strong, healthy 'glossy Starling' (Calornis metallica), caught fast in a Yellow spider's web, and he took the bird out alive and brought it on board the ship to be preserved."[5]

Vinson gives like testimony from observations made in the African Island of Réunion. The young spiders that encamp in innumerable

<hr>

[1] Novus Orbus Ionne de Laet, Ao. 1633, page 29. "Araneæ * * * quæ æstate ita validas telas nent, ut minores aviculæ illis irretantur."

[2] "Qui telas nent ita pertinaces ut vix disrumpi possint." Id., page 673.

[3] Natural History of Jamaica, Vol. I., page 196, A. D. 1725.

[4] The Malay Archipelago, Alfred Russel Wallace, page 437.

[5] A Naturalist on the "Challenger," page 382.

quantities among the large snares of Nephila swung between forest trees are sought by the birds who, in their too eager pursuit, strike upon the stout surrounding lines and are arrested. He had encountered these birds, particularly the beautiful Muscipeta Borbonica of Cuvier, entangled in these mammoth snares.[1]

Darwin speaks of the Brazilian forests as having every path barricaded with strong yellow webs of a species of Nephila similar to N. clavipes.[2] The late Prof. Orton uses precisely the same language of the spiders in the forests of the Amazon, and adds that some build nests in the trees and attack birds.[3] Prof. Wilder found that the orb of the Nephila of our Southern Atlantic coast would easily sustain a light straw' hat, whose weight is certainly greater than that of a young bird. My own experience with such webs in Texas is that they will sustain a weight quite equal to that, although I never made such a test. It is said by tourists that the woods of Southern California are barricaded in the same way as those of Brazil and the Amazon, by the webs of Orbweavers, so that it is often difficult to pass through them.

Two well authenticated cases of birds taken by a native spider have come under my notice in the vicinity of Philadelphia. A farmer belonging to the Society of Friends, Mr. Joseph Lownes, resident in the vicinity of Morton, informed me that he once found a bird, one of the smallest of our indigenous species of Kingster, entangled in the snare of a spider, which I judged from the description to be Argiope cophinaria. He watched for some time the movements of the bird, and believing that the latter would be finally overcome he benevolently released it from the web.

Argiope as a Bird Catcher.

Another case occurred on the grounds of the Philadelphia "Rabbit Club," near Fairmount Park, and was related to me by David J. De Haven, the custodian. He saw a large Argiope cophinaria (as it appeared evidently from his description) capture in her web a hummingbird. He watched the process of swathing the poor victim until it was completely wrapped around, when he slew the spider and rescued the bird, too late, however, for it was quite dead.

The above examples, which might be multiplied, show beyond question that the strength and mechanical advantages of an orbweb are sufficient to enable our large Orbweavers to capture small vertebrate animals. Whether or not they feed upon such captives one can only conjecture, particularly in the case of our native fauna. Certainly in the last case above cited the spider acted precisely as with all victims taken for food; but then, on the other hand, she might have done this and then have cut the hummingbird out of her snare without feeding upon its blood.

[1] Araneides des Isles de la Réunion, page xxi.
[2] Voyages of Adventure and Beagle, Vol. III., page 41.
[3] The Andes and Amazon, page 304.

The assertion must be taken with much allowance, that nets of geometric spiders are renewed wholly, or at least their concentric circles are replaced **Age of an Orbweb.** every twenty-four hours, even when not apparently injured.[1] In point of fact the renewal does not take place unless made necessary by the destruction or serious injury of the old snare. The reason assigned for this behavior by the same authors, viz., that the spirals rapidly lose their viscid properties by the action of the air, is not founded on fact, as is elsewhere shown.[2] The viscid beads retain their adhesive qualities under ordinary circumstances for a considerable time. It is doubtful if any orb becomes thus disabled in so short a period as that assigned—twenty-four hours—except when exposed to rain.

II.

At various times there have been placed on record accounts of the capture by spiders of small vertebrate animals, as snakes, mice, and birds. **Physical Power of Spiders.** Popular stories to the same effect have from time to time been sent the rounds of the daily press, and found utterance and often illustration, the latter sometimes of a most original and remarkable character, in popular magazine literature. The great seeming disparity in such cases between the size and vigor of captive and prisoner; the confusion of the various narratives in details as to the species and behavior of the spider, and the characteristics of her snare; the radical departure from known food habit of species that are insectivorous; together with the fact that the accounts all have come from lay observers, have been more or less lacking in scientific accuracy and minuteness of detail, and wholly without scientific verification—these considerations have caused such records and reports to be discredited by arachnologists and naturalists generally. But there are a few cases, confirmed by circumstantial evidence, and reported by observers of good reputation and careful habit, which deserve notice.

The physical powers of the Lycosidæ, the popular running, ground, or wolf spiders, is well illustrated by an instance recorded in the Proceedings of the Academy of Natural Sciences of Philadelphia.[3] The result as reported was achieved by pure strength and activity, without any of the mechanical advantages of a snare. Mr. Spring, while walking with a friend in a swampy wood, which was pierced by a dyke three feet wide, was attracted by the extraordinary movements of a large black spider in the middle of the ditch. Closer observation showed that the creature had caught a fish! She

---

[1] Kirby & Spence, Intro. Ento., I., page 419.   [2] See Chapter V.

[3] Proceedings, 1859. The account was presented by Mr. Lesley, from notes furnished by Mr. Edward A. Spring, of Eagleswood, New Jersey. It was confirmed by a personal interview with Prof. Spring, at Chautauqua in the summer of 1885, who repeated to me the details of the incident.

had fastened upon it with a deadly grip just on the forward side of the dorsal fin, and the poor fish was swimming round and round slowly, or twisting its body as if in pain.[1] (Fig. 219.) The head of its black enemy was sometimes almost pulled under water, but the strength of the fish would not permit an entire submersion. It moved its fins as if exhausted, and often rested. Finally it swam under a floating leaf near the shore and made a vain effort to dislodge the spider by scraping against the under side of the leaf.

A Spider Captures a Fish.

The two had now closely approached the bank. Suddenly the long black legs of the spider emerged from the water, and the hinder ones reached out and fastened upon the irregularities of the sides of the ditch. The spider commenced tugging at his prize in order to land it. The observer ran to the nearest house for a wide-mouthed

Fig. 219. A fish captured by a Dolomede spider.

bottle, leaving his friend to watch the struggle. During an interval of six or eight minutes' absence the spider had drawn the fish entirely out of the water; then both creatures had fallen in again, the bank being nearly perpendicular. There followed a great struggle, and on Mr. Spring's return the fish was already hoisted head first more than half its length out upon the land. It was very much exhausted, hardly making any movement, and was being slowly and steadily drawn up by the spider, who had evidently gained the victory. She had not once quit her hold during the period of a quarter to half an hour of observation. Her head was directed toward the fish's tail; she stepped backward up an elevation of forty-five degrees, drawing her captive with her.

[1] The figure has been drawn from a sketch furnished by Mr. Spring, who is a competent artist.

The observers were unfortunately unable to await the issue of the matter, and therefore caught the combatants in the bottle, partly filled with water. The fish swam languidly at the bottom of the vessel, and the spider stood sentinel on the surface, turning when the fish turned, **Relative Sizes.** and watching every motion. The bottle was set aside and visited after an interval of three hours. The spider was then found dead at the bottom of the jar, but the fish was alive and lived twenty-four hours afterward. The spider was three-fourths of an inch long and weighed fourteen grains; the fish was three and one-fourth inches long and weighed sixty-six grains. The spider was probably bruised by the catching. The spider referred to may have been an example of Lycosa lenta or L. fatifera, or more probably Dolomedes tenebrosus, all of which grow to great size along streams of water. I have seen very large examples of D. tenebrosus along the rocks of the Thousand Islands in the St. Lawrence River, and upon various streams in the vicinity of Philadelphia.

One of the most remarkable records of the physical and mechanical powers of spiders is made in Silliman's Journal.[1] **A Spider Ensnares a Snake.** The account is authenticated by the names and statements of a number of gentlemen resident in the vicinity of the occurrence, Batavia, New York. One evening Hon. David E. Evans found in his wine cellar a live striped snake, nine inches long, suspended by the tail in a spider's web between two shelves. The snake hung so that its head could not reach the shelf below it, by about an inch. The shelves were about two feet apart, and the lower one was just below the bottom of a cellar window, through which the snake probably passed into it. From the upper shelf there hung a web in the shape of an inverted cone, eight or ten inches in diameter at the top, and concentrated to a focus about six or eight inches from the under side of this shelf.

FIG. 220. A snake entangled in a spider's web.

From this focus there was a strong cord made of the multiplied threads of the spider's web, apparently as large as sewing silk, and by this cord the snake was suspended. A rude sketch of the serpent suspended in the web was made by an eye witness, and is exactly reproduced at Fig. 220. A close examination showed that the snake's mouth was entirely closed by a number of threads wound around it. Its tail was tied in a knot so as to leave a small loop or ring, through which the cord was fastened, as seen in the figure. The end of the tail above (cephalad of) this loop, to the length of half an inch, was lashed fast to the cord to keep it from slipping. As the snake hung, the length of the cord from its tail to the focus to which it was fastened was about six inches. A little above the tail was a round ball about the size of a pea, which upon inspection appeared to be a green

[1] American Journal of Science and Arts. XXVII. 1835. page 307. sq.

fly, around which the cord had been wound as a windlass, with which the snake had been hauled up. A great number of threads were fastened to the cord above and to the rolling side of this ball, to keep it (as the observers thought) from unwinding and so letting the snake down. It was conjectured that the cord must have extended from the focus of the web to the shelf below, where the snake was lying when first captured, and being made fast to the loop in his tail, was then carried up to the fly about midway of the cord. By rolling the fly over and over, the cord was wound around it, both from above and below, and the snake gradually hoisted until its head was one inch or more above the shelf. In this situation the snake hung alive for several days (three according to one statement, five according to another), when the web was broken by careless observers so as to allow part of the snake's body to rest upon the shelf below. Thus the serpent remained, unnoticed by the spiders after its fall, until eight days after its discovery, when some large ants were found devouring the dead body.

A Spider Windlass.

The witnesses state that when the snake was first observed "several large spiders were upon him sucking his juices;" that it "furnished a continued feast for several large spiders," until its fall; that "during the day no spiders were visible in or about the web, but at night there were three, much smaller than the common fly, seen feeding upon the body of the snake."

One might well be excused for withholding credence from such a story, although the acts were vouched for by abundance of respectable lay testimony. Accepting the account as true, or at least probable, I would make the following inferences: first, the description of the web, although sufficiently indefinite, leaves little doubt that the snake was originally taken in a snare of a species of Tubeweaver, and most probably by the Medicinal spider, Tegenaria medicinalis, Hentz.[1] The broad sheeted web of this spider is frequently found in cellars, which are favorite haunts. It builds near windows, in the angles and along the sides of walls, having its tubular den in a crack or opening laid along an angle. The sheet is usually drawn upward until its exterior margin is higher than the plane of the entrance of the tube. There is thus formed a sort of pouch within which insects often fall and so are readily captured by the spider, who mounts guard at the door of her den. Over the door the tube frequently rises into a sort of tower. (Fig. 221.) The webs of this species are sometimes of considerable length—eighteen or twenty inches—and those which have been standing for some time will be found overlaid by several successive thicknesses of silken sheeting, discolored by the soot and dust of the cellar. A specimen of this material may readily be taken and mounted upon white cardboard,

Who Snared the Snake?

[1] Probably the T. Durhami of Europe.

where it shows as a tissue of close texture. In the building of additions to the web, however, the new part shows as a quite open plane of mesh work.[1]

The webs of Medicinalis are often built in the angles of cellar windows, along the sill, and in positions quite similar to that in which the Batavia snake was caught. The strength of several snares, **Strength of Web.** found in the cellars of the Academy of Natural Sciences of Philadelphia, was tested as follows: two webs bore up under a pencil weighing sixty-eight grains; several small webs bore a weight of one-fourth and one-half ounce in corks spread over the surface, but

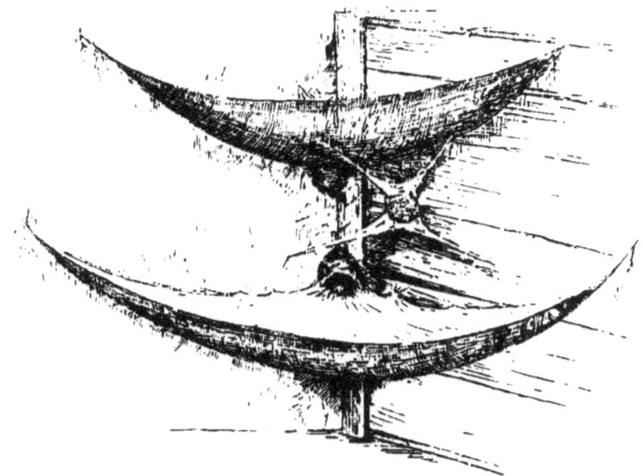

Fig. 221. The pouch, web, tower, and cocoon of the Medicinal spider, Tegenaria medicinalis.

broke down under an equal weight condensed into a small shell. One web bore up easily, and apparently would have carried for an indefinite period, the half ounce shell. It also sustained for a short period a weight of one ounce, and then gradually gave way by the breaking down of the thread attachments to the wall, without any yielding of the sheet itself.

The weight of a "striped snake," such as is alluded to, probably our common garter snake, Eutaenia sirtalis, Linn., is accurately fifty-five

[1] The two webs (Fig. 221) measured: No. 1 (upper). 14 inches long across the hypothenuse, by 10 inches deep; No. 2 (lower), 18 inches long across the sheeted part, 24 inches across the meshed extension, depth 9 inches.

grains for one ten and a half inches long, and fifty-one grains for one eleven and a half inches long.[1] The two together weigh less than a quarter of an ounce! Thus, a web of the Medicinal spider will sustain with perfect ease the weight of four such snakes, will even support six or seven readily, and will not break until the weight of eight snakes, each larger than the Batavia specimen, has been placed upon it. So far, therefore, the account is wholly probable.[2]

Weight of Snake.

The mechanical torsion caused by the struggles of the serpent would of course add to the natural effect of gravity, but would probably not counterbalance the excess of resistance in the web as here shown. The simple statement that a snake was suspended in a spider's web appeals to ideas and associations that produce at once wonder and unbelief. A snake?—that is a huge object! A spider's web?—that is a very frail thing! In point of fact, however, when the test of weights and measures is applied, our notions on both these points may easily be reversed; for some snakes are certainly very slight creatures, and certainly some spider snares have much strength.

The above incident does not stand alone. The late Dr. Asa Fitch, well known as an American entomologist, published an account of the entanglement and elevation of a snake, resulting in its death. The heroine of this adventure was also a New York spider, resident in the village of Havana, Chemung County, N. Y. She is described as "the common house spider;" "an ordinary looking spider of a dark color, its body not larger than a common house fly." These are such indefinite terms that they give little clue to the scientific name of the animal, and can hardly be excused as coming from a trained entomologist. However, several details are noted in the narrative which give good circumstantial evidence that some species of Theridium is meant, very probably our common Theridium tepidariorum.[3]

Theridium Snares a Snake.

This spider had woven its snare beneath the counter of a village store. A "common silk snake" about a foot long, which had been probably brought into the store in a quantity of sawdust, took up its residence on the floor underneath, two or three spans distant from the spider's snare. When first seen the spider had placed a loop around the serpent's neck, from the top of which a single thread was carried and attached to the under side of the shelf, whereby the head of the serpent was drawn up about two inches from

The Serpent Lassoed.

---

[1] Determined from alcoholic specimens in the collection of the Philadelphia Academy of Natural Sciences.

[2] The difference of weight between an alcoholic and living specimen is considered by Dr. Leidy so small that it need scarcely be estimated.

[3] The account is taken from the Annual of Scientific Discovery, 1862, page 331. The original record is not quoted.

the floor. The snake was moving about incessantly, in a circle as large as its tether would allow, wholly unable to get its head down to the floor or to withdraw it from the noose, while the spider was ever and anon passing down to the loop and up to the shelf, adding thereby an additional strand to the thread. Each new strand being tightly drawn, elevated the head of the snake gradually more and more.

As only the neck of the creature was at first entangled, Dr. Fitch thinks that the spider was exposed to attack as she ran up and down the cord, and that during the early stages of the conflict the snake did snap at the spider with its mouth. The latter, however, " with her hind legs, as when throwing a thread around a fly, had cast one thread after another over the mouth of the snake, so that he was now perfectly muzzled, by a series of lines placed vertically over the mouth ; these were held from being pushed asunder by another series "placed horizontally," as Dr. Fitch's informant states he particularly observed. " No muzzle or wickerwork for the mouth of an animal could be woven with more artistic regularity and perfection ; and the snake occasionally making a desperate attempt to open his mouth would merely put these threads upon the stretch. This strange conflict issued in victory for the spider. The snake continued his gyrations, his gait becoming gradually slower through weak-. ness and fatigue. The spider continued to move down and up the cord, gradually shortening it. At last the serpent was drawn up so far that only two or three inches of the tail touched the floor, when he expired, about six days after his capture was first noticed.

It is the above behavior, in swathing the victim with thickened strands of silk drawn out and thrown rapidly from the spinnerets by the hind feet, that determines the generic position of the spider with some certainty. The snare from the description was evidently not an orbweb, and this behavior, in connection with other details, points to

.**Theridium tepidariorum.** some Lineweaver as the hero of this exploit, either Theridium lepidariorum or Pholcus phalangioides—probably the former. Tepidariorum is a vigorous, active, and ferocious species. (See Chapter I., Fig. 7.) Her web is often spread over great spaces, and is strong enough to bear the weight of such a snake as here described. She shows unusual courage, strength, and skill in capture of prey, taking very large beetles and other insects, which she will raise through great (relative) distances to the centre of her snare.

It is worthy of mention, in connection with these incidents, that the belief that a special enmity exists between spiders and serpents is very ancient. Pliny says that the spider, poised in its web, will throw itself upon the head of a serpent as it is stretched beneath the shade of a tree, and with its bite will pierce its brain. Such is the shock that the creature will hiss from time to time, and then, seized with vertigo, will coil round and round, but finds itself unable to take flight or even to break the web in which it is entangled. This scene, concludes the author, only ends with the serpent's death.[1]

I had often wished for an opportunity to follow up critically one of the recurring reports of the physical powers of spiders. This wish was gratified in the summer of 1882. An article drifted through American newspapers which detailed the ensnaring of a living mouse by a Kentucky spider. I was fortunately able to trace the story to its origin in the Lebanon (Ky.) "Standard and Times." Correspondence with its intelligent editor, Mr. J. W. Hopper, brought me entire confirmation of the report from a number of trustworthy sources. I think the incident of sufficient importance to justify a somewhat detailed presentation. The original account as published by Mr. Hopper is as follows:—

Fig. 222. Diagram of a mouse hanging in a spider's snare.

"A very curious and interesting spectacle was to be seen **Mouse Snared by Spider.** Monday afternoon in the office of Mr. P. C. Cleaver's livery stable in this city. Against the wall of the room stands a tolerably tall desk, and under this a small spider, not larger than a common pea, had constructed an extensive web reaching to the floor. (Fig. 222.) About half past eleven o'clock, Monday forenoon, it was observed that the spider had ensnared a young mouse by passing filaments of her web around its tail. When first seen the mouse had its fore feet on the floor and could barely touch the floor with its hind feet. The spider was full of business, running up and down the line and occasionally biting the mouse's tail, making it struggle desperately.

"Its efforts to escape were all unavailing, as the slender filaments about its tail were too strong for it to break. In a short time it was seen that the spider was slowly hoisting its victim into the air. By two o'clock in the afternoon the mouse could barely touch the floor with its fore feet; by dark the point of its nose

---

[1] Pliny, Natural History, Chapter X., page 95.

was an inch above the floor. At nine o'clock at night the mouse was still alive, but made no sign except when the spider descended and bit its tail. At this time it was an inch and a half from the floor.

"Yesterday morning the mouse was dead, and hung three inches from the floor. The news of the novel sight soon became circulated, and hundreds of people visited the stable to witness it. The mouse was a small one, measuring about one and a half inches from the point of its nose to the root of the tail."

Mr. P. C. Cleaver, in whose office the incident occurred, wrote me the following statement: "I have two small rooms in my livery stable, one used as an office and the other as a bedroom for my clerk. In **Mr. Cleaver's Testimony.** the front room stands against the east wall a writing desk just tall enough for an ordinary sized man to stand and write on. When I first saw it the mouse was under this desk, fastened in the spider's web, with its head down and tail up. Eighteen inches or two feet above the mouse was a small spider, whose body was about the size of a small grain of sweet sugar corn, certainly not larger than would cover the nail of your smallest finger. It was of a dark color, but not black. I first saw it about one o'clock P. M., when the toes of the mouse barely touched the floor. The spider kept working it up until finally it was three or four inches from the floor, and was still alive when I left my stable to go home at night. I can give you no information as to the web that will satisfy you. It was long enough to reach to the floor, and there were a good many strands of it wound in many intricate ways that I do not understand. The web was very fine. I left the spider at work that evening at sunset, with orders that it should not be touched. But the web was knocked down that night—by some boys, I think, as a great many were there to see the sight, and my clerk thinks it was lost in that way. The spider, mouse, and web were all gone when I returned to the stable on the following morning." Mr. Cleaver emphatically declares the impossibility of any one about his premises having manipulated the mouse in any manner to secure its entanglement in the web. "I am as sure," he says, "that the spider caught and raised the mouse three or four inches from the floor by himself without the aid of man, as though I had been present from first to last."

Mr. Hopper, in addition to the printed article, sent me a written report of the incident, from which the following quotations are made: "As you will see from this account, no one observed the actual **Mr. Hopper's Testimony.** entanglement of the mouse. In a very short time after it was first observed I myself was informed of it, and went to the stable to examine it. This was Monday, August 22d, 1881. The office of the stable is a small room. The desk referred to is something over three feet high, four feet four inches long, and something over two feet wide. From the bottom of the desk to the floor the distance is two feet ten inches. The spider's web extended perhaps three-fourths the length of the desk next to the wall, and covered the bottom of the desk to the width of about fifteen or sixteen inches. It was about three feet long by sixteen inches wide.

"You will observe that the narrative in the news slip ends with Tuesday morning, August 23d. My paper, which is a weekly, went to press late Tuesday afternoon. The hoisting process continued all day Tuesday, and employés about the stable say that by dark Tuesday night the mouse was four or four and a half inches from the floor. Tuesday night a meddlesome boy entered the room in the dark and accidentally broke the web, and the mouse fell. Next morning, according to my recollection, the web was brushed away. I greatly regret that the spider was not allowed to complete his work, and that he was not captured and preserved. I was greatly mortified when I found how the affair had terminated.

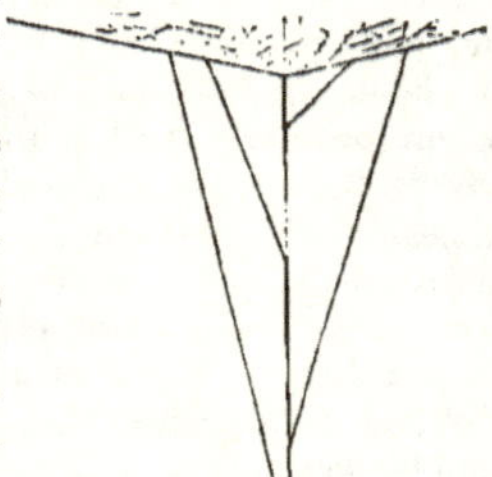

The Hon. J. Proctor Knott, then a representative in Congress from Kentucky, and later governor of the State, was one of the references given me by Mr. Hopper. He kindly wrote me from Washington, confirming the newspaper account. I quote from his letter the following: "When my attention was first called to the matter—about ten or eleven o'clock in the forenoon—the spider having made its thread fast to the end of the tail of the mouse, of perhaps fifty times its own weight, gradually hoisted its prey so that it could barely touch the floor with its fore paws, and was still busily 'hoisting away,' while the mouse was no less vigorously endeavoring to break loose. That afternoon, perhaps near five o'clock, in company with Mr. Hopper, the editor of the 'Standard,' I again visited the scene of the singular capture, and found that the mouse had been raised so that the top of its nose was precisely four inches from the floor, as I ascertained by actual measurement with a pocket rule. The spider was still actively at work and the mouse still struggling. The next morning I found the mouse dead, its nose about six inches from the floor, and the spider still at work. The thread was attached to the end of the tail. This statement, although written hurriedly and amid considerable confusion, you may use as you think proper."

The Hon. Proctor Knott's Testimony.

FIG. 223. A mouse suspended by a spider. (From a sketch by Hon. Proctor Knott.)

Governor Knott also sent me the foregoing (Fig. 223) memory sketch of the position of the mouse and the characteristics of the snare and the entangling lines.[1]

The testimony and observations thus obtained are of such a character as to establish beyond any doubt these facts: First, that a young living mouse was in some manner securely entangled in the **The Conclusion.** snare of a spider. Second, that the spider, by means of silken lines two or three feet long, hoisted the mouse through a perpendicular distance of four or four and a half inches. Third, that the mouse was entangled in the spider's web by the tail alone, and although it lived for at least ten hours, during which it struggled vigorously to escape, was unable to free itself, and finally died. Fourth, that the hoisting process continued during Monday from about 11 A. M. until the night of Tuesday following, a period of thirty-four hours, when the web was accidentally broken, and then brushed away. Fifth, that the specific identification of the spider heroine of this exploit was at first somewhat in doubt; and the credit seemed to lie between a Tubeweaver, the Medicinal spider (Tegenaria medicinalis), and the common Lineweaver (Theridium tepidariorum). The accounts of the captor's behavior during the hoisting of her victim, especially swathing her victim, and the opinions of the various eye witnesses to whom were sent descriptions and drawings of both species and their characteristic webs, point to the Lineweaver. I was much perplexed by the conflicting testimony inevitable in the reports of the several untrained observers. But persistent correspondence and the kindness of Mr. Hopper and others finally procured me specimens which were declared to be undoubtedly identical with the mouse catcher. These specimens are Theridium tepidariorum; to this spider, therefore, must be given the credit of the achievement.[2] Sixth, a comparison of the weight of a young mouse[3] with the actual power of resistance in webs of both Theridium tepidariorum and the Medicinal spider, as determined by a number of tests, shows that the incident on such grounds is not only plausible but much within the

[1] "The figure intended to represent the spider is larger in proportion to that insect than the mouse is to the unlucky little rodent it is supposed to suggest. The length of the line attached to the tail is much shorter in the sketch than in the original, where it must have been three feet or over, as the web from which it was suspended was woven upon the bottom of a writing desk, and, as nearly as I can remember, in the shape presented, but much larger."—Mr. Knott's letter.

[2] Specimens sent to me of the spiders supposed to be identical with the one that caught the mouse, taken from the same desk and from a web of similar construction, were the Medicinal spider. Also, a specimen of a web somewhat similar to the one in which the mouse was entangled, and a description with estimated measurements, of the extensive proportions of the original snare, point in the same direction.

[3] "A mature male mouse weighed three hundred and fifty-six grains. One half grown would probably weigh about one-sixth to one-fourth of this, say from sixty to ninety grains." Note from Dr. Joseph Leidy.

possibilities of the spinningwork of those spiders. Seventh, that a series of well and tolerably well authenticated cases, as well as observations of the habitual prowess of spiders in taking and securing their prey, justify the inference that the capture of a mouse or garter snake lies within the physical and mechanical abilities of both of the two species above named.

The space given the above facts may seem to some to be in undue proportion to their importance. But, apart from the value of positively determining any point in natural history, the discussion has this

A Conclusion. conclusion: The capture of small vertebrate animals by both Sedentary and Wandering spiders is possible; the one by the mechanical strength of their snares, the other by their physical strength. There is thus laid the foundation, at least, for the presumption that such animals may be or become natural food for the larger species of araneads. This is certainly a most important fact in the life history of spiders, and would greatly enlarge the range of their habits.

CHAPTER XV.

PROCURING FOOD AND FEEDING.

Food Taking Tools. THE Orbweaver's snare is its tool for trapping insects. It is a notable fact in the history of lower animals, that there is at least one order containing a large group of species which possess the power, otherwise the almost exclusive gift of man, to procure food by the medium of manufactured implements. The nearly universal habit of natural life is to imbibe nutriment directly, or to secure it wholly by means of the feet or mouth or other prehensile organs. The Wandering spiders fall into the general course of nature, and seize their food directly. The Sedentary spiders form an exception to this rule.

It is, of course, an interesting speculation how this remarkable habit originated, and how it came about that such a marked exception should exist in certain tribes of a natural order whose remaining tribes are wanting therein; but Nature thus far has yielded no light upon the subject. As far as we are able to judge from fossil spiders, the structural differences between such families as Epeïrids on the one hand, and the Lycosids and Attoïds on the other, have remained unchanged from the first apparition of spider life. It is a fair inference that the functional differences have also always existed; that Epeïrids have always captured their prey through the media of manufactured tools or snares, and that the Lycosids have stalked their prey and secured their food without any intervening instrument.

It has already been shown how well adapted an orbweb is for its chief purpose. Its combined strength and elasticity, its admirable arrangement for the free motion of the spider, its location and characteristics so well adapted to arrest the flight of insects, and its armature of viscid beads so completely suited to retain and disable the arrested victims—these all form an implement of tremendous facility to the aranead for procuring its natural food. **Handling the Snare.** The spider when ensconced within its nest holds by its claws to the tense trapline, and thus keeps its snare taut. When it is suspended at the hub the eight legs, stretched out and grasping points of the radii which command the entire snare, enable the spider at any time to contract its outlying lines around the centre, thus producing the same degree of tension.

I.

In this position, when an insect strikes a snare the impact as well as subsequent struggles set the web into violent agitation, which is at once communicated to the spider. Her conduct will be largely determined by the degree of agitation. Evidently the weight and size of the insect, and, therefore, its ability to defend itself, are gauged by the force of the agitation. If the insect appears to be a small one, or thoroughly **Insect Entanglement.** trapped, and the spider should be particularly hungry, she will rush immediately upon her victim. Ordinarily, however, the action is different. At the first signal, the spider will turn in an attitude of great muscular tension, as though to get the direction of the movement. She will often make a sharp pull, the whole body moving with muscular excitement. Sometimes only the fore legs will be thus twitched. Then a movement will be made toward the fly, which is conducted rather cautiously and at several stages, the spider meanwhile jerking the radii leading directly to the entangled insect. At each pause two or three quick

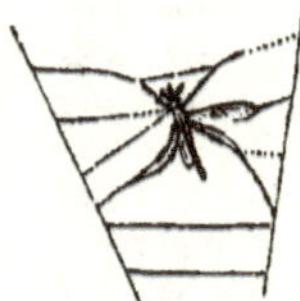

Fig. 224. Mosquito entangled by striking the net with full spread wings.

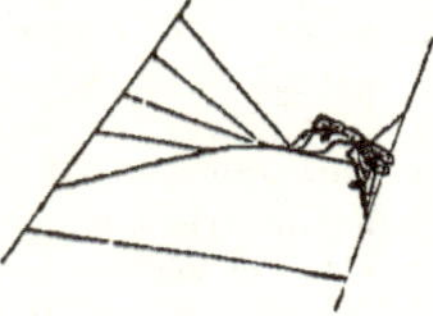

Fig. 225. Insect entangled by all the feet.

Fig. 226. A mosquito captured by several feet.

jerks are made. Sometimes, however, for various reasons, but chiefly through excess of caution, no doubt, she will fail to make any movement at all, and leave the insect to struggle until it is exhausted, in which case it may either be seized and eaten, or cut from the snare and thrown away.

The Orbweaver is not infallible in its ability to determine the character of the agitation. Sometimes the deft tickling of the web will produce **Accuracy of Perception.** a movement so much like the agitation of an insect as to deceive a spider, particularly if she be quite young or very hungry. A touch upon a dry insect hanging in an empty web once drew to the spot a young spider from an adjoining snare. It came straight to the point, as though directed by the agitation of the neighboring web, thus showing a sense of direction, and ability to determine the originating points of the movement; but also showing the fact that it was liable to be deceived as to the character of the movements of a living insect. Once, while observing an Epeira vertebrata, a small insect fell into the web. The spider ran towards it, seized it, and carried it to the centre. While feeding, two bits of wood from an overhanging vine dropped into the snare. Vertebrata at once rushed towards these, but finding by her touch that they were dead matter, instead of leaving the ob-

Deceived. jects she drew them towards her with her feet, passed them to her lips and palps, where they were held a moment until bitten entirely free from the lines. Then the fore feet were reached up, and by a sharp snap of the claws the pieces were thrown downwards out of the web. In this case, also, the Orbweaver was deceived. But very generally she is able to distinguish between an artificial agitation and that produced by an insect. At least, I have frequently failed to draw a spider from her retreat by my most skillful manipulation of her snare.

Blackwall is probably correct in his suggestion that the pulling motions which I have described are intended to determine whether objects entangled in the toils are animate or inanimate.[1] At all events, it is true that by jerking the radii immediately in connection

Use of Net Jerking. with that part of the snare in which the insects are entangled, and then suddenly letting go their hold, the spiders produce a vibratory motion in the net which seldom fails to excite action in the ensnared insect. Guided by the struggles of her prey, the Orbweaver runs along the most contiguous radii to seize her victim, avoiding contact with the viscid lines as far as possible, and drawing out after her a thread attached to one of the lines near the centre of her net, which serves to facilitate her return.

The manner in which insects are captured may be observed at any time, and yet one may venture to describe the method.

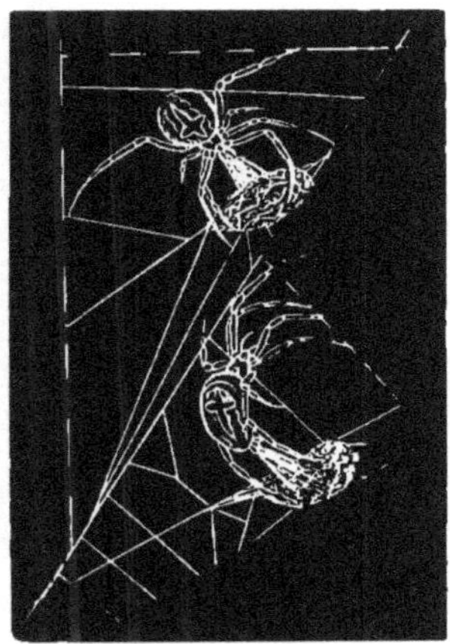

Fig. 227. Epeira revolving captured fly while enswathing it.

When the insect strikes the viscid spirals, one or more legs and one or other or both of the wings, or an antenna are usually first to

Insect Entanglement. feel the viscid grasp of the beads. The insect, at once arrested by the blow, begins to struggle, and finding itself fettered increases its efforts to be free. Sometimes, particularly if the viscid quality of the beads be somewhat abated or the entanglement be slight, the insect succeeds in escaping. This occurs more frequently perhaps than is ordinarily supposed. Very often, however, the struggles only result in fastening the victim more securely by bringing additional portions of the body into contact with the spirals. Sometimes the insect will strike broad on in its flight, or

[1] Blackwall. "Researches in Zoology," page 289.

with wings full spread, as represented at Fig. 224, and the whole under surface of the body will be first stuck to the spirals. At other times, as at Fig. 225, the feet will be seen gathered together in a little cluster, adhering at one point to the spirals. Several or all of these positions have been illustrated in the figures, accurately rendered from nature. A momentary entanglement is all that is required, for the spider is upon its victim ere it can succeed in releasing itself.

The mode of dealing with the entrapped insect when it is reached is

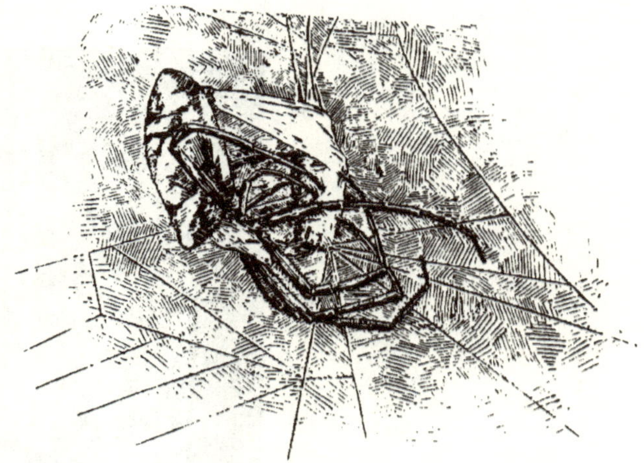

FIG. 228.   Argiope swathing a captured fly by a jet of silken filaments.

not always the same. Sometimes it is immediately seized and carried to the hub or den to be fed upon, the spider striding with it in her jaws over the lines of her orb. Occasionally the insect will be struck with the fangs, and the spider retreat instantly to await the effects of the stroke. This action may be repeated. At other times, several sharp squeezes of the fangs are given, as though to destroy the insect's life.

Treatment of Insects.

In the act of seizing a mosquito, an Epeira vertebrata was observed holding to the spiral lines with one hind foot, so that her operations might be unimpeded by contact with the viscid beads. The little cords by which she was thus held aloof were the shape of a pyramid, whose apex was within the claws of the spider. More commonly the victim is seized with the claws of the two fore pairs of legs. These are so long that they can be stretched out well forward of the spider's body, and grasp the insect without much danger.

With great rapidity the abdomen is then doubled under, and a jet of thick, white silk issued from the expanded spinnerets, and thrown out rapidly by the hind legs. At the same time the insect is revolved by the united action of the short third pair of legs, the two fore legs, and not infrequently by the aid of the hind pair also. There is much difference in this respect, but the first, third, and fourth pairs seem always to be used. As the fly is rolled around by the feet the swathing thread envelops it something after the manner of woolen yarns as they pass from a spindle to a reel. But sometimes the spider revolves her own body as well as the fly, thus facilitating the rapidity with which the victim is enswathed. There is, of course, a great difference in the amount of swathing thread used at different times. Sometimes a few threads suffice, so that the outlines of the insect's

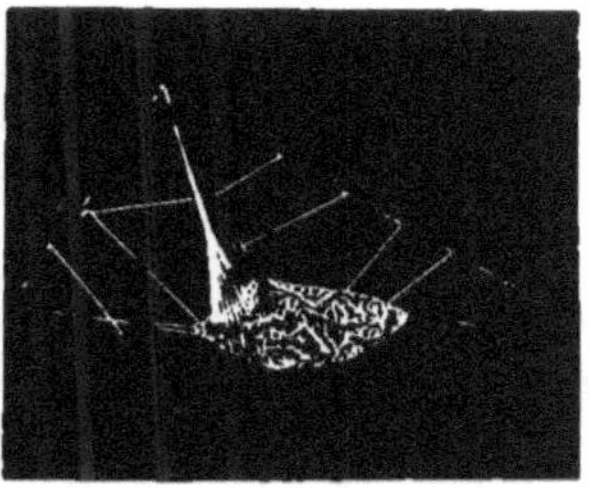

Fig. 229. A fly lightly swathed and trussed up.

body and limbs are clearly seen through them. (Fig. 229.) Again, the bandages will be a veritable winding sheet, and perfectly conceal the details of the victim, showing only a lumpy outline, a creature as truly mummied as was ever one of Egypt's sacred animals. (Fig. 235.)

Epeira trifolium was observed capturing a grasshopper. She approached very cautiously from above, and, as she drew near the entangled insect, threw out one fore leg and then another, drawing each back quickly as though feeling the character of the prey. Being satisfied, she dropped to one side and threw out two wide, thick streams of silk. These issued from either side of the spinning rosette, and each stream was fed evidently by the three spinnerets upon either side. (Fig. 230.) These two streams at once seized hold upon the limbs of the entangled grasshopper, and as the

Fig. 230. A double stream of swathing silk.

spider began to revolve the insect they were reeled out, rapidly covering the whole insect with swathing material. These streams of silk, after the first gush, were drawn out alternately by the two hind legs first one, and then the other, being used. Presently the spider dropped below her victim, and thence passed to the side opposite, continuing her operations until the insect was satisfactorily wound up. She did not strike it with her fangs at all, but retired to her den, dragging after her the swathing thread, which was widely divergent where it laid hold upon the grasshopper, but gradually converged as the spider moved away and closed her spinnerets, until it became a single thread. (Fig. 231.) This mode I have observed at various times.

If any emergency arise to require it, the spider can issue a jet of silk with such rapidity and of such volume that it is evident that strong muscular contraction has been used upon the silk glands, thus forcing the liquid material from the spinning spools without any aid of the feet in drawing it out. **Swathing.** That this is quite within the ability of Orbweavers I am perfectly satisfied by frequent observation of the action of Argiope cophinaria or Epeira insularis when taking a particularly large insect, such as a grasshopper or locust, moth or bluebottle fly. (Fig. 232.)

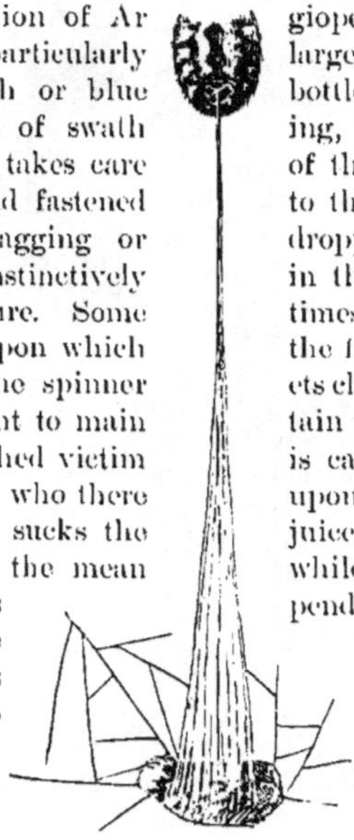

During the action of swathing, and without interrupting that work, the spider takes care of the broken radii, so that they are joined together and fastened to the perfect ones, thus preventing the orb from sagging or dropping apart. This protection of the orb goes on instinctively in the very midst of the passion of conquest and capture. Sometimes it is necessary to bite out the ends of the radii upon which the fly is entangled. In that case the rapid motion of the spinnerets closes the breach with irregular lines, but quite sufficient to maintain the tautness of the web.

Ordinarily the swathed victim is carried to the hub or den in the jaws of the spider, who thereupon settles herself in the usual **The Banquet Room.** position and sucks the juices through the enveloping threads. In the meanwhile the aranead, if upon her web, is suspended by the spinnerets and hind feet, the fore feet being used to hold and turn the carcass while it is being eaten. The fangs are also used to clasp the victim as it is turned by the feet or even more frequently by the palps. The return to the hub or den with the captured insect is occasionally accomplished by swinging outward from the point of capture upon the dragline which was carried after the spider when she rushed down upon her victim. Sometimes, instead of carrying the fly in the jaws, it will be fastened to the spinnerets by a short thread, and, thus burdened, the spider swings herself along, sometimes making one or two swings before she reaches her central point.

Fig. 231. The swathing narrowed to a single thread.

The feeding is done leisurely, and the juices so thoroughly squeezed from the carcass and imbibed that, when the spider is done with it, it is a little blackened ball of dried matter. The white silken enswathment has entirely disappeared, probably having been sucked in with the juices of the fly. The banquet over, the carcass is snapped out of the web by a sharp movement of the head and jaws.

I became much interested in the manner in which a nearly mature female Epeira vertebrata handled a moth which she had just captured. When the observation began, she was rolling the insect around as it hung from the centre of her web, the lower part of which was entirely torn away by the struggles of the large captive. When the swathing was com-

Deporting Swathed Insects. pleted, Vertebrata succeeded in carrying her prey to her shelter under some honeysuckle leaves two feet distant. She accomplished this at first by seizing the mummy with her hind feet, and partly by aid of the feet and partly by aid of the abdomen, bore it beyond the confines of the orb. When she struck the long bridge line connecting her snare with her den, she kicked her load loose from her feet and attached it to her abdomen by several lines about an inch in

Fig. 232. The Insular spider enswathing a captured locust.

length. With her prey thus hanging behind, she crawled hand over hand in the usual fashion along the line (Fig. 233), which swayed beneath its double load. As she approached her nest she reached a series of lines that converged upon the mouth of the den, whereupon she once more gathered her prize within her two hind feet, crawled into the den by use of the remaining feet (Fig. 234), and there began her banquet.

Evidently the principle of "laying by in store" for future use is well understood by spiders. Not, however, in any such manner as prevails among the ants and more highly organized animals, as Arachne's future is but a brief period.   Here is a young Argiope which on first observation had two insects trussed up, one on either side of her central web, near the outer margin of the orb.   On the second observation, an hour afterward, one of these was cut loose, and the spider held it under its jaws while fed upon it.   Here on a large insect, side of her shield, This is an observa

Another observa illustrate this point.

Trussing Captives.

she rested on her shield and there is another Argiope, engaged in feeding and has two other insects, one on either swathed and trussed ready for use. tion which is frequently made.

tion made upon Acrosoma rugosa will When the observation began Rugosa had just captured a fly.   A second fly struck the web, and the spider rushed to it, leaving fly No. 1 trussed up and hanging by a short cord.   She seized the second victim, held it a second or two, then slowly revolved it, using the third and fourth pairs of legs.   The fourth leg was also used in pulling out the enswathing thread.

Acroso- ma Trapping Flies

A slight enswathment was placed upon the insect, and it was left hanging in the snare. Rugosa then returned by a dragline to the carcass of No. 1, and feasted upon her, leaving No. 2 suspended to the top of the central.

Fig. 233. Carrying a moth by the spinnerets.

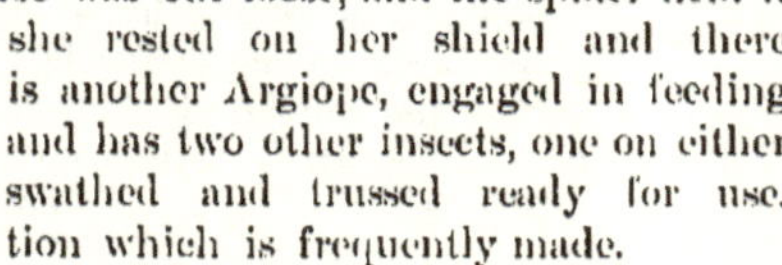

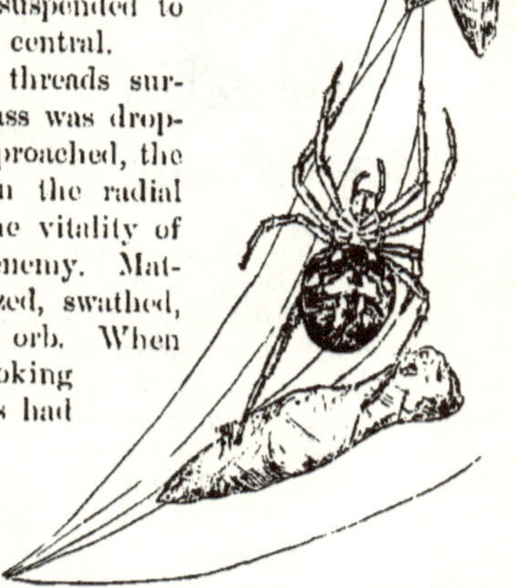

Fig. 234. Carrying a swathed moth by the feet.

When fly No. 1 was finished, the threads surrounding it were cut out, and the carcass was dropped from the snare.   No. 2 was then approached, the spider meanwhile cautiously pulling on the radial gangway by jerks, as though testing the vitality of the victim or the neighborhood of an enemy.   Matters being satisfactory, the fly was seized, swathed, and brought back to the centre of the orb.   When rejected, the carcass was a charred looking mass, out of which all the animal juices had been squeezed.

While preying upon No. 2 a third fly struck the web, whereupon No. 2 was at once flung out, as in Fig. 236, and hung by a thread to the lower margin of the hub. While waiting for prey, Rugosa clings to the upper part of the orb by the fourth pair of legs.   While engaged in feeding, the fourth and second pairs of legs are used to cling by, while the third and first pairs are used to turn and handle the flies.

Curiously enough the Orbweaver, although she makes her snare for the express purpose of capturing her food, sometimes shows a manifest **"A Time to Keep."** unwillingness to have it serve its purpose in any other than the regular and approved manner. On one occasion I saw an insect strike the orb of a Furrow spider, and on another occasion that of a Domicile spider, when the snares were only partly spun. Both animals acted precisely alike—they seized and swathed the flies, but, instead of feeding upon them then and there, hung them up for future use and resumed their net building. I have seen this act repeated many times

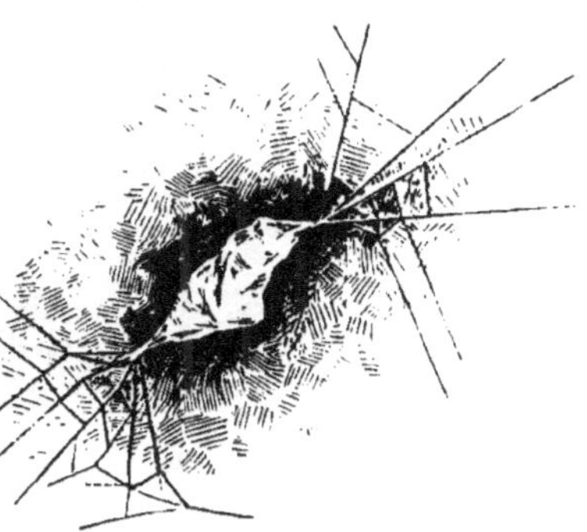

Fig. 235. A mummied fly trussed up.

by various species. Another spider (Epeira domiciliorum) having caught and wrapped up an insect that had struck her unfinished net, deliberately and, as I fancied, with a show of indignation, cut away and cast out the trussed captive from the snare! It was a most emphatic illustration of the proverb, "A time to keep and a time to cast away." I laughed heartily at the action, which I involuntarily associated with some ultra conservative human friends of mine, who are most unready to receive truth and other

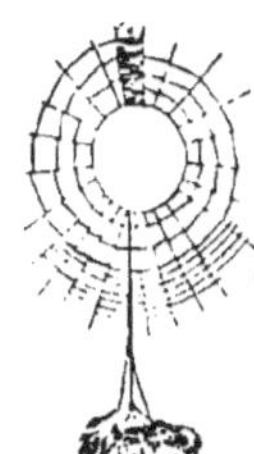

Fig. 236. A trussed fly hung out in Acrosoma's web.

blessings that do not come to them through the ordinary and approved channels. Doubtless the instinct of net building, in the above cited cases, when once excited, proved too strong to be seriously diverted or delayed by any ordinary conflicting sensation.

Influenced apparently by the same impulse, I have seen a Vertebrata and also Cophinaria stopping in the midst of laying in spiral lines to secure and swathe an insect which had struck the orb. In these cases, instead of leaving the insect swathed and trussed up for future use and then returning to the work of completing the spirals, the spiders held the captured prey within their mandibles, resumed their work, and carried the victim around during the entire process. The web completed, the quarry was taken to the centre and fed upon leisurely. In both cases about half of the spiral space had been finished before the insects struck the web and became entangled within its meshes.

These examples indicate that the ordinary instincts of spiders are held well under control. There are periods when certain instincts wholly dominate action, which at other times are held in subordination. One is not surprised to see this in such rare or unique **Subordination of Instincts.** instincts as the sexual impulse. But to see the same phenomenon in the sentiments that control daily life, and to see it frequently occurring, and so manifestly under the volition of the animal, is certainly more notable. In the examples just cited it is seen that the feeding habit is held in subordination by the industrial impulse when net making is in order; and a very complete subjection it surely is which constrains a hungry spider to truss up a fly or carry one about in its jaws until a snare is finished, or even cast it wholly out of the web.

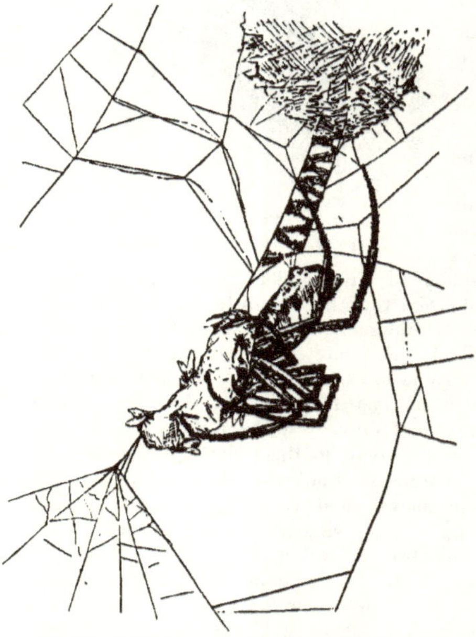

I once found a nearly mature Argiope cophinaria hanging in the centre of her orb engaged in **Laying by in Store.** sucking the juices from a fly, which she kept underneath her jaws and appeared to be handling entirely by the use of her palps. In the meanwhile she held attached to her fore feet on either side two swathed flies, one suspended by a single thread, and another by a double one. Evidently she

Fig. 237. Dwarf flies banqueting with a giantess spider (Argiope cophinaria).

was troubled with what the French call an embarrassment of riches. It is rare to see a Sedentary spider eating thus without the aid of the fore legs.

Another Cophinaria was observed with five flies, three of them large blue bottles, fastened at various parts of her web, most of them well towards the margin. Two of the blue bottles were completely wrapped in white swathing silk, and were covered from one end to another with a host of small black dipterous flies, that were trying to feed upon the carcasses of their huge, mummied congeners. Argiope appeared to be entirely regardless of the presence of these little creatures. They adhered so closely to the carcass that when the spider violently shook her web they rode back and forward like a group of children upon a seesaw, without being the least disturbed. Next morning I found that all the trussed up insects except one had disappeared; one (which I easily identified) remained in its former position, and even then several of the little Diptera were perched upon the carcass, apparently feeding. In the jaws of the spider was a swathed carcass, and even on that, as the spider held it within her mouth

Flies Banquet with a Spider. feeding upon it, were at least two of the little flies engaged with the greatest sang froid at their meal under the very jaws of their ferocious adversary! In the meantime a third fly was perched upon the middle of the abdomen of the spider herself, apparently enjoying the situation. Two days afterward I found the same curious state of things. It may be that the very diminutiveness of these creatures was their protection, especially as food was so abundant. It was certainly amusing, however, to see this seeming challenge of destiny. A few hours thereafter I saw one (or one of the same species) of these reckless Diptera trussed up near the spot where it had lately fed, although it was probably not eaten.

The same behavior was subsequently observed on several occasions and on different individuals; so that it was not the result of special sluggishness or personal peculiarity. Once, when a dozen or more of these little Diptera were hanging upon an enswathed captive, I saw Argiope brush away with her fore feet several that were crowding about her face. The action was most impatient—even angry—but none of the annoying and impudent intruders were hurt. On another occasion I observed two of the flies apparently held in the jaws of the spider. My first thought was that they had ventured too close, had been snapped up, and were being eaten by their giant hostess. But upon touching the point of my pencil to them, they at once disproved my theory by drawing back a little space and shaking themselves. They had not only ventured between Argiope's palps, but had pushed up to the very jaws, and were sipping the juices squeezed out by those organs! It was certainly a curious illustration of the old and famous riddle, "out of the eater came forth meat." (See Fig. 237.) I had never expected to see the spider and the flies peacefully feeding together upon the same carcass, but in nature, as in social life, it is often "the unexpected that happens."

II.

The efforts of spiders to take their prey are not destitute of adventures, sometimes of a very serious sort, sometimes approaching the ludicrous. For example, I chanced to get a sight of Argiope cophinaria just as she had captured a large honey bee and had begun to swathe it. I watched the struggles of the insect with interest, and found that the spider got the better of her antagonist very rapidly. Around and around the excited bee the swathing bands wound,

Special Incidents.

until at last it was completely enclosed within a silken bag. I concluded that all was over with the luckless insect, an opinion which Cophinaria evidently shared, for she laid on her final lines and clambered away to the centre of her shield, apparently with the intention of drawing her victim towards her to take a hearty meal.

Scarcely had she settled herself, however, ere the bee renewed its struggles. In a moment it succeeded in cutting a little opening at one end of the sac, out of which first issued jaws, then antennæ, then its head, and then its body. It was free. Instead of flying away, as one would have thought a reasonable insect ought to do, the bee turned with angry gestures upon the little ball of white silk into which had collapsed the enswathments out of which it had just escaped. Upon this she fastened her claws, thrust her sting ferociously into it several times, and then, as though she had satisfied her sense of justice and vengeance, spread her wings and began to ascend.

There was an angry hum in her wings, and an ugly look in the still outthrust sting, which led me to step back a pace or two lest I might come in for a share of her wrath. She followed me for a little distance, and then, changing her mind, mounted into the air, and in a moment or two was hovering over a fragrant honeysuckle blossom, apparently solacing herself for her recent insult by the sweets of nectar. What an escapade that was! And, if the bee only knew it, what a story of "hairbreadth 'scapes" she might have told to her comrades of the hive when she returned home.

A Bee's Escape from Bonds.

But how fared the spider? This question interested me. I stepped up to the web again, and after a few moments' waiting saw her go down her web lines to the roll of silken swathing. There seemed to be a slight movement of surprise at the character of the object; but if she was greatly disappointed she made little demonstration of the same. She seized the silken ball within her mandibles, turned upon her path, and carried it back to her shield, on the upper part of which she fastened it, somewhat after the manner of a trussed insect set aside for food. I could not satisfy myself whether she had noticed the escape of her prey before this return. But evidently she perceived it now. A little while afterward I found that the swathing cloth had disappeared, and I have no doubt that the spider took it within her jaws and comforted herself by feeding upon it; perhaps a poor substitute for the juicy morsel which she had anticipated, but nevertheless, even with a spider, I suppose, "a half loaf is better than no bread."

I observe that the location of the web makes a great difference in the amount of food obtained by the spider. Those webs which have a favorable position for the flight of insects, in the neighborhood of the honeysuckle blossoms of my manse yard, for example, or in positions on the ampelopis vines easily approached by insects, have an abundant supply of food. Others, less favorably situated, are seen feeding less rarely. In this matter of location the spider is very much dependent upon chance. The force or endurance of a current of wind **Location Controls Food.** during the first aeronautic flight, or the particular obstruction upon which the balloon may be arrested, will be circumstances determining the future habitat of the Orbweaver.

More frequently the range of life action is determined by the position in which the maternal cocoon is suspended, the natural tendency of spiderlings after egress being to distribute themselves in the immediate vicinity of their birth. But Orbweavers do crawl about from point to point and shift the site of their snares. I have known one to change its position by passing along one or two intervening city fences into an adjoining yard. The course and extent of these migrations are determined by the position and continuity of the foliage. But so strong is the sedentary habit of Orbweavers that they will suffer a great amount of privation before leaving the neighborhood, or indeed the immediate site of their snares. If for any reason this should happen to be poorly stocked with the creatures' natural food, their chance for growth and life is poor indeed; and I have no doubt that sometimes they perish from starvation.

In certain positions it is doubtless true that the excess of life goes to supply the lack of life nutrition. In other words, spiders are cannibals, and prey upon each other. The cocoons formed by female Orb- **Feeding on Each Other.** weavers usually send forth large colonies of younglings. As soon as they set up housekeeping for themselves they begin to prey upon each other and upon all other sorts of araneads. The strong, or skillful, or fortunate devour the weaker, less cunning, and the unlucky. A few only survive; the great majority must go to give nourishment to the few and secure the perpetuation of the species. Undoubtedly, in certain sites, this redundancy of life through maternal fecundity is an important, even an essential, factor in the food supply of spiders.

One who has observed the habit of spiders to spin their webs across cowpaths, footpaths, and the various trails leading through meadows, pasture lands, and woodlands, must have had occasion to reflect **Beating up Game.** upon the uncertainty of spider possessions, and perhaps have felt a touch of pity for the industrious creatures whose painstaking work is so continually broken down by passing animals and men. It is certainly true that great loss is thus caused, and that spiders are continually subject to the destruction of their snares by all manner of passing creatures; yet there is some compensation for this destruction.

I have often noticed that, as I walked back and forth over the fields, the grasshoppers, crickets, and other insects were stirred up by my movements, leaped or flew to this side or to that, and in their alarm and haste numbers of them struck the snares of the near by spiders, were at once entangled, and became the prey of the waiting proprietors. Thus it comes about that the very means of destruction to one proprietor becomes a means for furnishing abundant supplies to another; and doubtless that which at one time serves to destroy, at another time brings food to the larder of the same spider. There are not many animals that enjoy a like distinction of having human unfriends "beat up" the game for them as does the hunter spider silently seated at its araneal "run."

The ability of spiders to endure prolonged abstinence is very great, and to this end nature has admirably arranged their constitution. When **Long Fasting.** the abdomen is opened in dissection a large quantity of adipose matter comes into view, which supports and separates the different internal organs. This reservoir of fat is a storehouse of nutriment, which enables spiders to bear very long abstinence. When they have been deprived of food for a long time, the abdomen becomes smaller and shriveled up. I have at this writing in my possession one of our American tarantulas, Eurypelma Hentzii, which has had nothing to eat for a period of more than seven months.[1] During that time I have supplied it freely and continually with water, and it appears to be in entire health, and quite active. On several occasions I have preserved the same species quite as long without food. Longer periods of abstinence have been recorded by other observers. Of course, I do not refer to the period of hibernation, during which no food is required, but to abstinence during the seasons when spiders are wont to feed.

When an opportunity is given for feeding, they appear to be able to make up for lost time by consuming an extraordinary amount of food. **Enormous Feeding.** The number of insects which a healthy spider is able to devour during a day, without apparent inconvenience, has often been a great surprise to me. Before reaching maturity, such feeding rapidly produces a very apparent effect in growth. A half-grown spider, happening upon a location visited numerously by insects, will experience astonishing increase within a brief time.

III.

The manner of feeding among other tribes is not greatly different from that of Orbweavers. The Lineweavers swathe their captives in the **Comparative Feeding Habits.** manner above described, and eat them while they hang back downwards upon their snares, revolving the carcass and sucking its juices in the same manner as Orbweavers. In their mode of feeding, the Tubeweavers, although Sedentary spiders, quite resemble that which prevails among the Tunnelweavers and the Wandering tribes. That is to say, they simply seize prey with their paws and fangs, and feed upon them without swathing. Such Tubeweavers as Agalena nævia and Tegenaria medicinalis seize the insects as they drop

---

[1] From the latter part of October, 1888, until June 19th, 1889.

upon the outspread sheet, or into the sheeted pouch which forms the trap, and then dragging them to their tubular dens suck the juices. The Wandering spiders leap upon their prey, falling on them with the fangs, palps, and united claws of the front pairs of legs. Ordinarily, the first spring proves successful in capturing the victim, and, if it be not so, I believe that it is not often repeated.

I have frequently observed Hentz's tarantula feeding in confinement. When the spider was disposed to eat, an insect was seized with the fore legs, palps, and mandibles, which rapidly conveyed it to the mouth. In this position it was held by the palps, which, as the spider had occasion, also turned the carcass, aided by the mandibles, the latter organs mean-

Fig. 238.   Hentz's tarantula eating a locust.

while crushing the victim. (See Fig. 238.) During this act Tarantula was anchored to the rug on which it was wont to sit by several threads attached to the spinnerets. On one occasion, while in the act of eating a locust, a second locust approached near enough to be seized. It was struck upon the ground, where it was held down until the tarantula, moving slowly around, overspun and swathed it, evidently reserving it for future use.

I may say here that my experience in keeping other large spiders is that there is quite as much danger from overfeeding as underfeeding. I **Habits of Tarantula** have found the best success by giving a generous supply of living food during the summer and early autumn, and withholding food almost entirely during the remainder of the year. I was particular, however, to keep a vessel continually supplied with fresh water within the box. Spiders require water quite as much as other animals, and failure to keep them supplied will be fatal to health and life.

I have sometimes succeeded in tempting tarantulas to suck the juice of a bit of raw beef, but the only food that can be relied upon is living insects; and these spiders appear to be able to lay up within the four or five months of summer enough nourishment, in connection with a free supply of water, to last them during the entire year. These Mygalidæ do not become torpid in winter time, but remain active throughout the entire season, provided they are kept in a room heated to a moderate temperature. If exposed to a severe cold they are soon benumbed, but quickly recover when again brought into a warm atmosphere.

IV.

Although spiders can long survive without food it is absolutely necessary, as far as my experience extends, that they should be continually supplied with water. I have frequently received species of various **Need of Water.** tribes which had been shipped through the post office and were taken out of their packages apparently in the last stages of life. These I have often succeeded in restoring by applying them to water—placing them in such a position that their mouth organs would be near or over a drop of the liquid. In a longer or shorter time, according to the degree of exhaustion, but also, I think, varying with the peculiar constitution of the species, many of these would be restored and become as active as ever.

This is a common experience with those who have kept spiders in artificial conditions for the sake of observation and experimentation. Mr. Campbell says of the common English house spider, Tegenaria guyonii, that the habits of the females of this species, spending as they do an apparently sedentary life in dry places, render it difficult to see how they can obtain water except during their occasional excursions. Yet the frequent supply of water or a damp atmosphere is necessary for spiders. He had kept a Tegenaria guyonii for more than twenty-seven months without any liquid except that which she derived from insects. In one case a spider that he was keeping was found lying helpless at the bottom of the bottle with her legs drawn close to her body. He immediately filled a tube with water and dropped some on her back and in front of her. She quickly balanced herself, and, wetting the last joints of her palps, placed them to **Drinking.** her maxillæ. This she did five times and then advanced and lowered her whole body so that the maxillæ were dipped in the water. Thus she remained, apparently motionless, for a few seconds, when she raised herself to her normal position, and repeated the draught after an interval of a few minutes. Shortly afterwards she mounted to her usual roost at the shoulder of the bottle, with her abdomen considerably distended.[1]

[1] F. Maule Campbell, Jour. Linn. Soc. Zool., XVI., page 537.

This mode of drinking as described by Mr. Campbell accurately expresses the common method as I have observed it. In the case of large spiders that have long been kept from water, such, for example, as Hentz's tarantula, the spider will sometimes rush to the water, greedily drop the maxillæ and mouth organs into it, the body being partly sustained in the meantime by the outspread legs. Sometimes the mouth will be lifted up for a little while, and then again sunk into the water.

Many sedentary spiders, and indeed numbers of other tribes, must obtain a considerable supply of water during the process of cleansing themselves. The little drops of dew and rain which gather upon the hairs of the legs are brushed or squeezed into the mouth when the limbs are drawn through the mandibles in the process of toilet making, as described in Vol. II. of this work.

Cambridge observes that drought as well as excess of wet, but more especially the former, and unseasonable weather of all kinds have a strong effect in reducing the number of spiders. Some species found in marshy places are so susceptible to injury, from lack of moisture, that they cannot be carried alive in a box for more than an hour or two, unless a small portion of damp moss be placed with them. Others, on the contrary, appear to thrive best on the most arid spots, and in the hottest sun. As a rule, however, spiders are thirsty souls, constantly requiring water to drink.[1]

I have received one authentic report of spiders drinking milk. It was sent me by Mrs. Mary Treat, to whom it was communicated by one of her **Drinking Milk.** lady correspondents, Mrs. J. B. Harrison. The species referred to was not identified, but the statement made is that the spider spun a thread from the side of a box down to a milk pan, and then deliberately and carefully descended inside the vessel until it came to the milk, which it then sucked. This was observed in several cases. One cannot help wondering whether the spider's taste was sufficiently keen to distinguish between the milk and its ordinary drink. Probably not. The same lady speaks of a spider whose snare was on a pump in the yard, and which every night spun a delicate line just across the spout, and from this position procured drinking water.

Does the spider eat its web? is a question which has often been asked, and variously answered by both, scientific and non scientific observers. In **Eating Its Web.** point of fact, the Orbweaver does eat its web. It is its invariable habit to gather together the particles of its broken snare, when it clears away the wreckage to make a new web, and ball it underneath its jaws with its feet and palps. It then takes it into its mouth and apparently sucks from it all the viscid material and all the other nutritious matter—dealing with it, so far as I can observe, very much in the same way that it does with a fly.

The manner in which a fractured web is eaten may be frequently seen

---

[1] Cambridge, "Spiders of Dorset," Introduction, page xxxii.

after the morning is well advanced, or after the snare has been broken by the struggles of a large insect. The spider runs out upon her radial lines, and with great rapidity cuts here and there the supporting threads, gathering with a quick motion of her feet the various parts underneath her body and balling them around the mouth. Thence she runs back to the hub, whence she approaches another part of the web, as she moves clipping the segments and rolling the parts together with her feet. Her action is facilitated by the fact that when the supporting radii are cut the interradials collapse, and, by reason of the viscidity of the beads, mass together in a lump. This the spider seizes, condenses by a deft and rapid action of her feet, adds it to the little ball already gathered, then runs along a line which she is always careful to preserve, to a main foundation line leading to her shelter or nest, and settling herself imbibes the juices of her morsel at her leisure.

An English observer records a note which indicates that certain tube-weaving spiders consume their snares in winter time. A species of Agalena or Tegenaria was kept during the summer abundantly fed, **Agalena Eats Her Sheet.** its energy and excessive nutrition being largely consumed in increasing its web, adding layer to layer, one upon another, in texture almost as close as tissue paper. When the winter came and flies disappeared, the observer expected his pet to hibernate or become torpid. On the contrary, however, it seemed to be as active as ever in midwinter. It was then noticed that certain curious holes appeared in the web, which looked as if it had been cut away with some sharp instrument, and it kept on going and going, until altogether six or seven superficial inches of this paper like web had been devoured. The spider did not thrive on this food, and became very thin. It lived, however, until the following summer, and once more grew fat on abundance of flies.[1]

V.

The capture of food is always more or less disastrous to the snare of the Orbweaver, as may be easily seen by a study of the various figures representing that action. The insects themselves in their struggles thoroughly twist up the whole viscid section upon which they are caught, and thus **Wear and Tear of Snares.** throw it into a confused tangle of merged, crossed, and diverging lines, which extend in every direction. If the insect is a very large one, the amount of breakage is much greater. So also when the spider runs from her den or hub to seize the insect, her own action in swathing her prey increases the confusion of the lines. Frequently she is compelled to cut out the radii and portions of the spiral space in order to accomplish her capture; and after the insect is swathed a further damage frequently occurs by the act of the spider in cutting out

----

[1] Gilbert R. Redgrave, "Science Gossip," 1872, page 140.

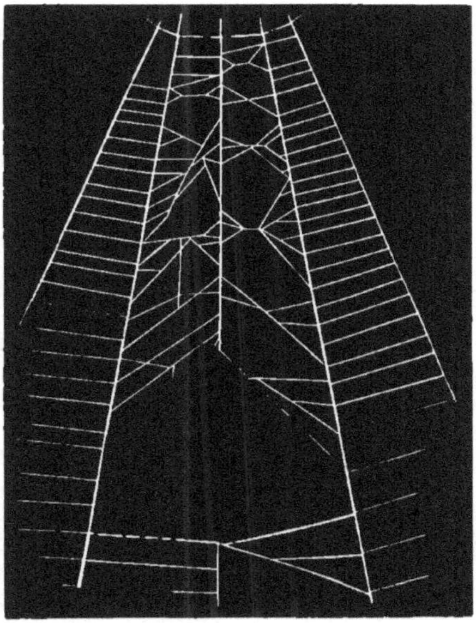

and transporting the mummied insect. If the day happens to be a very good day, viewed from the spider's standpoint, or a bad one from that of the flies; if the net site happens to be one where insects are numerous, the web will present a very forlorn appearance even early in the day, and by the time evening has come it will be but a tattered remnant of the beautiful object which caught the morning dew and glistened in the first sunbeams.

Fig. 239 is a sketch of a portion of web of Epeira strix, from which a freshly captured insect had been taken. The lines are drawn very accurately from nature.

In the act of capturing an insect it becomes necessary for the spider to

Fig. 239. Section of Epeira's orb after an insect has been captured.

piece together the parts of the web which are separated either by the breakage of the insect's struggles or the intentional cutting of the spider herself. This mending is done with great deftness and skill. The broken parts are held together by one or more of the feet, usually the hind feet. The claws on one side of the body grasp one portion of the armature, while those on the other grasp the opposite broken part. At the same time a thread is thrown out from the spinnerets, is attached to the margins of the fracture, and the rent is pieced together in a manner almost impossible to describe, and indeed to observe at all, so rapidly is it accomplished.

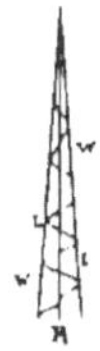

Fig. 240. Piece of broken radius spliced by Epeira strix.

Fig. 240 is a piece of a broken radius spliced by Epeira strix. R, represents the radius; L, L, lines which were run along either side thereof; and W, a zigzag cross line by which the three straight lines were warped together. At other times the angular points of the fracture on either side are simply held together by one or more lines, as the case requires, thus taking the place of the sundered radii and lost spirals by which the segments had been held together.

Mending Broken Webs.

It frequently occurs that the insects entangled upon a snare are never used by the spider; although a most voracious creature, her appetite is necessarily limited, and, at all events, she becomes somewhat dainty as her appetite is satisfied, and will not trouble herself with insects of a minor sort. Indeed, many large spiders, except when very hungry, pay no attention to the small insects strung upon their webs.

Unused Entangled Insects.

It is surprising how many of these will be arrested in the course of the day. I have counted as many as two hundred and thirty-six insects, great and small, hanging upon various parts of the web of Epeira sclopetaria, after the proprietor had abandoned the day's work and retired to her nest to await the evening meal. One day, while crossing the long bridge over Deal Lake, Asbury Park, I stopped to count the number of insects upon a web spun just beneath the bridge, and noticed that thirty-six mosquitoes had been entangled. Certainly this was a goodly amount of service for one spider to render a most unappreciative and ungrateful humanity.

A Mosquito Trap.

A friend has recently been deeply interested in the problem whether dragon flies, or, as they are sometimes called, mosquito hawks, might not be reared in sufficient numbers along the seashore to keep in check the immense number of mosquitoes that sometimes make life at our watering places very unsatisfactory to guests. There is no telling what artificial propagation may accomplish in this direction, and, at all events, all experiments in natural science are worthy of consideration until they are demonstrated to be impracticable. But I venture to suggest that the most effective natural checks upon the increase of insect pests are their natural enemies, the spiders. If men would abate the unreasonable prejudice which they have against this most friendly and helpful animal, they probably would suffer less from the raids of that piping and piercing pest, the American mosquito.

The spider is doubtless Nature's chief check against the undue increase of insects. Despised Arachne is entitled by her services to occupy the chief place among invertebrate philanthropists. She is, I might almost say, absolutely harmless to mankind. With the exception of an occasional alleged "spider bite" issuing in suffering or death, and delivered by the traditional and indefinite "black spider," I know of no evil that can be charged against her. True, as long ago the wise Proverbialist said, "The spider taketh hold with hands, and is in king's palaces."[1] She builds her cobwebs in our homes, but there is no harm in that. If one will take the pains to study the cobwebs, they will be found beautiful structures, and, at all events, the housewife can brush them away without encouraging hatred for the harmless creature

Nature's Check to Insects.

---

[1] Holy Scripture, Proverbs xxx. 28.

that makes them. For, be it considered, the spider only comes into our homes because mosquitoes and other insects also come! She comes, not seeking to harm us, but to help us, and therefore, for the sake of her motive, if she be not welcome, let her, at least, be thought of kindly.

The number of insects of all sorts and sizes destroyed by spiders simply passes calculation. If one will walk out on a dewy morning, with his eyes open for spider webs, he will be surprised to find how many there are, and how various, too, the forms of spinningwork that meet him. All over this new plowed field he will find them fresh spun; in yonder meadow, also, hanging by myriads upon myriads on the grasses. Along that hedge row they are nested, and have woven their dainty snares, and built their nests on the feathery ferns. In the branches of these shrubs and on the foliage of yonder trees are other hosts.

If one will push back the foliage, he will see yet others, spiders of the Wandering group, that stalk their prey as do the wild beasts of the forest, crouching on trunk and branches and lurking among the leaves. If one turns to the earth, other myriads are seen, whose homes are on the ground, or who build slight webs close to the surface. These have laid the axe at the very root of the tree, and are destroying the insects ere they rise from the surface to visit our homes.

Arachne the Philanthropist.

All these unnumbered multitudes of spiders are engaged, during every moment of their existence, in waging relentless war upon the insect world. When one considers how many spiders there are, and that they all thus feed upon their natural food, the insects, he may form some just conception of how needful they are to mankind. I do not hesitate to say that, unless Nature should provide some equivalent in the way of check upon insects, man could not dwell in many inhabited parts of the world were it not for the friendly service of spiders.

CHAPTER XVI.

EFFECTS AND USES OF SPIDER POISON.

WHAT are the effects of spider venom? Nothing connected with the life history of spiders has given rise to greater diversity of opinion than this question. The well nigh universal belief is that all spiders **Current Opinions.** are very poisonous and their bite apt to be serious and even fatal to human beings. It is this, doubtless, which maintains the most unjust popular dread of and hostility to these useful animals. On the other hand, naturalists have been generally inclined to an opinion quite the reverse of the popular one, and have held spiders as harmless to man.

I.

Let us first inquire what light anatomy can throw upon the subject. More than two hundred years ago Leeuwenhoek gave a substantially correct description of the fang of a spider, pointing out the small aperture through which the liquid poison is emitted. Since that time the poison apparatus has been frequently described, and any **Indications of Anatomy.** one with a microscope can easily satisfy himself of the facts. Whatever may be the effect of the secretion from the poison glands of spiders, it is certain that the organs and armature secreting and conveying the venom are formidable enough to suggest the idea of injury to creatures affected thereby. The fangs of Argiope cophinaria are shown in Fig. 211, where they are enlarged about fifteen times. The mandibles from which the drawing was made

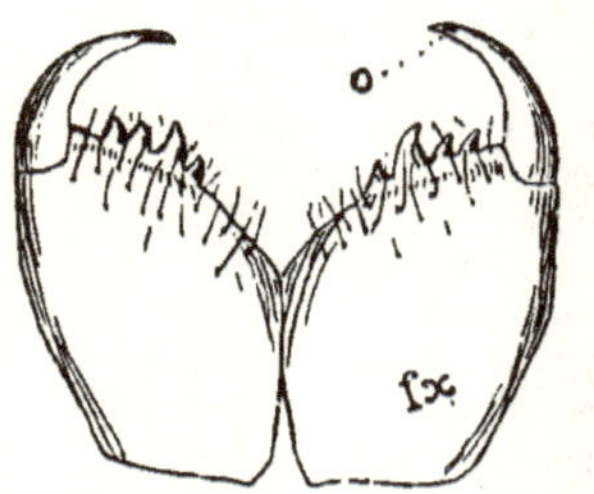

FIG. 211. View of the falces (fx) and fangs of Argiope cophinaria, from camera lucida drawing. The teeth on one side are shown in outline, and the opening (o) in the fang is shown. ✕ 15.

were taken from a nearly adult female. The falx, fx, was about two millimetres long and one millimetre wide. The fang itself was about one millimetre in length. When examined under the microscope it showed very clearly the matrix in which the poison gland had been placed, as seen in the outline drawing (camera lucida) at Fig. 212, g.m. One also sees the canal, cn, which contained the duct, and the little aperture at the extremity, o, from which the secretion of the gland issued.

The gland itself was well observed in a dissection made from Epeira domiciliorum, and represented at Fig. 243, multiplied about twenty-five times. The sac is covered with muscular fibre, as shown in the drawing, and yet more magnified in the camera lucida sketch of a portion of the sac at Fig. 244. This muscular provision implies a formidable arrangement for expressing the contents of the gland through the duct and its canal out of the opening in the fang, o.

Still another view is given at Fig. 245, the poison apparatus of Epeira diademata. The sac or poison gland, g, is inclosed in its coating of striated muscles; the duct, d, about the length of the gland, enters the falx and fang, f, and the outlet is shown at o, which appears to be along a little shallow groove in the outer surface of the inside face of the fangs. The outlet (o) is shown again at x, magnified about thirty times. The muscular fibres coil spirally and very regularly around the bag. The aperture is not only an oval slit, but the side towards the point is doubly beveled, thus facilitating the emission and direction of the venom.[1]

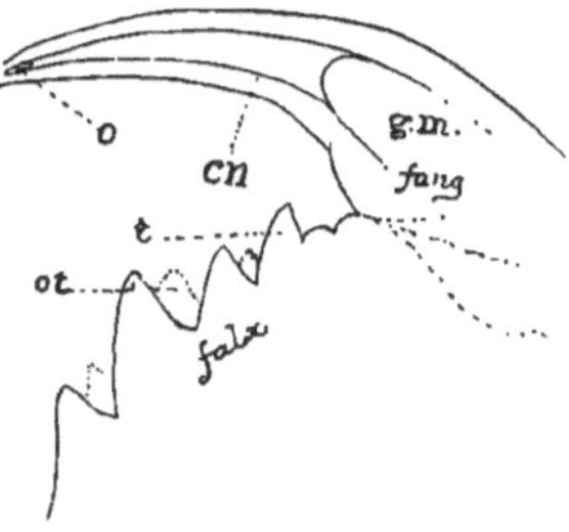

Fig. 242. Much magnified outline of the falx and fang of Argiope cophinaria. g.m., matrix of the poison gland; cn, canal which contains the duct leading from the gland; o, opening on the side of the fang; tt, the teeth; ot, dotted outline of the outer row.

As the discharge of the poison is not dependent upon the mechanical action of erecting the fang, as in the case of poisonous snakes, it is not improbable that the spider has the power of withholding the poison at will. As the emission of the venom depends on the compression of the muscles by the poison sac, and this compression is within the volition

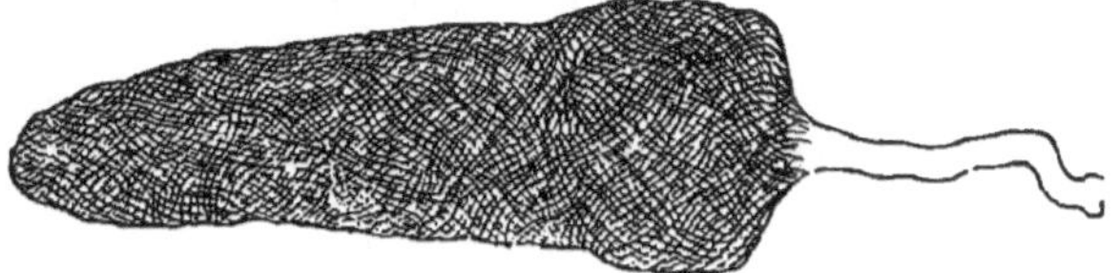

Fig. 243. View of the muscular system inclosing the poison gland of Epeira domiciliorum. Camera lucida sketch. × 25.

of the spider, we may well suppose that the animal often strikes without feeling the necessity of injecting poison into the wound, but destroys its prey simply by piercing. That this arrangement is general among the tribes of spiders appears by a similar examination of any other individual.

[1] From "Science Gossip," December, 1867, page 270, Mr. Henry Davis.

Fig. 246 shows the poison sac, gland, and one of the fangs of the
Mason spider (Nemesia cementaria) as dissected by Blanchard.[1] The vertical articulation of the fangs, or movement up and down, which characterizes this tribe of spiders,
may be noted in the cut. Fig.
247 represents the formidable
mandibles of the large Mygale, popularly known as the
"tarantula," drawn twice the
size of nature. The outlets
for the poison from the fangs
are here very manifest. They
are situated near the point of
the inner surface, and are of
the shape represented in the
figure. On one side of the

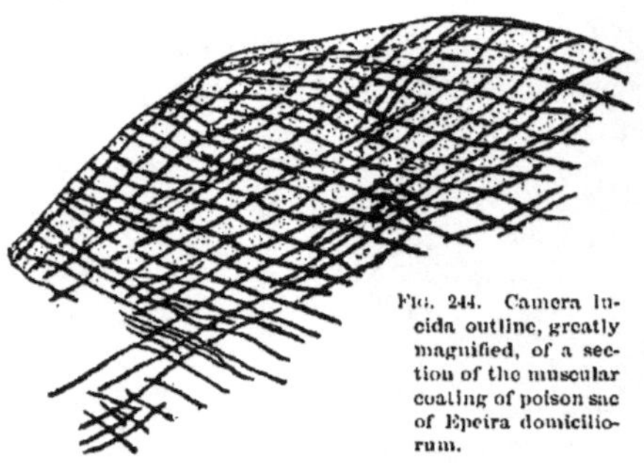

Fig. 244. Camera lu-
cida outline, greatly
magnified, of a sec-
tion of the muscular
coating of poison sac
of Epeira domicilio-
rum.

falx is a formidable row of ten teeth. The other side is protected by a
picket of closely placed stiff red bristles. It might be expected that such
a formidable armature would certainly inflict a grievous hurt, whatever
may be the case concerning the feebler armature of our ordinary familiar
spider fauna.

Another illustration of these organs is given at Fig. 248, which represents the fang and falx of an immature Drassus, multiplied about twelve
times, taken from a camera lucida drawing made by the late Mr. Richard
Beck.[2] The manner in which the falces and fangs are related to the mouth
organs is shown at Fig. 249, which is a view from
beneath of the cephalothorax of Epeira quadrata.
The lip is seen at the tip of the sternum, which
lies just under the maxillae, which organs in turn
are situated just beneath the falx.

The moults of spiders form admirable specimens
in which to examine microscopically the external
character of the fang. They not only show the
opening far more distinctly than the entire organ
taken from the animal, but they present the fangs
in a most favorable position for examination.

In view of the above results, we are free to say
that as far as the testimony of anatomy goes, it is
plain that spiders of all tribes are abundantly
provided with an armature for dealing an injurious

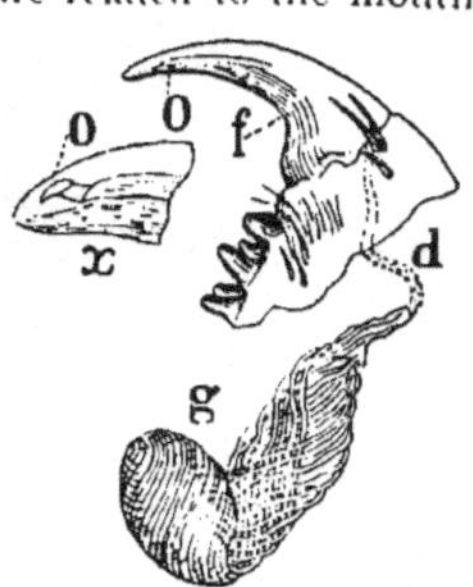

Fig. 245. Poison gland (g), duct (d),
and fang (f) of Epeira diademata. x, the point of fang yet
more enlarged, to show the external opening, o. (After Davis.)

wound to those whom they strike. One can hardly suppose that such a
gland as I have described, with such an attachment, is intended to secrete
any other substance than one which provides for the defense or nourishment of its possessor.

<hr>

[1] Cuvier, Regn. Anim. Arachnides.   [2] "Science Gossip," 1866, page 202.

II.

From the indications of anatomy we turn to the testimony of naturalists and other observers of the effects of spider venom. First in order of value, for their extent and thoroughness, are the experiments of Mr. Blackwall,[1] an abstract of which I present. The experimenter induced a female Epeira diademata to bite him on the inside of the left hand, near the base **Evidence of Effects.** of the fore finger. It continued to force its fangs deeper into the flesh, during a period of many seconds, and at last quitted its hold voluntarily, when a little blood issued from the wound. Though the spider was in a state of great excitement from previous irritation, Mr. Blackwall did not experience more inconvenience from its bite than from a puncture made near it at the same time with a fine needle. The effects of both injuries appeared to be very similar.

Fig. 246. The poison gland, duct, and fang of Nemesia cementaria. (After Blanchard.)

Again, a highly exasperated female Diademata was allowed to seize him on the inner side of the left fore arm near the carpus. It continued **Effect of Epeira Bite.** for more than a minute to bury its fangs deeper into the flesh, and, on quitting voluntarily, a little blood flowed from the wounded part, near which a puncture was made simultaneously with a fine needle. The effects of this and the preceding experiment were alike. In both cases the air was sultry and the temperature as high as seventy-five degrees. These two wounds were inflicted in the month of July.

Fig. 247. The mandibles of Hentz's Tarantula. ✕ 2. (From nature.) The bristles and teeth on the interior surface of the fang are shown, and the opening in the fangs through which the venom exudes.

In the latter part of August, a powerful and much irritated female Epeira quadrata bit Mr. Blackwall on the inner side of the left fore arm near the carpus. It retained its hold for the space of five minutes, occasionally forcing its fangs deeper into the flesh, and, on quitting it voluntarily, blood issued freely from the punctures. The effects of this bite did not differ materially from those of a wound made at the same time with a needle of average size, the intensity and duration of pain being very similar in both instances.

During the same month spiders of various species were induced, under the influence of excited feelings, to seize a piece of clean window glass with their fangs, when a transparent fluid, which escaped from the small aperture near their extremity, was deposited upon it. The application of this fluid to the tongue did not produce any sensible effect upon that organ.

[1] Linn. Trans., Vol. XXI., pages 31–37.

In order to compare the effects of spider venom with that of hymen-opterous insects, Mr. Blackwall touched to his tongue the poison emitted under like circumstances with the above from the sting of the common wasp (Vespa vulgaris), the hive bee (Apis melifi-ca), and the humble bee (Bombus terrestris). A powerfully acrid, pungent taste was the immediate consequence of applying the insect poison to the tongue.

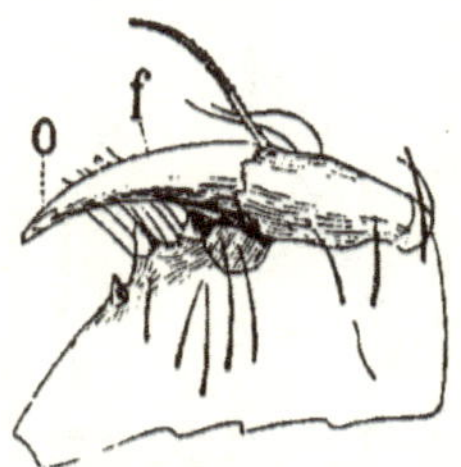

Fig. 248.   A falx and fang (f) of Drassus.   (After Beck.)

A contrast equally remarkable was evinced when these insect fluids were transmitted into the recent wound. That secreted by the in-sects caused inflammation, accompanied by acute pain, effects which, if pro-duced at all by that secreted by the spiders, were scarcely appreciable.

Inocula-tion Test.

Baron Walckenaer also experimented upon his own person, allowing himself to be bitten by the largest species of spiders around Paris without consequent swelling or reddening. The small punctures made by the spider's fangs gave him no other sensation than would have been produced by a pin or a needle thrust into the finger. It is his judgment that the venom of a spider has not as great an effect upon man as that of a wasp, bee, bed bug, flea, or even smaller insects.[1]

Walck-enaer's Witness.

Rev. Pickard-Cambridge often tested the absence of venom in some of the strongest British species.[2] Dugès made experiments upon himself with the largest spiders, such as Segestria and Tegenaria, without producing any physical pain or wound that could not readily be dissipated. M. Eugene Simon re-cords that he was struck in his finger by the fangs of Lycosa tarentula, which affected him after the fashion of the prick of two needles. The pain was lively, the blood flowed, but the little wound healed without any special ill effects.[3] A correspondent of "Science Gos-sip"[4] says that his son was bitten in his closed hand by a spider, which left two small blood stains. His wife was bitten, but there was simply a slight swelling. Another correspondent writes that a boy was bitten at

Fig. 249. The sternum and mouth organs of Epeira quadrata, viewed from beneath. (After Stave-ley.)

Cape Colony by a large spider, which is called a tarantula, so badly as to make his finger bleed, but no further effect followed.

Mr. George B. Lownes, a gentleman living in the suburbs of Phila-delphia, informed me that on one occasion, while walking through a lane,

<hr>

[1] Aptères, Vol. II., page 423.   [2] Spiders of Dorset, Vol. I., Introduction, page xxv.
[3] Histoire Naturelle des Araignées, page 27.
[4] G. B., Science Gossip, September, 1868, page 231.

he stopped to pick up a flat stone under which a ground spider (probably Lycosa scutulata) was nested in a little cave along with her cocoon. The spider sprang upon his finger, making a puncture like the prick of a pin. The wound bled, but had no other inconvenient effect.

My own personal experience with spider bites has been very limited, as I never but once could succeed in teasing my captives to bite me.

The Author's Experience. While roughly handling a large Epeira insularis, August 29th, I was struck by her in the ball of the thumb. The fangs left two slight punctures about one-eighth inch apart. At the mouth of each puncture on the skin was a little drop of transparent colorless liquid, evidently venom, which had been extruded from the poison gland. I waited a little space to allow this to enter the system, and then applied the liquid to the tip of the tongue. It had an acrid taste, leaving a remainder in the mouth something like the astringency of alum. Not the slightest inconvenience resulted from this wound. No irritation or swelling of any sort followed, and I was conscious of no pain except the very slight sensation produced by the original incision, which was no greater than that of the prick of a dull pin point.

III.

We turn now to some of the evidence that spiders do inflict a serious wound. Mr. J. M. Meek, of Waiwera, New Zealand, sent the following narrative of the effects of the bite of the katipo, or native spider,[1] which appears to be a species of Latrodectus: "On the morning of the 24th ult., at three o'clock, my son (a man of thirty-one years of age) was awakened from his sleep by the bite of one of those poisonous insects, and came into our bedroom about an hour afterwards, and exclaimed to his mother and myself, 'I am bitten by one of those spiders that the natives have so often spoken to me about, and am full of pain. See, here it is, in the bottom of the candlestick.' I looked at the insect, whose body was about the size of an ordinary pea, and in color nearly approaching to black. His mother, on looking at his back, saw the puncture the spider had made, and immediately commenced sucking the wound. I proceeded to the hotel, and obtained the services of Dr. Mohnbeer, when, on my return with him to my house, my son was suffering the most excruciating pain in the groin, the virus apparently working its way in that direction. After an application of ammonia by the doctor, the pain shifted from the groin and worked its way up the spine, affecting the arms and chest during the remainder of the day and lasting till the following morning, my son moaning with pain the whole time.

Venomous Spider of New Zealand.

"On Tuesday the pain became intense, the virus working its way into

---

[1] Popular Science Gossip, 1877, page 46.

his legs, causing the veins to swell very much. We applied turnip poultice to the wound, and when this was taken off a quantity of black fluid came from the sore. During the afternoon the pain in the legs and big toes still continued. Dr. Mohnbeer prescribed a liniment, which, after rubbing well into the legs, caused a black, inky colored fluid to emit itself through the pores of the skin in large drops, from which time my son began to improve, and has continued improving ever since, but suffers much from weakness. From the time he was bitten on Monday till the Friday following he lost exactly twelve pounds in flesh. I forgot to state that when he was first bitten I gave him small doses of brandy, at intervals during the first two days, which seemed to have the effect of greatly relieving the pain.

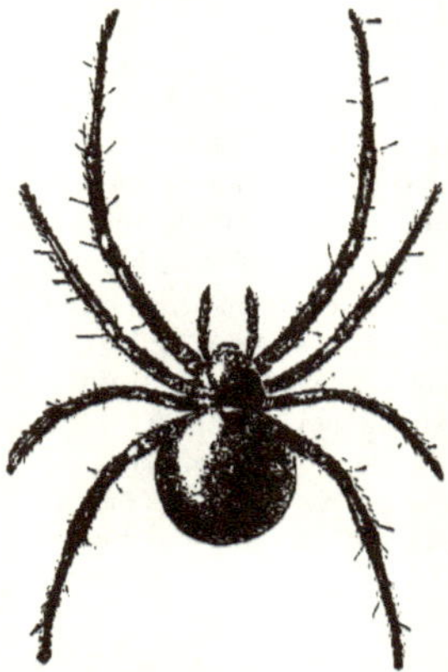

Fig. 250. Latrodectus mactans, adult female. Twice natural size.[1]

"I am informed by Te Hemera, native chief here, and also by other natives, that many fatal cases among their ranks have taken place by the bite of the katipo; they also believe the sufferer is sure to die if they cannot find the spider; but, on the contrary, if they find it and burn it in the fire, the patient gets well in three days. If they cannot find the insect, they set fire to the house and burn buildings, effects, and everything else. In this case the spider was found, and Dr. Mohnbeer has it preserved in spirits in his surgery. I write this to caution persons to look well to their bedclothes before retiring to rest, as I have witnessed persons suffering from the bite of snakes and other reptiles in Australia, but never saw any one in such agony as my son during the time the poison was taking effect."

Native Notions.

Notwithstanding this very clear and apparently trustworthy account and the examples which follow, M. Lucas, a well known naturalist, gives a testimony which is exactly the reverse concerning the venomous effects of the

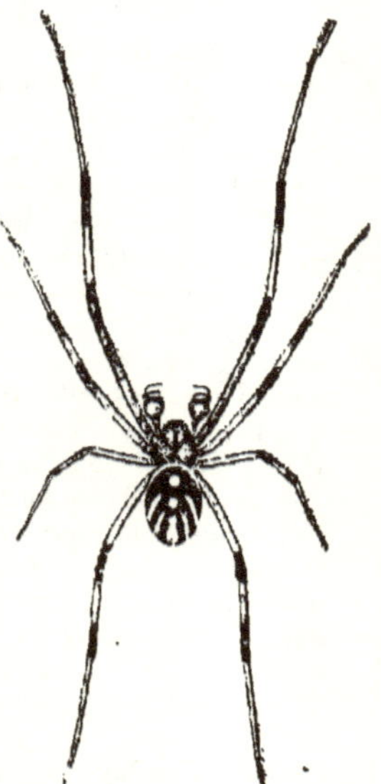

Fig. 251. Latrodectus mactans, male. Twice natural size.

<hr>

[1] For this cut and the two next following I am indebted to the courtesy of the Secretary of the United States Department of Agriculture.

very same spider. He states that he had studied the habits of Latrodectus in Algeria, where it is frequently found, and that he never observed
that its bite was venomous, although he himself had been bitten
several times without any bad effect.[1] Can it be that the very
state of mind in which the naturalist approaches the inquiry
neutralizes the poison by nullifying the effects of an excited imagination?

Lucas Denies.

In the entomological journal known as "Insect Life," issued by the
United States Department of Agriculture,[2] there is an excellent article
giving the evidence for and against the possibility of a fatal bite from
our common spiders. In this article two cases which appear to be well
authenticated are given of Latrodectus mactans, as the effects of the bite of
found in North Carolina. One of them resulted fatal ly, and the other seriously.
bite are fully detailed. Both The symptoms of the of the victims were negroes.
The same article quotes Wright,[3] who gives a num- from Mr. F. W. ber of cases from
one variety of and describes a hearsay of fatal bites by spider in New Zealand,
serious case in his own did not result in death.

New Zealand Katipo.

practice, which, however, He considers that the symp himself make it evident
fully affected by a narcot being absorbed into circu brain, and nervous system
tent, almost amounting to was treated with spirits of wound, and with ammonia
bined with brandy in con Mr. Wright adds that quainted with these spi
sidered their bite very dan toms of the case treated by that the man was power-
ic and acid poison, which lation affected the heart, to a very considerable ex-
fatal syncope. The man ammonia, applied to the and water, afterward com-
siderable doses internally. the Maories are well ac- ders, and have always con-
gerous. The tufts of sedge

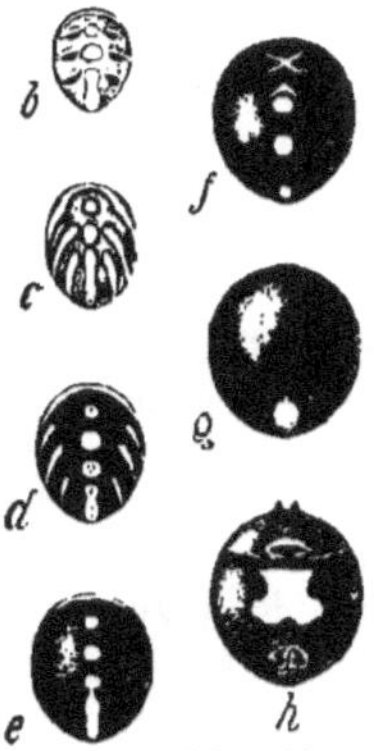

FIG. 252. Varied markings of the abdomen. b, c, d, e, f, g, upper side of abdomen; h, under side of the specimen marked g; e, f, g, h are enlarged two, c and d three times, b four times the original.

upon the sea beach are the favorite haunts of the red spotted variety, and
the natives avoid sleeping in such places. Half a stone's throw inland,
however, they do not fear the "Katipo," as they call the aranead. This
statement appears to me to throw discredit upon the entire testimony of
the natives, for it is not possible to believe that the venomous character
of the spider can be affected by a simple removal from the sedgy growth
along the seashore to the herbage half a stone's throw inland.

Mr. Gosse[4] records the effect produced upon one of his servants who

[1] Annals Entomological Society of France, 1843, page 8.
[2] Insect Life, Vol. I., No. 7, pages 204-11.
[3] Transactions of the New Zealand Institute, 1869.
[4] P. H. Gosse: Naturalist's Sojourn in Jamaica, page 241.

was bitten by one of the large, beautiful Nephilas who spin their huge orbwebs in the forests of Jamaica. Coming through the woods at early dawn his face came into collision with one of the strong webs. He stopped to brush it off, and immediately felt some large insect run down his body, which presently bit him on his great toe. The pain was less severe than that following the sting of a wasp, or even the puncture of a Tabanus; but the man described it as having three distinct paroxysms—if one may use such a term for so small a matter. The pain was not of long duration. Here, as in so many other cases, the record fails positively to show that the wound was really inflicted by a spider, but that may be inferred.

An English gentleman records that while removing some old boxes he felt a sharp nip in the hand between the fore finger and thumb, and found a large spider fastened on his hand, which at first he could not push off, as his fangs were fastened in the skin. After killing the spider he found two small holes, one twenty-fourth of an inch apart, filled with blood. There was a tingling sensation in the part for eighteen hours afterward, with a tenderness in the wound.[1]

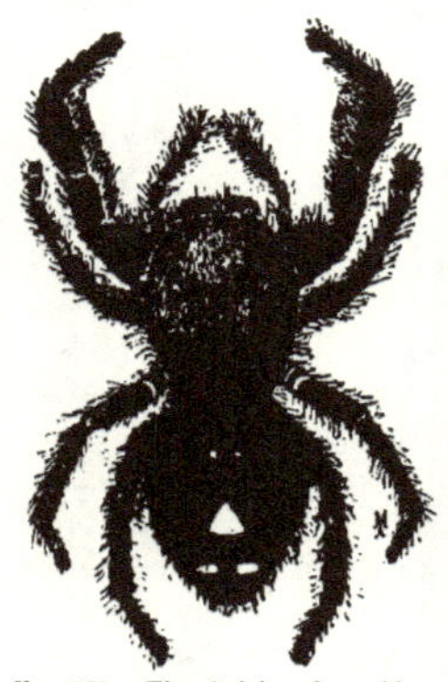

Fig. 253. The Saltigrade spider, Phidippus morsitans (Walck.), much enlarged.

It must be confessed that the experiments of naturalists, as well as their observations, are unfavorable to the popular belief in the dangerous character of the spider's stroke, except in the case of the very large species, such as our American tarantula. I can only say for myself, that having handled thousands of living spiders, taking them up with my fingers, and permitting them to crawl on hands or face, I have never experienced the slightest inconvenience, and have only been consciously bitten two or three times. Other than this, if I have been pricked by the fangs, the wound has been so insignificant as entirely to escape notice.

Yet the belief in the venomous, if not fatal, character of the spider's stroke is so deeply rooted in the popular mind that it would be almost impossible to eradicate it. The question arises, is not this general belief worthy of credence? If it were unsupported by facts, I certainly should not hesitate to answer, no! There is so much ignorance, amounting even to absurdity, as to the dangerous character of many insects and other inferior animals, and ignorance has so often shaded into superstition, that one is justified in holding even a widespread popular opinion of no value until the contrary is demonstrated. However, the problem is much confused by what appear to be

The Popular Notion.

<hr>

[1] Science Gossip, page 165, 1868.

authentic facts concerning wounds inflicted from time to time by certain spiders. I have met many cases recorded in public prints, in magazines, and personal letters. It is true that in most cases the testimony can hardly be regarded as reliable. It amounts, usually, to this: That some one was bitten by an insect, the result being either serious or **Indefinite Testimony.** fatal; that a "black spider" was seen somewhere near the individual, or near the couch or bed or seat upon which the individual rested; that the said black spider (it is always a "black spider," with no further description) was immediately killed, and therefore no specimen of the individual could be obtained. The indefinite character of such testimony at once excludes it as evidence.

But cases somewhat better authenticated are also reported, several of which appear to be worthy of credence. In these examples the same "black spider" figures. But something more definite appears after a little cross questioning; and it is important to note that in most of such cases the testimony centres upon two spiders. One is a well known and widely distributed Lineweaver, Latrodectus mactans, Walck. (the L. verecundum of Hentz), and the other a large black Saltigrade spider which is probably Phidippus morsitans (Walck.).[1] In most cases Latrodectus is the offending party. Concerning this species there is a very general concensus of popular feeling that it is extremely poisonous, and this feeling is found not only among the colored people and others of the United States and the West India Islands, but in communities in the old world where the genus has representatives. The testimony above quoted concerning this aranead certainly seems to justify the popular belief; yet the well known naturalist, M. Lucas, as we have seen, was bitten by Latrodectus without the least discomfort! (See Appendix for additional facts.)

IV.

Separate from the question as to the effect of spider venom upon the human organization, is the question, what is its effect upon the natural enemies and prey of the spider? One writer[2] says that five **Effects on Insects.** or six flies which he fed to an Orbweaver, were trussed up successively after having been apparently killed. After the lapse of fifteen or thirty minutes, these began to revive, and before the hour was completed, most of them had extricated themselves and got away. The flies which recovered were the last ones thrown into the web.

Another observer[3] describes a conflict between a lineweaving spider and a species of Epeira, in which the latter was wounded by the former, the fangs being sunk into the leg, where the biter hung on like a bull dog. From this moment, Epeira, though much larger, made no attempt to

[1] The Attus audax and A. sexpunctatus of Hentz.
[2] Edward Sutton, "Science Gossip." 1868, page 45.   [3] "Science Gossip." 1876, page 255.

retaliate upon its puny assailant, but commenced to pull with all its force to liberate the imprisoned limb. This was accomplished after a few seconds, when it hurried to its corner and began to work at the wounded limb with its palpi, falces, and labium. At first he had the impression that it was trying to suck the poison from the wound, but was surprised to see the spider pull the wounded limb out of its socket and cast it away. On picking up the discarded leg, a small globule of what seemed to be poison was seen glistening on the place where the spider had fastened. This case of voluntary amputation may have been caused by consciousness of the effect of the poison, but just as likely by the hurt of the puncture and crushing alone.

Voluntary Amputation.

Mr. Blackwall directed his attention to the effects of the poison of spiders upon their own order. The following examples will show the unvarying result of his investigations. A female Epeira diademata, in a violent struggle with a female Cœlotes saxatilus, pierced her abdomen in the medial line of the dorsal region, about one-third of its length from the spinnerets. The wounded spider did not exhibit any marked symptoms of distress, and speedily resumed its accustomed habits. Two female Diadematas were engaged in a severe contest, when one of them was seized by the fangs of her antagonist near the middle of the right side of the abdomen. A brown fluid flowed from the punctures and soon coagulated. But the spider appeared to be only slightly and very briefly affected by the injury. Another female Diademata in a highly excited state bit itself near the middle of the femur of the left anterior leg. A transparent fluid flowed copiously from the wounded part. Coagulation, however, quickly ensued, after which the spider manifested no unfavorable symptom whatever.

Spider Venom versus Spiders.

A male Tegenaria civilis, in a violent struggle with a female of the same species, deeply inserted his fangs near the middle of the dorsal region of her abdomen, and retained his hold for several seconds. From the punctures thus made a brown fluid issued copiously, and in a few minutes coagulated. The injured spider appeared to suffer very little from the severe wounds it had received, as it speedily constructed a small web in a phial in which it was confined, and continued for more than a year to feed freely on the flies introduced to it.

Tegenaria and Lycosa.

A female Ciniflo atrox was bitten by an exasperated female Lycosa agretica near the middle of the cephalothorax. The Lycosa retained its hold for many seconds, and, on quitting it voluntarily, a transparent fluid flowed from the punctures and coagulated. The wounded spider, apparently regardless of the injury it had received, spun a web with which it long continued to ensnare its victims. It thus appeared that the injuries inflicted by spiders, in a number of genera and species, seem to exercise no greater degree of influence upon other spiders than upon the human species.

Mr. Blackwall then directed his attention to the effects of spider wounds upon insects. His observations were made upon a number of genera of **Effects on Insects.** spiders in their assaults upon such insects as wasps, bees, flies, and grasshoppers. The result of these observations, which are recorded in considerable number, is that all these insects survived after the infliction of the spider's stroke for a period of time, in some cases, as high as three days.

The experiments did not present any facts which appear to sanction the opinion that insects are deprived of life much more quickly when pierced by the fangs of spiders than when lacerated mechanically to an equal extent by other means, regard being had in both cases to the vitality of the part injured—a circumstance upon which the suddenness of death largely depends. It is true that the catastrophe is greatly accelerated if spiders maintain a protracted hold of their victims. But this result is attributable to the extraction of their fluids, which are transmitted, by oft repeated acts of deglutition, into the stomach.

Mr. Cambridge does not hesitate to say that the bite of a spider is undoubtedly poisonous when inflicted upon its prey.[1] And he supposes that at least one effect of the bite in most cases is to benumb or par- **Cambridge's Opinion.** alyze the insect, which, if not at once devoured, remains in a state of insensibility, and is available as fresh food for some hours and perhaps for several days. I do not know upon what grounds this distinguished arachnologist bases this opinion, as he gives no facts bearing upon the matter, and qualifies his opinion by the word "probably." Perhaps he has reasoned from the analogy of the effect of a wasp's sting upon a spider, which is precisely that which he supposes to result to the victim of the spider's bite. But analogy is not argument, and while it may guide us to a safe conclusion, cannot be received as a sufficient demonstration in a matter of this sort.

For myself, I may say that I have never seen a single case that would justify Mr. Cambridge's conclusion. It is undoubtedly difficult to make a decisive observation, because in the case of Sedentary spiders, the habit of swathing the prey in a thick shroud of white silk prevents one from observing whether the stroke of the spider's fangs has produced any special effect. This swathing is done so rapidly, and the limbs and wings of an insect are so effectually wrapped up, that it needs no suggestion of paralyzing venom to account for the creature's utter immobility. Moreover, I have often seen insects struggling within their enswathment a little while after they had been captured.

Nor is it the unvarying custom of Sedentary spiders to strike their victims when they capture them. My observations convince me that the stroke is perhaps more frequently omitted than given, the insect being

---

[1] Spiders of Dorset, Introduction, page xxv.

at once seized by the fore feet as it struggles in the web, swung around towards the spinnerets, and wrapped up. It is only in the case of partic-

Prey Not Always Struck. ularly large and formidable insects that the stroke is administered, and that after they have been partially disarmed by enswathment. In fact, I believe that Orbweavers, at least, are quite chary about coming into such close quarters with large insects as would permit the use of fangs. It is true, as I have fully illustrated, that spiders do hang an enswathed victim to a portion of their snares that they may feed upon it at their leisure; but even when immediately fed upon, as is ordinarily the case, the same enswathment is practiced.

If we turn to the Wandering group of spiders, who stalk their prey, it is doubtless true that when one springs upon its victim it often strikes it with its fangs. But this is certainly not the universal practice, for I have often observed insects simply seized by the feet and at once carried around to the mouth and eaten without any more ceremony. This is commonly the case with the large Mygalidæ from our Southwestern States kept by me in artificial conditions. Grasshoppers fed to them, for example, are generally struck down or seized with the fore feet without any application of the fangs. Perhaps the superior vigor of the spider in this case renders such action entirely unnecessary.

On the whole view of the subject I must say that I am in doubt as to what special use the poison gland and apparatus can be to the spider in

A Reserve Weapon. ordinary cases, and am inclined to think that it is a sort of reserve weapon for special exigencies, and is sparingly used. It appears to be unnecessary for ordinary purposes of capturing food, especially with the Sedentary groups, but is apparently of greater importance to the Wandering groups, who stalk their prey afield. Yet, even in such cases, it would seem that the puncture of the fangs without any poisonous injection is sufficient to fulfill every requirement for sustaining and defending life.

Nevertheless, the fact remains that the spider is furnished with a poison gland and apparatus somewhat resembling that of venomous serpents,

Influence of Physical Condition. and I have too much confidence in the wise economy of force and material in nature, to suppose that so perfect an organ could be without some useful function in the life economy of the aranead. Reasoning from analogy of other venomous animals, serpents for example, it is probably true that much of the effect of spider venom depends upon the condition of the spider itself as to degree of irritation, etc., at the time when the stroke is given. On the other hand, the physical condition of the person bitten also largely determines the effect of the bite. That which is harmless to one individual we know is often injurious or fatal to another; and that which at one period of life may produce serious results, at another time is comparatively harmless. It is therefore probably true that there are a few of our indigenous spiders, as Latrodectus mactans and Phidippus morsitans, which at certain times may inflict an injury upon certain individuals which may be serious and even fatal. But in the great majority of cases, there is no more, and indeed is less, reason to apprehend danger from a stroke or bite of a spider than from the sting of a bee or probe of a mosquito.

In the case of the immense creatures (Mygalidæ) known as tarantulas, the matter, of course, is different. It would be strange, indeed, if such large animals, with so formidable fangs and such a considerable supply of venom in the poison glands, should not be able to inflict a serious wound. The cases which have been reported to me of injury resulting from the stroke of these large spiders I consider sufficient to establish this fact, and to warrant the general feeling that they are animals to be handled with great care. Yet even concerning them I must say that I have never experienced much difficulty in capturing them, and, as a rule, I believe they are more inclined to run away from man than to attack him. Nevertheless, I have well authenticated instances of our southwestern Mygalidæ springing upon individuals, and even upon horses, when specially irritated.

The Tarantula.

It is a common amusement (I have been informed) among the Texas cowboys to set two Tarantulas to fighting. They surround the combatants in a ring, after the fashion of frequenters of the cockpit, and freely bet their money on one or the other. I have never heard of any injury suffered by the managers of these aranead gladiatorial duels; and the reports would seem to indicate that the big fellows are of rather a sluggish temperament.

V.

It would be quite impossible, and indeed undesirable in a work of this character, to enter at length upon the strange superstitions which have grown up around belief in the fatal character of spider venom. The prejudice is a very ancient one. Diodorus Siculus records that there borders upon the country of the Acridophagi a large tract of land, rich in fair pastures, but desert and uninhabited. Aforetime the region was inhabited, but there fell an immoderate rain, which bred a vast host of spiders and scorpions. Whoever was bitten or stung by these creatures immediately fell dead. The whole nation arose and attempted to destroy these implacable enemies of their country, which so rapidly increased that they threatened to depopulate the land. In point of fact, they did this, for the inhabitants were unsuccessful in their warfare, and were forced to fly to another place.[1]

Superstitions.

The supposed effects of the Italian tarantula are well known, and

---

[1] Diodorus Siculus, Book III., chapter 2. This wonderful story may also be found recorded in Strabo's Geography, Book XVI., chapter 6, section 13.

travelers in Italy, for a small sum, may see the "tarantula dance" executed in the very best style, either with or without the original accessory of a spider's bite. The superstition is doubtless a very ancient one, probably handed down from early Roman times. A species of Lycosa, which takes its name from Tarentum, near which it was supposed especially to abound, is the spider to which tradition ascribes the peculiar effects to be described. The modern scientific name is Lycosa tarentula. When one is bitten by this spider, so the story goes, at first the pain is scarcely felt; but a few hours after come on a violent sickness, difficulty of breathing, fainting, and sometimes trembling. Then he is seized with a sort of insanity. He weeps, he dances, he trembles, laughs, cries, skips about, breaks forth into grotesque and unnatural gestures, assumes the most extravagant postures, and, if he be not duly assisted and relieved, after a few days of torment, will sometimes expire. If he survive, at the return of the season in which he was bitten, his madness returns.

Italian Tarantula Dance.

Some relief is found by divers antidotes, but the great specific is music. At the sound of music the victim begins the peculiar movements which are known as the "tarantula dance," and continues them while the music continues, or until he breaks into a profuse perspiration which forces out the venom. Thereupon he sinks into a natural sleep from which he awakes weakened, but recovered. Such in substance is the story generally told, believed, and until comparatively modern times unquestioned, which has found its way into the works of many travelers and naturalists of the earlier sort. It may be worth while to print an example of these stories. Here is what one old writer has to say :—

"Alexander Alexandrinus proceedeth farther, affirming that he beheld one wounded by this Spider, to dance and leape about incessantly, and the Musitians (finding themselves wearied) gave over playing: whereupon, the poore offended dancer, hauing vtterly lost all his forces, fell downe on the ground, as if he had bene dead. The Musitians no sooner began to playe againe, but hee returned to himselfe, and mounting vp vpon his feet, danced againe as lustily as formerly hee had done, and so continued dancing still, til hee found the harme asswaged, and himselfe entirely recovered. Heerunto he addeth, that when it hath happened, that a man hath not beene thorowly cured by Musique in this manner: within some short while after, hearing the sound of Instruments, hee hath recouered footing againe, and bene enforced to hold on dancing, and never to ceasse, till his perfect and absolute healing, which (questionlesse) is admirable in nature."[1]

An Ancient Tale.

Goldsmith, who seems to have been well informed on this point, does

---

[1] Quoted from "Treasurie of Ancient and Modern Times," page 393, in Mr. Frank Cowan's "Curious Facts in the History of Insects."

not hesitate to declare that the whole matter of the tarantula poison is an imposition of the peasants upon travelers who happen to pass through that part of the country, and who proffer then a trifle for suffering themselves to be "bitten by the tarantula." Whenever the peasants find a tourist willing to try the experiment they readily offer themselves. They are sure to counterfeit the whole train of symptoms which music is supposed to move.[1]

An Imposition.

It is not to be wondered at that notions such as these were formerly fixed in the minds of common people, when we remember that it is but a comparatively short period since learned men and physicians were under the dominion of kindred errors as to the deadly effects of spiders. Dr. James, in his Medical Dictionary, thinks it worth while to give a number of examples of this sort. He tells seriously of a woman who was possessed with a cruel passion for destroying spiders by burning them in the flame of a candle, but who was cured by a remedy quite as remarkable as the disease. One night while the persecutor was destroying a large black spider it burst with a great crack, and the animal fluids were thrown into her eyes and upon her lips. Thereupon she flung away her candle and cried for help, fancying herself killed with the poison.

Credulous Doctors.

In the night the woman's lips swelled excessively, and one of her eyes was much inflamed. Her gums and tongue were affected, and a continual vomiting attended. For several days she suffered the greatest pain, but a cure was eventually effected with a preparation of plantain leaves and cobwebs applied to the eyes, and taken inwardly two or three times a day.[2] It is a pity that people in this age of vaunted science and intelligence, and who are not far removed from the folly and cruelty of this woman, could not like her at least fall under the sway of a kindred fear, and thus be moved to spare the unfortunate creatures whom they slay.

The same medical authority records that several monks in a monastery in Florence are said to have died from the effects of drinking wine out of a vessel in which there was afterwards found a drowned spider. One perhaps might be persuaded that in those "good old days" even monks may have been found who "died from the effects of drinking wine." But modern judgment would probably decide the aforesaid story of the spider's fatal offices a case of "post quod" rather than "propter quod."

These curious examples of intellectual bondage and credulity among learned and unlearned alike might be greatly multiplied, and no doubt would be interesting. But they belong to the natural history of man rather than of the spider. Let us hope that the emancipation of our race from all errors concerning spiders may soon be complete.

---

[1] "Goldsmith's Animated Nature." Philadelphia edition. 1795. Vol. IV., page 153.
[2] A Medical Dictionary, by R. James, M. D., Lond., 1743, Vol. I., "Araneus."

CHAPTER XVII.

NESTING HABITS AND PROTECTIVE ARCHITECTURE OF ORBWEAVERS.

THE spinningwork of spiders may be classified generally as, first, the Snare, spun for the capture of prey; second, the Enswathment, by which insects are disarmed and prepared for food; third, the Gossamer, used for purposes of aqueous or aerial locomotion; fourth, the **Forms of Spinning-work.** Cocoon, spun for the propagation and protection of the species; and, fifth, the Nest, which is a domicile more or less elaborate and permanent within and under which the aranead dwells for protection against the exigencies of weather and the assaults of enemies. It is not

Fig. 254. Nest of Insular spider in clustered leaves of blackberry.

implied by this classification that a difference in quality marks the material used in spinning the above forms, although to some extent this is true. In point of fact the silk used in all modes of work is substantially the same, and the difference in results is chiefly one of quantity, condition, color, and manner of application. The present chapter will describe that form of industry which secures for the orbweaving species a domicile or temporary retreat, which is popularly known as a den, tent, or nest. This domicile is usually wrought of clear spinningwork, or some adaptation of foliage.

One who studies these nests of rolled leaves and silken tubes must often have suggested to him the habits and spinningwork of many larvæ **Analogy.** of true insects, particularly the Lepidoptera. It would almost seem that one were marking a survival of manners which might justly characterize the immature period of a race, while the race itself has swept on to maturity. Thus, it is not in the function of spinning alone that spiders raise a suggestion of the larvæ of insects.

(284)

I.

Among the Orbweavers the leaf rolling habit is perhaps most decided in the Insular spider. She invariably domiciles upon shrubs, bushes, and bushy trees, and commonly chooses a site within five to eight feet

FIG. 255. Folded leaf nest of Epeira insularis.

Spectacle Spider's Nest. of the ground. above and gener and is a series of tied as at Fig. 254, or a sin as at Fig. 255. The form may perhaps be character The leaves have been pulled fastened together by cross ternal surfaces at the mar which the spider dwells is less thickly with silken at the summit of the dome, the abdomen rests, appar ray of threads adhering to

The cluster-leaf nest of Fig. 256. This was made tall grass, whose **Cluster Leaf Nest** were so woven to shaped or "Lib figured. The lower and quite delicately spun of in place the graceful foli the crown of this dainty sconced, holding by the line which joined the snare

Another nest (Fig. 255) rolled-leaf nest. It is a **Rolled Leaf Nest** fastened at the the example giv between four and and wider end opened two-thirds of the distance tain (Fig. 257) stretching

Her tent is located always ally to one side of her snare, leaves drawn together and gle leaf rolled up and tied of nest shown at Fig. 254 ized as the cluster-leaf nest. down at the free ends and threads drawn over the ex- gins. The concavity within frequently lined more or sheeting, which is heaviest against which the apex of ently secured thereto by a the spinnerets.

sometimes takes the form in a clump of weeds and stalks, leaves, and blossoms gether as to form the helmet erty Cap" domicile here open part of the tent was lines that united and held age of the grasses. Within nest the spider was en- fore feet to the taut trap- at the hub.

may be characterized as the large leaf folded over and edges by overlaid lines. In en (Fig. 255) the leaf was five inches long; the lower toward the snare. About within the tent was a cur- from the floor to the roof

along one side of the den. The curtain was three-fourths of one inch high, and one inch wide. Against this curtain the spider had pushed the apical part of the abdomen. She was preying, when found, upon a hornet (Vespa maculata), a very good proof of her vigor.

It sometimes happens that the single leaf within which the spider is nested will be stayed by lashings which unite it to an adjoining leaf,

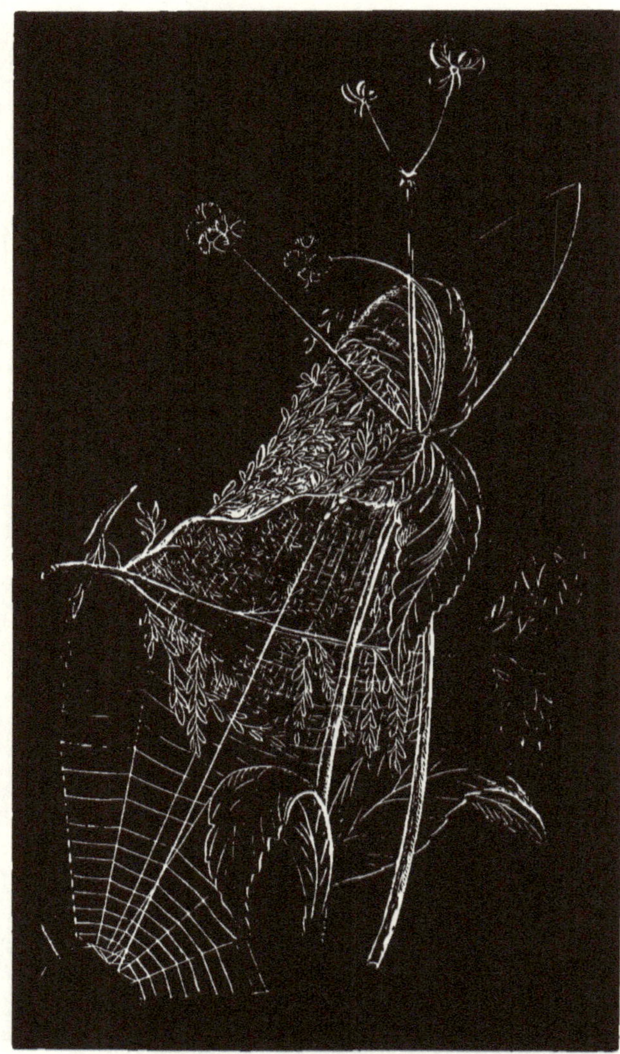

Fig. 236. Nest of the Insular spider, woven with grasses and leaves. The spider's
foot is shown outthrust from the nest and grasping the trapline.

as in Fig. 258. Indeed, constant regard is had in the nest architecture
to the stability of the leafy domicile. Stay lines of various
Stability of Nest. lengths and thickness are thrown out to adjoining objects until
the nest hangs firmly poised, and is thus thoroughly inter-
woven with the spinningwork system of the occupant.

A third form of nest may be designated the woven leaf nest. It is
shown at Fig. 259, where it is seen to be a close textured silken bell,
woven between the needle like leaves of a pine tree. The mouth
Woven Leaf Nest opens downward and toward the snare. This silken tent does
not appear to be woven as closely as that often spun by the
Furrow Spider, but affords good protection to the inmate, and shows her
ability to deftly adapt her spinningwork to her environment.

These three forms of nest, tent, or den will be found to indicate, with
more or less accuracy, the spinningwork of Orbweavers, and, to some extent, of all the Sedentary spiders, as applied to arboreal nest architecture.
The terms cluster-leaf nest, rolled-leaf nest, and woven-leaf nest may therefore be used in the above sense, although without attempting to establish
anything like a rigid classification.

To these may be added a fourth type, the woven nest, which is well
illustrated by the close textured tubular den spun by Epeira strix and
Epeira sclopetaria against exposed parts of human habitations.
Woven Nest. This form of nest is sometimes cylindrical, as with the nests
woven by Strix and Sclopetaria. This is composed of a close
textured sheet of spinningwork rolled as in Fig. 260, and stayed by guy
lines attached to various parts of the surrounding surfaces. Often the
nest is quite egg shaped. The spider inhabits this tube, having her face
toward the opening, and holding as usual to her trapline. Sometimes the
nest is simply a square patch of thick white silk stretched across an angle
or corner, open in the direction of the snare, and either open or closed at
the other end. Many nests of this sort have been seen on the verandah
of a gentleman's cottage at Niantic, Connecticut, spun by Epeira patagiata
and E. sclopetaria. During the day the spiders keep closely to cover, and,
as the afternoon declines, creep out and weave their snares. They have a
weird look as they swing to and fro against the darkening sky.

Again, the woven nest is bell shaped, and open as with the tent of
Epeira domiciliorum (Fig. 261) when she chooses a similar site. The lower
part of this nest is spun of open linework, and is supported
Domicile Spider. by silken guys hung upon thick foundation lines or directly
attached to the surrounding surfaces. The upper part is closely
woven, and thus affords protection to the spider who rests within, and
particularly to the soft abdomen, which is the most vulnerable and least
defensible portion of the body, and which, as it occupies the topmost part
of the tent, is, of course, most protected from assaults of raiding Hymenoptera.

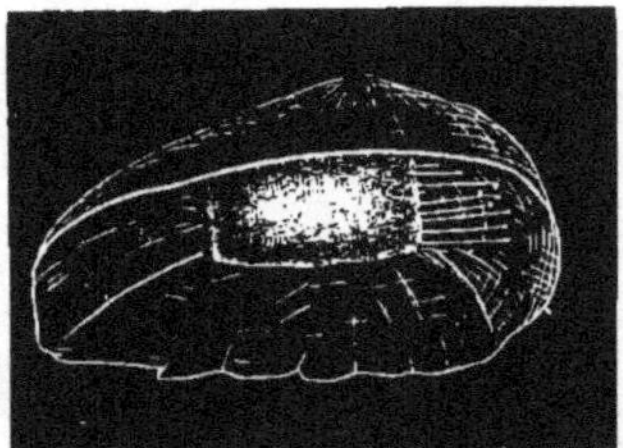

Fig. 257.

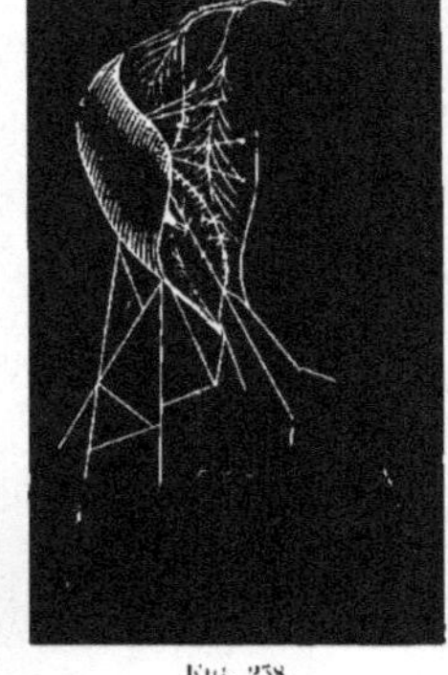

Fig. 258.

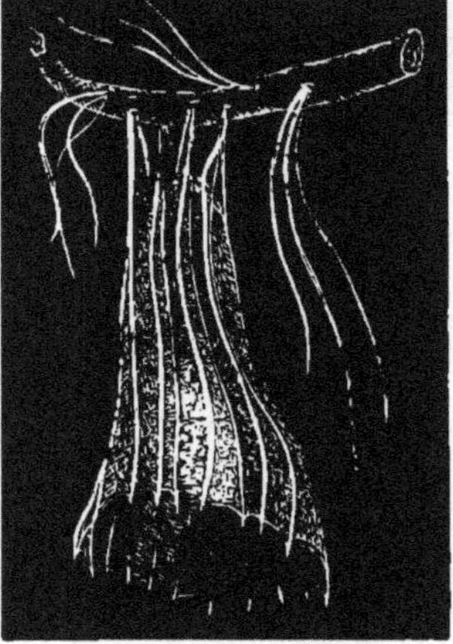

Fig. 259.

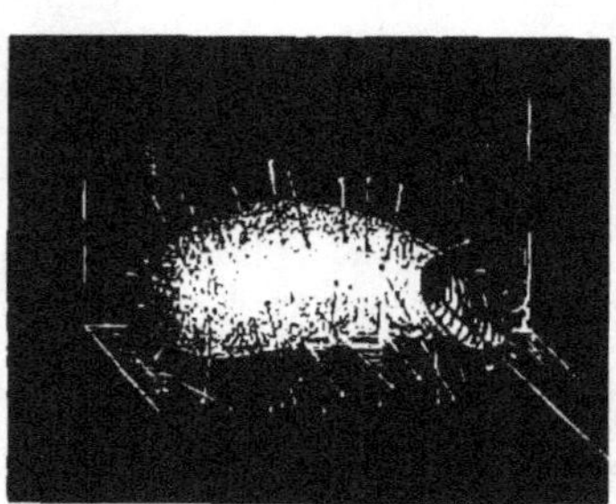

Fig. 260.

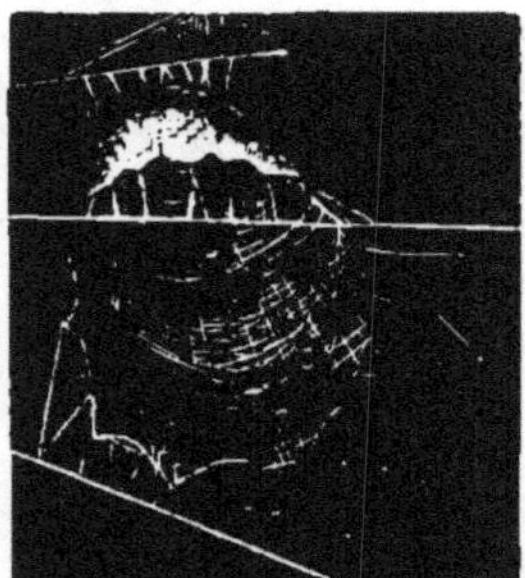

Fig. 261.

Fig. 257. The curtain or silken lining of the upper part of nest.   Fig. 258. Nest lashed to an adjoining leaf. (Epeira insularis.)   Fig. 259. Woven leaf nest of Insularis.   Fig. 260. Tubular nest of Epeira strix.   Fig. 261. Bell shaped nest of Epeira domiciliorum.

II.

As a rule, the various groups of Orbweavers differ from each other and agree within themselves in characteristic nest forms. The form prevailing in each family is substantially the same; each species seems to **Architec-** adhere quite steadily to one characteristic form; but there are **tural Va-** some marked variations in the habit of certain species, as in **riations.** the Insular spider, whose nest architecture we have seen is not constant in form among the individuals of that species. Indeed, the variation extends without a doubt to the habits of the same individual under different circumstances. This opens a most interesting feature in the story of spider industry, which may as well be kept in mind as we proceed with the description of these nesting habits. It will be obvious that some of the variations are adaptations

Fig. 262. Nest of Strix within a rolled leaf.

to changed environment. Some of the most decided of these variations have been observed in the nest architecture of Epeira strix. I observed two of this species domiciled in the beautiful hedgerows of a New England meadow, within nests of several rolled leaves, which had an inside lining quite like that which is made by Insularis. Both nests were below the orb, one ten inches below. The second example had for her nest a very bright red rolled leaf with a tube inside of it, which made a strikingly pretty object.

The ordinary nest of Strix when domiciled in the open field or wood is a rolled leaf. A single leaf is taken, the edge pulled up, drawn under, and fastened by adhesive threads into a rude cylinder, within **Varia-** which the spider hides during the daytime. (Fig. 262.) A **tions and** thread connection with the foundation lines of the snare is **Adapta-** sometimes maintained; but rarely with the centre of the orb by **tions.** a taut trapline, as is the habit of the Insular spider. For this reason I have often been greatly puzzled, and not infrequently foiled, in searching for Strix in the neighborhood of her orb, which one comes at

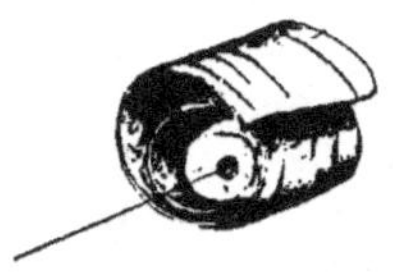

Fig. 263. Nest of Strix within curled birch bark.

last to recognize on sight with tolerable accuracy. This severing or concealing of her trail threads is undoubtedly a protection against raiding naturalists; but I cannot imagine any security which it gives against natural enemies. This cylindrical nest will often be spun within any convenient cavity, as, for example, a bit of curled birch bark, Fig. 263, a specimen found on an island in St. Lawrence River.

A second form of the nest of Strix varies from the rolled leaf nest in having the edges of the two adjacent leaves bent towards each other and lashed together on the exterior at the juncture by silken cords, and on the interior by adhesive tissue web. An oval opening is left at the united points of the leaves, through which the connecting line passes to the snare. The spider domiciles within the leafy cavern thus formed.

Again, the spider avails herself of small holes in wood or stone, openings in fences, the interspaces between curled bark on the trunk of old trees, or some like cavity, which she appropriates as a nesting place. A slight lining will generally be found upon the concave surface. I have noticed that in such cases the snare is sometimes diverted from its normal shape in order to give a convenient approach thereto from the den. One such example was found spun between a side of the Peace Fountain in Fairmount Park (Philadelphia) and a stone wall adjoining. In order to pitch her tent within a hole in the rock, the spider diverted one of the radii from the plane of the orb and extended it backward to the hole. The spirals which passed over this radius thus made an elbow, which was nearly a right angle, and gave the orb an odd, broken appearance. The radius, of course, served as a bridge line by which Strix passed from her den to her snare.

Another variation, or rather series of variations, was noted upon the side of Brush Mountain at Bellwood, Pennsylvania. Several young pine trees had been cut away and tossed from the mountain to a bank of the Juniata River below. The foliage had withered and fallen from the boughs, whose branches stretched out dry and bare, and among them a colony of young Furrow spiders had pitched their tents and spread their snares. One specimen happened to spin her web near the axil of several goodly sized branches, which were formed into a natural shelter by the inverted position of the bough. The spider had recognized this vantage, and made her nest at the point of juncture, or rather took shelter there, for there was little artificial nesting beyond a faint tissue spread over the bark at the point where she sat.

Shelter Tent.

A second specimen had lodged at a point near the tip of a small branch, whose delicate, dry twigs gave no sufficient shelter, and, besides, were directed upward. Accordingly, a silken tube, funnel shaped, was spun between the twigs, within which young Strix nested. (Fig. 264.)

A third spider, lodged in a similar site, had made a silken sack for a tent, whose mouth had apparently originally opened directly toward the snare. But a Saltigrade spider had fastened a parasitic tubular nest upon one side of this sack, and accordingly the mouth was found closed and the door shifted to the opposite side, as though to avoid interference with a troublesome neighbor. A fourth individual had woven a silken cover or screen, behind which she lodged. A fifth had pitched her tent upon a stray leaf, beneath which a similar cover, a small rectangular piece of silk canvas (suggestive of the military bivouac or "dog tent"), was stretched by lines attached to the sides and corners, and fastened to the leaf surfaces and surroundings. Between this sheet and leaf the spider was ensconced, having the usual bridge line connection with the orb. (Fig. 265.)

Two of the above colony had established nests in tufts of a parasitic moss fastened upon dead limbs. One of these was very pretty and ingenious. The moss grew in a bunch about the size of a hickory

Tent in the Moss. nut; this was pierced at the top, and the filaments pushed aside sufficiently to allow an interior cavity large enough to house a spider. An oval door or opening was formed near the top by bending and binding back the fibres of the plant. A secure and tasteful retreat was thus obtained at the only really available spot in the vicinity of the snare. (Fig. 266.)

Fig. 264. Funnel shaped nest of Epeira strix.

When the Furrow spider weaves her orb upon the exposed surfaces of human habitations, as the cornices of porches, outhouses, etc., her nest takes a form quite different from any above described. A tube of stiff, silken fibre is spun against

Tubular Nest. the surface, to which it is lashed at all sides. This cylinder is about an inch long and half an inch thick, and at the end toward the orb has a circular opening about a quarter of an inch in diameter. (See Fig. 260.) The stiff texture of this nest appears to be necessary to make the walls self supporting, inasmuch as there are

Fig. 265. Shelter tent of Epeira strix.

no supports like the twigs and leaves found at hand in arboreal sites. Moreover, the open position of the domicile exposes the spider very freely to the assaults of the mud daubers who frequent such localities, to birds, and other enemies, so that a canvas is needed of tougher texture than that required in sheltered sites.

Nevertheless, it may be remarked that Strix will often spin a quite close tube even within a rolled leaf of two or three thicknesses.

In this summary of the nest architecture of the Furrow spider it is manifest that while there is a general regard to protection of the spider's person, there

Intelligent Adaptation. is a modification over quite a wide degree of variation in the form of the protective nest. Further, that this modification appears to be regulated, more or less, by the accidental environment of the domicile, and in such wise as to show no small

Fig. 266. Tent in the moss. E. strix.

degree of intelligence in adapting the ordinary spinning habit to various circumstances, and to economizing labor and material.

III.

One of the most interesting sights in the way of spinning industry which it has been my privilege to see was observed upon a rocky hillside in the neighborhood of Niantic Bay, Connecticut. The field had formerly been a wooded slope, but all the timber had been cut away, and in its stead an undergrowth of sumac, huckleberry, and laurel well nigh covered the surface. The characteristic stone fences of New England marked the margins of the slope, along which clumps of ferns, golden rod, raspberry vines, and various other wild plants were thickly aligned. Standing upon the crest of the hill, one could see in the distance the shimmering waters of the bay melting into the ocean beyond, covered with the white sails of passing ships. The permanent abodes and summer habitations of human beings were scattered along the crescent lines of the beach. The river wound in sinuous course at the foot of the hill, and emptied into the bay a mile or two beyond.

A Fair Spider Encampment.

The scene was a beautiful setting for a picture that warmed the heart of an arachnologist. For all over these bushes that covered the rocky slope was encamped an innumerable host of spiders of various species. It has never been my privilege to see so many and such fine examples of the order established within so limited a space. The largest and most beautiful of our indigenous fauna were there represented in vast numbers. Argiope cophinaria hung in the centre of her white shield, which with its zigzag cords above and below glistened in the sunlight and marked distinctly the habitation of its proprietor. The black and yellow of the immensely distended abdomen (for the time of ovipositing was near) and the mingled black and brown of the outstretched legs showed in striking contrast against the pure white silken shield.

Here and there one noted the orbs of our other species of Argiope (A. argyraspis), whose web scarcely differs from her congener, but whose abdomen of glittering silver, crossed with lines of black and yellow, at once mark her as peculiar and exceeding in beauty among the tribes of Arachne. Here a delicate snare of the Hunchback spider, Epeira gibberosa, hung among the laurels, the bright green of the aranead herself, as she swung beneath the hub of her snare, scarcely distinguished against the background of the leaves over which it was extended.

If one reached out a hand to this side or that, he could touch the beautiful orbs of two of our most persistent nest building species; but the spiders themselves were not in sight, and their great round snares seemed deserted. They hung to thick threads of yellow silk, constituting the upper foundation line, thicker than an ordinary pack thread, of a glossy yellow color, and stretched sometimes three feet, four feet, six feet, eight feet from point to point in the midst of the open spaces between bush and bush. Where are the occupants of these empty webs? What destroyer has been abroad that so many of them should stand deserted at this evening hour?

Tent Makers' Orbs.

Lay your hand upon this trapline, fastened to the centre of the orb,

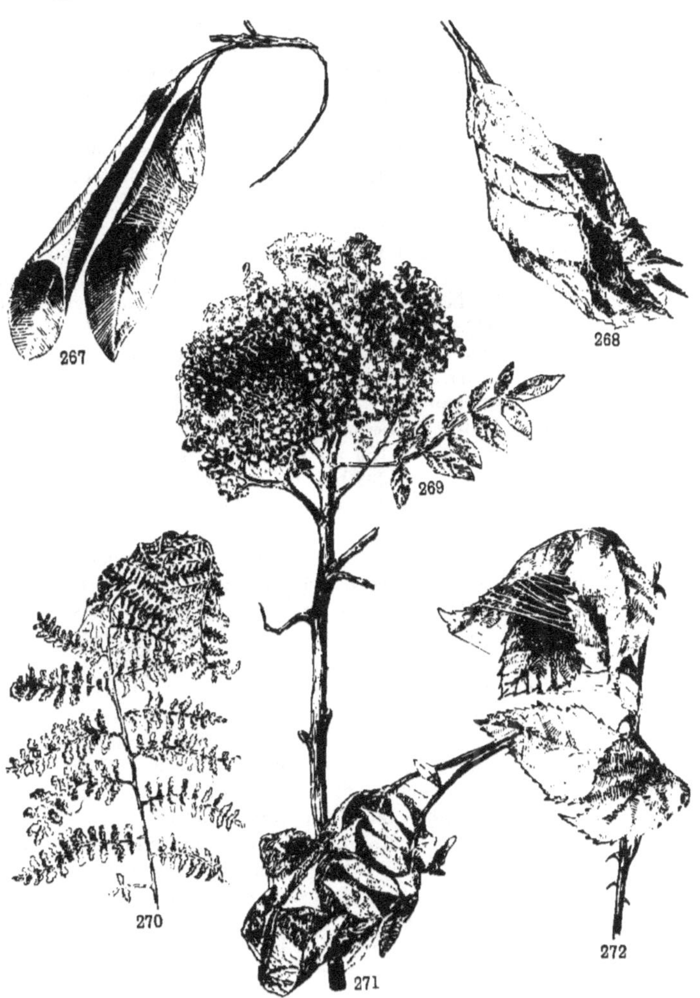

Various Nests of the Shamrock Spider.

holding every radius taut, though slightly bagging at the hub. Carry the finger outward to this clump of bushes. What is this? A nest! The leaves have been spun together deftly until they make a beautiful cap shaped or helmet shaped habitation, within which, if you will take the pains to stoop a little, you may see the goodly proportions and the fair colors of the Insular or the Shamrock spider. These nests are built on every side, and vary in their forms according to the character of the plant of whose leaves they have been constructed.

The closing days of August have already begun to tint some of the bushes. These sumacs have assumed their party colors of red and crimson and brown, so that our aranead dwells within a habitation of divers hues like the tabernacle in which ancient Israel worshiped. Of course, the spider had no part in the selection of these varied colors for her tent, and has no share in the enjoyment of the discoverer who notes the pretty effect it has on her domicile. Nevertheless, it adds to the pleasure of the scene, and helps to impress the observer with a sense of the fitness of all the surroundings not only, but of these industrious creatures in the midst of their surroundings.

Tinted Nests.

I had never thought it possible that by any combination of favoring circumstances so many of these handsome spiders could have been preserved in so limited a space. But here everything appears to have united to protect them from their natural enemies. These bushes are just the sites in which spiders love to spin. This slope, with its sunny outlook towards the east and south, has protected from winter chill the eggs within cocoons, and warmed them into life when springtime came. With them have come also swarms of the insects which form their natural food. The place, too, is a lonely one as far as man is concerned; for, besides the farmer's occasional visits, only now and then a straggler, or a lover of fields like myself, happens along. A cow or two may sometimes feed here and pick up the bits of pasture that grow between clumps of bushes and outcropping boulders of granite. Here, too, come, in the summer season, the women and children to gather huckleberries. But the very vision of the many spider webs, and particularly of the great Argiope swinging at the centre of her hub, is enough to cause them to shy away and leave unplucked the tempting clusters of berries that hang around the dreaded snare.

A Spider Paradise.

Other than these, few visitors come to the spot; and thus, largely delivered from destructive enemies, warmed and cheered into life by the favoring slope, with abundant provision for spinning sites that give good and easy access to the low flying insects which supply Arachne's larder, these creatures live and feed and grow and prosecute their loves, their wars, their maternal duties and cares, and die amidst the glowing foliage of autumn, having fulfilled as happy a destiny as one could reasonably hope for a child of the spider world.

In the neighborhood of Philadelphia the Shamrock spider is somewhat
rare, but here her huge orbicular snare is hung on every bush.
Sham-rock Spiders. Without passing the limits of a single field I could collect hundreds of specimens of females, whose large, rounded abdomens
show that they are approaching the crisis period of motherhood.

During the entire day, with rare exception, these araneads keep themselves closely to their nests, leaving them only in the late evening hours
to station themselves at the centre of their orbs for the more convenient
trapping of prey. The nests are in most respects well suited as a domicile for the occupants. They vary in style and proportion according to
the character of the plants upon which they are spun. Often they consist
of a single leaf, in which case the edges of the leaf will be brought together
and fastened close to the stem. The lobes of the leaf also, as far as practicable, will be joined in the same manner, but with a wider interval between the tips, the interspace being spanned by threads or by a thin tissue
of spinningwork.

The laurel is a strong, tough leaf, yet even that will be rolled and sewed
together by this spider's art. (Fig. 267.) Sometimes, as though to save the
Nests in Laurel. effort required for the bending of such stiff material, several
laurel leaves will be adjusted in a manner somewhat peculiar.
One leaf will be selected as the roof, and without being curled
will be fastened across the edges of two other leaves, which have been so
disposed that they stand with their flat surfaces almost upright. Thus
both roof and sides are flat, as though they had been built of inelastic
boards, and within this cubical refuge the spider fixes her home. On the
sumac plant, whose leaves are lanceolate and very pliable, a number of
leaves are chosen, and these are overlapped and the tips bent downward
until they form a wigwam, within which the spider dwells. (Fig. 268.)
Its blossoms also (Fig. 269) are pressed and spun into nests.

Here, again, in this natural fernery, which straggles along the borders
of the stone fence, one has a good opportunity to select nests that are
Fern Nests. strikingly beautiful in form. The delicate tips of the ferns,
sometimes one spray, sometimes more, are drawn together, overlaid and interlashed, until a domicile is constructed that might
attract even the Queen of the Fairies to fix her palace therein. (Figs.
270, 271.) Hard by, a neighbor Trifolium is ensconced beneath a bower
of rich brown blackberry leaves. (Fig. 272.) Thus, it will be observed that
the spiders have wrought upon their material as practical architects, adapting methods and accommodating plans to the quality of their material.

The nest of the Insular spider differs very little from her congener
Among these bushes scattered over the rocky slope she pitches her tent
and makes her home side by side with the Shamrock spider. Perhaps, if
I were asked to name a distinction, I would say that Insularis is rather
more fond of an open wooded location than Trifolium, and is somewhat

more inclined to select a loftier site for her habitation. For example, let us climb these bars into the adjoining woodland and walk along the

Nest of Insular Spider. wagon trail, which is absolutely embowered by the young overhanging trees. We find on all sides large, round webs, swung to long foundation lines that stretch from the lower branches of the trees to the ground, or to the low undergrowth. Long traplines extend upward to a leafy cell, within which one can see the orange and yellow colors of Insularis, as she crouches, with legs drawn up around her face, against the upholstered end of her chamber. The great leaf of the young hickory, or the long, palm shaped leaf of the oak, are often chosen by this spider, and they make a roomy dwelling place.

On a closing day of August one sees hanging near by the nest of the female Insularis another curled leaf, not quite so artistic and complete, perhaps, but showing the outward signs of a spider habitation. Turning

Courting. back the tip he sees a male Insularis who has come a-courting, and he has pitched his tent as near that of his lady love as circumstances seem to allow. He is not the only lover on the premises, however, for on the opposite side of my lady's bower is another courtier; and just below, swinging to some straggling ratlins stretched against the stem, a third attendant is found. These are the days of mating, with all their joys and sorrows, their successes, and their perils. Yes, perils I must say, for twice to-day, at least, I have seen the unfortunate gallant rolled up within silken swathing, dangling at the jaws of his lady love, who thus proved how greatly she liked him, after the shocking fashion of the cannibal islanders.

Let us pluck one of these Trifolium nests, that we may examine its interior. This requires a little care, for the tips and other parts of the leaves are so stayed by numerous lines, radiating to this side and to that, flaring downward, and attached to the upper foundation cable of the snare as well as to adjoining foliage, that, if one is not careful to clip the threads all around the leaf, it will be torn as he draws it away from the stem. The nest, of course, is always open downward, never upward, always facing the centre of the orb, so that the trapline can pass directly out of the nest to the hub. No obstruction, therefore, is permitted at the door of the tent, or, if one so please to phrase it, at the mouth of the den. But the opposite end is always closed, usually by a thick curtain of silk which entirely shields the abdomen, and makes a comfortable resting place for that part of the body. All around the sides of this end of the chamber one sees, especially if the nest has been occupied several days, little white patches of thickened silk, which show where the spinnerets of the spider have attached the dragline which it is the invariable habit of the species to use as an anchorage whenever it moves. These little white spots, scattered all around the inner surface of the cell, and showing within the lighter silken lining of the leaf, have a very pretty effect, and one might think at the first glance that they had been thus distributed with æsthetic intent. They are, however, simply the result of accident, caused by the restless movements of the spider around and around her room, and by the habit just alluded to. Out of the front door stretches the trapline, to which the fore claws of the spider are clasped; and towards the back part of the room, fastened to the spinnerets and probably clasped occasionally by the hind feet, there is another line which anchors the spider to her nest. Thus, both fore and aft, this truly domestic creature has strong attachments to her home.

In order to test the ability of Insularis to adapt her nesting habits to change of plant environment, I selected several that had made nests in

Adaptations of Nesting Habit. several leaves of oak and in clustered leaves of sumac. These I transferred to some coniferous trees (spruce) standing upon a lawn. The spiders proved themselves competent to meet the emergency. Their first movement was to station themselves beneath the branches of the pine, and in the course of time they chose themselves a site at the points where several twigs united. It was impossible, of course, to treat the situation after the fashion to which they were bred among the clumps of huckleberry and sumac bushes, or in the grove of young oaks. The needle like leaves of the pine would permit of no such treatment, but it was not long before the upholstering art of the spider had overcome the difficulty, lashed the prickly leaves into some respectable semblance of smoothness, and covered them all over with silken tapestry.

FIG. 273. Adapted Nest of Insular Spider.

Finally, a hemispherical nest was placed within the joints, partly protected on three sides by the twigs, and at the exposed points spun of such close tissues that it formed ample protection. In this particular the pliability of the spider's architectural instinct was fully demonstrated.

I have repeated the experiment many times, and always found that these two nest making species when transferred from one plant to another, no matter how different the foliage may be, as in the above cases, are able completely to adapt themselves to the new circumstances and spin a habitable home. (Fig. 273.)

In the Domicile spider the habit of leaf tenting is not quite so firmly fixed as in the above species. She often builds a leaf nest which does

Domicile Spider. not differ from those of her congeners already described, but I have frequently found her without any such domicile. In Woodland Cemetery (Philadelphia) are great numbers of this species, who find a favorite web site in the interspaces of a barbed iron fence. Very many dried leaves are seen in late summer, pierced by and clinging to the barbs, and within these the spiders establish a congenial but not very artistic domicile. (Fig. 274.) Others have a rude nest of rubbish at one side, under the sheltered parts of the fence. From these dens several trap-lines, in an irregular series, frequently stretch to the orb centre. Like Insularis she also spins a bell shaped tent when a suitable arboreal shelter is not convenient to her site. Indeed, her habit in this respect appears to form (if one might so say) a connecting link between the confirmed leaf nesting behavior of Insularis, whom I have never seen without a leaf nest, and the habit of those species that persistently occupy snares and have no tented retreat.

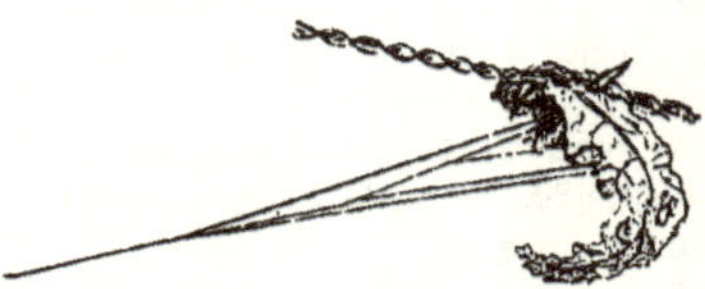

Fig. 274. Nest of Domicile spider in dried leaf.

I have always found Epeira trivittata upon a vertical web, with a meshed hub and the usual characteristics of Epeira strix and that group of Orbweavers. I do not remember to have seen her dwelling in a nest of a very perfect character, **Epeira trivittata.** but she makes a simple shelter at the side of her orb, in which she spends part of her time. One female (Massachusetts) was seen hanging in a sprig of golden rod at one side of her snare, having several lines extending therefrom to the web. (Fig. 275.) Another was resting, with her back upward, in a little nest in the leaves of an adjoining golden rod plant. A series of slight irregular lines connected the hub with the stem of the bush on which the orb was spun. Trivittata[1] is closely related to Domiciliorum in general structure and habit. This spider is distributed throughout the larger part of the United States, its locality having been determined from New England to Wisconsin, and from Florida to Texas and California.

A quite persistent nest maker is Epeira vertebrata,[2] a spider which is naturally grouped with the last named. I have received numerous specimens from

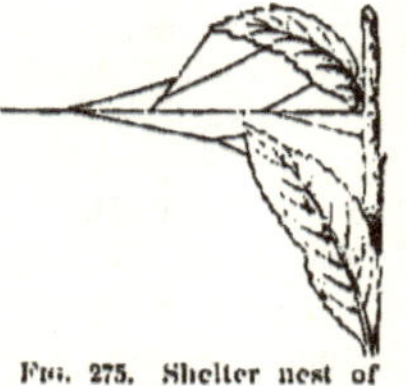

Fig. 275. Shelter nest of Epeira trivittata.

Epeira vertebrata. the Pacific coast, and from cocoons sent me by Mrs. Rosa Smith Eigenmann (San Diego) have raised a number of specimens upon vines in my manse yard. These all made nests of rolled leaves, but they are evidently not as persistent and artistic nest builders as Trifolium and Insularis. Early in the afternoon they would make snares, and usually wait at the hub for prey, instead of watching from their den.

---

[1] E. arabesca, Walck., Nat. Hist. Aptères, Vol. II., page 74. E. trivittata, Keyserling Sitzungsberichte der Isis, 1863.

[2] McCook, "Descriptive Notes of New American Species of Orbweaving Spiders." Proceed. Acad. Nat. Sci., Philadelphia, 1868, page 196.

The nesting habits of all the Angulata group of Epeira known to me are like those of the Insular and Shamrock spiders. I have always found Epeira bicentennaria and E. sylvatica within rolled leaf nests precisely resembling those heretofore described and figured. This group is distributed over the entire continent, and may be distinguished by two conical processes, more or less prominent, one on each side of the anterior part of the abdomen. The Diadem spider, the well known Epeira diademata of Europe, heads the group, and may have been an importation in the vast trains of human emigrants who have sought our shores. The far western Epeira gemma, and Epeira cinerea well scattered over the Northeast, belong to the same group. All have probably the same nesting habits, and are closely related structurally.

The Angulata Group.

The brief descriptions of the nests of Epeira diademata, quadrata, apoclisa, and other European and exotic species made by Blackwall, Menge, and Walckenaer, for example, permit us to assert their identity in nesting habit with American species. It will probably be found that this characteristic is cosmopolitan, and that all nest making species of Orbweavers throughout the world have substantially the same architectural methods within affiliated groups, and that their tents, dens, domiciles, or nests closely resemble each other, the variations depending largely upon the nesting site and the material available for manipulation and underspinning.

Unity of Habit.

IV.

It is difficult to observe all the steps in the construction of a leaf nest, inasmuch as the process is not continuous from beginning to completion, but is gradual and accumulative. There is certainly a difference in this respect; some species, like Insularis, having a stronger disposition to provide a well protected nest from the outstart of any settlement in a new site. But many spiders content themselves with a comparatively rude shelter at first, and, as occasion or disposition may prompt, proceed to add to their domicile.

How Nests are Built.

At one time the leaf or leaves will be drawn closer together; at another, the roof will be overspun with fresh silk; again, the supporting lines will be strengthened, and the silken approaches extended, or the outlying warp receive additional woof, so closing up the walls of the tent. Thus the nest is likely to be perfect in proportion to the time that the occupant has been upon the premises. In the intervals of trapping, eating, and snare spinning, the aranead architect occupies herself in adding to her house and perfecting its appointments.

The Process Gradual.

Nevertheless, one may have opportunities for seeing the spider's architectural methods, and by piecing together various observations can know the entire process. I have been favored with several views of the various stages of the work, and therefore proceed to record my observations. A typical example of methods was given by a female Domicile spider.

First Stages. The first foundation line of her orb was already stretched when I began the observation. She passed over this once or twice, and then, without waiting to spin an orbweb, near one of the extremities began preparing a nesting place from two leaves of the honeysuckle vine upon which she was located. When the work commenced the leaves presented the appearance of Fig. 276. The first steps consisted in stringing a number of lines (L L) between the inner surfaces of the two leaves, at the upper part thereof. This work was done rather slowly, the spider striding across from one leaf to the other until a little maze of lines was thus formed between the inner surfaces. Any pressure

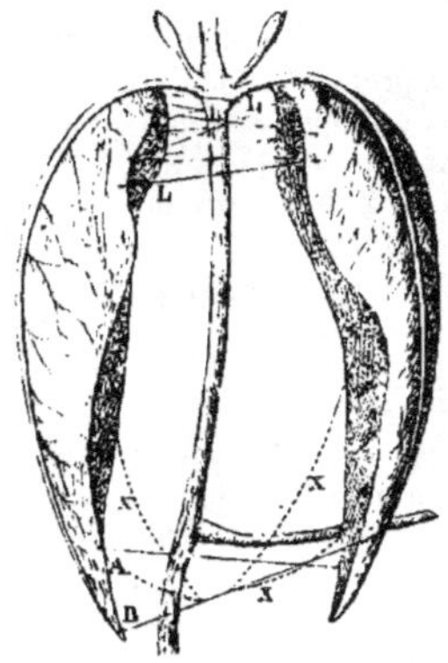

Fig. 276. Process of nest making; first stages. L L, lines joining edges of leaves; X X, position of tips after lines A, B, etc., are drawn taut.

upon these lines, in the way of tightening or shortening them, tended to approximate the tops of the leaves. The next step consisted in attaching a line (A, B) to the edge of one of the leaves near the tip. Striding across to the other leaf, dragging out the line after her, the spider threw the legs on one side of her body around the outer surface of the leaf, then attached the line and began slowly to shorten it.

Joining Edges. This movement, of course, drew the tips of the two leaves towards each other. The edges of the leaves on the opposite sides were treated in the same manner. Thus, by fixing a line to one leaf and pulling the opposite leaf towards this point, and then attaching thereto the other extremity of the line, the leaves were approximated, as indicated by the dotted lines X X, and the preparatory stages of a nest accomplished. When the nest was completed it presented the appearance of Fig. 277.

The spider stayed in this nest for several days without making any marked additions to it, which was due, perhaps, to the fact that heavy rains were falling most of the time. After this work of nest construction was over, she dropped from the projecting stem of the leaves by a dragline, threw out a swinging basket, and issued a thread from her spinnerets, apparently with a view to seeking a foundation. This thread attached itself to the vine at an opposite point about a foot distant, but for some reason was in a little while loosened and floated away before the spider crossed over and strengthened it. At this point I was compelled to cease observation.

A half grown Insular spider colonized upon an arbor afforded another opportunity to note the first stages in nest building. After she had been placed upon the vines, she spent a considerable length of time in wandering back and forward over the leaves, climbing upward all the while,

Beginning a Nest. never downward, which may be said to be a common habit of spiders under such circumstances. Finally, she reached a spot well to the top of the vine covered arbor, which seemed to suit her. Several leaves, closely clustered together, drooped over in such a way as to form a natural shelter, and underneath these the spider began arranging her tent. She passed backward and forward under the surfaces of the several leaves in the cluster, stretching lines from one to the other in the manner already described. Her motions seemed to be really aimless. She appeared to be guided by no special principle in extending any single thread, and it was difficult to observe what bearing her work might have upon the end manifestly in view. After a long time spent in this kind of spinning, a confused mass of lines was left upon the upper part of the inner surfaces of the clustered leaves.

In the meantime, however, the process had evidently drawn the leaves somewhat together, at least had compacted them into a closer cluster, holding one against the other so tightly that they were not separated by the currents of wind. The spider then placed the end of her body, the abdomen, against this maze of threads. The details of her behavior thereafter were not accurately marked, but the substance of her method appeared to be as follows: she pushed against the lines with her abdomen, moving the spinnerets back and forward at the same time, until a slight concavity was formed, and the mass began to assume the shape of an inverted bowl.

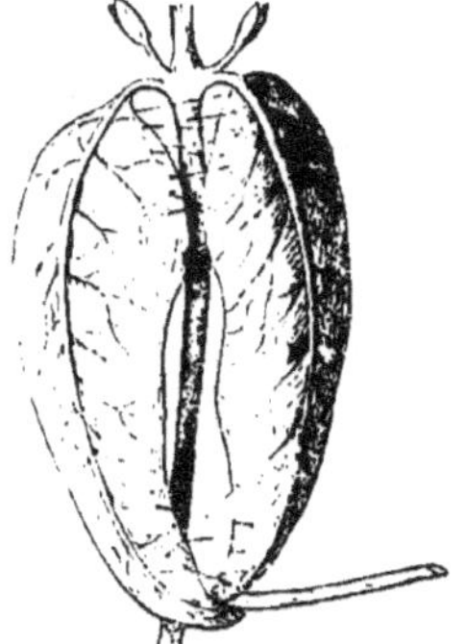

Fig. 277. Last stages of nest making.

The same movements that produced this effect, by pulling upon and tightening the weft, drew the leaves still more closely together, and forced them into the shape of the clustered leaf nest represented at Fig. 254.

From this shelter the spider departed, and proceeded to spin her orbicular snare, carrying her trapline into her den, from which she awaited,

Upholstery. as usual, the trapping of her prey. In the course of time, had the spider not been disturbed, the mass of crossed lines would have been reduced to a texture of close white silk, and the whole would have been moulded into a dome like tent as a lining to the inner surface of the leaves. Further on, the margins of this lining would have been stretched out towards the tips of the leaves, the edges of the leaves would have been agglutinated or sewed in the manner above described, and thus the nest would have been completed.

An interesting illustration of the method of sewing was given by a large Epeira insularis, whose nest I had opened by breaking the threads near the lower margin. The inmate reached her claws over the upper edge of the leaf, pulled it downward toward the lower edge, and, while holding the two edges together, elevated the spinnerets, and threw out a ray of threads, which immediately adhered to and cemented them together. The process is not really a "sewing," as it is popularly called, at least in the sense that the leaf is perforated and the thread drawn through the holes. That word, however, is the best that we have, and, perhaps, sufficiently characterizes this behavior.

The fastenings are evidently made in part, at times, from without, as the threads show application to the outer surface of the leaf. This spin-

Mode of Sewing. ningwork is well shown at Figs. 254 and 255, in which cases the spider has crawled over the outside of the leaves, swinging her abdomen alternately from one side to the other, touching the spinners to the surface at each movement. Again, the nest presents the appearance of having been sewed from within in the same manner. In such cases the spider evidently applies the liquid silk to the tangent or approached edges of the leaf, which, when released from the pressure of the spider's claw, spring back and stretch out the thread, leaving an open seam across which the lines run. Sometimes this seam is subsequently entirely closed. The character of the sewing of this and other Orbweavers is shown at Fig. 255, into which the threads have been drawn very accurately from the natural specimen. The sewing habit obtains among the nest makers of all tribes, and the mechanical methods are in all quite identical with those of the Orbweavers as above described.

Passing now from the spiders whose snares are full orbed, we find the nest making habit existing, with some modifications, among the smaller

Zilla: Nest of Young. group that weave a sectoral orb. Of these the most numerously represented in species is the genus Zilla; her nest is sometimes simply a rude den of netted lines, so arranged as to leave a concavity in the centre of the mass sufficient to shelter the spider. The young Zillas quite invariably weave such a shelter tent when they first set up housekeeping. (See Fig. 133, Chapter VIII.)

Among the adults of the genus the dome shaped silken tent, such as has already been described (Fig. 261), is very common. This tent is swung

Domed Tent. in various positions, according to the location of the spider, and may or may not have a screen of tented leaves. At other times, as I have often seen with Zilla x-notata, in New England, the shelter is spun underneath leaves, and occasionally the leaves are used as a protection, without a very decided woven tent. On the whole, my observations of the habit of Zilla show that it is not strongly inclined to avail itself of the protection of leaves in the manner of Epeira trifolium and others of that group. However, it occupies its home, and uses its trapline in the manner of the nest making Epeiroids.

Closely related to Zilla in the character of its snare is Epeira thaddeus, but in this species the nest making habit appears to be more strongly de-

Nest of Epeira thaddeus. veloped. It may often be found nested in the angle of a door or window, or other like situation, on the outhouses of farms and rural buildings. Here it spins a white silken tube of close texture, which is generally a quite exact cylinder. In this respect it differs from the nests of Zilla and Epeira triaranea, which are almost habitually in the shape of an inverted bowl or dome. The cylindrical tent of Thaddeus varies in length from three-fourths of an inch to one and one-quarter inch, the latter being the length of the nest represented at Fig. 278. The cylinder is stayed by a series of lines attached to it at various parts and stretched to numerous points in the surrounding sur-

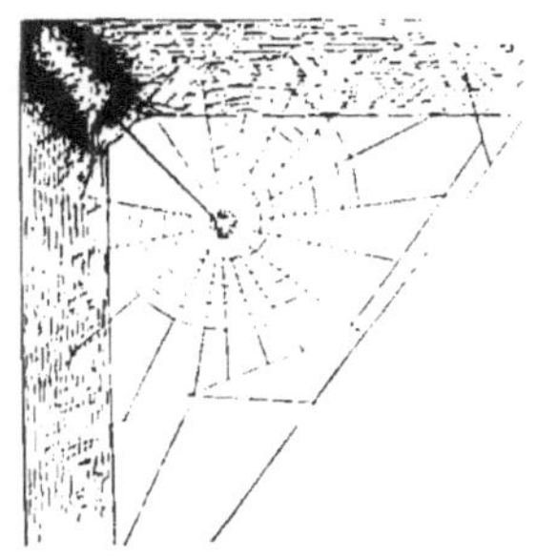

Fig. 278. Cylindrical nest of Epeira thaddeus, spun in the angle of a door.

face, thus holding it intact. Within the cylinder Thaddeus sits holding her trapline, through which all agitation upon her sectoral orb is communicated.

She has learned, however, the value of screening her cylindrical tent beneath a shelter of clustered leaves, as at Fig. 280. In this case the leaves are agglutinated by threads spun upon the inside or sewed upon the outside, precisely as in the case of the Insular and Shamrock spiders.

I have found this cylindrical nest spun within the needle like leaves of the pine tree, and the manner in which it was stayed, and preserved in sufficiently rigid attitude for the practical uses of its occupant, was a good example of the ingenuity of this species. (Fig. 279.) In the above examples the nest is visible by the observer, but at other times it is wholly screened from view, being spun beneath and within the concave surfaces

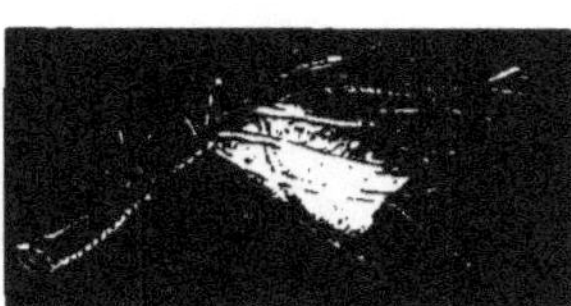

Fig. 279. Cylindrical nest of Thaddeus in pine leaves.

of two attached leaves whose edges have been sewed together, and the entire shelter stayed by means of lines stretched to adjoining leaves and the common stem. If the stay threads be cut and the leaf turned back, the cylindrical nest will be seen inside as represented at Fig. 280.

Again the cylindrical tent of Thaddeus will be woven underneath a cluster of several leaves (Fig. 281), which overarch it like a rounded roof, making a pretty and effective shelter. Beneath this dome the silken cylinder may be seen projecting, the external end stayed by lines fastened to adjoining leaves, and the trapline stretched out taut to the centre, or the sectoral snare hung among the foliage underneath. One would certainly think that a spider thus domiciled has secured for herself the highest attainable security and comfort within the compass of aranead nidification. At other times her den will be found within the point of a single leaf, which has been curled over and sewed together.

It will thus be seen that the nesting habit of Thaddeus is closely related to that of the group represented by Insularis and Trifolium, the principal difference being, that in the last named species the silken part of the structure seems to be rather the lining, while in the former the silken tent is quite distinct and the leaf shelter appears to be rather a secondary matter. At all events, no matter how complete may be the security afforded by the clustered leaves or rolled leaves, the cylindrical tent of Thaddeus may nearly always be found entire, and in a well secured retreat.

In the case of Triaranea the use of the leaf in nidification is extremely rare. Such, at least, is the result of my own observations, although I should not be at all surprised to find that in other geographical provinces the spider may be found to resort to the aid of leaves and other material quite as freely as some of her cogeners. Nevertheless, it is probable that the maze of netted lines within which she swings her bell shaped tent answers all the purposes of a leafy protection, and as long as her home is protected by such an environment she will be less likely to resort to the additional protection of leaves.

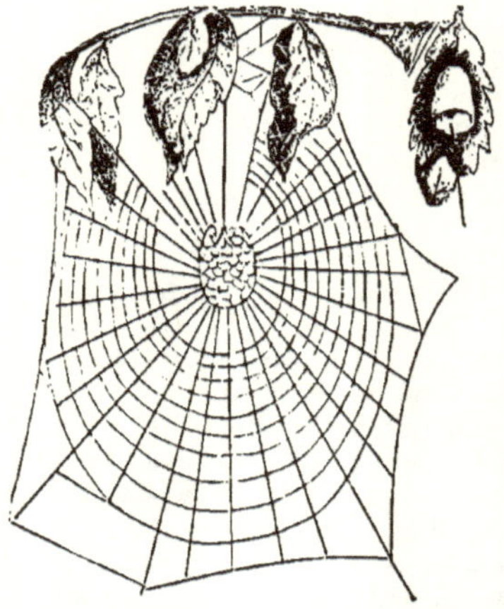

Fig. 280. Nest of Epeira thaddeus within leaves. The tube is shown uncovered at the upper right hand of the cut.

Be that as it may, her home is a silken dome, swung within a mass of netted lines supported upon the foliage of trees, or stayed upon the surrounding surfaces of her nest site. It is open downward toward the orb, to which the home is connected by the ordinary trapline. The mass extends well below the mouth of the tent, and a little free space is usually left between the maze and the orb. Sometimes the tent is decidedly bell shaped, widest at the mouth, and is much larger than the occupant herself, as at Fig. 282. Again, I have seen a tubular passage way or vestibule extending from the mouth of the nest entirely through the length of the maze, thus affording a sheltered passage for the spider along her trapline, well nigh to the point of approach to the orb at its hub. (See Chapter VIII., Figs. 123, 132.) It often happens that Triaranea selects a site that enables her to dispense with much of her shelter. In stone walls along Niantic Bay (Connecticut) and Cape Ann (Massachusetts) many of this species are domiciled. They spin their nest upward against the boulders built into the wall, and avail themselves of the little cavities and rugosities therein. Thus sheltered above and from within they need less protection, and accordingly their silken tents are generally very scant and rudimentary.

Closely related to Triaranea in the character of her nidification is the Labyrinth spider, **Labyrinth Spider's Nest.** one of the most interesting of our indigenous fauna. Labyrinthea weaves a silken dome, hung within a maze of crossed lines, precisely like that of Triaranea. I have marked a difference in the character of the trapline, which seems to consist of a number of threads more commonly than in the case of Triaranea. There is one feature,

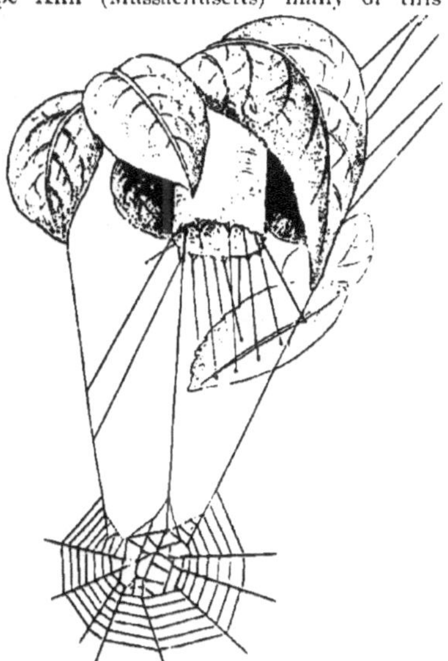

Fig. 281. Cylindrical nest of Epeira thaddeus woven beneath a tent of clustered leaves.

however, which seems to be peculiar to this species. Within the midst of her maze will almost always be found a dry leaf; and underneath this the spider rests, sometimes without much interposed spinningwork, but at other times within the ordinary silken dome. (See Chapter VIII., Fig. 114.) The leaf may frequently fall within her retitelarian snare, and probably is not, as a rule, brought there by the action of the spider, although I cannot affirm this. But it is certain that, the leaf being within her maze, she does draw it to some central place and cluster the netted lines around it as a central point, and then establishes herself beneath the leaf, against which, in the course of time, she proceeds to abut the summit of her silken dome. (Fig. 283.) She has thus secured additional protection from assaults made from above.

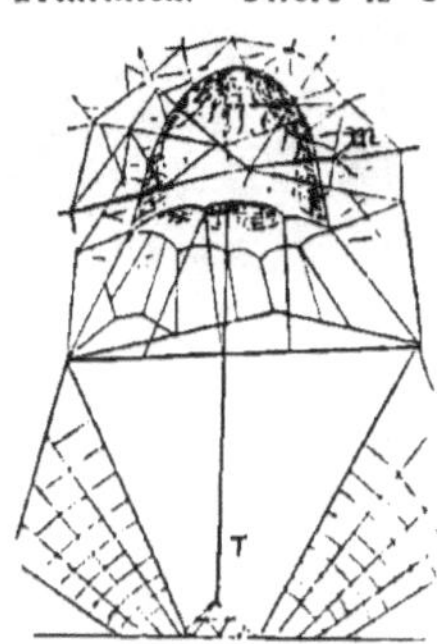

Fig. 282. The bell shaped silken nest of Epeira triaranea. m, the retitelarian mass; T, trapline.

In some cases the concavities of the leaf are utilized, and the spider, creeping within them, finds an additional shelter, and makes such concavities the site for the location of her silken dome. (Figs. 284, 285.) Labyrinthea is able to avail herself of other roofing material than a leaf, for I have more than once found her snare in the pine forests of New Jersey, having in the centre of the maze a mass of miscellaneous material, such as fine sawdust, or the castings of moth larvæ, or drifted rubbish of various sorts, which had probably fallen upon the tangle of crossed lines, and had been gathered by the occupant into a mass,

Leafy Roof.

Fig. 283. Leaf roofed dome of the Labyrinth spider.

which, being agglutinated by the viscid threads, was finally shaped into a solid shelter, beneath which the spider rested and eventually constructed her silken dome.

Labyrinthea is a most persistent dweller within her domicile. I think the female rarely leaves the confines of her web, limiting her life to living within her tent, spinning her orb and trapping flies upon it, and wandering back and forward in various duties of housekeeping and house repairing through her retitelarian maze. She may make excursions into adjoining foliage and surroundings, as some other Orbweavers do; but, if so, I have never been able to find her abroad. She even spins her cocoons within the limits of her netted snare, and there her young are hatched and frequently occupy the site for a while after egress, and subsist upon the microscopic insects that are entangled upon the lines.

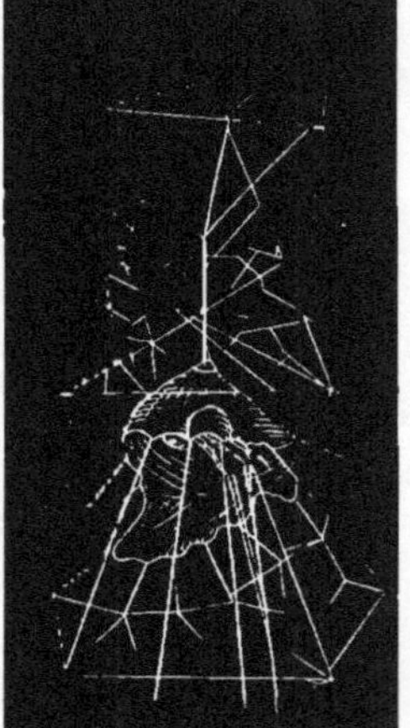

Fig. 284. Leafy canopy of Labyrinthea, hung within the maze.

The nesting habits of the Hunchback Epeira (Epeira gibberosa) have already been referred to (Chapter IX., page 154, Fig. 145) in connection with the makers of horizontal orbs. The nest is simply a hammock or net of crossed lines, commonly stretched between the edges of a leaf, which are pulled up so as to make a slight concavity. Beneath this spinningwork the spider suspends herself, back downward, after the fashion of the Theridioids and the spinners of horizontal orbwebs. Her face is outward toward her snare, and the feet

Gibberosa's Hammock Nest.

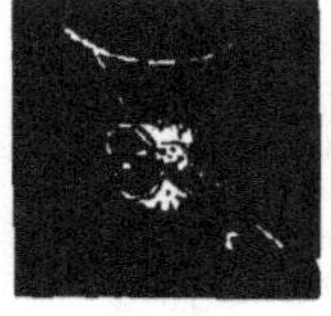

Fig. 285. A den in a leaf. a, trapline.

clasp the trapline leading thereto. The occupant is sheltered beneath and on both sides by the leafy walls, and, as her hammock shelters from attacks coming from above, she may be regarded as well protected. A front view of Gibberosa's nest is given at Fig. 286, and a side view at Fig. 287; the nest is shown even more plainly at Fig. 145.

V.

Nesting Industry Protective. The various forms of nest architecture described above may be said to have developed around the instinct of protection. In other words, the spinningwork of spiders used for domiciles is protective industry. It may be well, with this in view, to make a summary of the nesting habits of Orbweavers as above described, and briefly compare them with those of other tribes of the order.

It may be said, at the outset, that the portion of the body which is most assailable by enemies and least defensible by the spider is that which is invariably especially protected. That part is the soft abdomen. Around this the tube, tent, or screen, or whatever characteristic defense is provided, will

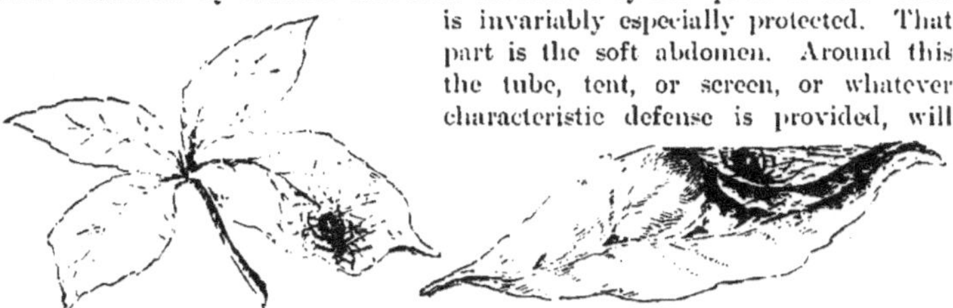

FIG. 286.   Hammock nest of Gibberosa on a leaf.   FIG. 287.   Nest of Gibberosa; side view.

certainly be spun. It is this part that parasitic enemies assail; it is this which forms the juicy bit coveted by birds, frogs, lizards, and other arachnophagous animals. The legs and even the face will therefore be thrust out of the entrance of the nest or be left partially unprotected, while the abdomen is entirely screened. One cannot suppose that this coincidence is accidental. Evidently the animal is conscious that the abdomen is the portion of its body which most requires protection, and has directed its industry to that end.

The following are some of the varied forms of protective industry:
1. Spiders protect themselves by leafy tents, that is to say, tents, coverings, or screens made of bits of a leaf, of a whole leaf, or of several leaves united. The Labyrinth spider, for example, appropriates a dry leaf that may drop into her snare, or which she secures for that purpose. It is placed in the midst of her labyrinth of crossed lines, frequently with the concavity downwards. Underneath this she stations herself, pressing the abdomen upward against the leaf. Insularis and others of the group represented by her protective industry make a

Leafy Tents.

more artistic use of the leaf. Several leaves will at times be drawn together, being united by the edges and tips so as to give a bell shaped tent; sometimes one leaf alone is used, the edge being folded over like a grocer's cornucopia; sometimes sprays of grasses and blossoms are united with a leaf or two, making a very pretty effect. The concavity of these structures is silk lined, and within it the spider sits, her abdomen forced inward and generally rested against a silken cushion or sheet. The face looks towards the snare, and the spider's feet grasp a trapline which is joined thereto.

2. Again, protective industry takes the form of silken tents. These are woven inside of leafy tents, as in the case of the Insular and Shamrock spiders, or under a leaf or other objects, as with the Labyrinth spider. Some species make tents of pure silk. The Domicile spider sometimes spins a bell shaped tent, opening downward, the apex of which is fixed within the angle of a house or against the trunk of a tree or leaf. This dome is quite large; from one to one and a half inch in length and breadth at the mouth. Indeed, it may be stated generally that the size of the dwelling corresponds with the size of the aranead inhabiting it. There is not much waste of spinning energy. There is little room for obtrusive enemies to enter into the door and share with the lawful inhabitant the unoccupied space. This applies only to silk nests, as the leaf ones are often very roomy. It is noticeable that spiders which make use of curled leaves for domiciles can, when circumstances require, dispense with these leaves and provide themselves with silken tents or tubes as their sole defense.

Epeira thaddeus makes her tent against, or under, or even within a curled leaf, or within the needle like leaves of the pine. It is ordinarily cylindrical, instead of bell shaped. Others, again, as the Furrow spider, make a close cylinder or tube a little longer than their own length, with a small opening at one end looking towards the orb.

3. Another phase is represented by such spiders as Labyrinthea and Triaranea, in whose webs the protective industry appears to have reached its most complex development. In the case of the Labyrinth spider there is, first, the leafy roof or screen; there is, next, the little tent or tube spun against the leaf, whose mouth opens downward toward the orbweb; and then, encompassing the whole, is the maze or labyrinth of crossed lines, which forms in itself a very complete protection against raiding insects. The same form of industry substantially characterizes Epeira triaranea, except that this spider never provides for her silken tent a leafy roof or covering of miscellaneous material.

4. Protective industry assumes the form of wings, or aprons, or fenders of crossed lines thrown out upon the flanks of the snare. The retitelarian maze by which the Labyrinth spider and Triaranea protect themselves may,

in part, be seen upon the webs of our two large indigenous species of Argiope. On either side of the orb these spiders are in the habit of throwing out wings of crossed lines, which extend, as a rule, beneath the lower margin of the hub upon which the spider ordinarily hangs, thus securing industrial protection from every direction except from below, which point is guarded by the defensive organs and armor. In point of fact, Argiope thus encloses herself within a rude tent of straggling lines. These lines ward off assailants, or check or entangle them, and give warning of danger in time to escape. Their purpose is manifestly protective, since they are apparently too open to serve for catching prey, and otherwise do not seem adapted to that end. The Orchard spider, Argyroepeira hortorum, resorts to the same mode of protection, but, inasmuch as she makes a horizontal web and hangs upon the under part thereof, the protective apron is thrown beneath the orb, and thus secures the aranead against the approach of enemies from the exposed quarter.

Protective Wings

5. The central shield of thick spinningwork, which is found beneath the Banded and the Basket Argiope, may also be regarded as protective; and it is probable that the thick scalloped and pointed ribbon decorations characteristic of the Banded Argiope and also of Uloborus, serve some protective purpose besides the strengthening of the net. At least, it is the habit of the spider to place herself behind these screens, which thus protect her from the exposed point, the shrubbery and other objects against which the snare is fastened being the protection from the other side.

6. Another protective use of simple lines may be seen in the case of the Hunchback orbweaver, Epeira gibberosa, who makes a hammock tent, swung between leaves. She spins a series of straight lines quite thickly between the edges of a leaf, or several leaves, and hangs underneath them, communicating with her snare by the usual taut trapline. She is thus protected beneath and on all sides by her leafy site, and above by her hammock.

7. In addition, and generally, it may be said that almost all the orbweaving families will avail themselves of any chance cavity or projection for temporary shelter or as a permanent site. Therein they hide themselves, either with or without additional protection of spinningwork, and remain until appetite prompts them to spin their snares and place themselves upon them to procure food. In some cases, as with the Furrow spider, such a shelter is habitually preferred; a hole or depression, or even more frequently a dry curled leaf or bit of bark, being chosen.

In point of fact, spiders appear to live continually in dread of enemies, and their whole life is spent in a defensive industrial warfare for the protection of their persons, or in offensive war upon those insects which furnish them their natural food. In the former case they are habitually in hiding; in the latter, in ambush.

VI.

The subject of nesting architecture could hardly be considered complete without a glance at the curious habit of nest parasitism, as it may (somewhat loosely) be termed. The facts in my possession are **Nest Parasitism.** not numerous, but are enough to indicate that more, and more interesting ones, may await future observers. Saltigrade spiders are very much in the habit of attaching the silken cell in which they live to the nest of Orbweavers, and, indeed, I may say, of other tribes. One may find a little Saltigrade snugly ensconced, as in Fig. 288, on the silken dome of Epeira, with the mouth of the cell opening almost next door to the exit of her host's house. It seems strange, at first thought, that the two would pass to and fro without molesting and destroying one another; but they manage to do this.

Again, I have often found underneath a bit of loose bark, or a flat stone, the tubular nest of Epeira strix, surrounded on all sides and even overlaid by the cells of various Saltigrade species, in some of which the mother would be found dwelling with her young. Here, again, the wonder is that the colonists dwelt together in unity.

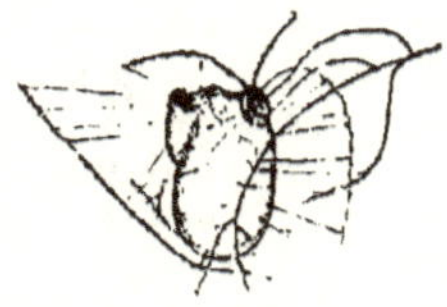

Fig. 288. Parasitic nest of Saltigrade spider upon nest of Epeira strix.

It is not an unusual thing to find the little silken cell of Clubiona and various Drassids spun underneath some portion of curled leaf or leaves, which are used by the Insular or Shamrock spiders for nests. Indeed, these ubiquitous Tubeweavers feel free to attach their cells to any object, in almost any site, **Squatter Sovereignty.** without the slightest regard to the equity of squatter sovereignty. Observations of this kind are so frequent that I have fancied that during the hours of rest within the domicile the predatory nature of araneads may be in abeyance, and that there may be a mutual understanding—a sort of modus vivendi—that in such cases the ordinary cannibalism of their kind is to be suspended.

Vinson gives an interesting account of the manner in which the little Linyphiæ of the African islands whose fauna he has described, take up their dwellings upon the huge snares and extended foundation lines of large Orbweavers, mostly of the genus Nephila. Here they remain quite at home, and apparently undisturbed by their gigantic hostess, and support themselves by picking up the small insects ensnared in their neighborhood, and which are too minute to satisfy the appetite of the proprietor of the snare.[1] This appears to be quite a fixed habit among the smaller species of Africa. A similar phenomenon I have often observed among our American fauna, and shall allude to it in a following chapter (Vol. II.), upon the Babyhood of Spiders. The little ones of a recently escaped

---

[1] Aranéides des Iles de la Réunion, etc., page xix.

brood will occupy the abandoned snare of an adult Orbweaver, and, clearing out the space between the radii, spin their own minute orbs. I have seen a brood of young Epeira patagiata attempt this sort of squatting upon the premises of an adult Zilla x-notata, very much to their own discomfort. For, although the little fellows succeeded in getting positions for their minute orbs, the original proprietor, by skillful management, was able to dislodge and one after another devour them, until she had eaten up nearly all her guests.

Moreover, among certain species of the Retitelariæ, the habit has become fixed of invading the snares of other species for the purpose of **Piratical Invaders.** destroying the occupants. Argyrodes trigonum, for example, will invade the nest of the Labyrinth spider, whose maze forms an admirable retreat, and therein will establish herself. Another species of Argyrodes, which I have described as A. piratica, was sent to me from California, and is said by Mrs. Rosa Smith Eigenmann to be an habitual depredator upon the premises of the Orbweavers of San Diego. The little creature will fearlessly invade the snare; attack, destroy, and devour her huge opponent. The particulars of this habit I reserve for the chapter (Vol. II.) upon the Enemies of Spiders.

The abandoned nest of Orbweavers is often occupied by Tubeweaving spiders. Agalena nœvia especially finds it a pleasant retreat, and makes it the centre of her broad, sheeted snare. So also I have found the rolled leaf nest of a young Epeïroid occupied by a Saltigrade. I have no evidence, however, that any of these spiders deliberately dislodges the owner in order thus to take possession. Nor have I ever seen one Orbweaver make a raid upon the premises of a congener for a like purpose.

Mrs. Treat records[1] a case which looks very much like nest parasitism. An interesting Lycosid, Dolomedes scriptus, appeared to take a special fancy for the nest of a female Shamrock spider. For more than two weeks, while the Dolomede was carrying her cocoon, her favorite resting place was on the top of the Orbweaver's tent, and often, when the latter left her domicile to seek prey upon her orb, as is her custom, Dolomede would stealthily slip inside. But she always seemed to know when Trifolium was about to return, and would quickly emerge and take her place on the outside. The only wonder to me, in this case, is that the Lycosid, which is a large and powerful spider, abundantly able to cope with and destroy Trifolium, did not at once make a meal of the Orbweaver whose home she coveted, and, after the fashion of human creatures, take possession of the premises from which she had dislodged the rightful occupant.

On the whole, I am inclined to think, although the facts are certainly inadequate to form a just conclusion of any sort, that cases of proper nest parasitism are rare. That is to say, it is not often that one

____

1 " My Garden Pets," page 24.

spider will deliberately appropriate a part of the nest of another, or dislodge another in order to possess the whole place.

The fact is that the construction of a nest is not a very difficult matter. Orbweavers, at least, are apt to change their position when in anywise made uncomfortable, and build a new home. Material costs **Facile Nest Making**. nothing, for leaves are plenty and free as fuel in an Adirondacks forest; and, as to tapestry and other hangings for her abode, she possesses an unfailing manufactory within her own person, and at her own command. Moreover, there is a wholesome fear of results which, in the absence of any moral sentiment, is apt to restrain a covetous aranead from assaulting a spider who is ensconced within her own castle, and has the advantage of being on the defensive; for, even in spider world it is easier to defend a fort from an assailant than to attack it upon scaling ladders.

CHAPTER XVIII.

NEST MAKING: ITS ORIGIN AND USE: DEVELOPMENT IN VARIOUS TRIBES.

I.

A STUDY of the modes of construction described in the preceding chapter suggests the thought that the habit of nest making may have originated among the Orbweavers in an accidental way. The tendency is natural and universal, among spiders of all kinds, to shelter themselves underneath arboreal or other surfaces. They know instinctively that they are exposed to enemies. The under surfaces of leaves, or the little domes formed by clusters of drooping leaves, are most common and natural shelters for spiders when living on arboreal sites. With such creatures, that subsist by means of the spinning habit, and constantly protect themselves by fastening draglines to the surfaces over which they move, and thus never venture any distance without leaving an attachment behind them, and a thread by which they can return, it would be the most natural thing conceivable to attach themselves in like manner by outspun threads to surfaces beneath which they had thus sought shelter.

In the restless movements of the body back and forth, numerous attachments would be made, and so a rude silken shelter would easily result; and it would inevitably follow, without premeditation or purpose of the spider, that the leaves, by the very action of the threads, would be held together, and in the course of time drawn closer together into the various nest shapes which we see. These forms might thus be made without any fixed purpose or definite movement of intelligence. That it is often so I am well satisfied. That the more perfect habit could have originated in this seemingly accidental way, and have become fixed in the course of time by heredity, appears not an unreasonable theory.

At all events, it is certain that in the selection and adjustment of material in the nidification of Orbweavers, one does not see such a deliberate and intelligent purpose as is found, for example, among some of the Lycosids. The turret spider, Lycosa arenicola Scudder, deliberately seeks and selects the bits of straw and sticks out of which she rears her little tower so like an old fashioned log cabin chimney. (Fig. 289.) There is here a deliberate choice and bringing of material to the nest site.

The same aranead, when building on the seashore, will show intelligent adaptation in the use of the material at hand. I have often found her burrow, when dug within the sand, with a course or two of small quartz pebbles laid around the rim, upon which, as a sort of foundation, the usual chimney or turret of straws would be raised.

If one will thrust a twig down the burrow, which goes straight downward six, eight, or ten inches, and will dig away the sand on either side, he will see the delicate silken lining of the burrow clinging to the twig, as shown at Fig. 290. It is a delicate fabric, with whose strands the grains of sand are interblended. But it serves, in part, to keep the tube intact.

Lycosa carolinensis constructs from the needle like leaves of the white pine (as in the cut Fig. 291), or from other available material, by bending and pasting, domiciles which more closely resemble birds' nests than anything that I have met in aranead architecture. These are pasted together by a process not unlike a rude sort of basket weaving. In this case, also, one must assume a deliberate and intelligent action on the part of the spider.

The selection of the pine needles as they lie scattered over the field; **A Basket Weaver.** bringing them to the nest site; ar-

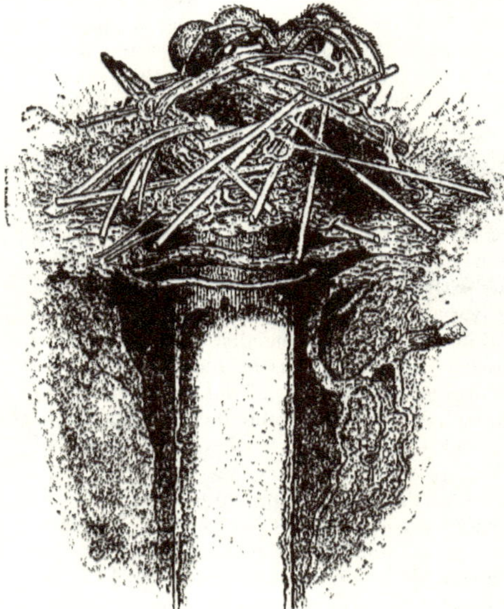

Fig. 289. The Turret spider's nest. The earth is represented cut away, to show the burrow.

ranging them in the little fasciculæ or bundles which may be seen in the cut (Fig. 291); the bending of these into place to form the basket like vestibule or dome above the burrow—all these actions, not to speak of others, imply a process of selection and adaptation more or less deliberate and intelligent.[1]

On the contrary, in studying the nests of Orbweavers and noting their manner of constructing them, one cannot escape the conviction that chance has had quite as much to do as design in the outcome of some of the beautiful forms illustrated in the foregoing chapter. It is in the act of

[1] The nest of Carolinensis from which the figure has been drawn was contributed to my collection by Mrs. Treat, and was made by a New England spider.

sewing together the leaves, after the nest site is selected and the preparatory stages wrought out, that one sees most evident marks of intention on the part of the architect. There can be no doubt that here is manifest the deliberate purpose to effectually enclose the dwelling and secure it from intrusion of enemies and inconvenience of weather changes.

Design in Sewing.

II.

If now we come to compare the protective industry of Orbweavers with that of other tribes of spiders, even those which most widely differ from them in structure and general life habit, we shall find less essential difference than might have been anticipated. The germinal form, or prevailing type of protective architecture, for all tribes, is the tube or some modification thereof. The entire tribe of Tubitelariæ, for example, domicile within tubes which do not differ in essential particulars from that which is woven by the orbweaving Furrow spider and others of kindred habit, or by Epeira thaddeus.

Comparative Studies.

Fig. 290. Upper figure: Turret spider's tower built on a pebble foundation. Lower figure: inside lining exposed by digging out the sand.

Indeed, the open dome shaped tent of Epeira domiciliorum and other spiders is only a modification of the architectural type. The little tube of the Drassids (Fig. 292), and numerous species of Tubitelariæ that construct kindred domiciles, scarcely differs in any regard from the tube of the Epeiroid Thaddeus and Furrow spiders. In the case of the Speckled Agalena, whose funnel shaped web is known to all familiars of our fields, the tubular part thereof is really the spider's domicile, and the broad sheet outstretched upon leaves, grass, or surrounding surface of its site may be regarded as a portion of the snare. The same spider protects herself, as is the case with many Orbweavers, by a maze of straight lines spun above the separating sheet, and which also serves in part to sustain it, and acts besides as a snare to arrest prey.

Tube-weavers.

If, again, we take such an example as the Medicinal spider, Tegenaria medicinalis (or Durhami), whose web is so frequently found in cellars and shaded outhouses, the same fact meets us. There we see the thick sheet, not spread out broadly as in the case of Agalena, but rather pouched; thus forming a good receptacle for dropping insects, who are apt to roll easily into the little round opening at the apex of the snare. Above this opening is spun a short tubular tower, which also is prolonged a little way beneath the opening. Within this peculiar structure the spider protects herself, precisely as in the case of the Orbweavers above described. (See Fig. 221, Chapter XIV.)

Fig. 291. The nest of Lycosa carolinensis, built from the needle like leaves of a pine tree.

If we pass next to the Saltigrades we find the same fact. The jumping spiders, whose bright forms and animated movements are familiar around our houses and yards, spin for their domicile thick white silken tubes, which differ very little in form and structure from those of the orbweaving Furrow spider or the tubeweaving Drassid, Disdera, or Segestria. (Fig. 293.)

Salti-grades.

The Lineweavers, although such close neighbors to the Orbweavers in structure, and having remarkable points of approach in certain features of the snare, are somewhat defective in points of architectural resemblance as far as the nesting tube is concerned. But they have some striking representatives of the prevailing type. There is, for example, the little lineweaving Theridium zelotypum which I have often observed along the trails in Adirondack forests, living in a little tent whose roof was the gathered leaves of a young pine tree, and whose interior was a silken tube or bell shaped dome quite resembling the nest of the Insular spider. Within this tent the mother Theridium domiciles, and with her dwell a number of her young. (See Fig. 294.)

Line-weavers.

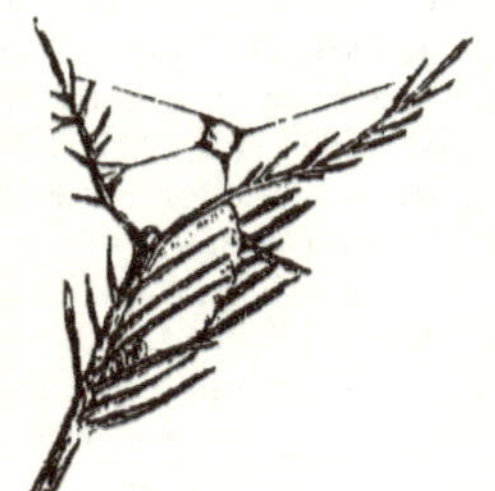

Fig. 292. Tubular nest of Drassus.

When the habits of American Lineweavers shall be studied more carefully, it will probably be found that Zelotypum is not alone in the matter of nidification. At least, we know that among the European Theridioids there are some species who almost equal the Epeïroids in the perfection of their nests. Theridium nervosum is one of these; in the midst of her pyramidal snare of interlacing lines, or, at other times, sheltered underneath a growing leaf, she prepares a perfect little nesting tent, which is fastened by silken cords into a dome **European** like frame. The tent is lined with white silk, and is covered **Therid-** with small dead leaves or flowers, or the stamens of larger flow- **ioids.** ers, or anything which has presented itself. It is decorated with the wings or other parts of insects, among which the beautiful wing cases of the nut weevil are often found. This tent is not used for a domicile alone, but as a receptacle for the cocoon.[1]

Theridium riparium builds a nest which Black-wall thus concisely describes: She fabricates a slender, conical tube of silk, of a very slight

Fig. 293. The tubular nest of a Saltigrade spider, in a rolled leaf.

texture, measuring from one and a half to two and a half inches in length, and about one-half inch in diameter at its lower extremity. It is closed above, open below, thickly covered externally with bits of indurated earth, small stones, and withered leaves and flowers, which are incorporated with it, and is suspended perpendicularly, by lines attached to its sides and apex, in the irregular snare constructed by this species. In the upper part of this triangular domicile the female spins several globular cocoons of yellowish white silk, of a slight texture, whose mean diameter is about one-eighth of an inch, in each of which she deposits from twenty to sixty small spherical eggs, of a pale, yellowish white color, not agglutinated together. The young remain with the mother for a long period after quitting the cocoons, and are provided by her with food, which consists chiefly of ants.[2]

In point of fact, this English Lineweaver possesses the faculty of nest building to as remarkable a degree as any known spider. I therefore insert at length a series of interesting observations recorded by Mr. Edward H. Robertson, of Brixton, England.[3]

Riparium has a great antipathy to strong light, and usually completes her nest under **Material** the shade of overhanging banks, **Used.** seldom making her appearance during the day, and becoming active as darkness creeps on. The nest is a

Fig. 294. Nest of Theridium zelotypum.

tube varying in length from one to two and a half inches, closed above, but open at the lower end, the diameter at the mouth being about one-half

---

[1] Staveley, British Spiders, page 145.

[2] Blackwall, "Researches in Zoology," page 356. Also, Spiders of Great Britain, Introduction, page 9.

[3] "Science Gossip," January, 1868, page 12 sq.

inch. The materials of which it is composed externally are small particles of hardened earthy pebbles, twigs, withered leaves, etc., rather slightly attached by threads. This tube is lined with silk, forming a comfortable home. However irregular in appearance the nest may be externally, the interior is always smooth.

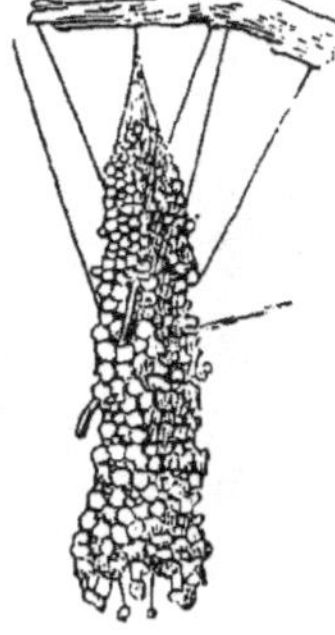

Fig. 295. Nest of Theridium riparium, made of pellets of clay.

Mr. Robertson examined sixty or seventy nests, and kept a dozen of them under glass cases for closer observation. Most of the nests were suspended under the leaves of raspberry and gooseberry bushes and like situations at a distance of from two to four inches from the earth; in a few instances they were suspended in the angles of old walls. When built above the soil the pebbles alone seemed to be used. When built near a wall particles of mortar were taken. In the latter case, the nests were the most regular in form. When withered leaves were near, these and small twigs were used, and the nests formed of such materials were the least symmetrical. It is thus manifest that the mechanical finish of the domicile depends largely upon the building material available.

In order to test the capabilities of these little architects, the observer supplied those which were in confinement with small twigs cut in lengths of about one-eighth inch, mixing with them larger pieces. He **Artificial Supplies Used.** was surprised to find that the smallest pieces were not often selected, and apparently the most unsuitable pieces were frequently chosen by the little architect. Figs. 298 and 299 are examples of nests formed by these twigs. The upper parts, above the marked line in the cuts, were built before they were transferred to cases. Fig. 298 was constructed in the course of three weeks. Fig. 299 was built by a wonderfully industrious mother of two large families, who subsequently made a neat little residence of particles of chalk.

While the eggs remain unhatched, the nest seldom exceeds one inch in length. No sooner, however, does the mother find that she has to accommodate a large family than she is seized with a building impulse, and may be seen to descend suddenly to the earth. **Mode of Building.** She then takes a seemingly purposeless scramble over the material beneath her nest. Passing by much building material apparently well fitted for her purpose, without any attempt at examination, she fixes upon a twig or other object which

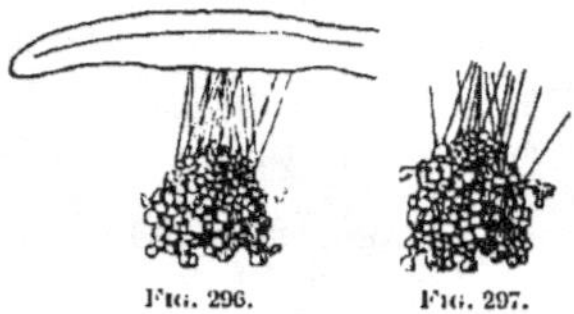

Fig. 296.   Fig. 297.

Nests in their earliest stages.
(Theridium riparium.)

often appears disproportionate to her size and strength. To this she attaches a line, and quickly scrambles back again, dragging the twig after her.

This dragline she fastens to one of those which connect with the mouth of her nest, and which just serve to suspend the object. Returning, another thread is attached, and the piece is suspended midway between earth and nest. A third trip serves to fix the substance at the mouth of her domicile, to be afterward more neatly arranged. Several objects are thus frequently suspended at one time, giving the nest a rather unfinished appearance, as represented in the figures.

Nests built in the open air are almost impervious to light, while those built in confinement admit the light through the various interstices left by angular pieces of the building material. The little creature seems unable to remedy this, doubtless because the natural site affords her better opportunity for the selection of material adapted to her wants.

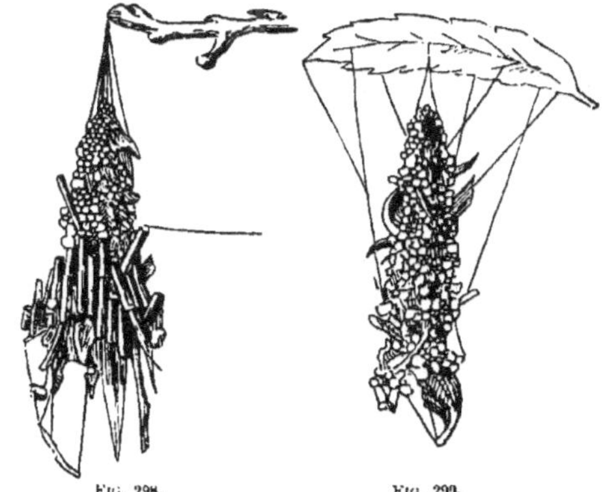

FIG. 298.   FIG. 299.

FIG. 298. Nest made of materials artificially supplied; the lower part of sticks. (Theridium riparium.)   FIG. 299. Nest with dead leaves, twigs, etc., intermingled with pellets of earth. (Theridium riparium.)

The objects used are invariably built into the inner surfaces only; and Mr. Robertson scarcely ever observed one of the busy little workmen on the exterior of its house, excepting when forming a slight covering of silk on the upper part, which is sometimes done.

The snare of the spider is spun downward from the mouth of her tubular nest. The lines are the ordinary intersecting threads of her species, which are so disposed that they enclose an inverted funnel shaped space, the mouth of the nest representing the point of the funnel.

The Snare.

From some unknown cause these spiders sometimes left their homes with their broods, built on the inside of a branch irregular structures, one of which is figured. (Fig. 300.)

FIG. 300. A rudimentary refuge, or experimental nest. (Theridium riparium.)

Riparium's nest is not simply a domicile for the proprietor, but is a nursery and home in which to rear the young. The mother spins several nearly spherical cocoons of yellowish white silk, the diameter of each being about one-eighth of an inch, within which are contained from thirty to sixty eggs. When the young are hatched, they remain with the mothers until they gain a considerable size—a period of several weeks. The first, and probably the second, moult take place within the nest, the third occurs after the spider has commenced life on its own account. Although so numerous, the juvenile Ripariums in Mr. Robertson's artificial nests appeared to be on very good terms, seldom engaging in any quarrels—not so frequently, he thought, as the same number of boys in a school would have done. The mother Theridium exhibits wonderful affection for her eggs and young.

Domicile and Nursery.

The food of the spider is principally ants, and many deserted nests were literally full of the remains of these insects. House flies, when trapped upon the snares, are held very tenaciously by the viscid globules which, Mr. Robertson asserts, are dispersed over the intersecting lines. It is most interesting to watch the proceedings of the juveniles when the mother is endeavoring to catch a fly. Hearing or seeing a disturbance, a young spider cautiously descends a line, followed at a distance by another and another. These approach the victim, evidently as anxious to assist the mother as children are to use their little fingers when they see others busy. The fly struggles in its toils, and away scamper the young spiders as fast as tiny legs can carry them, repeating this process until they can make a meal off the fly. When an insect is captured it is usually enswathed and drawn up within the nest to be devoured.

Food.

These examples would seem to indicate that among our American Theridioids we may expect to find the nesting habit much more strongly developed than has heretofore been supposed. At all events, it is seen that this tribe has in some of its representatives fair rivals of the Orbweavers in the perfection of the nesting habit. The difference in the use, in the case of Theridium, appears to be that the nests of Orbweavers are habitually the dwelling places of their builders, while those of Lineweavers are not so much permanent dwelling places as retreats for the cocooning season. However, the Orbweaver's nest is also occasionally used to house her cocoon.

One may find rude examples of the nesting habit in the genus Linyphia. There is no more common or more interesting snare along the skirts of our American woods, especially in the Middle and Atlantic States, than that of Linyphia marginata. This consists of a dome of open meshwork which is stretched in the midst of a maze of crossed lines. It looks not unlike a miniature umbrella minus a handle and hung by innumerable cords to the foliage. (Fig. 157.) Within this structure the spider has her abode, hanging inverted, close to the ceiling, ready to dash through the flimsy fabric and seize the unfortunate victims that drop down upon the roof through the labyrinth above.

Nesting Snares of Linyphia.

Linyphia communis spins a nest precisely like the above in structure, but differing from it in that the concavity of the dome is invariably

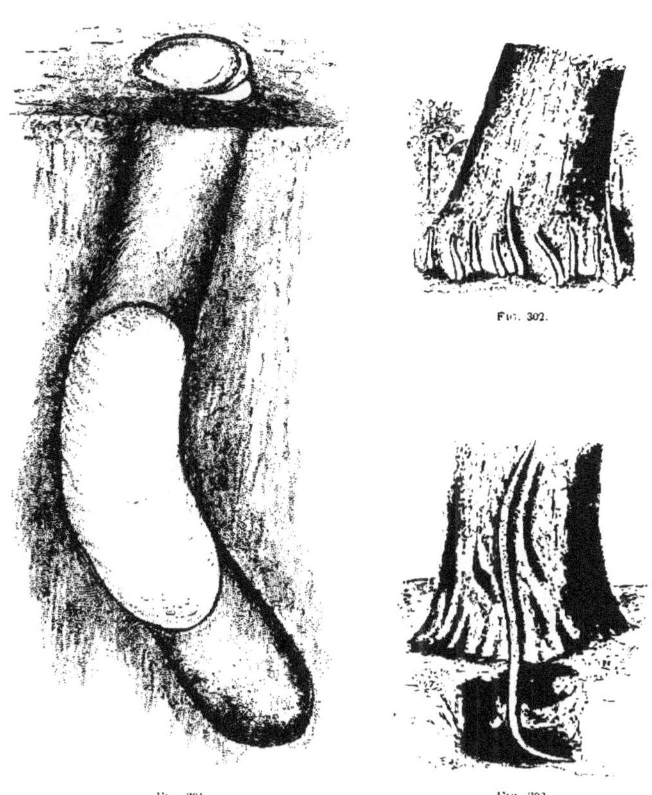

FIG. 301.

FIG. 302.

FIG. 303.

FIG. 301. The silk lined burrow or nest of the American Trapdoor spider, Cteniza californica. The earth is cut away, giving a vertical exposure of the tube and its lining. FIG. 302. A colony of Purseweb spiders' nests on a palmetto trunk. FIG. 303. Purseweb spider's tube; soil removed to show underground burrow.

turned upwards instead of downwards. (See Fig. 156, Chapter IX.) The spider rests, as in the case of her congener, beneath her tent, and waits for the prey that, striking upon and arrested by the labyrinth of crossed lines stretched above, drop into the inverted silken bowl, beneath which the watchful aranead hangs. Thus among the Linyphia, also, the Line-weavers have fair representatives of that nest making habit which we have regarded as germinal and typical of the nesting architecture of all the tribes.

Among the Territelariæ the tube making habit has a very high development, particularly in the genera Nemesia, Cteniza, and Atypus. All these spiders make tubular burrows beneath the surface of the ground, which are lined with a thick sheeting of silk that really constitutes a tube within a tunnel. (Fig. 301.) The genus Atypus carries this tube above the surface, attaching it, in the case of Abbot's Atypus,[1] to the surface of trees (Figs. 302, 303), while Atypus piceus fastens her tube to the surface of weeds and grass into which or along which it is carried. Thus we find that in this large and interesting tribe the tube is also made the architectural type of the domicile.

Territelarian Tubes.

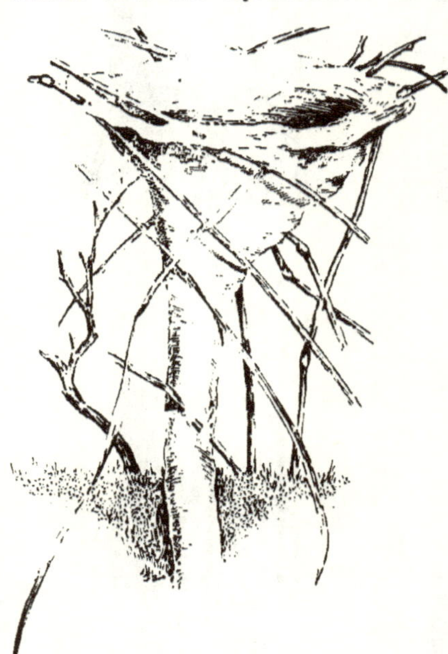

FIG. 304. The tubular, funnel shaped nest of Cyrtauchenius elongatus. Elevated above the ground, and suspended to grasses. The earth is opened to show a section view of the subterranean tube. (After Moggridge.)

The nest of Cyrtauchenius elongatus, as described by M. Eugene Simon, closely resembles that of Agalena nœvia in the character of the tube alone; but this tube is enclosed within a deep cylindrical burrow, and is prolonged upward for about three inches above the surface of the ground, and enlarged into a funnel shape, so that it becomes from two to three inches across at the orifice. (Fig. 304.) This aerial portion is snow white, and at once attracts the eye, even from a considerable distance; the nests, rising up amid sparse grass, which serves to support but not conceal them, present the appearance of scattered white fungi. Cyrtauchenius

---

[1] Atypus Abboti Walck.

belongs to the Territelariæ, and appears to be nearly related to Atypus and Nemesia. Mr. Moggridge classifies its nest among those of the Trapdoor spiders, characterizing it as the funnel shaped nest.[1]

Among the Citigrades we find a resemblance in general habit to the Tunnelweavers. The burrowing habit is quite identical, and the tube making habit, although not so highly specialized, nevertheless exists. It

Citigrades. is chiefly displayed, however, in spinning a tubular lining to the little tower prolonged above the burrow, as in the case of the interesting nest of the turret spider,[2] Fig. 289, or the silk lined, dome shaped vestibule of the Tiger spider,[3] composed of moss or various scraps of miscellaneous material, which is wrought into an entrance to the sloping burrow that

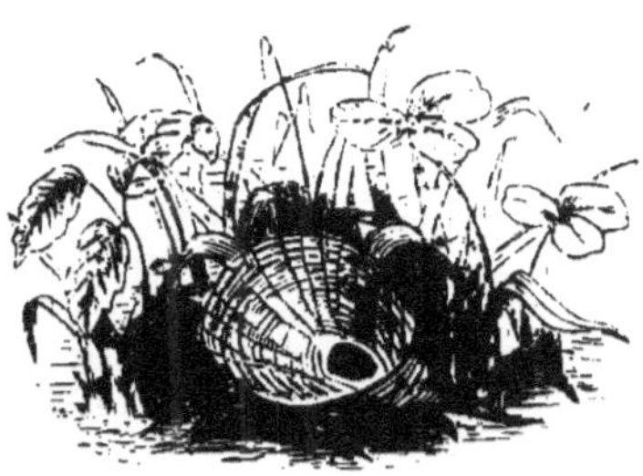

FIG. 305. Vestibule of Lycosa tigrina (McCook).

extends beneath the surface of the ground. (Fig. 305.) The silk lined tower of the turret spider may be said to resemble very closely the tubular nest of such Orbweavers as Epeira domiciliorum and E. thaddeus, when they build within the leaves of a pine tree or weave their tent in like situations. The silk lined vestibule of the Tiger spider is not unlike the leafy nest constructed by the Shamrock spider and others of the group to which she belongs. (Compare Fig. 259, Chapter XVII., with Fig. 305.)

Coming finally to the Laterigrades we find here the nest making habit less developed than in any other tribe of the order. These araneads stalk their prey afield; use no sort of spinningwork for their capture: and, as far as I know, make no fixed domicile of spinningwork for their permanent abode. I

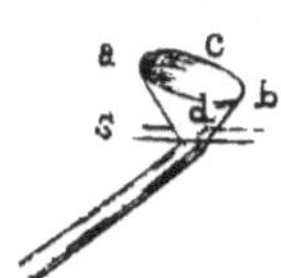

FIG. 306. Outline nest of Lycosa tigrina. s, surface of ground; the course of burrow is indicated beneath; a, b, c, d, the vestibule or upper part of nest.

Laterigrades. have, however, found Laterigrades, as Philodromus and Misumena, dwelling with their cocoons beneath tubular structures of delicate texture, which served both as a cover to the spider and her cocoon. In form and spinningwork these differed in no essential particular from the tubes of Drassids and Epeira and the cocooning tents of Orbweavers. This, I believe, is a common habit, particularly with the mother Laterigrade at the cocooning period. So far, then, as she may be said to possess in any degree the instinct of nest building, she displays a tendency to adopt the typical form, and screens herself within a tube.

[1] Moggridge: Harvesting Ants and Trapdoor Spiders, page 183, pl. 13.
[2] Tarentula arenicola Scudder.   [3] Tarentula tigrina McCook.

As a result of the above comparative study of the nesting industry of the spider fauna, we may conclude that there is one germinal or typical

One Typical Form. form of nest among all the tribes, which form is the tube. Around this common and rudimentary form the greatly varied and widely divergent nests of spiders, whether known as domiciles, dens, tents, tunnels, or caves, may be grouped in series of more or less modified forms.

It may be allowable to say, using the language of accommodation, that all these variations have been developed in these various species around this typical and germinal form; but the statement cannot be said to rest upon any demonstration of actual facts, and must stand simply as a convenient and appropriate formula for expressing certain relations. It is, however, a sufficiently interesting discovery that, amidst so many forms which at first sight appear to be widely different, one is able to trace with striking and manifest clearness a common plan.

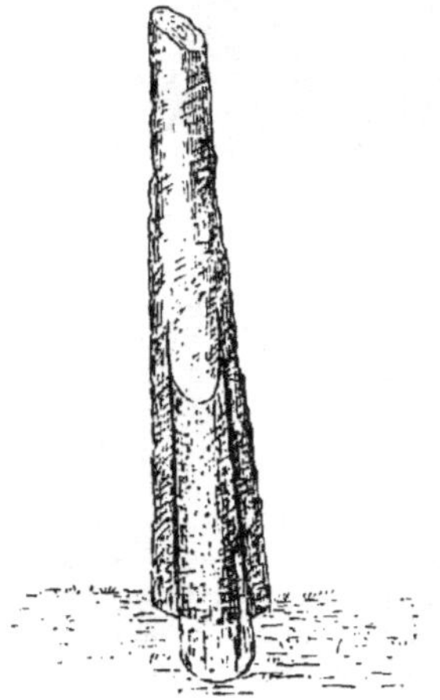

Fig. 307. Partly covered and sanded frame of Atypus Abboti.

As one considers them, he is conscious of something like the feelings with which he wanders through the studio of an artist of fecund and versatile genius. Variety of invention and detail in execution are certainly manifest; but everywhere, also, are apparent to the critical student traces of a single mind, whose dominant characteristics inevitably assert themselves in its products. The details vary; the Author's style is one. Perhaps this unity of plan is not to be wondered at, when we reflect that the physiological characteristics of spiders in all tribes and species are not widely different, and hence the functions might be expected to find very similar expressions, at least in certain fundamental points.

III.

In comparing the detailed studies of the manner in which the various tribes of spiders construct the typical tubular nest, one reaches the conclusion that there is little or no difference in the processes as

Uniform Manufacturing Method. pursued by individuals. When Epeira constructs a tubular den, she proceeds in her work in precisely the same way as Agalena when laying out the tubular part of her snare, or as Abbot's Atypus, the Purseweb spider, when constructing the long tube within which she spends her life. So, also, the Basket Argiope, when spreading the thickening shield which forms the centre of her orb, has the same method as the Speckled tubeweaver or the Medicinal spider when spreading out the carpet like structure or the pouched bag which form respectively the snares of those species.

I have described at length the method in a paper upon the habits of the Purseweb spider,[1] and it will fairly represent the action of all other species making similar dwelling places. The characteristic tube **Method of Atypus** of the Purseweb spider is spun against the trunk of a tree, extending several inches above the surface of the ground and about an equal distance beneath it. (Fig. 303.) The first stage in constructing this tube is to stretch a series of lines about two inches from the surface of the ground to various points on the surface of the tree, until a circular or nearly circular row is formed, extending from the tree to the

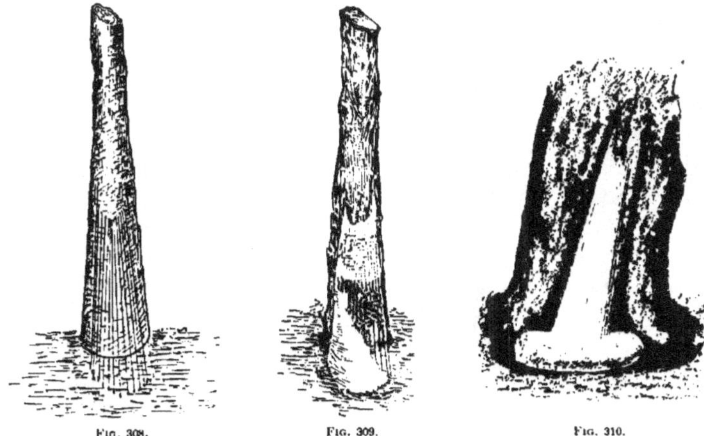

FIG. 308. FIG. 309. FIG. 310.

FIG. 308. The frame of original lines stretched against a stock. FIG. 309. The frame partly covered over; the spider is seen within putting on the weft. FIG. 310. The completed tube, with a small cross tube woven at the base.

ground. This forms a frame of straight lines, which is the foundation of the tube. (Fig. 308.) The spider now passes within this structure, and, clinging to the threads with her feet, moves her abdomen simultaneously backward and forward and up and down, meanwhile issuing from the spinnerets thickened lines, which adhere to the framework. In other words, the framework constitutes the warp, and the lines issued thereafter the woof of her texture. (Fig. 309.) As the threads are drawn out from the spinnerets they are beaten down upon the frame lines by the

[1] Proceedings Academy Natural Sciences, Philadelphia, 1888, pages 203–18. "The Nesting Habits of the American Purseweb Spider."

spinnerets, not interwoven with them. When a sufficient number has been laid upon the original frame, by the repeated spinning and beating action of the spider, the whole presents the appearance of a thickened sheet wrought into the form of a tube. (Fig. 310.)

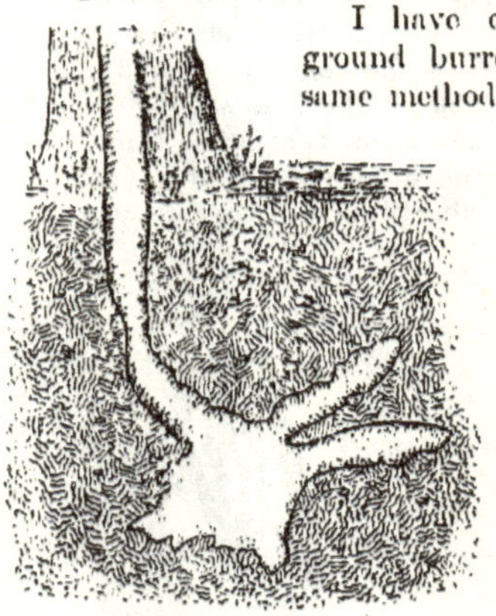

I have observed the overspinning of an underground burrow by a Purseweb in a glass jar. The same method was followed, except that the frame lines were spun against the concavity of the burrow and the inner surface of the glass. The spider then proceeded to thicken over the frame by spinning against it little ribbons of silk and beating them down with her long spinnerets. When hanging head downward, with claws clasping the frame lines, and spinning upward against the roof of her burrow (Fig. 312), she presented to the observer a rather odd appearance. No doubt this is the mode by which the spider silklines the underground part of her tubular snare which extends beneath the sand sometimes as far as above the surface, and is either single, or branched, after the manner represented in Fig. 311. (See also Fig. 303.)

Fig. 311. Purseweb spider's nest. View below ground, as well as above. The subterranean terminus is expanded and branched.

The same method of spinning is used by our American tarantula, Eurypelma hentzii, in weaving the rug upon which it often loves to stay when in artificial confinement. In the act of spinning, the long posterior spinnerets are curved upward and forward (which is, indeed, an habitual position with this tribe), and from the spinning tubes along the exterior part of the spinneret are given

The Ta-rantula's Rug.

out numerous fine threads. These are pressed to the ground by the downward motion of the spinnerets. The abdomen is then lifted up, and by this action the threads are drawn out. Again the downward motion is repeated, and simultaneously the end of the abdomen to which the spinnerets are attached receives a lateral

Fig. 312. Purseweb spider working the weft on an underground frame.

motion that causes the threads to be spread over the surface of the ground. At the same time the animal slowly moves its whole body around, as upon a pivot, thus dispersing the silk over a circular patch of surface about equal in diameter to twice the length of its body, or to the spread of its legs.[1]

Thus the thick texture of the sheeted web is produced by the act of beating downward with the long spinnerets, repeated motions of which up and down make little loops, which thicken over the surface and are beaten down and then smoothed over by the spinnerets. (Fig. 313.) It will be seen that this action does not differ from that of all other spiders while engaged upon similar spinningwork.

The spinning habit is not greatly developed among the Lycosids, although that group of spiders furnishes some interesting examples of nest making. **Among Lycosids.** Nevertheless, in the work of making the cocoon, in which its spinning industry is most conspicuous, we find Lycosa dropping into the common method of fabrication. I have observed and described the mode of spinning a cocoon, which is as follows: A circular cushion of beautiful white silk about three-fourths of an inch in diameter is the piece out of which the round egg bag of Lycosa is made. In spinning this the spider's feet clasp the circumference of the cocoon, and the body

Fig. 313. Tarantula putting the weft upon her rug. (Eurypelma Hentzii.)

of the animal is slowly revolved. The abdomen is lifted up, thus drawing out short loops of silk from the extended spinnerets, which, when the abdomen is dropped again, contract and leave a flossy curl of silk at the point of attachment. The abdomen is also swayed back and forward, the filaments from the spinnerets following the motion as the spider turns, and thus an even thickness of silk is laid upon the eggs.[2]

I have seen Saltigrades engage in the same act of spinning their cocoon and silken cylindrical nest, and the words used for describing the above might be almost exactly applied to the behavior of the Attoïd. The details of these methods of cocoon making will be reserved for the proper chapter in the second volume of this work. But, in the meanwhile, this reference to the method falls into the purpose of present thought.

[1] See my notes on the Age and Habits of the American Tarantula. Proceed. Acad. Nat. Sci., 1887, page 377.

[2] See my note on "How Lycosa Fabricates her Round Cocoon." Proceed. Acad. Nat. Sci. Phila., 1884, page 138.

If we turn to the Tubeweavers we find a varied and interesting field of spinning industry in the making of snares, nests, and cocoons. In all of these it may be confidently said that the methods, as far as known, are substantially the same as those described as prevailing in other tribes. A few illustrations show this fact.

Methods of Tubeweavers.

The interesting and well known water spider of Europe, *Argyroneta aquatica*, weaves in water a bell shaped tent (Fig. 314), within which she dwells, deposits her egg sac, and rears her young. The following observation indicates that even in this seemingly unnatural element the same general method characterizes the spider's weaving. Fig. 315 represents a patch of spinningwork made by this water spider upon a glass within which she was confined, and drawn by Mr. Underhill.[1] On examining the central part of this patch, it appeared, both to the naked eye and to the microscope, like a piece of the spider's cocoon. Certain broad threads at the edge of the patch at once explained the method by which this close and even texture was obtained. They are represented by Fig. 315, c, as they appeared under the microscope. They seem to have been produced, as in the cases above described, by the spider erecting or placing, parallel to one another, a series of spinning tubes, which emitted separate and parallel threads, instead of lines directed towards one point.

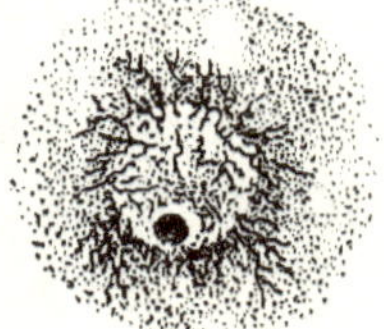

Fig. 314. The bell shaped nest of Argyroneta or the water spider, under water.

The Water Spider.

These bands Mr. Underhill supposed to be the product of the anterior spinnerets, while the other two threads, a and B, are emitted by the posterior and middle spinnerets.

When Agalena nævia wishes to extend the borders of her sheet like snare, she proceeds in the same way, carrying first various lines beyond the margin to the desired distance, which lines are stretched across the foliage or other surface that forms the nest site. When the desired number of these lines has been laid down, the Tubeweaver moves backward and forward over them, spinning out all the while a stream of silk, at the same time moving her long spinnerets up and down from the surface of the

Agalena's Method.

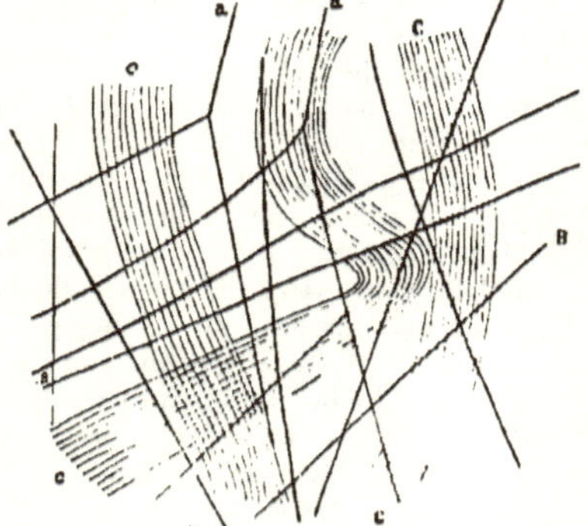

Fig. 315. Highly magnified piece of the Water spider's web. a, a, B B, the single original or warp lines; c, c, c, the banded filaments forming the weft.

[1] "Science Gossip," 1875, page 134.

frame, by this vertical movement drawing out the thread and beating it back again, thus thickening the weft upon the lines. In this manner a sheet of thin texture is rapidly formed, and this, in the course of time, is thickened by a repetition of the same mode of spinning. This is exactly the method, as I have heretofore shown, pursued by Argiope cophinaria in thickening her shield. (See Chapter VI. and illustrations.) It is the manner in which the dome like tents of all the Epeïroid spiders are constructed. When the method of procedure has been ascertained in one spider, the arachnologist may be assured that he has the key to the methods practiced among all the tribes.[1]

IV.

The tube making faculty appears to be, as far as secondary causes are concerned, the natural result of the instinct of self protection. It is, perhaps, most natural that the lower animals should seek to protect **Origin of** themselves within barriers formed by their body secretions, as is **Tube-** the case among the larvæ of many insects. The restless move-**weaving** ments of the body, characteristic of these creatures, conjoined **Habit.** with the instinct to cover themselves up, to protect themselves from unfavorable weather changes and from the approach of enemies, may be a sufficient natural explanation of the origin of the tube making habit.

Thus, the silk moth larva, while secreting silk from the glands which open on the upper lip, moves backward and forward, continually distributing its secretions, and at the same time, by the motion of its body, limits them to the borders of the space around which it moves. In the same way the social caterpillars have learned to shut themselves within their well known tent, which presents so largely the appearance of a designed structure, but which, in its origin at least, may have been quite as much the result of accident, the silken secretion simply hardening around the limits of the space through which the restless creatures move, and which by their motions they keep free from threads.

In like manner the larva of the ant, at the moment when nature brings upon it the sense of the great change from its larval to its pupal state, moves backward and forward within a narrow space, secreting its **Tube-** delicate silk, which by its movements is pushed away from di-**making** rect contact with its body, and hardens into the little case or **Larvæ.** pouch in which itself at last is encompassed. Thus we may suppose that, in an entirely natural way, the Supreme Overforce, while

---

[1] It took many years of observation, numberless experiments by day and throughout many nights of careful watching among the various species, to reach this conclusion. But I am so confident that I have fully demonstrated it, that I have no hesitation in declaring the general principle here announced. I have little doubt that subsequent studies of other species in all the tribes will verify the generalization.

Fig. 316.

Fig. 317.

Fig. 316. The rolled leaf nest of a Tortricid moth larva, made among ferns   Fig. 317. A rolled
leaf nest of the Shamrock spider, made among ferns.

governing all creatures and all their actions, has developed in certain arthropods the habit of spinning tubes or cylinders as a protection to the body.

Among the spider fauna this habit is particularly prominent. It does not exist, as with insects, in a larval state, but in the perfect animal, the only one, with possibly one exception,[1] of which we have knowledge. **Psocidæ.** The belief has been expressed that both sexes of the Psocidæ possess the power of spinning a web which McLachlin affirms is not distinguishable from that made by spiders.[2] This habit, which characterizes the larvæ of insects, is carried forward to the perfect animal among the Araneæ, and, as we have seen, the habit of protecting themselves by tubular spinningwork, in one form or another, exists among some species of every tribe of spiders.

One who is conversant with insect architecture cannot but be struck with the resemblance between the nests of spiders and those made by the larvæ of certain insects. Brief allusion has already been made to this, but it may be worth while to call attention more distinctly thereto.

Very often I have met, along the seashore in New Jersey, a species of leaf roller Tortricid moth, whose species I do not know, that has reminded me of the nests of Epeira trifolium spun among the ferns, and **Epeira and Moth Larva.** which is one of the most beautiful examples of the nesting habit to be found among spiders. The two objects may sometimes be seen almost side by side, and even the most casual observer would scarcely fail to note that they must have been constructed upon the same fundamental principles of architectural instinct. There are, of course, differences which one may note without very acute perception; but the resemblances are certainly worthy of consideration, and it is to these that I have here wished to call attention. (See Figs. 316 and 317.)

The nest of Theridium riparium is constructed on very much the same principle as that of the larva of the caddis fly, or case worm, a Neuropterous insect which is very well known, and whose remarkable **Theridium and the Caddis Fly.** architectural habit has excited the interest of naturalists. Several illustrations of the nests of this insect are given.[3] The first represents a case made of bits of moss, and is the work of Limnophilus rhombicus. (Fig. 323.) The second represents the case worm, found in great abundance by Professor Packard in Labrador, and which he supposes to be the work of Limnophilus subpunctulatus, the most abundant species found in Labrador. The case is straight, cylindrical, and built of coarse gravel, and the larva is a thick, cylindrical, whitish worm. The next figure (Fig. 320) represents the nest of Limnophilus

---

[1] *Psocus sexpunctatus.* See a note of the author in Proceed. Acad. Nat. Sci. Phila., 1883, page 278.

[2] Monograph British Psocidæ, Entomological Monthly Magazine, Vol. III, 1866-7, page 268.

[3] These are copied from Packard's "Guide to the Study of Insects," page 617.

flavicornis, a European species which is often constructed of small shells; and Fig. 324 illustrates the case or nest of the European Limnophilus pellucidus, which is formed of large pieces of leaves laid flat over each other.

I am not familiar with the larva's method of putting together these nests, although I have some very interesting ones in my possession, not greatly differing in construction from those which are here illustrated. The principle on which the various particles of material are collected and placed together to form the perfect cover made by the little worm cannot differ greatly, judging from architecture alone, from those which regulate

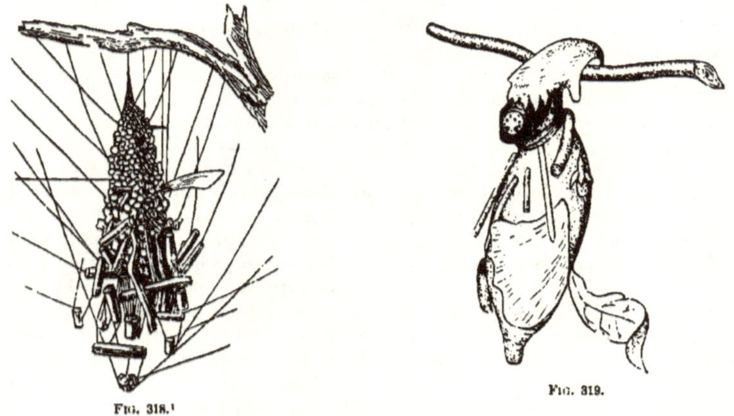

FIG. 318.[1]

FIG. 319.

Nests of Theridium (Fig. 318), and the Bag worm (Fig. 319).

the behavior of Theridium riparium when she builds the nests described upon the preceding pages. (Fig. 318.)

A like reflection is suggested by the work of the well known bag worm, or basket worm, Theridopterix ephemeraeformis. (Fig. 319.) This is the caterpillar of a species of moth, sometimes known as the house builder moth (Oiketici). The insects are also called Canephorae, or basket carriers, and the Germans call them Sackträger, or sack bearer. The baskets of the above species are among the most familiar objects in this geographical district, and may be seen hanging in multitudes to the limbs of trees after the leaves have fallen in autumn. I have been greatly interested in studying the whole process by which these interesting objects are made, and have described it elsewhere.[2]

Theridium and Bag Worm.

---

[1] The part above the horizontal line on the left of the figure was made of pellets of clay in natural site; that below of material artificially supplied. "Science Gossip," January, 1868, page 12, sq.

[2] In my "Tenants of an Old Farm," Chapter XIX., "Housekeeping in a Basket."

The material which is fastened upon the internal silken sack consists of particles of the food plant upon which the caterpillar is reared. These are the stems and other rejected portions of the plant, left when feeding, and which hang to the silken bag on the outside. They are sometimes so thickly placed that the silken sack is entirely covered, as at Fig. 325, which is a specimen from the Southern States in my collection of insect architecture.

One might extend these comparisons much further and find that the striking resemblances between the protective architecture of spiders and that of the larvæ of insects might be carried to the very lowest forms of life. Prof. Joseph Leidy, in his monumental work upon the Rhizopods,[1] has presented numerous forms of these creatures, that lie so far down in the scale of animated being, which at once call to mind the habits of the caddis fly larva and the larva of the house builder moth. Fig. 326 represents the Rhizopod, Difflugia urceolata, a common form found in ditches in the neighborhood of Philadelphia. Ordinarily the shell of this Difflugia strikingly resembles the ancient Roman amphora. The body of the shell varies from a globular shape to a more or less ovoid form; the principal extremity or fundus is more obtusely rounded, or more or less acute; and sometimes it is rounded and more or less acuminate. The shell is composed, as is generally the case in other species of the genus, of colorless angular particles of quartz sand, mostly of larger ones scattered with more or less irregularity, while the intervals are occupied with smaller ones. Frequently larger stones occupy the larger shell; but, passing this, they gradually become smaller, approaching the edge of the rim or reflected lip.[2]

Another Rhizopod which suggests at once the architecture of the bag worm is represented at Fig. 327. Difflugia acuminata is one of the most common forms of Rhizopods, and is very generally distributed. Not unfrequently, as in the figure, the shell is composed of colorless, chitinoid membrane incorporated with quartz sand, alone or with this and intermingled diatoms. In this the grains of sand are usually closely placed in juxtaposition at and near the mouth of the shell, but are elsewhere scattered and separated by wide intervals. In some cases the shell is more or less covered with large diatoms, which are generally adherent in the length, and diverge upward beyond the boundary of the shell.[3]

Not only do we find these striking resemblances in the external architecture of these widely separated creatures, but apparently we find the same purposes originating the architecture. The house builder moth larva constructs her thatched domicile in order to cover over its soft body;

---

[1] "Fresh Water Rhizopods of North America," Washington, 1879.
[2] Op. cit., page 107, and pl. 14, Fig. 3.
[3] Leidy, Idem, page 111, pl. 13, Fig. 21.

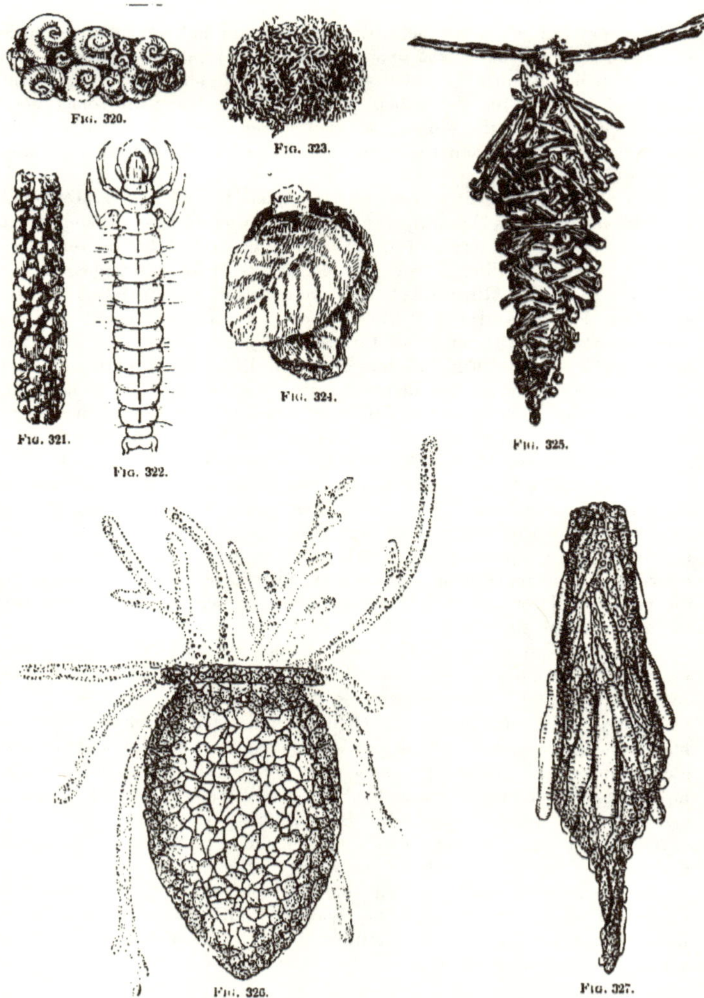

A COMPARATIVE VIEW OF THE NESTING ARMOR OF RHIZOPODS, CADDIS FLIES, AND BAG WORMS.

FIG. 320. Case of Caddis (Limnophilus flavicornis), made of minute shells.   FIG. 321. Case of gravel, made by the larva (FIG. 322) of a Caddis fly.   FIG. 323. Case of Caddis worm (Limnophilus rhombicus), made of moss.   FIG. 324. Case of Caddis (Limnophilus pellucidus), made of pieces of leaves.   FIG. 325. The basket or thatched bag of the Bag worm (Theridopterix).   FIG. 326. Shell of a Rhizopod, Difflugia urceolata (variety amphora), built up of quartz sand. > 100 diameters. (After Leidy.)   FIG. 327. Shell of Rhizopod, Difflugia acuminata, composed of quartz sand and diatoms.   200 diameters. (After Leidy.)

the caddis fly builds over her body her tiled tube of shells or pebbles, or covers it with thatched moss, for the same purpose. The animated body of

Common Architectural Aim sarcode known as a Rhizopod evidently is moved by the desire to preserve its protoplasmic structure, when it gathers diatoms and bits of sand from which to rear around itself its beautiful architectural armor or encasing wall. The nest making spider, Epeira trifolium or Theridium riparium, is manifestly moved by the same disposition to shelter the soft abdomen, which is the most assailable and vulnerable part of her body.

From the lowest form of Rhizopod, through these more highly organized insects and arachnids, we may ascend to man, who occupies the sum-

Man's Architecture. mit of the zoological pyramid, the crown and king of creation, and note the same outcome of life. In the great cathedrals which he rears to the Almighty, or in the humble cottages which he builds, alike in stone wall, in tiled or shingled or thatched roof, we may see the methods of his humbler fellows of the creature world, only carried out upon a loftier scale and with a nobler purpose.

Thus, in the nesting architecture of living things, the naturalist may see, as on so many other fields of observation, the harmony which pervades creation.

> " From harmony, from heavenly harmony,
>   This universal frame began :
> From harmony to harmony,
>   Through all the compass of the notes it ran,
>   The diapason closing full on Man."

What is the meaning of this harmony? By what dominating Force, through what natural laws has it been accomplished and is it main-

Universal Harmony tained? These are problems which have occupied the thoughts of students of nature, and upon which they have honestly and earnestly divided. We may indulge the hope that when the realm of life has been sufficiently explored, from the larger knowledge of facts there may issue, in this matter also, substantial harmony.

By whatever theory one may account for these facts, certainly the facts themselves show that an unexpected degree of harmony pervades all the home building industry of the smaller creatures that inhabit the globe in common with more highly organized animals. The traces everywhere appear of one common origin, or (as many would prefer to express it) of one Originating Mind, whose Will, the source of all natural forces, is expressed in the infinite variety of forms and methods which these natural forces are working and have wrought through all the ages of time.

CHAPTER XIX.

THE GENESIS OF SNARES.

It now remains to trace the relations which exist between the various forms of spinningwork treated in detail or alluded to in this volume.

Spinning-work Relations. In attempting this I am well aware that great difficulties lie in the path, and am not unmindful of the fact that one is inclined in such a task to give greater or less play to imagination.

Moreover, the limited knowledge of the spinning habits of our spider fauna hinders me from tracing the connecting links that would perhaps show intimate relations between industries which now seem widely separated. Nevertheless, one cannot well resist the effort.

In considering the natural relationships of snares it is at least convenient to proceed from the standpoint of a gradual evolution or development of the spinning habit. In justice to my own belief, it is proper **A Hypothetical Standpoint.** to state that such a course is entirely hypothetical. As far as I have been able to grasp the subject and reach conclusions therefrom, there appears to be no ground, either in the habit of existing fauna or in the records of geologic ages, to justify the assertion that any one tribe of spiders has been the parental stock out of which the others have proceeded, or that any one form of spinningwork has been the germinal form from which all the varied aranead industries have had a natural and gradual growth.

Nevertheless, in that scientific use of the imagination which is a most advantageous and often a necessary factor in exhibiting the relations of things, it is proper for one to so far take advantage of current beliefs as to express certain relationships, which very clearly and beautifully appear, as though they had originated through diverging or interblending lines from one common source. Doubtless many of my readers, certainly most of my scientific friends, will think that my tentative standpoint expresses the real state of things; and if the truth rests with them I shall be glad to thus help them make it appear.

I.

As the starting point of our first comparative view I take the Trapline. The simplest use of the thread or combination of threads thus denominated may be seen in the habits of such a spider as Epeira strix. This aranead, like the majority of her congeners, forsakes her web during the day and seeks some near by retreat. This may be a curled leaf, the shelter of a projecting bit of bark, a recess in the rocks, or other like refuge, in which she is measurably protected from her enemies. As she **Genesis of a Trapline.** abandons the centre or hub of her orb, upon which she has been hanging during the night and early morning, she leaves behind her the precautionary thread which is habitually drawn out after spiders when they move, and which I have called the dragline.

This thread is carried from the hub to the point of retreat. It can nearly always be traced by a careful examination of the orb, and by means of it the practiced spider hunter can frequently trace this **A Simple Trail.** most secretive species to her snare. This is not universally the case, however, as I have sometimes been foiled in attempting to find Epeira strix by her dragline. However, the custom prevails, and, with less secretive species, the line can more readily be used as a trail to the spider's retreat. I do not know that this line serves any other purpose than a sort of gangway by which the spider leaves her web and returns to it when the evening shades begin to fall. Nevertheless, one may recognize in it, perhaps, the germ of the trapline.

With other species, such as Epeira trifolium and Epeira insularis, the trapline is more

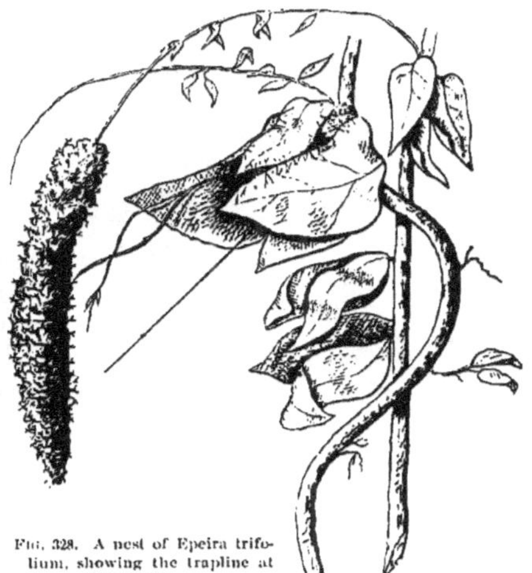

Fig. 328. A nest of Epeira trifolium, showing the trapline at the nest terminus.

sharply differentiated from the snare itself, and is specialized in its uses. It is a line connected by more or less deltated branches with the **Trail and Telegraph** retreat of the spider in her leafy or silken tent. This is habitually a single line in the species just named. The end by which it is connected with the hub of the orb diverges into several branches,[1] forming a delta or triangular pyramid, the basal lines of which seize the hub at several points. The opposite extremity enters the nest and is held by one or more of the spider's feet (Fig. 328); usually one of the front legs is extended and grasps the line with the claw. In this manner the trapline is held very taut. The branching portions draw

---

[1] See the various figures in Chapter XVII. illustrating this point.

up the various lines of the snare, so that all the radii, particularly, are held in a tense condition.

This tension of the trapline and radial lines makes the whole web an efficient telegraphic instrument for conveying to the spider in her den or domicile any vibration caused by insects entangled upon the snare. When by such telegraphy the capture of an insect is communicated to the sensitive feet of the spider, she immediately rushes along her trapline to the hub, and from that point to her prey. Thus, in the typical Orbweaver's snare, the trapline serves the two purposes—first, of communicating to the proprietor the presence of entangled insects; and, second, of affording a gangway to the net and back again to the tent. In short, the incidental dragline appropriated to the uses of a gangway, in Epeira strix, is here specialized into a trail and a telegraph.

As far as I can positively affirm, no other than these two purposes are served by the trapline in these species. However, it is the habit of spiders who thus use this specialized instrument to frequently pull upon it, increasing the tension by drawing it towards themselves and then letting it go again, making a series of rapid jerks. I have never been able to observe that this motion had any purpose or effect to increase the entanglement of an insect, and have always regarded it simply as a means of determining the presence, weight, and energy of the victim, and thus estimating the degree of caution necessary in approaching it. If the insect be quiescent, as often occurs, the pulling and sudden relaxing of the trapline is quite sure to set it in motion again.

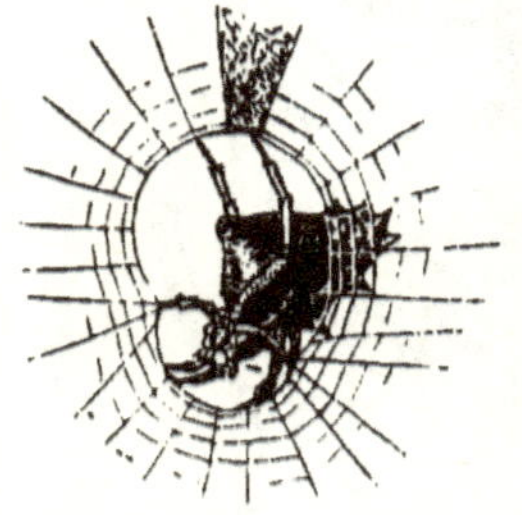

Fig. 329. *Acrosoma rugosa* hanging at her hub, to show the radii clustered on the claws.

Jerking the Trapline.

It might, perhaps, be observed in this connection that even when the spider is hanging on guard at the centre of her orb, she spins a series of deltated lines, the apex of which is grasped by several claws of the legs, and the opposite ends of which are attached to the radii in such a way as to cause a direct communication between all parts of the orb and the sensitive feet within which these lines are thus converged. Examples of this are especially observable in the various species of Acrosoma. Fig. 329 shows the manner in which Acrosoma rugosa, when hanging upon the open hub of her snare, thus gathers converging radii into her claws. A like habit in the cases of Acrosoma mitrata and spinea is illustrated by Figs. 112 and 113, page 127. In the same manner that the trapline is jerked by nest building Epeiras, in order to tighten it and test the presence of insects, this series of footlines is also frequently jerked, and apparently for the same purpose.

Footlines.

While I cannot record observations which justify me in asserting that this use of the trapline, or the similar use of the footlines, aids in entangling insects, I can very well believe that it may frequently contribute more or less to this result. This may be done either by the mechanical momentum of the lines which are swung around the insect by the sudden tightening and releasing thereof; or by exciting the insect and causing it to move its wings and legs, thus entangling it more and more within the viscid spirals.

A young Epeira domiciliorum well illustrated the general tendency in this direction when under special compulsion of circumstances in the capture of prey. When observed, her web had been badly damaged **Utilizing Web Fragments.** by insects. At the sides all the spiral lines had disappeared, and a few patched radii alone remained. On the upper part of the orb were a few spirals. A segment remained in tolerable condition on the lower part of the snare, but it also was greatly damaged by the fracture of some of the radii. The spider had spun a number of lines from the hub to the spinning space, and these, with the remaining radii, were gathered together in all the fore feet and pulled very taut. The upper part of the web was also tightened, but to a less extent, by the action of the two hind feet. But on the sides the web appeared to hang loose, and, taking a side view of it (Fig. 330), one could readily see how the whole action of the spider was bent upon keeping the valuable portion of the web in a taut condition, ready for service, while the other parts were left to take care of themselves. This spider had little more space available for the capture of prey than a Triangle spider with a complete web. I

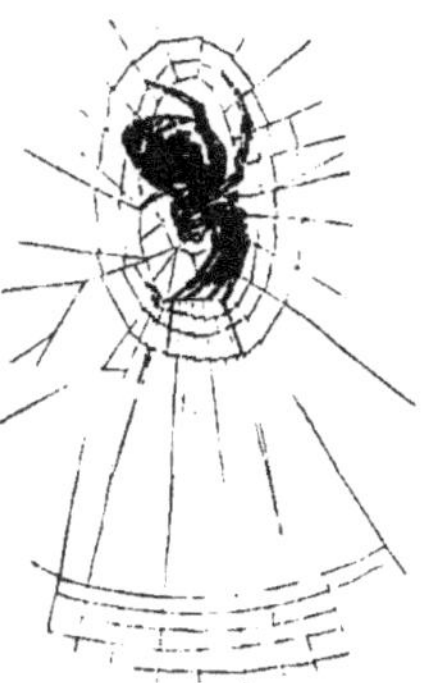

Fig. 330. Epeira domiciliorum, trapping with a fractured snare.

have no doubt that, had I waited to see an insect strike the sector thus controlled by the fore feet, I should have seen this Orbweaver let go the clustered traplines held in her claws precisely as the Ray and Triangle spiders habitually release their single traplines.

Another example was afforded by the snare of a full grown Stellate spider (Epeira stellata), which by some rare ill fortune had lost the entire central part of the orb. Yet the animal was not discouraged, but **Epeira stellata.** held her place at the hub with her legs doubled up in the manner usual to the species, and holding quite taut her little remainder of a web out on the margin, together with the connecting radii that had survived the wear and tear. Here, again, a few sectors quite disconnected from the hub were doing duty for trapping insects, as is habitually the case with the Ray spider. (See Fig. 331.) (Compare Fig. 331 with Fig. 187, page 196.)

In certain species the trapline consists of several threads, as, for example, in Epeira labyrinthea. In other species, where a single trapline is the rule, the same habit will be sometimes observed, as, for example, in the case of Zilla, whose trapline becomes a strangely complicated series of threads. (See Chapter VIII., Fig. 118.) **Multiplex Traplines.** Labyrinthea connects the central portion of her orb with the silken dome or leafy shelter within her maze of intersecting lines, by a series of straight lines sometimes quite numerous. These make a little bridgeway between the tent and the orb. When the spider is within the tent the feet are reached beyond the borders and grasp at various points these lines. Sometimes the lines are twisted into a strong and single thread, either accidentally or by the voluntary action of the spider.

When one takes a side view of the orb (see Fig. 116, page 138) he almost invariably finds the centre **Bowing Orbs.** drawn inward and upward towards the spider's retreat, thus causing all the radial lines to bow inward or toward one another. In this position the snare in its general outline has a striking resemblance to that of a Ray spider when it has been bowed by its proprietor in the manner described and illustrated at Fig. 190, page 196. Epeira triaranea

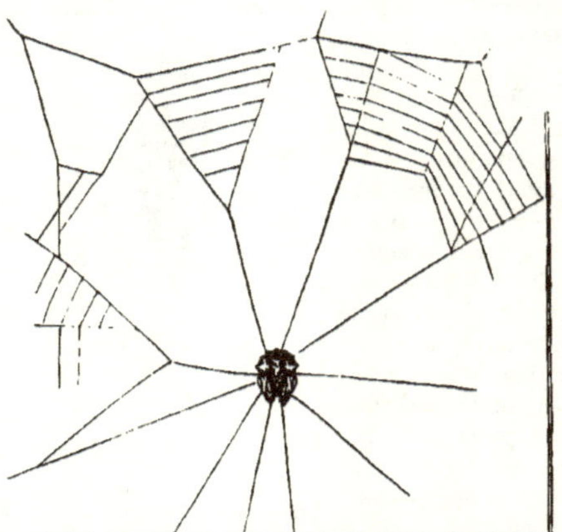

Fig. 331. The Stellate spider trapping with the scant remnants of a snare.

has the same habit of bowing her web upward and inward towards her den, and, indeed, such is the case with some other species; necessarily, more or less of this bowing of the orb must result from the habit of holding the trapline taut. But in the case of Labyrinthea the bowed condition of the web is more striking, I think, than in any other species with whose spinningwork I am acquainted, and is so noticeable that the most casual observer may see it.

We come now to the use of the trapline as it is even more highly specialized in the habit of the Triangle spider. Here the line serves not only the purposes common to the species already described, but **Hyptiotes' Trapline.** becomes a real instrument in the spider's hands for springing her net. Such Orbweavers as Epeira strix and Epeira trifolium, when they are drawing their traplines taut, necessarily leave a little slack line between the point of seizure by the fore claws and the point at which the inward end of the line is fastened to the tent or stays. But this loop is only incidental, and serves no special purpose (as far as we know) in securing the entanglement of prey. But with the Triangle spider the coil is a prominent and special feature of the net. It is always found between the hind legs and the third pair of legs, and when the snare is sprung, as already described, this coil instantly straightens out, permitting the whole net to shoot forward, and the forward motion sends every line around the entangled victim and adds to the degree of its entanglement.

When we consider the Ray spider's habit we find the trapline here even more highly specialized. It has, first, the uses common to the typical Orbweaver, that is to say, it serves for telegraphy and transition. Second, it acts as a regular trap, inasmuch as it has a prominent coil of slack line ready to be sprung at any time. **Ray Spider's Trapline.** But, further, it unites all the separate sectors of the orb into one common system, thus serving not only to spring a single net, as in the case of Hyptiotes, but a series of united nets of the same sort.

Moreover, this spider possesses the habit of moving its trapline from point to point, instead of keeping it fixed as in the case of the Triangle spider—certainly a remarkable adaptation. Further, by a simple but ingenious system of "locking" the web, that is, twisting the axis of the several rays around the extremity of the trapline, the spider causes the trapline to hold her whole snare in workable position while she resorts to any part thereof to seize her prey. Thus, also, as the daily wear and tear in capturing food destroys in succession various parts of the web, the trapline holds together and intact the remaining parts, even though quite opposite to each other.

We have thus traced the natural history of this important and useful member of the Orbweaver's web, from a simple dragline by which the animal escapes from and returns to her snare, through an interesting series of variations, to this quite specialized and complex use which marks the trapping habit of Theridiosoma gemmosum.

Thus, as a dragline it serves, first, the cautionary use of escape from danger by swinging to an anchorage; second, it affords a trail for retreat to the place of departure; third, it serves to telegraph agitation **Summary** of the snare to the proprietor; fourth, it holds the snare taut, and thus maintains its efficiency; fifth, it acts as the spring line of a genuine trap; and, sixth, it binds and locks together the united or the dissevered parts of a snare, which at the same time it also springs separately or together as need requires. Of course, I do not pretend to intimate that there has been anything like a development of the use of the trapline in the sense that there is any traceable genetic connection between the various adaptations here pointed out. So far as I know, and, perhaps, as far as can be known, every species preserves its own habit quite independent of any relation to other species of its tribe. Yet it is certainly interesting to observe the varieties of use to which this implement has been placed, and to observe that a seemingly rudimentary implement and incidental service in one species, as Epeira strix or Epiblemum scenicum, become in another and widely separated species a special instrument and a complex and permanent habit.

II.

In the foregoing section we have traced the connection between the primitive dragline and the traplines by which snares are operated, and have noted the relations or points of resemblance between the various forms of trapline among Orbweavers, from the simplest to the most complex. We may now attempt a like service for the entire system of trapping spinningwork known as the snare. In this undertaking I propose to go beyond the field of orbwebs, and take into the view the characteristic snares of all the aranead tribes.

Genesis of Snares.

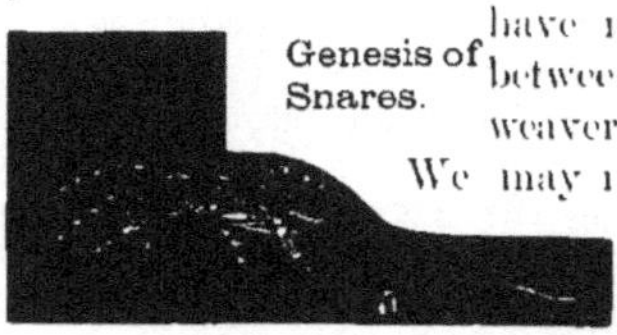

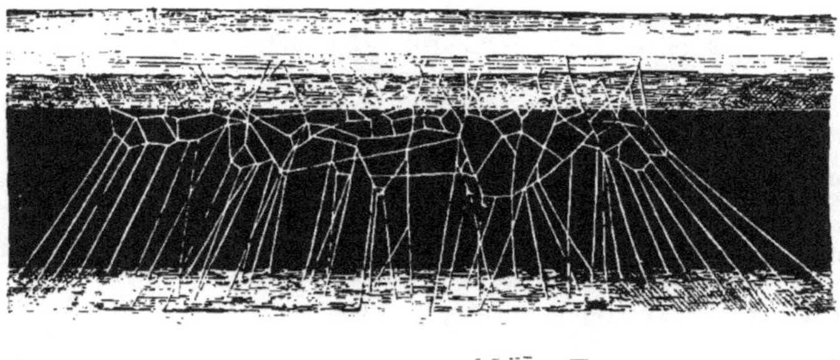

Fig. 332. The original spinning thread—the dragline, a.

Let us suppose, again, that the original form of spinningwork was the single line which has been alluded to as the dragline, and whose relationship we have just traced into the various forms of snares made by Orbweavers. If now we venture further to suppose that the spider always possessed the habit which is strongly apparent in such tribes as the Lineweavers and Orbweavers, of moving restlessly to and fro between twigs and leaves, spinning out a single thread,

The Original Spinningwork

Fig. 333. The meshed snare of Theridium, thickened at the top, and supported by silken trestles.

and making anchorages and attachments as it moves (Fig. 332), we easily arrive at the form of snare characteristic of Lineweavers.

These straggling lines, crossed at all angles, would soon, and without any apparent purpose of the spider, drop into a maze of interlacing single threads, which would present in crude form the typical snare of such

Theridium's Parental Snare. genera as Theridium, Pholcus, Ero, Neriene, and others of the Retitelariæ. That web is, in point of fact, just such a snare as I have seen other spiders make, notably the Orbweavers, by such purposeless moving back and forward as I have mentioned. To be sure, the snares of Theridium and Pholcus, as we now see them, have a little more finished character than that of the crude cobweb

FIG. 331. The sheeted web of Linyphia costata.

described, but the difference is not very great, and it therefore implies a rigid persistence in habit throughout an immense period of time.

We take another step in the development of web making, confining ourselves still to the tribe of Lineweavers. I have already described, in the chapter on Engineering Skill, the manner in which Theridium tends to thicken that portion of her snare in which she hangs back downward. This is a most natural action, resulting from several facts. First, as she passes from her resting point to the various parts of her snare in which insects are entangled, she spins out an anchorage for the dragline, by which she is sure to connect herself to this roosting spot.

Again, when she returns with her prey, she swings her abdomen around several times, before finally settling for her banquet, and at each time she ejects a similar jet of silk and unites the thickened spots by a little thread. (See Fig. 59, page 61.) Still further, in her restless movements back and forward over her web, around this central roost, she throws out similar anchorages and lines. Thus, this spot and its vicinity in a little while become much thicker than the surrounding portions of the snare.

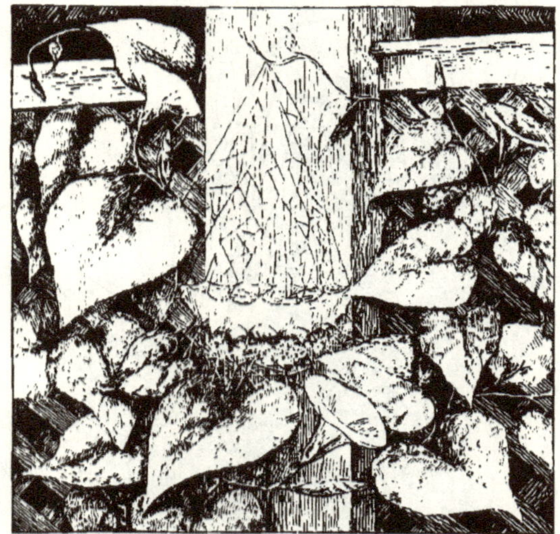

Fig. 325. Linyphia's snare among the morning glories.

Here, now, we have the germ of the typical snare of the genus Linyphia. In point of fact, it consists, as I have already shown (Chapter IX.), of a sheet like bit of spinningwork, whose fibres are very open, or, as one might otherwise express it, of a netted **From Theridium to Linyphia.** sheet of spinningwork, whose meshes are very close. Our original snare of irregularly crossed lines has thus advanced a step toward a meshed sheet like snare. In many species of the genus Linyphia the snare is simply a netted sheet, more or less horizontal, having outgoing straight lines, which support it above and below. It thus very nearly approaches, in the habitual form of its snare, that form which, as I have shown, incidentally results from the long use of Theridium's web of intersecting lines.

The step is not a large one by which we may conceive the snare just described to be transformed into that of the dome shaped web of Linyphia marginata, or the bowl shaped web of Linyphia communis. It **From Sheet to Dome.** only needs, in the former case, a little more downward pressure upon the cords at the edges, and in the latter a little more pressure upon the marginal cords upward, to complete the process. (Fig. 335.) We may now pass from Lineweavers to Tubeweavers. A glance at the snare of Agalena nœvia, for example, as represented in Fig. 215, page 217, and Fig. 336, will show how close is the resemblance between it and the snares of Linyphia already described. Agalena has a sheeted web of open spinningwork, or of close, irregular meshwork, as one may choose to put it, whose weft becomes much thickened in course of time by frequent overlaying. It also has the crossed lines extending upward, for the most part, but often downward also, representing the original rude intersecting lines of our supposed primitive snare. This retitelarian feature of the web is a most important factor in the daily capture of prey, by signaling their presence to the waiting proprietor; by arresting and trapping them so that they fall upon the sheeted premises beneath; and by actually entangling them.

Fig. 336. Sheeted web and tube of Agalena nœvia, woven on a hedge.

This most highly organized of all the Tubeweaving species has therefore substantially a Lineweaver's snare. To this structure is added the tube, which, in point of fact, is not the snare, but the nesting place. I have already shown, in the chapter on Nesting Habits (Chapter XVII.), the manner in which this feature of the snare may have been gradually developed by the natural action of the spider. In point of fact, the tube is the typical nest of all species, and is naturally formed by the movements of the spider within a limited space, spinning out as it moves the silken material which it secretes.

Theridium, and still more habitually and definitely Linyphia, will form a little tube like structure by the mere gravity of the body as it hangs **From Dome to Tube.** upon its snare in this manner: The eight legs reach upward, forming what may be called the sectional outline of a tube cut horizontally. The weight of the spider, aided by the violent agitation of its snare when struck by an insect, pulls down these eight points in such a way that a little conical or dome like tent is formed just above the spider's feet. This is illustrated at Fig. 157, page 167. The same effect is produced by the stay lines which are attached above, and which often draw up parts of the surface, as at Fig. 337, into little domes. We might almost think of these as the germinal form of the tube as it is seen in the Lineweaving species. But still more distinctly we may see the habit naturally engrafted upon such an interesting species as Theridium zelotypum or Theridium riparium, whose beautiful nesting habits are described in Chapter XVIII. In these species the inside lining of the nest of gathered sticks and rubbish is a distinct tube, which is sometimes prolonged beyond the mouth of its den.

Indeed, whenever a Theridioid spider takes its place beneath a leaf or

Fig. 337. Snare of Linyphia costata, showing tent like elevations.

other shelter, as it often does, especially under stress of continued bad weather, it is sure to spin above and around its abdomen a little **Growth of a Tube.** conical mass of lines, which, by the pressure upwards of the animal, is compacted or beaten into a concave form. If the weather continue unfavorable, or the spider is undisturbed for a considerable length of time, this little rudimentary tube will gradually make encroachments upon the leafy shelter, and will be prolonged outward and downward. Now, when the sun comes out and invites anew to web spinning, it is inevitable that the snare will be spun just beneath or close in the neighborhood of this tube like shelter. Thus it becomes easy to explain the appearance of a tubemaking habit, not only in Lineweavers, but in Orbweavers and Tubeweavers. The same is true of the Saltigrades, who persistently live in tubes; of the Laterigrades, who occasionaly form them; and of the Citigrades and Tunnelweavers, who make silk lined tubular burrows in the ground.

Among the causes that would lead directly from a simple lineweaving to a tubeweaving habit are the maternal function and instinct. The mother seeks retirement when the time of ovipositing draws near. **Influence of Maternity.** Beneath some ledge, or leaf, or stone, or twig, or other convenient shelter, she takes refuge, and there remains until the last act of maternal care. The very continuance in one place would naturally lead to the formation of a rudimentary nest in the manner just explained. The mother's promptings to protect her progeny by overspinning the eggs would lead almost inevitably, in many cases, to herself sharing the provided shelter, or extending or adapting it for her own benefit.

Fig. 338. The cocooning nest of a Laterigrade spider, Philodromus.

How natural is such a step appears from the fact that such spiders as the Laterigrades, that never (or but rarely) use any sort of snare or shelter, resort to a tubular cell for the protection of their eggs and young, and dwell within it themselves during the hatching season. (Fig. 338.) So, also, **Laterigrades and Lycosids.** Lycosids, which habitually wander in the open in pursuit of prey, when the time for cocooning comes make a burrow or nest in the ground or beneath a rock, which they silk line and use as a domicile. Thus, also, Dolomedes, which is persistently nestless and webless in ordinary habits, is drawn by maternal instincts to spin among the leaves, or in like situation, one of the most complete nests that can be found in the whole range of aranead spinningwork.

Having thus pursued the line of analogy from the Lineweaving to the Tubeweaving species, we may return upon our course for a moment to **Analogy Between Lineweavers and Orbweavers.** trace the analogies between the Lineweaving and Orbweaving species. Already, in a preceding chapter (Chapter VIII.), I have fully illustrated the peculiar habit of certain Orbweavers to combine with their typical orbicular snare the typical retitelarian snare

Fig. 339. The cocooning nest of Dolomedes sexpunctatus.

of the Lineweavers. Conspicuous examples of this are Epeira labyrinthea, Epeira triaranea, and most of the species belonging to the genus

Zilla.   In point of fact, the Lineweaving habit seems to drop into the spinningwork of all the Orbweavers with more or less facility.   Such a genus as Argiope is able to swing out from either side of its orb a snare which, considered separately, is entirely characteristic of the Lineweavers. (Chapter VI., Fig. 96.) It will probably be sufficient in this connection to refer the reader to the figures and facts contained in Chapter VIII. (See Figs. 115 and 123.)

Fig. 340.   Coöperative housekeeping between Epeira labyrinthea and Linyphia communis.

An interesting illustration of this commingling of typical habits was once observed upon a bare, dead branch of a bush. Within the branching limbs a Labyrinth spider had established her peculiar snare.

Coöperative House-keeping.

The delicate orb swung at one side, and a maze of crossed lines containing the nesting tube was woven above the orb. Close by a female Linyphia communis had spun her snare, which consists of a bowl of loose sheeted spinningwork and a maze of retitelarian lines hung above it. Now, it so happened that these two neighbors wrought their snares so close to each other that they really interblended. The cross lines of Labyrinthea and the cross lines of Linyphia were so interwoven that it was impossible for me to determine the

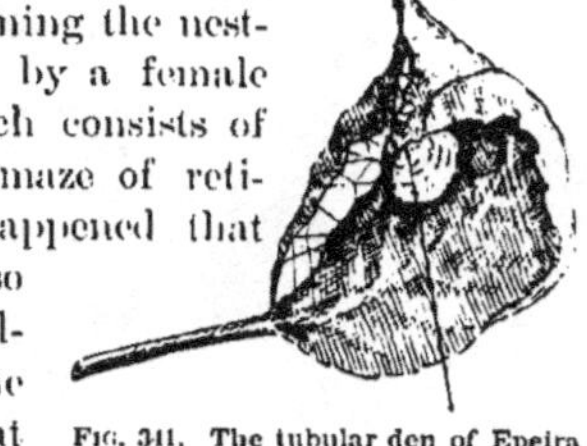

Fig. 341.   The tubular den of Epeira thaddeus within a sewed leaf.

boundary line between the two webs, or to say at what point the work of the one ended and the other began. (Fig. 340.) It was a case of coöperative housekeeping, something like that which I have already illustrated in the case of two Labyrinth spiders (see Fig. 120, page 135), the difference being that in this case the coöperation was between species of different tribes, instead of the same species. Nothing could better illustrate the community of habit, in the particular of spinning retitelarian snares, than such a juxtaposition as this.

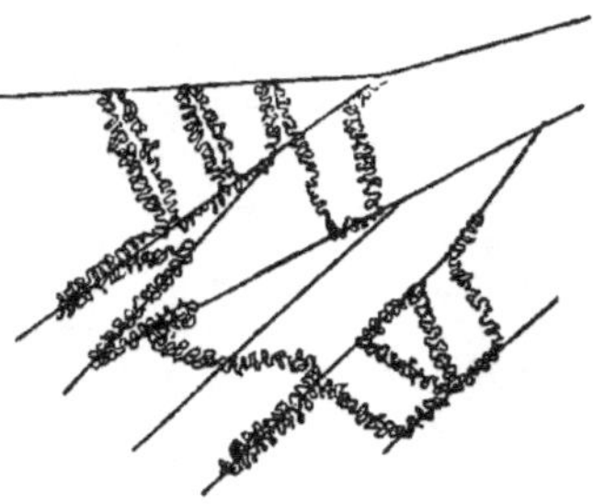

Fig. 342.   The curled thread of Dictyna on its supporting radiating lines. (After Emerton.)

We have already seen how the tube is used habitually by certain species of Orbweavers, as, for example, Epeira strix, Epeira triaranea, Labyrinthea, and Thaddeus (Fig. 341), and, indeed, by all the nest making species, such as the Furrow, Insular, and Shamrock spiders. This feature of their spinningwork is readily accounted for, and appears most closely to connect that tribe with the other tribes of the spinning fauna. It is, however, far more difficult **Origin of Orbwebs.** to explain the origin of such a remarkable habit as the construction of an orbicular snare of that geometric character with which the reader is now familiar. We approach it, however, from the direction of the Tubeweaving genera, as Dictyna and Clubiona. The fact has heretofore been alluded to, that they are provided with special organs, the cribellum and calamistrum, for the exudation and preparation of a flocculent thread out of which their trapping lines are spun. These threads are placed upon lines composed of ordinary spinningwork, which usually diverge with more or less regularity from some common point. The manner

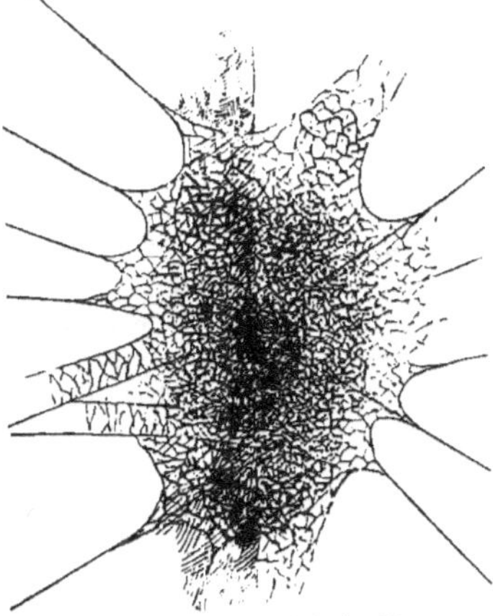

FIG. 343. The snare of the Wall loving Dictyna, woven on a Philadelphia city wall.

of placing them is well illustrated by Fig. 342, where the curled thread is seen spread along its supporting lines, and passed from one line to another, and so back and forth throughout the snare.

This would seem to be a most natural movement. It is precisely the one which, as we have explained (see Fig. 95, Chapter VI.), is re- **Dictyna's Curled Spiral Thread.** sorted to by Argiope cophinaria and Argiope argyraspis when they form the zigzag band which adorns and characterizes their round web. It is

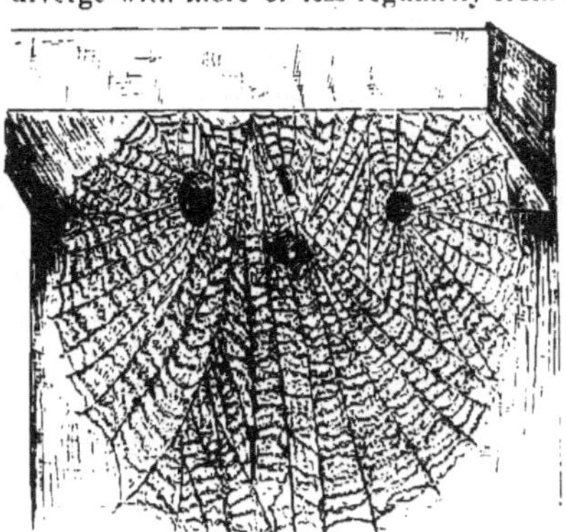

FIG. 341. Orb like snare of Dictyna philoteichus, woven against a wall.

naturally produced by the striding movement of a spider between two lines, swinging her abdomen backward and forward as she moves. In some cases, as in the web of a species of Dictyna which abounds in Philadelphia and vicinity, and everywhere spins upon our walls and fences, this peculiar snare takes upon it, in a rude way, the outlines (Fig. 343) and even in greater detail the general form of an orb, as may be seen by consulting Fig. 344. In other words, this wall loving spider starts from its little tubular nesting place and drags its lines out to surrounding adjacent points. Between these lines it then extends its flocculent thread, carrying it downward to the circumference and backwards again towards the centre, and so back and forth, until, as we have said, the rude outline of an orbweb is formed.

Now, it is of interest to know that among the Orbweavers we have two well defined families who are provided with the calamistrum and cribellum, and spin the same kind of a thread as that just described. **Orb-weaver's Curled Spirals.** Hyptiotes, or the Triangle spider, makes a web whose four diverging lines, with their interlacing flocculent spiral, might very well be represented by a section taken from the web of Clubiona or Dictyna. We are not able to trace a close relation between these two families, along any structural lines (apart from the cribellum and calamistrum), but the relation between their spinningwork is very apparent.

Yet, further, we have among the Orbweavers the family Uloborinæ, whose species construct an exact orbicular snare, in every essential respect resembling the snare of such Orbweavers as the Orchard spider (Argyroepeira hortorum) or the Extended spider (Tetragnatha extensa), except that the spirals have the teased or flocculent characteristic of Clubiona, instead of the viscid beaded armature common with Orbweaving species. Thus our sectoral snare of Hyptiotes with its flocculent spiral lines has become a complete orb; or, in other words, the circular sector appears as a full circle, retaining its flocculent interradials.

It is interesting here to note, that while the Triangle spider, on the one hand, is connected with the Tubeweavers by this peculiar flocculent thread, and, on the other hand with the species that spin full **The Ray Spider's Link.** orbs by the same characteristic thread, it is connected with the Orbitelariæ at another point by the interesting species known as the Ray spider. That is to say, the Ray spider has the viscid armature common to the Epeïroids, and its snare is arranged in orbicular form, like that of Uloborus and other Orbweavers. But, strangely, the various sectors of the circle are so combined that they can be managed wholly or in part in the same peculiar manner which characterizes the Triangle spider. That is to say, the trapline is held with a coil of slack thread above the two hind feet, and the various sectors of the circular webs are snapped off separately or unitedly by the same spring movement that marks Hyptiotes, and which is fully described in Chapters XII. and XIII.

In considering the relations which the snares of Orbweavers bear to those of other tribes, one cannot overlook the important characteristic **Viscid Lines.** which has been considered under the chapter relating to the viscid armature. That is to say, the characteristic snare of the Orbitelariæ consists of a series of straight lines covered with viscid beads, and disposed in the form of spiral concentrics, or spiral loops upon radiating lines lacking this viscid quality.

Is there any trace of this remarkable characteristic in the spinningwork of the other tribes? We have seen that the webs of Uloborus and Hyptiotes are destitute of this peculiar armature, substituting therefor the flocculent thread which has been heretofore described. We have also noted that in this particular the spinningwork of the Orbweavers finds its homologue in the snares of certain Tubeweavers, as, for example, Dictyna and Amau- **Dictyna.** robius. Concerning Dictyna, it may be stated that so careful and distinguished an observer as Bertkau, for example, offers the opinion that this genus is provided with certain glands which secrete viscid material that must be intermingled with the flocculent spinningwork which forms the cross lines of the typical snare. Undoubtedly the amount of viscid material must be very small; nevertheless, it is an interesting fact that the organs for producing it should be found among the Tubeweaving genera armed with the calamistrum. That the same organs exist in Uloborus and Hyptiotes, the Orbweaving genera provided with calamistrum and cribellum, I take for granted.

As to the snare of Amaurobius, I think that no one who has ever examined it will hesitate to say that it is provided by the spider which spins **Sticky Web of Amau- robius.** it with a considerable amount of viscid material. The way in which it sticks to one's fingers, and the entire characteristics of the thread when examined carefully, go to establish this point. I have not examined the genus by dissection, and cannot, therefore, speak from anatomical observation, but have no doubt at all that Amaurobius will be found possessed, in a yet more decided degree than the genera just noticed, with organs for the secretion of viscid material.

One other fact remains to be noted, and I confess that I speak of it with considerable hesitation. On one occasion, while studying the snare of **Are Therid- ium's Threads Viscid?** a species of Theridium which I took to be T. differens, I was surprised to find it distinctly marked with viscid globules. (Fig. 345.) They were of an irregular character, but were manifestly similar to those which form upon the snares of Orbweavers. Thinking that I might have been deceived by a little twist in the line forming natural nodules, I examined carefully and often, with the same conclusion, that the lines were beaded as with the webs of Orbweavers. I have never met with a similar case, and scarcely know what to think of this. Could it have been an abnormal act on the part of the spider forming the snare, resulting from some morbid physiological condition? Could it be that an Orbweaver had straggled upon the web of this Lineweaving species, and left some traces of her presence by emitting her peculiar viscid beads which, forming upon the retitelarian meshes, left the traces of the stranger's presence? Could I have been mistaken?

I should not have ventured even to mention this experience had I not noticed the statement made by Mr. Edward H. Robertson,[1] that the snare of Theridium nervosum in England is characterized by a similar armature. He states positively that house flies when trapped upon the snares of this species are held very tenaciously by the viscid globules which are dispersed over the intersecting lines. I do not remember to have noticed this feature attributed to any Lineweaving species by any other observer. That it must be a rare phenomenon is manifest from this fact; but may it not be that a more careful examination, with this point distinctly in view, will show results of a more decided character?

Theridium nervosum.

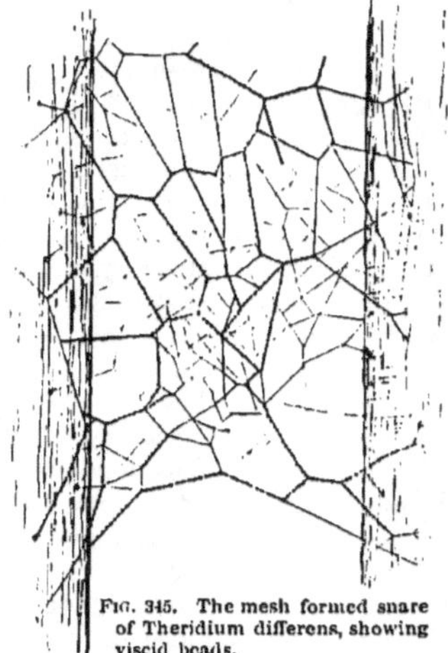

FIG. 345. The mesh formed snare of Theridium differens, showing viscid beads.

At all events, it is proper to say that there remains the possibility that one of the most striking industrial characteristics of the Orbweaving spiders may have been bestowed in some degree upon the tribe of Lineweavers whose species are most closely related to the Orbitelariæ, both in structure and economy. Thus in this particular, also, we are able to trace, though it must be confessed in a not very decided manner, an analogy between Orbweavers and at least two of the other tribes of Araneæ, viz., Tubeweavers and Lineweavers.

III.

In the preceding section I have shown how one may rise to the complex orbweb from the simplest form of snare—a few lines. It will perhaps equally illustrate the general harmony of habit which I have frequently pointed out, and the danger of fixing any arbitrary point from which development has progressed, if I show that one may reach the same terminus from a very different starting point, viz., the tubular snare. Indeed, my first conclusions settled upon this as the most natural point of departure, since (as I have heretofore shown) the

Another Starting Point.

[1] "Science Gossip," January, 1868, page 12.

tube is probably the most rudimentary form of nest. Moreover, the Tube-weavers are quite generally thought by systematic arachnologists to include the species that rank lowest in organization. Their characteristic web might, therefore, with considerable confidence be assigned the lowest place in an order of industrial development.

Our alignment of facts from this point will necessarily require the use of the same material, only shifting the relative positions. But in the movements one may catch new views of the factors concerned, their **Tube-** values and relations. Let us, then, start with some form of **weavers.** tube as the typical snare and retreat of the spider in its most rudimentary phase of life. At one end of the tribe of Tubeweavers we find the most lowly organized families, such as Gnaphosa, who limit themselves to simple tubes with the few lines which are necessary to fix them to their surroundings. At the other extreme we find the highly organized and interesting spider, Agalena nœvia, whose tube has developed from its outer extremity into a widespreading sheet or pouch. This, again (which is another manifestation of spinning habit), is supported by outgoing straight lines, which intersect each other at various points.

If now we pass from the Tubeweavers to the Lineweavers, we observe that the sheeted snare, which forms so important a part of Aga-**Tube-** lena's web, appears as the sole snare of certain species of Liny-**weavers** phia, as, for example, Linyphia costata, whose web is a simple **to Line-** netted sheet with lines above and below to support it. In other **weavers.** words, it is the snare of Agalena minus the tube.

Again, in the same genus of the Lineweavers, we observe that the intersecting lines, which are but a subordinate feature in the snare of Agalena, are a prominent feature in such species as Linyphia communis and Linyphia marginata, which, however, also retain, but in a less developed form, the sheeted portion of the snare. This part assumes the form of a bowl in the one case, or of a dome in the other. The meshes of the spinningwork lack the closeness of texture commonly observed in Agalena nœvia or the closely related Tegenaria medicinalis.

Once more, in the same tribe of Lineweavers, we find that the intersecting lines of Agalena's snare appear in the genus Theridium, where they are developed into a well organized mass of netted intersecting lines, forming a formidable snare for the capture of insects. The position of the spider within this web is entirely like that of Linyphia, and is wholly different from that of Agalena.

It must be observed, however, that even in the case of Theridium the intersecting lines have a strong tendency to approximate each other at the central point where the spider rests, until, as in the case of Theridium tepidariorum and Pholcus phalangioides, the spinningwork approaches closely that of Linyphia's dome, and more remotely the sheeted spinningwork of Agalena.

Thus we see that it is possible to trace a close resemblance and apparent relation between the spinningwork of the Tubeweavers as represented by Agalena and the principal genera of the great tribe of Lineweavers.

Let us start again, but from another standpoint, in the tribe of the Tubitelariæ. The Clubionidæ represent a very important and interesting group, many of whose genera are characterized, as we have learned, by the special spinning organs known as the cribellum and calamistrum. Let us take, for example, the genus Dictyna, a species which I have heretofore described as the Wall loving Dictyna (D. philoteichus). It is very common in the city and suburbs of Philadelphia. Its interesting snare is spun everywhere upon fences and walls, in the angles of outbuildings and upon leaves of vines and various plants. The central point is a little tube woven against the site in which the snare is pitched. From this outgoing lines proceed, diverging as they go, somewhat after the manner of the radii in an Orbweaver's web. Between these lines is spun a flocculent thread, consisting of minute filaments which have been teased by the calamistrum. This curled thread is laid in between the radii quite after the fashion of the zigzag ribbon characteristic of the orb of Argiope. That is to say, it crosses diagonally from one diverging line to another, as repre-

Dictyna's Orb like Web. sented in the Fig. 344. It is the habit of Dictyna to overlay one snare with another until the strata of spinningwork, if I may so call them, are laid several deep. I have often observed them upon the walls and fences in Philadelphia thus spun out from the central tube in all directions, until they present so strikingly the appearance of a lace collar that the most casual observer at once notes the resemblance. I think one cannot fail to see in the form of this snare a suggestion of the round web of the Orbweaver, with its radiating lines diverging from the centre.

From this peculiar snare of a representative genus of the Tubeweavers we may be easily led, by the analogy of spinningwork, to a family that confessedly lies on the very margin of the Orbweaving genera,

The Uloborinæ. namely the Uloborinæ. In the genus Hyptiotes the Triangle spider has a snare consisting of four diverging lines, or a single sector of an Orbweaver's web. Now, we are compelled to observe that the threads by which these diverging lines are united is precisely of the character of that used by Dictyna in uniting her diverging lines, and this thread is spun out by precisely the same kind of spinning organs—the cribellum and the calamistrum. We have thus established a striking relation on this side of the circuit between the Tubeweavers and the Orbweavers, as on the other side we showed a relation between the Tubeweavers and the Lineweavers.

The progress of these analogies may be further traced. Hyptiotes shows but a single sector of a circle, whose radiating lines are united by the teased thread characteristic of the tubemaking Ciniflonidæ; but we find in the same family another species, Uloborus, whose snare is a complete circle, with lines radiating from the centre all around to the circumference, precisely in the manner of Argiope and Epeira. These **Curled Spiral Threads.** lines, however, instead of being united by viscid concentrics, are united by a spiral thread precisely like that used by Hyptiotes and Dictyna. Here we see the flocculent thread upon radiating lines which appears in a genus of the Tubitelariæ, planted upon the radiating lines of a full orbed web. In other words, Dictyna may be said to have given to Hyptiotes a fraction of her habit, which Hyptiotes has developed into her fixed and characteristic snare, and in turn has handed on to Uloborus, which has multiplied the circular sector of Hyptiotes into a complete orb, while retaining the characteristic interradials of the Tube-weaving Dictyna.

But we are enabled to trace another resemblance and another variation in the habit. The most interesting spinningwork of the Ray spider, **The Ray Spider.** Theridiosoma gemmosum, may be said to be constructed fundamentally upon the plan of Hyptiotes. But that plan has been enlarged by multiplying the number of sectors. In this respect, it approaches the spinningwork of Dictyna, as represented at Fig. 344. But these several sectors or rays have been so united that they form, under certain aspects, an orbicular web. This web, by means of the trapline and the special habit possessed by the spider, can be bowed until it assumes the form of the dome shaped web of the Lineweaving Linyphia.

Here appears a remarkable variation. While the fundamental character of the Ray spider's web unites it most closely to Hyptiotes, and thus backward to Dictyna; the interradial lines show marked divergence in the direction of the Orbweavers. They are covered with viscid beads, precisely like the webs of the Epeïroids. Thus we are led from the Tubeweavers, by way of the genus Dictyna, along the line of the Triangle spider, Uloborus, and the Ray spider, to the great tribe of Orbitelariæ, whose habits and industry we have especially considered in this volume.

We can now connect these two wings of habit, which from the one extreme of the Tubitelariæ have departed towards the Lineweavers, and from the other extreme towards the Orbweavers. Let us go back for a moment to the intersecting lines which support the sheeted snare of Agalena. These, as we have seen, appear in the genus Theridium and allied genera **Agalena and Theridium.** as a well developed web of interlacing lines, massed in a labyrinthean snare. It is but a step from this spinningwork across the border into that portion of the web of Epeira labyrinthea which is known as the labyrinth or maze. This, in every respect, is a Retitelarian snare. If we were to sever the orb of the Labyrinth spider from its composite web, we should find the residuum in no respect differing from that of the typical web of Theridium tepidariorum.

Nor is Epeira labyrinthea alone in the possession of this characteristic lineweaving adjunct to its web. We have seen it in the case of Argiope, though not so strongly developed and not universally possessed by the individuals of that genus. We have seen it more decidedly and permanently fixed upon Epeira triaranea and Epeira thaddeus. But, to a greater or less extent, it may be said that the lineweaving habit belongs to the Orbweavers, though by way of association with and subordination to their typical orbicular snare.

Epeira and Theridium.

It may further be worth noting, in this connection, that not all the Epeiroids make use of a round snare. There is a wide difference between the mere sector of an orb made by Hyptiotes and the web made by Epeira triaranea or Epeira labyrinthea, and which I have denominated a sectoral orb. Yet the last named snares are only larger sectors of circles, like that of Nephila, for example. By turning to the description of the manner in which the interradials of Nephila are woven in, it will be seen that it substantially resembles that used by Hyptiotes and, indeed, by Dictyna, when placing in its spirals of flocculent thread. In other words, the sectoral orb is made by a series of loops passing over the sector of a circle larger or smaller, as the case may be.

Sectoral Orbs.

Moreover, a very considerable group of the Orbweavers spin horizontal orbs; and it is interesting to observe that Uloborus, which is related to Orbweavers generally by its round web, and to the Tubeweavers through Hyptiotes and Dictyna by their nonviscid armature of flocculent spirals, spins a horizontal web like that group of the Epeïrinæ to which the Orchard and the Hunchback spiders belong.

Horizontal Orbs.

Thus it has been shown that one may pass by natural gradations, through forms more or less distinctly marked, from the simpler and seemingly more primitive spinningwork, to the various orbicular snares, which may be considered the most complex of all known webs. These relationships are often very striking, and, on the whole, beautifully indicate the industrial unity of the entire order Araneæ.

The Conclusion.

Nevertheless, no one better knows than the student of spider habits how vast are the intervals which, at many points, have no more substantial bridge than that which imagination or analogy may supply. When arachnologists shall have more thoroughly wrought out the natural history of spiders, some of these interspaces may be united or more nearly approached. Perhaps some species have disappeared whose spinningwork might have furnished missing industrial links. Nevertheless, the veritable facts of science can go no further than to show the points and degree of approach, and exhibit the general harmony, one might almost venture to say the germinal unity, of industrial habit which marks the children of Arachne.

Unity of Industrial Habit.

THE END.

APPENDIX.

WHILE revising the index for this volume I received a note from Professor Thorell, calling my attention to a paper by Dr. Carl Apstein upon the spinning organs of spiders,[1] and particularly to a point (referred to in Chapter XIX.) on which we had had some correspondence. The paper had escaped my notice, having but recently reached the library of our Academy of Natural Sciences. Had I seen this valuable and interesting paper a few months sooner, it would have enabled me to revise and in some places correct matters which appear in certain chapters of my book. As, however, my sheets are printed, and the type distributed, it is only permitted me to make use of an Appendix Note to call attention to what I deem very important.

NOTE A.—ON THE SPINNING ORGANS.

(CHAPTER II.)

Dr. Apstein, in the paper above alluded to, has wrought out with great pains the scheme of study which years ago I had proposed to myself, as I have already intimated in my preface. He has observed with care, and presented in his plates, the exterior spinning organs of various species from the several tribes. He has also made studies and drawings of the internal spinning organs. It is most interesting to note both the agreements and the differences as thus indicated. I venture to present facsimiles of several figures, one giving the spinning organs in situ of Epeira diademata, which the reader may compare with my own partially diagramatic figure of Argiope cophinaria, page 39, Fig. 30. I also give some reproductions of the spinning spools, which Apstein has been able to locate in their connections with the various glands. This identity has heretofore been very much in doubt.

Dr. Apstein believes that the material, which forms the viscid beads upon the snares of Orbweavers and some of the Lineweavers, is secreted by the Aggregate glands. He thinks that the Tubuliform glands secrete the cocooning stuff, or the threads which envelop the eggs. The curled threads

---

[1] Bau und Function der Spinndrüsen der Araneida. Von Carl Apstein. Archiv für Naturgeschichte, 1889, pages 29-74, Plates III., IV., V.

characteristic of Uloborus, Hyptiotes, and Dictyna are secreted by what he
calls the Cribellum gland. The Lobate glands prepare the threads by
which the insect is swathed previous to being eaten. Possibly, however,
several glands take part in furnishing the swathing bands. The Pyriform
glands secrete the spinningwork which forms the snare proper, or the
seizing tissue, together with the dragline and trapline. I would venture to
add to this the suggestion that the same glands must also secrete the filaments which form the ballooning thread and floating strands known as
gossamer. The function of the Aciniform glands and Ampullate glands,
according to Dr. Apstein, is not known. (See Figs. 348–354.)

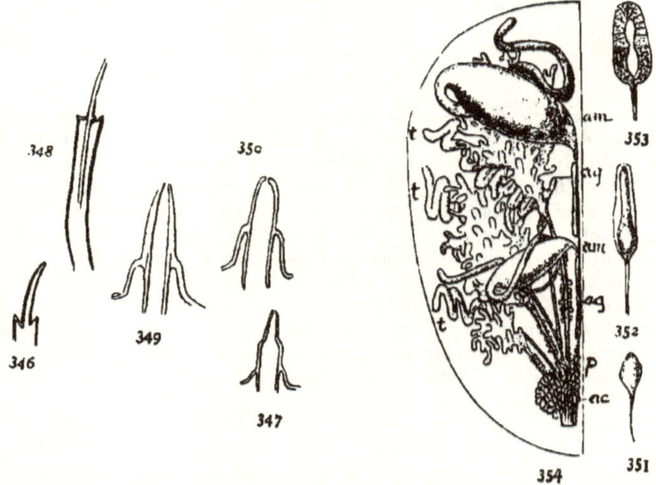

FIG. 346. Spinning spool of Epeira diademata pyriform gland. × 188. FIG. 347. Longitudinal section of
a spool of the aggregate gland. × 188. FIG. 348. Spinning spool of the glandula aciniformis. × 188.
FIG. 349. Longitudinal section of a spool of the ampullate gland. × 188. FIG. 350. Longitudinal section of spool of glandula tubuliformis. × 188. (After Apstein.) FIG. 351. An aciniform gland. × 30.
FIG. 352. A pyriform gland. × 105. FIG. 353. Longitudinal section of pyriform gland. × 105. FIG.
351. The spinning glands of Epeira diademata in natural site. × 9. (After Apstein.) ac, aciniform
glands; p, pyriform glands; am, ampullate glands; ag, aggregate glands; t, tubeformed or tubular
glands (glandulæ tubuliformes.)

NOTE B.—SECRETION OF VISCID BEADS.

Dr. Apstein is inclined to think that the foundation thread is created
from the "Aciniform gland." As soon as the foundation is stretched the
spools of the Glandulæ Aggregatæ (the Aggregate or Treeform Glands) are
pressed on it, and leave on it a little drop of viscid secretion. The three
spools stand close together on the superior spinneret—that is to say, their
mouths lay close together. If now the two superior spinnerets be pressed
to the foundation thread, the six spools of the two sorts will embrace it,

and the secreted drops can unite and thus surround the thread upon all sides. In order that the minute drops remain, it is necessary that the foundation thread be dry when the Aggregate gland places its secretion upon it. As the foundation thread is very strong, it will dry more quickly if it consist of numerous fine threads instead of a single strand. For this reason Apstein believes that the Aciniform gland secretes the foundation thread. In the same way one can believe that the Pyriform gland forms these threads. The foundation thread is more elastic than the dry threads composing the snare itself. As the last named are formed from the Pyriform glands, there seems to remain only the Aciniform gland for the secretion of the foundation thread.

Note C.—Viscid Threads of Lineweavers' Snares.
(Chapter XIX., Page 351.)

The viscid drops form, in masses close together, a large glutinous spot, upon which small insects adhere. With Epeïroids the spirals of the snare are formed of this thread. Among the Retitelariæ Dr. Apstein found these threads on the large, loose meshed web above the habitation of the spider. If an insect flies into this roof formed web it sticks to it. By its efforts to escape the loose threads are broken, and the animal falls into the home web, where it is seized by the spider. In no other web did he observe these threads, and no other spider possesses these glands.[1]

The bearing of these facts upon the relations between the spinning-work of Orbweavers and Lineweavers is manifest. Dr. Apstein confirms, both from the standpoint of histology and field observation, the statements concerning the viscid character of the web of Theridium, which I have made with so great reserve. (See page 351.) He thus immensely strengthens the plausibility of supposing an easy passage from the spinningwork of Lineweavers to that of Orbweavers, or in the reverse direction. Had these observations reached my hand in the summertime, I should certainly have made a thorough examination of the snares of Linyphia and Theridium. At this date the matter is impossible, and must go over for another year.

Note D.—The Swathing Thread for Insects.

The Lobate or Lobeformed glands[2] occur only in Theridium steatoda and some others of the above mentioned Retitelariæ. They have, therefore, only a limited extension, less so than the Aggregate glands. The swathing threads are produced by the Lobeformed glands, as the spider has, in her great lumen, always a large quantity of this material in reserve.

---

[1] Apstein, op. cit., page 63.

[2] Lappenförmige. These appear to be the Bulbous or Tuberose glands of Meckel, figured Chapter II., page 44.

Besides, this spinning material can flow off through a wide spool and produce the necessary spinningwork for throwing on the animals. Pholcus has a large gland and a wide spool. Apstein believes that this gland serves to throw threads on the animals in the web, and keep them there.[1]

NOTE E.—MEDICINAL PROPERTY OF SPIDER WEBS.
(PAGE 95.)

Dr. James, in his Medical Dictionary, introduces his article Araneus[2] with this statement: "Both Spider and the Web are used in Medicine. The Spider is said to avert the Paroxism of Fevers if it be applied to the Pulse of the Wrist, or Temples, but is peculiarly recommended for a Quartan, being inclosed in the Shell of a Hazle-nut. The Web astringes and conglutinates, and is therefore vulnerary, retains Bleeding and prevents any Inflamations."

NOTE F.—EFFECTS OF SPIDER POISON.
(PAGE 281.)

Dr. James, in his Dictionary, quotes from the works of Harvy the following sentence, which shows that the distinguished discoverer of the circulation of the blood was a fearless experimenter and an earnest searcher after Truth: "Having for Trial's sake pricked my hand with a Needle I after rubbed the point of the same Needle with the Tooth of the spider, and perforated the Skin therewith in another part of my Hand, but could distinguish no Difference in the Sense of the Punctures. However there was one remarkable enough in the Skin, for in the Envenomed Puncture the same was soon raised up into a Tubercle looking red with Heat, and Inflamations rising up as it were to shake off the inflicted."

Doleshall shut up small birds with Mygale javanica and M. sumatrensis, both large and strong spiders, and the birds died in a few seconds after being bitten. One of the spiders was left for ten days without food, and then was made to bite another bird, which was injured, but in six hours recovered. The same author was bitten in the finger by a Jumping spider. The pain was severe for a few minutes, and was followed by lameness of the finger, and gradually of the hand and arm, which soon went away entirely.[3]

Bertkau allowed spiders to bite his hand. On the ends of the fingers the skin was too thick to be penetrated, but between the fingers they easily pricked it. The bite swelled and smarted for a quarter of an hour, and then itched for some time, and for a day after itched whenever rubbed, as mosquito bites will do. He also experimented on flies, which died in a

---

[1] Apstein, op cit.   [2] Med. Dict., Vol. I., London, 1743.
[3] Quoted by Emerton, "Structure and Habits," page 34.

few minutes after being bitten. Of course, however, experiments of this kind are greatly invalidated by the fact that it cannot be determined whether the death of the insects resulted from poison, or from the mutilation produced by the entrance of so formidable a weapon as a spider's fangs.

Dr. Alfred Dugés gives an account of a little girl patient who had been bitten by one of those enormous spiders, quite common in Guanajuato, Mexico, which Mr. Leon Becker has named Metriopelma breyeri. The wound presented an oblong, tumefied border, about three lines high, of a livid violaceous color, filled with a serosity which he was not able to examine. The centre of the tumor was concave, and filled with red pus. Eight days after the accident there was little pain, but no general symptoms. Dr. Dugés was not able to follow up the case, but thinks that if there had been any serious consequences of the bite the child would have been brought back to him for further treatment.[1]

[1] "Insect Life," Vol. II., No. 2, 1889, page 47.

LIST OF SUBSCRIBERS

Up to November 1st, 1889.

Note.—All subscribers contained in this list are entitled to the special terms as specified in the original prospectus. To all others the price is $30 for the set of three volumes, $10 payable upon the receipt of each volume.

SCIENTIFIC SOCIETIES AND PUBLIC LIBRARIES.

Free Public Library, Worcester, Massachusetts.
The Brooklyn Library, Brooklyn, New York. (W. A. Bardwell.)
The Bronson Library, Waterbury, Connecticut. (H. F. Bassett.)
Mercantile Library, Philadelphia. (C. H. Hart.)
Yale University Library, New Haven, Connecticut.
Auburn Theological Seminary, Auburn, New York. (Rev. Prof. E. A. Huntington, D. D.)
Case Library, Cleveland, Ohio. (S. E. Chamberlain.)
United States Department of Agriculture, Washington. (Ernestine H. Stevens.)
Harvard College Library, Cambridge, Massachusetts. (William H. Tibbinglast.)
Kenyon College Library, Gambier, Ohio.*
Theological Seminary, Princeton, New Jersey.*
Washington-Jefferson College, Washington, Pennsylvania.*
Library of Supreme Council of the Thirty-third Degree Ancient and Accepted Scottish Rite
    of Free Masonry, Washington, District of Columbia. (Albert Pike.)
University of Petersburg. (Voldemar Wagner, Polytechnique Museum, Moscow.)
Public Library, Indianapolis, Indiana. (Charles Evans.)
Public Library, Detroit, Michigan. (H. M. Utley.)
College of New Jersey, Princeton, New Jersey. (Frederick Vinton.)
Peabody Institute, Baltimore, Maryland. (N. H. Morrison, Provost.)
New Jersey Agricultural Experimental Station, New Brunswick, New Jersey. (Irving S. Upson.)
State University of Nebraska, Lincoln. (Lawrence Bruner.)
Cornell University, Ithaca, New York. (G. W. Harris.)
Public Library, Toronto, Canada. (James Bain, Chief Librarian.)
Free Public Library, New Bedford, Massachusetts. (R. C. Ingraham.)
University of Kansas, Department of Natural History, Lawrence. (T. H. Snow.)
Williams College Library, Williamstown, Massachusetts. (Charles H. Barr.)
Academy of Natural Sciences of Philadelphia. (Dr. Edward J. Nolan.)
Accademia de Fisiocritici, Siena, Italy. (Prof. Giulio Chiarugi.)
Library of the United States Senate, Washington.
The Mercantile Library, Astor Place, New York. (W. T. Peoples.)
Public Library, Milwaukee, Wisconsin. (K. A. Linderfelt.)
Altoona Mechanics' Library, Altoona. (Dr. C. B. Dudley.)
Pennsylvania Railroad Trainmen's Library, Broad Street Station, Philadelphia. (Y. D. Cramer.)
K. K. Naturhistorisches Hofmuseums, Vienna, Austria.

* Presented by Col. John J. McCook, New York.

LIST OF SUBSCRIBERS.

INDIVIDUALS.—FOREIGN COUNTRIES.

Thomas Workman, Belfast, Ireland.
F. M. Campbell, Hoddesdon, Herts, England.
Rev. Dr. W. H. Dallenger, F. R. S., Ingleside, Lee, London S. E., England.
S. Chatwood, Esq., Irwell House, Prestwich, Manchester, England.
Cecil Warburton, Christ's College, Cambridge, England.
Dulau & Co., Soho Square, London. (F. K. Justen.) Six copies.
Loescher & Co., Libraj, Rome, Italy.
Rev. C. J. S. Bethune, Port Hope, Ontario, Canada.
The Earl of Derby, K. G., Knowsley Hall, Prescott, England.
Gerold & Co., Vienna, Austria.
De Erven Loosjes, Haarlem, Holland.
Otto Harrassowitz, Leipzic, Germany.
Prof. T. Thorell, Museo Civico Storia Naturale, Genoa, Italy.

INDIVIDUALS.—THE UNITED STATES.

Joseph Jeanes, Philadelphia. (Three copies.)
Col. John J. McCook, New York. (Four copies.)
Willis F. McCook, Esq., Pittsburgh.
James Spear, Wallingford. (Two copies.)
Frank K. Hipple, Philadelphia.
Hon. W. N. Ashman, Philadelphia.
Rev. W. J. Holland, D. D., Ph. D., Pittsburgh.
John Eyerman, Easton.
Thomas MacKellar, Philadelphia.
J. L. Forwood, M. D., Chester.
H. F. Bassett, Waterbury, Connecticut.
Gen. Anson G. McCook, Washington. (Two copies.)
William J. Latta, Philadelphia.
Col. R. P. Dechert, the City Hall, Philadelphia.
Lucien M. Underwood, Syracuse, New York.
Lieut. Col. O. C. Bosbyshell, the United States Mint, Philadelphia.
Marcus A. Hanna, Cleveland, Ohio.
John M. Shrigley, Lansdowne.
Horace F. Whitman, Philadelphia.
Hon. Levi P. Morton, Vice-President of the United States, Washington.
Henry Howson, Philadelphia.
Robert H. Lamborn, New York.
E. K. Medara, Philadelphia.
F. M. Webster, Lafayette, Indiana.
Col. Elliott F. Sheppard, New York.
W. B. Clark & Co., Boston.
Rev. R. H. Fulton, D. D., Philadelphia.
Rev. Prof. John J. McCook, Hartford, Connecticut.
Samuel H. Scudder, Cambridge, Massachusetts.
Wistar Morris, Overbrook.
James F. Magee, Philadelphia.
Alfred Pell, Highland Falls, New York.
John H. Redfield, Philadelphia.
S. A. Ellis, Rochester, New York.
William Sellers, Philadelphia.
Mrs. Mariné J. Chase, Philadelphia.

Lawrence Bruner, Lincoln, Nebraska.
Otto Lugger, Ph. D., St. Anthony's Park, Minnesota.
John Baird, Philadelphia.
T. H. Snow, Department of Natural History, University of Kansas, Lawrence.
W. P. Drew, Philadelphia.
Hon. Joseph Allison, Philadelphia.
Hon. Eckley B. Coxe, Drifton.
James Angus, West Farms, New York.
Archibald McIntyre, Philadelphia.
Edwin S. Gault, Philadelphia.
Mrs. William Slade Clark, Philadelphia.
Mrs. T. K. Gibbs, New York.

ADVERTISEMENT.

With the issue of the first volume of "American Spiders and their Spinningwork," the author (who is necessarily the publisher also) announces the withdrawal of the special terms offered to subscribers in the prospectus of August 1st, 1889.

The price will be $30 for the set of three volumes. Payment is expected for each volume, $10, as it is delivered. No volume will be sold separately.

The several volumes will be mailed at the publisher's expense, bound in stout cloth suitable for ordinary library use, but with uncut edges for the accommodation of those who wish special library binding.

"The Author's Edition" is strictly limited to *two hundred and fifty copies*, which will be numbered consecutively in the order of subscriptions, as received.

The first two volumes are devoted to a description of the Industry and Habits of Orb-weaving spiders, both separately and in their relations to the spinning economy of other aranead tribes. The First Volume treats particularly of Snares and Nests. The Second Volume will treat of the Cocooning Industry, Maternal Instincts, and General Habits. These volumes are liberally illustrated by drawings from Nature, the First Volume alone containing three hundred and fifty-four figures. The Third Volume will be devoted to descriptions of the Orbweaving fauna of the United States, accompanied by a large number of lithographic plates, painted by hand in the colors of Nature.

All business communications and subscriptions may be addressed directly to the author or to

"AMERICAN SPIDERS AND THEIR SPINNINGWORK,"

ACADEMY OF NATURAL SCIENCES.

LOGAN SQUARE, PHILADELPHIA.

—

The author's published works upon the ants may be had on the following terms:—

"The Natural History of the Agricultural Ant of Texas." Octavo, bound in cloth, pp. 312, plates XXIV. $3 00

"The Honey Ants of the Garden of the Gods, and the Occident Ants of the American Plains." Octavo, bound in cloth, pp. 188, plates XIII. 1 50

"The Mound Making Ants of the Alleghenies. Paper, pp. 56, plates VI. 75

These will be mailed to any address for the above prices, or the three works for . 5 00

Address, "ACADEMY OF NATURAL SCIENCES,"

LOGAN SQUARE, PHILADELPHIA.